HISTORIANS, STATE AND POLITICS IN TWENTIETH CENTURY EGYPT

This book explores the relationship between historical scholarship and politics in twentieth century Egypt. The changing roles of the academic historian, the university system, the state and non-academic scholarship, and the tension between them, are examined in contesting the modern history of Egypt.

In a detailed discussion of the literature, the study analyzes the political nature of competing interpretations and uses the examples of the Copts and resident foreigners to demonstrate the dissonant challenges to the national discourse that testify to its limitations, deficiencies and silences.

Anthony Gorman has taught at Macquarie University, the University of Sydney and the American University in Cairo. He now lectures at the School of Oriental and African Studies at the University of London and is currently working on aspects of the resident foreign presence in modern Egypt.

HISTORIANS, STATE AND POLITICS IN TWENTIETH CENTURY EGYPT

Contesting the nation

Anthony Gorman

RoutledgeCurzon
Taylor & Francis Group
LONDON AND NEW YORK

First published 2003
by RoutledgeCurzon
11 New Fetter Lane, London EC4P 4EE

Simultaneously published in the USA and Canada
by RoutledgeCurzon
29 West 35th Street, New York, NY 10001

RoutledgeCurzon is an imprint of the Taylor & Francis Group

© 2003 Anthony Gorman

Typeset in Sabon by
Integra Software Services Pvt. Ltd, Pondicherry, India
Printed and bound in Great Britain by
Biddles Ltd, Guildford and King's Lynn

British Library Cataloguing in Publication Data
A catalogue record for this book is available
from the British Library

Library of Congress Cataloging in Publication Data
Gorman, Anthony, 1959–
Historians, state and politics in twentieth century
Egypt : contesting the nation / Anthony Gorman.
p.   cm.
Includes bibliographical references and index.
1. Egypt—Historiography.   2. Nationalism—Egypt.
3. Historiography—Egypt.   4. Egypt—Politics and
government—20th century.
I. Title: Historians, state and politics in 20th century Egypt.
II. Title.

DT107.824 .G67 2002   2002068284
962'.007'2—dc21

ISBN 0–415–29753–2

TO MY PARENTS MAURICE AND
DULCIE GORMAN AND THE
MEMORY OF MY SISTER JUDY

CONTENTS

CONTENTS

PREFACE

This book could not have been completed without the help and encouragement of many people. The principal debt is to my parents for their unfailing moral and material support over the years and for instilling in me a strong sense of what can be achieved. To them, and to the memory of my sister Judy, I dedicate this book.

I owe special thanks to Bob Springborg, who served as my doctoral supervisor from close at hand and afar, and has continued to prove an unfailing source of advice and encouragement. To the many Egyptian historians who gave freely of their time and thoughts I wish to acknowledge particular gratitude. Ra'uf 'Abbas was especially generous with his knowledge and helpful in facilitating contact with many of his professional colleagues. I also wish to express thanks to Ahmad 'Abd al-Rahim Mustafa, 'Abd al-Mun'im al-Jumay'i, 'Asim al-Disuqi, 'Afaf Lutfi al-Sayyid Marsot, 'Abd al-'Azim Ramadan and the late Salah al-'Aqqad for helping me come to an understanding of my subject. The debt I owe to them and the other Egyptian historians who assisted me will be evident in the text. Although they may not agree with my conclusions, I hope they will consider this study in some way as a recognition of their contribution to historical scholarship.

Most of the field research for this study was undertaken during my time as an exchange student at the American University in Cairo in 1993–4 and was supplemented by research carried out while I was a member of staff at AUC in 2000–01. While a student at AUC my time was made easier through the skills of Enid Hill and Mahmud Farag, who dealt with some early bureaucratic difficulties. My teachers, especially Samia Mehrez and Walid Kazziha, and the library and librarians at AUC, were helpful in pointing me in the right direction when required.

Over the years I have been much sustained by the personal encouragement, inspiration and exhortation of many friends and colleagues. Maria Varvaressos, Chusnul Mariyah, Didier Monçiaud, Katerina Trimi and my colleagues and comrades in Cairo sustained me with their support, friendship and patience. Michael Carter has always been a reliable source of advice. My thanks also to Samir Raafat and Magid Kamil (Dar al-Kutub). In Alexandria,

I was given every assistance by Alekos Vlakhos, librarian of the Mikhailides Collection at the Greek Consulate. In Athens, I wish to thank the Greek Literary and Historical Archive (ELIA) and its staff for their guidance and good humour, Efthimios Souloyiannis for being so generous with his knowledge and the hospitality of the Nordic Library.

For those that endured early drafts and provided constructive and encouraging comments, my thanks to Robert Springborg, Christine Asmar, David Christian, Dan Crecelius, David Waldner, Pam Stavropoulos and Geraldine Herbert-Brown. My appreciation also to Don Reid, Richard Pennell, Nancy Gallagher and Ulrike Freitag who provided useful criticism on later versions of the manuscript. Nevine Gobran helped with some Arabic translations.

Finally, despite the view put forward in this study that historical scholarship is the product of an array of political forces, social influences, intellectual traditions, institutional pressures, and indeed, economic considerations, I nevertheless feel compelled to respect the custom of asserting personal responsibility for any shortcomings in the text.

I have employed a system of transliteration based on that of the *International Journal of Middle East* Studies without the use of diacritical marks for long vowels and the emphatic consonants; ' indicates *ayn*, ' represents *hamza*, except initially when I have avoided it. This system has been used with rigour in the use of personal and place names except where the existence of an English convention made such a practice seem ill-conceived, such as Nasser, Cairo and so on. This has occasionally meant some inconsistency when an author has published in more than one language. Reference to the bibliography should clarify any ambiguity. In the transliteration of Greek I, on the whole, have followed the system suggested by the *Journal of Modern Greek Studies*.

ABBREVIATIONS

ASU	Arab Socialist Union
Barakat, *QF*	'Ali Barakat, 'al-Tarikh wa'l-qadaya al-manhaj fi misr al-mu'asira', *Qadaya fikriyya* 11–12 (July 1992) 73–90
CPSS	The Centre for Political and Strategic Studies at al-Ahram
Crabbs, *WH*	Jack A. Crabbs Jr, *The Writing of History in Nineteenth-Century Egypt, A Study in National Transformation*, Detroit: Wayne State University & Cairo: AUC Press, 1984
EAHS	Egyptian Association for Historical Studies
HADITU	Democratic Movement for National Liberation
HAMITU	Egyptian Movement for National Liberation
HISS	Higher Institute of Socialist Studies
IJMES	*International Journal of Middle East Studies*
JUQ	*Jama'at al-umma al-qibtiyya* ('Society of the Coptic Nation')
MTM	*al-Majalla al-tarikhiyya al-misriyya*
RCC	Revolutionary Command Council
Reid, *CU*	Donald M. Reid, *Cairo University and the Making of Modern Egypt*. Cairo: AUC Press, 1991
RGS	Royal Geographical Society

INTRODUCTION

Political struggle, social upheaval and national uncertainty characterize the history of Egypt in the twentieth century. In less than 50 years and in the course of two revolutions, Egypt moved from a monarchical system of government, formally part of the Ottoman Empire albeit under occupation by British forces, to an independent republic governed by a military regime claiming to rule in the name of all Egyptians. This political transformation was accompanied by major economic, social and cultural changes. Over time, the image of Egypt as a loose aggregation of Islamic, Arabic, Egyptian, Mediterranean, and European elements that existed at the beginning of the century gave way, particularly after 1952, to an increasingly restrictive, sometimes chauvinist, and certainly contested conception of Egyptian national identity.

This study examines the development of historical scholarship in Egypt from the late nineteenth century until the end of the twentieth century against the backdrop of the struggle for independence and the conflict between domestic forces to construct a national identity. Through a discussion of the emergence of an academic historical tradition, the influence of public institutions, and the role of non-academic historical writing, it draws together important elements in the contest between political power, historical interpretation and social diversity within a national framework. It proposes that the state and the academy, while the principal architects of the historiographical mainstream, have been regularly challenged by the work of non-academic historians and dissident historical currents in a way that has reflected the debate in the political arena. More than this, the conceptual limitations of national discourse have muted and even excluded historical voices in Egyptian political, economic, social and cultural life. The study therefore highlights the critical tension between scholarship and political power in the construction of the nation and the implications that restrictive national categories have on our understanding of social complexity.

Studies of the development of historical scholarship have been framed by two broad schools. One approach, generally favoured by historians, has been to emphasize the emergence of a mature historiography as part of the process of modernization. Under the increasing influence of Western culture, this approach stresses the prominence of secular scholarship as an indicator of cultural and intellectual progress.[1] Often framed around figures who embody this modernist trend, this perspective is informed by the liberal ideal of the historian as an autonomous individual, disinterested if not detached from his or her political and social environment.[2] The historian is an agent of modernization, contributing to the intellectual development of the country and playing the role of educator or cultural technocrat.[3] Its institutional expression is the modern university system and its practitioner, the academic historian. A more refined version of the modernist approach gives greater consideration to the political environment, particularly the process of state building, and the social milieu from which historians emerge.[4] While acknowledging a greater interplay between historical scholarship and political forces, this view is nevertheless preoccupied with the Western model of intellectual progress that has employed unflattering cultural stereotypes in non-Western contexts.[5] Moreover, the focus on the construction of the national narrative grants is little concerned with trends that run counter to the emergence of the state or the national society.

The second approach, more often employed by political scientists, emphasizes the political utility of historical scholarship in the service of a regime. Here the historian is a servant of state power, and historiography is an ideological tool used to maintain the legitimacy of the political system. In this analysis, the focus is on the role of state power which may operate in an enabling sense, by dint of its financial resources and patronage to promote a particular historical vision, or in a coercive way, by censoring or suppressing dissenting, 'subversive' views. Far from the autonomous historian, this school of thought is most concerned with the relationship between state intelligentsia and state power. This model has most often been applied in authoritarian states, such as the former Soviet Union,[6] Africa,[7] and South East Asia,[8] and has been influential in discussions of scholarship in the Middle East, especially in the post-colonial era, where regimes have sought to cultivate a national historiography in order to bolster their political legitimacy and territorial integrity.[9]

While these two broad approaches illuminate important aspects of the practice of historical scholarship, they have their limitations. Emphasis on the historian as a detached intellectual and on history as a disinterested record of events neglects the political and social processes of which the historian and scholarship are both part. Stressing the instrumental role of history in the service of state power restricts the historian to being a member of a specialized state intelligentsia and disregards historians beyond the influence of the state and the existence of oppositional or dissident discourses.

More recently there has been an increasing interest in other factors that affect the pattern and development of scholarship, such as the institutional culture of the university system and the associational life of the historian.[10]

More attention has been given to the dynamics of the interplay between history and political ideology, the politically partisan dimension of scholarship and the impact of contemporary political context on historical interpretation.[11] Yet if there has been increasing recognition of some political contingencies, the focus on the interests of the state and its academic counterpart, the university system, has seen a relative neglect of other forces in society that have generated contesting or dissident interpretations. Discussions have focused on the ideal, if not always the practice, of the academic historian, as the legitimate scholar in contrast to the partisan nature of the non-academic. There has been an attendant failure to appreciate the positive contribution of non-academic scholarship and the social forces and institutions that have nurtured it. In short, there has been little acknowledgment of the common enterprise of academic and non-academic scholarship. It is argued here that non-academic historians, as a more diffuse and varied group, have been less constrained by certain political factors and have reflected a more accurate representation of society's diverse character. Certainly, they have challenged the academy and pioneered new historical interpretations.

The priority that has been accorded the academic historian mirrors the priority given to the nation as the primary object of discourse. As an idiom of political identification and legitimation, national historiography has acted as an instrument that brings together diverse elements to construct a discrete, verifiable tradition invoked to confirm a particular political and social vision. This has taken on a particularly energetic character in countries where the legacies of colonialism, the existence of sectarian and tribal loyalties, a diversity of cultural traditions and the impact of modernization have posed different and often conflicting points of reference. In Egyptian historical scholarship, the nation has remained largely unchallenged as the principal discursive object. Scholars have preferred to divine the character of national unity, employing such concepts as 'normative consciousness' (Safran), 'community of discourse' (Gershoni and Jankowski) and 'collective consciousness' (Krämer) and 'Egyptianity' to distil unity from diversity.[12]

Couched in terms of the struggle for national independence, this conceptual unity takes on an idiom of liberation. In the context of domestic politics it has come to represent a more ambiguous practice as a field of political struggle and an instrument of coercion. Its totalizing nature has routinely overlooked or minimized other levels of social identification and spheres of social activity. Political, social and cultural elements that speak of diversity, such as community affiliations, ethnic organizations, regional and religious groups, have often been devalued or ignored. Where acknowledged, they are regarded as objects in the midst of the nation, not subjects or constituents of it: at best quaint but irrelevant sideshows or vestiges of an earlier age, at worst, alien and obstacles to national integration.

Over the last two decades there has been an attempt to break the bearhug of this hegemonic national discourse. The *Subaltern Studies* project launched in 1982 proposed to combat the repressive effects of national discourse by putting non-hegemonic historiography on an academic footing.[13] Minority discourse drew attention to alternative modes of thought and identity whose existence have been muffled, suppressed and marginalized by national mainstream discourse.[14] Rather than a basis for unity, these projects have regarded the national mainstream as an oppressive ideology that attempts to conceal or marginalize minorities. It further charges the hegemonic culture, and more specifically, government policy, with having presided over a process of 'institutional forgetting' which stifles or conceals the memory of minority culture and excises the existence of particular groups or issues from the historical record. In exploring the possibilities created by a disassembling of a monolithic, totalizing view and highlighting the multifarious complexity of culture, society and identity, this study seeks to bring to light alternative frameworks which challenge the dominant ideology.

The potential of these new approaches has been most realized in the field of social history and cultural studies. It has made less headway in the field of political history where étatist perspectives and nationalist fetishism have been more resistant to a dispersal of political power beyond the prescribed limits of national discourse and its corresponding state structures and institutions. This is particularly true of Middle East historiography where the political imperative of national unity remains strong and exercises an unmistakably strong influence on scholarship. Following the appearance of *Minorities in the Arab World* just after the Second World War, Albert Hourani recalled the hostile reaction,

> At that time I was very much criticized by Arab nationalists who said, 'You ought not to be writing about this, you are dividing the people. This is a time when you ought to talk about unity, not about division.' The general feeling was that I ought not to have written it.[15]

Thirty years later, this political sacred cow was still firmly in place,

> When it comes to the problems of minorities and local democracy, he [the Arab intellectual] must cease from censoring himself for fear of imperiling an apparent national unity. The Arab revolutionary intellectual has too long applauded the call to unity, the while accepting and sometimes justifying the fragmentation that is reality.[16]

In Egypt, at least since the time of Lord Cromer, Egyptian nationalists have insisted on the indivisibility of the Egyptian nation.[17] Competing configurations of political and social forces sought to define, refine or altogether recast the character of this collective national identity according to their particular perspective. Rival political tendencies of the left and right, religious and secular forces, and diverse cultural traditions asserted and continue to assert their own national vision. The emergence and practice of historical scholarship in modern Egypt has been an integral part of this process and an arena in which battles, no less fierce than those of conventional politics, have been fought over the ownership of the national heritage. As a country of heterogeneous political and cultural traditions, and extraordinary diversity in class, national, religious and communal affiliations, Egypt presents an unusually vigorous case of this complex interaction between historical discourse, political power and social diversity.

Some scholars, noticeably but not exclusively based in the West, have endeavoured to critique the totalizing aspects of national discourse by focusing on alternative points of reference. A growing body of work on women in Middle Eastern history has proved one important inroad into the bastion of national, and largely male, discourse. Critical of mainstream Middle East historiography for its inadequate recognition of the contribution of women within national movements, it has sought to undermine the prevailing uniform and stereotyped image of women in public life.[18] Significantly, it has been largely left to women historians to produce detailed studies of feminist movements and highlight the contribution of individual activists in this struggle.[19] New work in other areas such as the labour movement,[20] the capitalist class,[21] and the peasantry,[22] has appeared, seeking to disarticulate, if only to a limited extent, class consciousness from hegemonic national discourse. There has, however, been less movement in areas of ethnic or cultural identity.[23]

These new approaches have not gone unchallenged. If one scholar took a certain fatalistic tone in stating, 'Since a national history is extremely rare, well-documented and well-argued national(istic) history is probably the best we can reasonably expect',[24] others, such as Vatikiotis, stridently resisted the challenge to state hegemony and defended the centrality of the nation-state in the historical narrative.[25] Amongst *academic* historians in Egypt, the conceptual possibilities raised by these new studies appear to have had limited impact. The construction of an (explicit or implicit) Egyptian national experience has witnessed a general rejection of a historical vision of pluralist or multi-ethnic society and maintained a firm grip on the markers of national identity.[26] Those views that have challenged this national hegemony and espoused a more communitarian or cosmopolitan perspective have not been extinguished but they have emerged from within Egyptian civil society or from the Egyptian *mutamassir* diaspora and not the academy.

In seeking to examine the development of both academic and non-academic historiography, this study proposes a more complex model of the interaction between historical scholarship, state and society. Rather than confining historians to the monolithic roles of elite intellectuals, managers of legitimation or class representatives, it takes a view of historians as representing a broad spectrum of diverse social, political and cultural voices. It proposes that historical scholarship is the product of a matrix of both state and non-state intellectual, social, institutional and political forces. Within the framework of its own political economy inside and outside the academy, historical scholarship interacts with the public sphere in its engagement with political ideas, attitude towards state authority and organic relationship with social diversity. As a discourse of representation embedded with a number of political variables, historical interpretation offers a variety of responses, based on its own assessment of political values that are expressive of a heterogeneous and contested picture of public national and non-national identity.

While all historical scholarships reflect some or all of these characteristics, contemporary Egyptian history offers a particularly fertile arena in which to explore these themes.[27] The diversity of academic and non-academic work offers considerable range and character of intellectual and political influences. Moreover, the contemporary period, as the time most immediate to the political struggles and social interaction of the present, where the interests of the state are most sensitive and the efforts of oppositional political currents most energetic, represents the clearest illustration of the critical relationship between historiography and politics. This study is based on a wide-ranging reading of contemporary Egyptian historiography, supplemented considerably by a large number of interviews with prominent Egyptian academic and non-academic historians in order to gain an appreciation of the enterprise of the historical work and an understanding of the political and social circumstances.[28] It crystallizes the conjunction between political forces and historical interpretation by examining a number of national schools or currents of thought influential in contemporary Egyptian historiography, namely the royalist, liberal, materialist, Islamic and feminist currents.[29] Each is expressive of a particular conception of the nation, locating political power, social forces and cultural identity in a distinctive arrangement and rooted in the contest for national supremacy between political forces. This contest is not simply in ideological or party political terms but is a function of broader trends of thought, state and institutional power. When influential, they have been supported with the considerable resources of the state. As oppositional discourses they have been sustained, on a much smaller scale, by political parties, private think-tanks, religious foundations and other organs, sometimes in the face of state repression. Nevertheless, as national discourses, they have attempted to apply a general framework to capture the basis of historical change in Egyptian society. Coexistent with these currents are those who have sought to represent voices of Egyptian society dissident from the national mainstream. Contemporary Coptic, feminist and *mutamassir* historiography, generated by alternative social forces and institutions, have both supplemented the historiographical picture and challenged the claims of the grander national narratives to comprehensively represent the character of the Egyptian nation and the dynamics of its historical transformation. The elucidation of these non-national discourses, therefore, sheds light on the diversity and contestation of historical representation, and the complexity of Egyptian identity.[30]

Despite, or perhaps because of, the diversity of Middle Eastern societies, historians of the area have often been intent on the unity of national discourse and used the nation as an ideological totem in order to establish the parameters of what is politically and historically legitimate. Other elements of social identity have been marginalized for contravening national aims and sensibilities or have been subsumed within the shadow of the nation. While the potency of national discourse cannot be dismissed, it has frequently obscured or ignored the presence and claims of other levels of association and identity by making exclusivist and totalizing claims. A broader and more heterogeneous conception of the historian and historiographical discourse extends the scope of legitimate history beyond the limits of the prevailing national idiom and recognizes a pluralistic, multi-centred mode of historical interpretation, where power is dispersed across society and where its development is multi-dimensional rather than linear. An awareness of a diverse conception of Egyptian historiography illustrates more clearly the organic connection between historical and political discourse operating within and beyond the national framework. In bringing together a consideration of both the context and text of historical scholarship in Egypt, this study seeks to capture an important dimension of this political struggle.

In Part I of the study, I examine the political economy of historiography and the construction of national discourse. The first three chapters deal with the social and political development of modern Egyptian scholarship addressing three different sites of production: the academy, the state and the non-academic scholarship of civil society. Chapter 1 traces the emergence of the academic tradition from the bureaucrat-historians of the nineteenth century to the professional academic historians of the twentieth century. It suggests that, while there has been a process of professionalization of the historian, far from conforming to a model of the disinterested, apolitical scholar, they have often been politically involved intellectuals, participating in various currents of national politics, and playing a part in the consolidation of the state-building process. Chapter 2 examines the relationship between scholarship and the state arguing that in the learned societies of the nineteenth century and the universities and academic institutes of the twentieth century, government authority has played a critical role in the direction, restriction and formation of historical scholarship. Chapter 3 argues for the significance of non-academic history in its discussion of the political origins and development of the liberal, materialist, Islamic and feminist currents of historical thought. Often dismissed as inferior and partisan, non-academic historians have used the advantages offered by their less institutionalized situation to present a diverse and vibrant historiography that has often operated as an innovative influence on historical ideas within the universities. It suggests that the greater volatility of non-academic history is a more representative reflection of the diversity of historical and political perspective in society. Chapter 4 compares the different historical discourses of contemporary Egypt in the liberal, materialist and Islamic schools. It argues each conceives of the constituent elements of the nation in different ways, giving priority to certain elements of Egyptian society as the true representatives of the nation, and precedence to particular political and social values. In this equation the historiography of Egyptian women has served as both a supplement and, perhaps increasingly, as a dissonant voice.

In Part II, I examine the historiography of two subaltern or non-national groups in Egyptian society which have been marginalized or excluded from mainstream historical discourse: the Copts, the native Christian population of Egypt, and the *mutamassirun* or 'Egyptianised' resident foreigners. After providing a brief historical background, each group is considered within the interpretations of the liberal, materialist and Islamic currents and is then examined according to some of its own scholarship. In arguing that historical writing on these groups has been neglected by the academy as indifferent, even contrary, to the ideological claims and political interests of the state, the discussion reinforces the relationship of complicity between academic historians, state institutions and political power.

Part I

HISTORIANS AND THE NATIONAL DISCOURSE

1

THE EMERGENCE OF THE ACADEMIC TRADITION

The work confirmed the view I had long held that history...
derive[s] as much from the historian as from the documents.

AJP Taylor[1]

The emergence of the academic historian in Egypt in the period following the end of the First World War has been regarded as heralding a new age in the development of Egyptian historiography. From this time on, according to this account, the model of the bureaucrat-historian of the nineteenth century gave way to the academic historian of the twentieth century when Egyptian scholarship took on a new maturity and began to develop a sound, politically disinterested and professional tradition.[2]

This view needs to be qualified. Although, strictly speaking, academic historians do not precede the establishment of the modern university system, this study argues that the bureaucrat-historians in Egypt, the so-called 'amateurs' of the nineteenth century, were the forerunners of the academic historian of the twentieth in their relationship to political authority. Serving in important government positions that involved them intimately in matters of state and especially education policy, their personal and professional interests were dependent on and aligned with those of the chief political authority, the palace. The tone of this relationship between political authority and historical scholarship would influence the development of the academic historian of the twentieth century. From the 1920s onwards, with the establishment of a modern state university system, an academic tradition developed which, while less dependent on personal patronage and more insulated by the relative autonomy of the university, produced historians who were regularly involved and even immersed in public life. The academic historians of the twentieth century, like those historians of the nineteenth century, continued to be part of the process of the establishment and consolidation of a state-centred, national discourse, not merely its observers and chroniclers. Far from being scholars aloof from the political debates and issues of the day, it has been common for academic historians to be active in politics as party apparatchiks, government bureaucrats, political agents or otherwise publicly engaged intellectuals.

11

EGYPTIAN HISTORIOGRAPHY AT THE BEGINNING OF THE TWENTIETH CENTURY

An overview of the development of nineteenth century historical scholarship in Egypt is appropriate here in order to assess the position of the discipline and the milieu from which it emerged at the beginning of the twentieth century. In this, the work of 'Abd al-Rahman al-Jabarti (1754–c. 1825) stands as an important reference and starting point. His history of the period 1688–1821, 'Aja'ib al-athar fi al-tarajim wa'l-akhbar, has been lauded as an outstanding achievement both in its quality and scope. As the best contemporary witness for the end of the Ottoman period, the arrival of the French in 1798 and the consolidation of the rule of Muhammad 'Ali, his work is an invaluable account of a critical period in Egyptian history. Cast as the isolated, brilliant individual against the backdrop of a period of decline, one scholar fulsomely described al-Jabarti as 'one of the greatest historians of the Muslim world of all times, and by far the greatest historian of the Arab world in modern times'.[3] In fact, increasing knowledge of the substantial debt al-Jabarti owed to eighteenth century sources has tempered some of the grander claims made of his genius.[4] Nevertheless, his position as a commanding figure in Egyptian historiography and his status as the finest and final product of the classical tradition of Islamic historiography are secure.[5] Born into a notable family of Azhari shaykhs, al-Jabarti was a member of the social and cultural elite, well-connected and a man of considerable personal means. Although he held no government post, he had served for a time as a member on one of the governing councils set up by the occupying French forces.[6] Thereafter, he appears to have withdrawn from public life, describing himself as 'secluded... in the corner of obscurity and neglect and retired from employment unlike other people'.[7] He used this time to compile a vivid account of a time when the country was in political upheaval, drawing on his own observations and official papers, court and council records, supplied to him by personal contacts.

Given the generally favourable assessment of modern scholars, it might seem surprising that al-Jabarti cannot be said to have propagated his own historical school either in method or spirit but the reasons are not difficult to ascertain. Unlike almost every historian of the nineteenth century, and many of the first half of the twentieth century that followed him, al-Jabarti was exceptional in his unequivocal disapproval of the rule of Muhammad 'Ali. Indeed, 'Aja'ib al-athar was so critical of the Egyptian ruler that the court ordered the destruction of copies and the work was not published in full until 1879–80.[8] Al-Jabarti's hostility to the Egyptian ruler was not confined to his historical writings. Disgusted by the cruelty of Muhammad 'Ali's rule, al-Jabarti had refused to sign a shaykhs' petition calling for his retention of the governorship of Egypt.[9] In fact, there were rumours, apparently unfounded, that al-Jabarti was killed by Muhammad 'Ali.[10] In contrast, al-Jabarti's historiographical successors supported the legitimacy of the ruling family to a man. Writing at a time when the dynasty of Muhammad 'Ali was firmly in place, they were government officials, acting as intellectual and managerial agents in forging the administrative and political coherence of the state. Their world-view and personal interest militated against a critical view of state authority and the positive portrayal of the Egyptian regime guaranteed the unimpeded publication of their works.

The prototype for this new kind of historian was Rifa'ah Rafi' al-Tahtawi (1801–73). Rising from humble origins to a position of very considerable wealth, al-Tahtawi's public life encapsulated many of the characteristics of the bureaucrat-historian. His initial appointment as religious head of the first educational mission sent by Muhammad 'Ali to France in 1826 established a pattern that would thereafter provide the training and inspiration for many young Egyptian scholars. Upon his return to Egypt 6 years later, he embarked on a long and distinguished career in government service, serving as editor of the official Egyptian newspaper, *al-Waqa'i' al-misriyya*, and director of the School of Languages. At one time he was the only permanent member of the Egyptian Board of Education and edited *Rawdat al-madaris*, a journal dealing with Arabic language and culture.[11]

Among a large number of books and translations, al-Tahtawi wrote *Manahij al-albab al-misriyya fi mabahij al-adab al-'asriyya*, a somewhat haphazard history of Egypt from early times until his own day.[12] Described as 'a treatise on national progress', the work was motivated by al-Tahtawi's insistence that 'it is the duty of every citizen to assist his community, and do whatever he is capable of for the furtherance of his country's interests'.[13] The community, in al-Tahtawi's view, *was* the state, and its progress was fostered by the extension and consolidation of its institutions. The special task of education was the inculcation of patriotism as the best way of forging a sense of community.[14] According to al-Tahtawi, the state's interests were those of the ruling family and his attitude of 'discreet and conventional flattery' towards rulers Sa'id and Isma'il was therefore quite appropriate.[15] Thus, if al-Tahtawi can indeed accurately be claimed as 'the first Egyptian who saw Egypt as a nation distinct from the general body of the Islamic community',[16] this was an Egypt constructed in statist terms.

The pattern of bureaucrat-historian continued with the career of 'Ali Mubarak (1823–93), who enjoyed an even more prominent public profile than al-Tahtawi.[17] Like al-Tahtawi, Mubarak benefited from time spent in Paris on an educational mission and once back in Egypt, launched a public career, as technocrat and politician, studded with important posts. As Minister of Education, a position he occupied on a number of occasions, he established two important institutions of public education, the Dar al-Kutub (National Library) and the Dar al-'Ulum (Teachers' College). His service as Minister of Public Works and Waqfs left a lasting physical imprint on the city of Cairo. Politically Mubarak allied himself with the anti-'Urabi camp,

13

a position that ensured the continuation of his successful career in the first decade of the British occupation when he served in the Cabinet on a number of occasions.[18]

Mubarak's massive contribution to Egyptian historiography, the 20 volume *al-Khitat al-Tawfiqiyya*, reflects his close association with authority.[19] A traditional encyclopedic form presenting a wealth of historical detail rather than a historical narrative, the *khitat* belongs to a literary tradition of collecting information for the purposes and management of the state. As Mehrez observes, 'from the very start this genre of historiography [i.e. the *khitat*] has been directly linked to the authorities: it originated for administrative purposes and therefore by definition had a patron whose interests it served and represented'.[20] Some sections of *al-Khitat al-tawfiqiyya* go even further, expressly praising Muhammad 'Ali and his family in a way that identifies Mubarak unmistakably 'as a historian who represents the political and ideological interests of the authority in the city'.[21]

By the late nineteenth century the model of the bureaucrat-historian established by al-Tahtawi and 'Ali Mubarak was well in place. Others followed even if their public careers were less eminent. Ya'qub Artin (1842–1919), an Armenian Egyptian, spent a lifetime dedicated to the cause of government service. Beginning as a tutor to the children of Khedive Isma'il in 1873, Artin rose to the position of undersecretary of the Ministry of Education in 1884, where he was a significant player in educational matters until his retirement in 1906. He later sat on the administrative council of the private Egyptian University.[22] His contribution to Egyptian scholarship consists of two major works, *L'Instruction publique en Égypte*, and *La Propriété foncière en Égypte*, both written in French (though soon after translated into Arabic), and a large number of articles for the *Bulletin* of the Institut d'Égypte.[23] Although written in a more modern form than Mubarak's *Khitat*, Artin's work shared its heavy reliance on official documentation, the strong emphasis on administrative detail and the centrality of state institutions.[24]

What Artin did for the history of Egyptian public education and landed property, Isma'il Sarhank (c. 1854–1924) did for Egyptian naval history, and Jirjis Hunayyin for its taxation system.[25] Each could draw on personal experience of their chosen subject: Sarhank had held a number of posts in the Navy and Ministry of Marine, and Hunayyin had served as a former superintendent of the Egyptian treasury. However, their efforts were dwarfed by the most ambitious project of all, *Taqwim al-Nil* by Amin Sami, a history of Egypt from the arrival of Islam until the reign of Isma'il in six volumes.[26] Sami again had a wealth of administrative experience having served as head of the Dar al-'Ulum between 1895 and 1911 and as director of the *Mubtadayan* School, a prominent preparatory school, for more than 24 years.[27] Like the writings of the bureaucrats before him, he relied heavily on a barrage of official documents, statistics, graphs and lists, so much so that parts of *Taqwim* have been compared to a telephone directory.[28]

The bureaucrat-historians form the central tradition of scholarship in nineteenth century Egypt and the political milieu from which they emerged is critical to an understanding of their work. Writing from the perspective of government officials, their analyses stressed the primacy of state institutions, administrative procedures and government authority. Their heavy reliance on state archives and statistical information, a feature particularly characteristic of the genre in its later stages, reinforced the legitimacy, authority and bureaucratic apparatus of the state. Intimately involved in the field of public administration, their careers depended on the favour and continued patronage of the palace. Their historical scholarship was an expression both of their professional preoccupations and a means of advancement. They were state builders concerned in their public duties and in their writings with the emergence of the modern state, its description and affirmation of its institutions. Their writing perforce legitimized the ruling dynasty and was in complicity with it. This need not necessarily mean that they always wrote approvingly of every action of the Egyptian ruler, though that was generally the case, but their conceptual approach had a certain inherent justification, a view that the increasing strength of the state and its institutions was a natural and desirable progression.[29] Above all, it reflected the political milieu of which they were part: modernization and the emphasis on the unity of the nation are the dominant motifs; the centre of political power is the palace, the institutional framework is the state.

THE ROYALIST SCHOOL

With the end of the First World War and the dissolution of the Ottoman Empire, Egyptian nationalists resumed their demands for British withdrawal and national independence. Ultimately, the aims of the 1919 Revolution were frustrated: after fruitless negotiations Britain unilaterally granted Egypt a measure of self-government in 1923 while retaining ultimate power for themselves. Yet even this concession was enough to reinvigorate the domestic political scene and provide the stage for a triangular contest between the mass-supported Wafd, a palace intriguing with minor parties and individual politicians, and the British government. The Egyptian elements in this troika were almost exclusively drawn from the propertied classes, and the result was an unsatisfying, often sterile, series of political manoeuvres and coalitions asserting their claims to govern in the name of the nation.

Against this background, King Fu'ad actively cultivated a group of scholars, the royalist school, whose work would dominate the interwar period. Its practitioners were both Egyptian and European historians, academic and non-academic, who wrote histories of Egypt favourable to the dynasty of Muhammad 'Ali and by implication, and sometimes explicitly, of Fu'ad's own rule.[30] Having been educated in Switzerland and Italy, the king had a deep admiration for the virtues of European scholarship and had also shown a marked interest in matters of education. Before becoming head of state, he had served as the founding rector of the private Egyptian University in 1908 where he had presented his own lectures.[31] More than this however, Fu'ad had a deep personal appreciation for culture and the political utility of its patronage.[32] In 1915 in his inaugural address as president of the Royal Geographical Society Fu'ad hinted at his intentions

> Il faut maintenant nous mettre à l'oeuvre et établir avec méthode notre programme. Notre but doit consister à donner à la Société dans le mesure de nos efforts un essor nouveau, digne des grands noms qui l'ont illustrée.[33]

A central part of this programme was the cultivation and propagation of historical scholarship sympathetic to the monarchy. When Fu'ad became ruler of Egypt in 1917 following the death of his brother Husayn Kamil, he was in a more powerful position to promote this vision. Throughout the 1920s until his death in 1936 he nurtured a scholarship congenial to his and his family's interests, promoting publications, sponsoring conferences and granting those favoured with privileged access to state papers.

Archives, and particularly diplomatic records, played a conspicuous role in the royalist school since they reinforced a state discourse and emphasized the centrality of the ruler. Of those records in the possession of the Egyptian government, the most important were the Royal Egyptian Archives, supervised by Joseph Gélat Bey, Director of the European Section of the King's cabinet.[34] Fu'ad was just as keen to make use of the potential of foreign state archives, and European consular archives were a particularly favoured source material. The approach made to the Greek government was probably typical. In January 1929, the Greek ambassador, Metaxas, wrote to Athens informing the foreign minister that he had been approached with a request to allow publication of the Greek consular archives in Egypt from the period 1833 to 1870. Metaxas asked that authorization be granted not only because it would be prestigious for Greece but it would '... particularly please His Majesty, King Fu'ad, who shows a great interest in this'.[35] Two studies based on the documents pertaining to the last years of Muhammad 'Ali's rule duly appeared.[36] Based on this type of material, a large number of historical works and edited collections of documents relating to the Muhammad 'Ali dynasty were commissioned and published throughout the 1920s and 1930s.

Foreign scholars figured largely in this project. Most favoured were the French but Italian, British, Greek and American writers also participated. The case of Angelo Sammarco is illustrative.[37] Born in Naples in 1883, Sammarco first came to Egypt in 1922 to take up the position of history teacher at the Italian Lycée in Cairo. From this time on, he dedicated himself to the study of Egyptian history, conducting research, writing and giving lectures at learned societies such as the Institut d'Égypte and the Royal Geographical Society. In 1925, following the death of Eugenio Griffini, Fu'ad offered Sammarco the vacant post of librarian of 'Abdin Palace and asked him to continue the task of reconstructing the history of contemporary Egypt. In 1929, Sammarco published his ambitious plans for a monumental work on modern Egyptian history in 30 volumes (in the end, only four were completed). He continued to write prolifically during the 1930s, concentrating particularly on the reign of Muhammad 'Ali and the construction of the Suez Canal. Following another initiative of Fu'ad, Sammarco undertook the compilation of a four volume work, *Histoire d'Égypte moderne depuis Mohammed Ali jusqu'à l'occupation britannique (1801–1882)*.[38] The outbreak of the Second World War interrupted this schedule and Sammarco returned to Italy where he died in 1948.

While Sammarco came from a plausibly academic background, the career of Georges Douin (1884–1944) was even more reminiscent of the earlier bureaucrat-historians. Born in France in 1884, Douin entered the French Navy at an early age and while stationed in China established a reputation as a scholar of Chinese.[39] In 1919 he was engaged by the Suez Canal Co. in the position of *contrôleur de navigation* and rose to the position of principal agent at Port Said in 1927. Douin had begun publishing history in 1917 but it was only after the appearance of his book on Bonaparte's fleet in Egypt in 1922 that he attracted Fu'ad's attention. Following a request from the king Douin prepared a large series of documents from the reign of Muhammad 'Ali for publication, particularly consular correspondence written by French, English, Austrian, Prussian and Russian representatives. Over the next 4 years he maintained his focus on Muhammad 'Ali authoring a number of works on his military campaigns in Syria. In the 1930s, Douin turned his attention to Khedive Isma'il who, he believed, had been neglected by historians. 'La foule, oublieuse ou ingrate, semble avoir perdu jusqu'au souvenir de ses [i.e. Isma'il's] grands bienfaits. Et aujourd'hui, l'homme couché dans la tombe attend toujours la justice, son oeuvre, un historien.'[40] He took the task on himself, covering the achievements of the ruler in three volumes titled, *Histoire du règne du Khedive Ismail*. For these efforts Douin was rewarded with honours both in France and Egypt, including the *cravate* of the order of Isma'il.

Isma'il was a particularly significant figure for the royalist school because it was the alleged economic incompetence of his reign that was used to justify British intervention and ultimately the invasion and occupation of the country in 1882. Pierre Crabitès (1877–1943), an American judge of the Mixed Tribunal in Cairo and later Chief Judge, undertook a similar defence of Isma'il.[41] In his history titled pointedly, *Ismail, the Maligned Khedive*, he took Lords Cromer and Milner to task for their negative portrait of the Khedive as 'a spendthrift, a voluptuary, and a thief'.[42] There was another reason to defend the Khedive: he was Fu'ad's father. The point was not lost on a contemporary reviewer, 'This book is not concerned with Ismail as Khedive alone. It is Ismail as an ancestor of sovereigns to be whose vindication is asserted.'[43] Crabitès duly followed up with a biography of Ibrahim, the father of Isma'il and grandfather of Fu'ad.[44] Above all, however, Muhammad 'Ali, as the founder of the dynasty and modern Egypt, remained the favoured subject. Henry Dodwell (1879–1946), after a long career in the Indian Educational Service, then as Professor of the History and Culture of the British Dominions in Asia at the University of London, wrote a glowing account of his rule, later translated into Arabic, for which he received the tidy sum of LE 500.[45]

Never one to miss a timely opportunity, Fu'ad used the occasion of the 15th International Congress of Navigation in Cairo in 1926 for the publication of yet another laudatory volume. *L'Égypte, Aperçu historique et géographie gouvernement et institutions vie économique et sociale* was edited by the secretary-general of the Congress, Yusuf Qattawi (1861–1942), a man close to the King at this time, having been Finance Minister in 1924, and later appointed by Fu'ad to the Senate in 1927.[46] In the preface Qattawi explained the genesis of the book, 'Répondant au désir de Sa Majesté, une phalange d'éminentes compétences á gracieusement prêté son concours pour tracer cette esquisse de l'Égypte contemporaine.'[47] The eminent persons were not wholly unqualified for the task but they were largely palace or government officials. Qattawi opened proceedings with a historical survey; 'Ali Pasha Jamal al-Din, the undersecretary of the Ministry of the Interior, wrote on the pilgrimage to Mecca; Ahmad Lutfi al-Sayyid, contributed a section on the origins and organization of the Egyptian University of which he was Rector: Dr Isaac Levi[48] dealt with commerce and industry. Georges Douin and Gaston Wiet, appointed at this time as head of the Museum of Arab Art at Fu'ad's personal direction, also contributed.[49]

A more ambitious collaborative work was launched with the *Précis de l'histoire d'Égypte*, a three-volume work, later extended to four volumes, in the early 1930s.[50] This brought together the talents of a number of European scholars in a survey of Egyptian history from prehistoric times until the reign of Isma'il. Édouard Driault, already a stalwart of the royalist stable with a considerable body of historical work to his credit,[51] and Sammarco contributed the chapters on Muhammad 'Ali and his successors. The fawning preface in the first volume by Muhammad Zaki al-Ibrashi Pasha, a court official and trusted palace confidant, struck the appropriate tone, praising Muhammad 'Ali, Isma'il and Fu'ad as 'les trois principaux artisans de la restauration égyptienne' and thanking the king for his 'inépuisable générosité'.[52]

The *Précis* was the forerunner of a much grander project. The seven volume *Histoire de la nation égyptienne*, was in some sense the crowning achievement of the royalist school. Funded by a royal subvention of over

LE 8000, the *Histoire* received the imprimatur of the Académie française, being edited by Gabriel Hanotaux, a former French Foreign Minister (and later Dean of the Académie).[53] In the last volume to appear Hanotaux recalled the King's original instructions,

> On a beaucoup parlé des vieux Pharaons dans les histoires de l'Égypte. Mais, maintenant, si on se mettait aux temps modernes ... L'histoire de mon grand aïeul Mohamed Aly est à peine connue: racontez-la. Parlez du génie militaire d'Ibrahim, des grandes transformations qui se sont accomplies sous Säid, sous Ismäil, mon père ... Voyez mon pays, sa richesse, son ardeur, sa bonne volonté, ses aspirations, et ses oeuvres actuelles. Tout cela mérite aussi d'être raconté, expliqué. L'opinion est-elle bien renseignée sur nous? Avertissez-la. Rendez-nous justice par la vérité. C'est un beau sujet que je vous confie, Monsieur Hanotaux. Je vous le confie. Que puis-je dire de plus.[54]

The massive *Histoire* was the work of a number of French scholars modelled on the *Histoire de la nation française*.[55] Again, it provided a historical survey of Egypt, this time on a more imposing scale, from the earliest times until the Montreux Conference in 1937. The modern period, covered by François Charles-Roux, French Ambassador to the Vatican, was a standard diplomatic account which focused principally on the actions of the rulers, although there was some discussion of the Egyptian national movement under Mustafa Kamil and the emergence of the Wafd. Whereas the *Précis* had been published while Fu'ad was alive and had only dealt with the period up to the death of Isma'il, by the time the last volume of the *Histoire* appeared, Fu'ad had been dead for 4 years and the book opened with a suitably eulogistic section on the late monarch by Henri Dehérain titled *Un Mécène royal*.

Even if it had lost its most fervent patron, the royalist school did not end with Fu'ad's death but continued in less lavishly-funded fashion and with less reliance on European scholars. Its leading figure in the 1940s was Jacques Tagher (1918–52). Born in Cairo of Syrian background, Tagher had graduated from the University of Paris and began to add to the canon of royalist histories with his work on Muhammad 'Ali in 1942.[56] By 1946 he had been rewarded with an appointment as the Keeper of the King's Private Library. In that year, with the head of the Historical Archives of the King's Cabinet, Georges Guindi Bey, he edited a collection of documents from the reign of Isma'il, marking the 50th anniversary of the Khedive's death. The Arabic translation appeared the following year.[57] Over the next several years, he continued to write on many different aspects of nineteenth century Egyptian history, editing the memoirs of Clot Bey and authoring a book on Copts and Muslims.[58] In 1948, Tagher became secretary-general and founding spirit of a new journal *Cahiers d'histoire égyptienne*. Again a royal anniversary provided the impetus for the event, this time the centenary of Ibrahim Pasha's death. The journal, funded in part from donations from the French Embassy, the Suez Canal Co. and private individuals, along with the proceeds from subscriptions, was dedicated to matters of Egyptian political and diplomatic history, as well as relations between Europe and America with both the ancient and modern East. Intended for a foreign audience and published in French or English, the editorial committee was international in character bringing together local and foreign scholars, a mix that was reflected in the contributions to the journal over the succeeding years.[59] Despite Tagher's sudden death in 1952, *Cahiers d'histoire égyptienne* continued to appear regularly throughout the 1950s, producing work characterized by a conservative tone.[60]

Certainly after, but even before 1952, the royalist school was roundly criticized by Egyptian commentators and historians. One consistent accusation was that its works were the product of venal commissions rather than genuine works of academic integrity.[61] The regular format of many of these histories did little to dispel this impression: the frontispiece often featured a photo of the King with a specific dedication to the monarch. Authors consistently thanked the 'wise patronage' and good services of the king, or, in one case, 'that fearless quest for truth which characterized His Late Majesty's interest in the history of the dynasty of Muhammad Ali'.[62] Putting aside the personal motives of the historians themselves, Fu'ad's intentions were unmistakable. He expressly fostered, encouraged and patronized the cultivation of a historical school which proclaimed the benefits and benevolence of the reigns of, less the whole royal dynasty, than his own direct forebears, his father (Isma'il), his grandfather (Ibrahim) and his great-grandfather (Muhammad 'Ali). In return for his support, the authors were granted the access to various private and official papers, that would have been otherwise unavailable to them, and were well-paid for their efforts.[63]

More significantly, the histories of the royalist school were charged with failing to provide an accurate account of Egyptian history.[64] As primarily diplomatic or military narratives which dealt with the relations between Egypt and foreign governments, or accounts that focused on the achievements and perspective of the palace, the historical analyses of the royalist school tended to be top-heavy with little consideration given to the role of other players, and most importantly, the great majority of Egyptians. This elitist view, while not unremarkable for the time, was exacerbated by the fact that some of these historians also wrote on the contribution of the resident foreign communities in Egypt in the modern period: Sammarco on the Italians, Crabitès on Americans, and Politis on the Greeks.[65] At a time when the legal and economic privileges of the Capitulatory Regime and indeed the position generally of the foreign communities rankled the national movement, this compounded the impression of a historiography that failed to genuinely present the national history.

However, it was above all the charge that *foreigners* were hired to write Egyptian history that was to be repeated most tellingly from the 1940s onwards.[66] This was not entirely accurate. Trusted Egyptians from circles close to the palace also wrote from a pro-monarchy perspective. Ahmad Shafiq (1860–1940) was the son of an Egyptian father and Circassian mother, who enjoyed a long career in the Khedival court, particularly distinguished during the reign of 'Abbas Hilmi II.[67] Active in the national movement before the First World War, he departed for Constantinople following the declaration of hostilities in 1914 and was not permitted to return to Egypt until 1921. In 1924, the first of ten volumes of *Hawliyyat misr al-siyasiyya*, a chronicle of the period 1914–30, appeared.[68] Another study by Shafiq, published in French in 1931, discussed the period from Isma'il until the present praising the Khedive's political vision, if not his financial skills, and providing mixed assessments of 'Urabi and Sa'd Zaghlul.[69] Amin Sami, active in public education since the time of Isma'il and a member of Majlis al-Shuyukh in the 1920s, produced his final work, *Misr wa'l-nil min fajr al-tarikh ila alan* in 1938, which presented a positive image of the royal line and was likely commissioned by the palace.[70] Yusuf Qattawi's contribution to the royalist school has been noted; his son, René (1896–1994) also wrote on the reign of Muhammad 'Ali.[71] Finally, a member of the royal family, and Fu'ad's own second cousin, Prince 'Umar Tusun, produced a respectable history of the 'Urabi revolt among other works.[72]

A number of the royalist works written in foreign languages were translated into Arabic but it is in part ironic that the criticism levelled at the royalist school for being a foreign scholarship overlooked work that was written in Arabic and therefore more accessible to the Arabic-reading public.[73] Nevertheless, the accusation did accurately identify the preference given to foreign scholars. Even palace toady Karim Thabit felt obliged to acknowledge this point in the introduction to his own book on Muhammad 'Ali. Citing the great number of works in foreign languages but the small number available in Arabic as the main reason for his own contribution, he promised to shed new light on an old subject and ended with the inevitable praise for Faruq and his father.[74]

However, the campaign to discredit the royalist school was less about numbers and more about the identity of the historian and the political tone of the scholarship. Muhammad Rif'at, one of the new generation of Egyptian historians, put the point more mildly than some, '... in my opinion, it is the nationals of a country who are best fitted to express the true feelings and reactions of their fellow-countrymen to the ideas and the events that confront them'.[75] The overall impression of the royalist school, as with the bureaucrat-historians of the previous century, was of a body of work that sought foremost to justify the legitimacy of the monarchy and second, gave primacy to state institutions over the Egyptian people themselves. This historiographical imbalance, which in the early part of the twentieth century had already provoked a response from writers of the liberal school, proved an important catalyst to the academic works of the 1940s and 1950s.

THE FOUNDING FATHERS: RIF'AT, GHURBAL AND SABRI

Since the reign of Muhammad 'Ali, Egyptian students had been returning from Europe with an array of qualifications in military science, law, languages and other subjects. Despite the steady improvement in technical skills, by the early twentieth century the Egyptian education system was still incapable of producing local historians comparable to European standards of scholarship. It was not until the 1920s when the first modern historians with specialized academic training began to return from study in Europe that a local academic tradition started to take root. With the establishment of the Egyptian University in 1925, which offered the institutional base, over time they laid the foundations for an alternative perspective less beholden to the interests of the palace. Expressive of, and often personally engaged in, the complexities of the Egyptian political scene, they served as articulators and participants in the establishment and propagation of a national historical discourse.

There is no agreement as to who can claim to be the first Egyptian academic modern historian. Three candidates deserve consideration for the title: Muhammad Rif'at Bey, Muhammad Shafiq Ghurbal and Muhammad Ibrahim Sabri.[76] Each studied in Europe and from the 1920s came to play significant albeit contrasting roles as teachers, administrators and scholars in promoting new historical ideas and formulating public education policy in Egypt. It is somewhat ironic that of the three, Rif'at, whose claim is perhaps the weakest, was the only one who initially wrote in Arabic.[77]

Muhammad Rif'at was from an aristocratic Turkish family and preceded both Ghurbal and Sabri in obtaining postgraduate qualifications abroad. Sent to England by the Ministry of Education just prior to the First World War, he graduated with a Masters degree at the University of Liverpool under the supervision of Sir Charles Webster, probably at his family's expense.[78] On his return to Egypt, he became professor of history at the Higher Teachers' College and wrote the first volume of *Tarikh misr al-siyasi fi al-azmina al-haditha*, a study of the period from 1798 to 1841, which was published in 1920. In due course a second volume followed in 1932 which took the narrative up to 1882.[79] The work appeared in three editions and multiple printings, becoming the prescribed text at the Higher Teachers' College in 1927, where it remained until 1952.[80] For a time Rif'at taught at Alexandria University and, during the 1940s and 1950s, he wrote regularly on various international and regional issues. However, it was in the field of education policy that he had greatest influence. After holding a series of positions in the Ministry of Instruction, he became General Director of Secondary Education in 1946, and undersecretary in the Ministry of Education. By 1952 he held the title of Pasha and was appointed the Minister of Education in the two administrations of Ahmad Najib al-Hilali in that year. It was in his dedication to the task of the Arabization of history textbooks that Rif'at combined his roles of historian and bureaucrat.[81] Clearly a policy inspired to counter the foreign language tradition of the royalist school, he explained his own decision to write in Arabic with characteristic simplicity, '...I felt it my duty to translate my acquirements into Arabic with only occasional articles or lectures in English.'[82]

Muhammad Shafiq Ghurbal (1894–1961) was undoubtedly the key figure in putting modern Egyptian history on a firm academic footing.[83] Born in Alexandria to a merchant family, Ghurbal graduated from the Higher Teachers' College in Cairo in 1915. His talents were recognized when he was awarded a Ministry of Education scholarship to study at the University of Liverpool, where he took a Bachelors degree with honours in 1919. After 3 years' teaching at a high school in Alexandria, he returned to England where he enrolled in a Master of Arts at the University of London, working under the supervision of Arnold Toynbee at the London Institute of Historical Studies.[84] The research carried out during both degrees was to provide the basis for his first book, published in English in 1928, *The Beginnings of the Egyptian Question and the Rise of Mehemet Ali*.[85]

Following his return to Egypt in 1924, Shafiq Ghurbal taught for some years at his old college before being appointed as assistant professor of modern history at the Egyptian University in October 1929. Originally established as a private institution, the university had been nationalized by the government in 1925. Since its foundation the staff had been predominantly European but Ghurbal's arrival was part of a changing of the guard. Slowly British, French, German and Italian scholars gave way to Egyptians usually with European qualifications. Under the rectorate of Ahmad Lutfi al-Sayyid the university became both a symbol and a force in the growing nationalist movement. In 1935 Ghurbal succeeded the Englishman Arthur J. Grant and became the first Egyptian professor of modern history. The succession was important not simply because Ghurbal was Egyptian. Grant's tenure had come at the end of a long career as a historian of nineteenth century European history.[86] Ghurbal was a relatively young historian of great promise more than 30 years his junior and a specialist in nineteenth century Egypt. The appointment thus represented an important step both for Egyptian academics and for modern Egyptian historiography. Thereafter, the university's practice was as a rule to appoint Egyptians to its modern history staff.

From his position as professor of modern history, and then dean of Arts, Ghurbal proceeded to nurture a generation of Egyptian students and wield considerable influence as a public educator. Over more than 20 years at the university from the 1930s until the late 1950s, he was a source of knowledge and inspiration for many history graduates. Indeed, he preferred to concentrate his academic energies on the supervision of students and his influence was to be observed more in the work of his students than in his own published work.[87] Among them would be Ahmad 'Izzat 'Abd al-Karim, Ahmad al-Hitta, 'Ali al-Jiritli, Amin Mustafa 'Afifi, Abu al-Futuh Radwan and Ibrahim 'Abduh, who between them would produce pioneering work in the fields of Egyptian political, social and economic history.[88] The influence Ghurbal exercised as teacher rather than published scholar was captured politely in his *Times'* obituary, 'Shafiq Ghorbal was the best and the most highly respected – although not the most productive – of modern Egyptian historians.'[89]

One reason for Ghurbal's relatively modest publication record was undoubtedly his considerable public career outside the university. In 1940 his appointment as assistant deputy director (*wakil musa'id*) in the Ministry of Education marked the beginning of more than a decade of involvement in the administration of public education. The move, reminiscent in some ways of the careers of the bureaucrat-historians in the previous century, was an indication of Ghurbal's administrative talents and dedication to public service, as well as his political connections.[90] The Ministry of Education at this time was notorious for its political and bureaucratic intrigues. Only 2 years earlier Taha Husayn had commented,

> I can testify without fear of contradiction that no other ministry in Egypt is so ridden by fierce rivalries, hatreds, suspicions, and intrigues as the Ministry of Education... [It] has become a clear, or rather murky, mirror of political life in Egypt with opinions that change daily depending on the minister and party requirements.[91]

Ghurbal's initial appointment by an anti-Wafdist coalition government is therefore particularly significant. Though apparently never a formal member of a political party, his career in the ministry indicates close sympathies with the Sa'dists, a splinter group from the Wafd towards whom it preserved an active antipathy. Led by Ahmad Mahir, Mahmud Fahmi al-Nuqrashi and Ibrahim 'Abd al-Hadi, the group also maintained close links with the palace.[92] During the 1940s Ghurbal voiced his general support for the monarchy in a number of articles and recognized that, while the country had problems, gradual reform was the best way to deal with them.[93] Certainly, Ghurbal was no friend of the Wafd. Following the return of Mustafa al-Nahhas to office by the force of British tanks in February 1942, Ghurbal withdrew to the university in December following some disagreement with the government.[94] With the fall of the Wafdist government at the end of 1944 and the appointment of Ahmad Mahir as Prime Minister, Ghurbal returned to the Ministry of Education in January 1945 as technical adviser (*mustashar fani*).

He subsequently served as adjunct undersecretary in the government of Isma'il Sidqi and permanent undersecretary in the second al-Nuqrashi government. For a time he was deputy undersecretary of the Ministry of Social Affairs, ultimately returning to the Education Ministry as undersecretary to Muhammad Rif'at when the latter was minister and staying on until 1954 when he reached retirement age. At some time during the 1940s he was granted the rank of Bey.[95] In addition to these duties Ghurbal was the member of several learned associations and served on a great number of committees that testified to his role not just in matters of academic scholarship but as an active public intellectual.[96]

The third major pioneer in the Egyptian academic tradition in modern history was Muhammad Ibrahim Sabri (1890–1978).[97] In contrast to the English training which Rif'at and Ghurbal received, Sabri was a historian of the French school, obtaining his *licence* (1919), then his doctorate (1924), at the Sorbonne, from which he earned the sobriquet, al-Surbuni.[98] A prolific writer, Sabri ranged across a wide variety of subjects of nineteenth and twentieth century Egyptian history, and extended himself to literary criticism from the pre-Islamic to the contemporary era.[99] Despite the fact that he held formal academic qualifications of higher standing than Ghurbal, Sabri did not enjoy the same esteem amongst his colleagues nor exercise the same influence amongst his students. Indeed, his profile as a historian was almost the inverse of Ghurbal's, since he had greater stature as a writer than as a teacher. The reasons for this appear to be both personal and institutional. Although he first published in Arabic, Sabri's historical studies for the first half of his professional life were largely written in French.[100] This practice, which had been quite common among Egyptian scholars up until the First World War but became increasingly less so during the interwar period, inevitably limited Sabri's readership in Egypt.[101] Not until 1948 did he decide to write consistently in his native tongue, as he put it, 'until he paid his debt to his country'.[102] Nor did Sabri enjoy the same institutional stability and support as Ghurbal. Both, in fact, returned to Egypt in 1924 and taught for a period at the Higher Teachers' College. Initially, it appears that Sabri was preferred since he was offered a position at the new Egyptian University but differences with King Fu'ad precipitated his departure and he moved to the Dar al-Ulum in 1927.[103] The next year his history of modern Egypt was removed from the curriculum of the Higher Teachers' College and replaced by Muhammad Rif'at's text. In 1937, Sabri was appointed the director of the education mission in Geneva but he was back in Egypt by 1946 as the deputy director of the Dar al-Kutub. He taught briefly at Cairo University in 1950 then, in the following year, was nominated director of its Institute of Documents and Libraries.[104]

More than his academic contemporaries, Sabri demonstrated strong nationalist inclinations. A disciple of the exiled nationalist writer Ya'qub Sanu' (Abu Naddara) by 1907, he had publicly supported the latter's slogan of 'Egypt for the Egyptians'.[105] It was not until after the First World War that Sabri applied his historical training to an articulation of this theme. His book, *La Révolution égyptienne*, was the first nationalist interpretation of the events of 1919.[106] It bore the mark of two important influences, one intellectual, the other political. Its emphasis on revolution as a historical theme and the realization that the study of history was important in raising the consciousness of the people bore the mark of Alphonse Aulard, a renowned historian of the French Revolution and Sabri's supervisor at the Sorbonne.[107] The political influence was avowedly Wafdist. While in Paris Sabri had become acquainted with members of the Wafd and had many conversations with Sa'd Zaghlul, for whom he worked as a translator and secretary during the critical period 1919–21.[108] Contrasting assessments of *La Révolution égyptienne* reflect these two aspects. For one historian the work is 'the beginning of professional Egyptian historiography';[109] for another it is, 'a propaganda pamphlet intended to convince the European public of Egypt's right to full independence'.[110] However we might evaluate Sabri's work, it undoubtedly marked the beginning of a career of over 40 years that exercised considerable influence over Egyptian historical studies.

The mixture of scholarship and politics that we observe in the careers of Ghurbal, Sabri and Rif'at was not an aberration of the period. In the generation that followed them, academic historians were routinely involved in the world of contemporary politics as activists, advisers, commentators, critics and sources of expertise. The career of Muhammad Fu'ad Shukri (1904–63) combines the roles of academic and political agent. Shukri had graduated from the Higher Teachers' College and, like Muhammad Rif'at and Shafiq Ghurbal before him, had gone to Liverpool University where he obtained a doctorate in 1935 for a thesis on Isma'il and slavery in the Sudan.[111] On his return to Cairo, Shukri took up a position teaching modern history in the Faculty of Arts at the Egyptian University. In some ways, he was a foil to his colleague, Shafiq Ghurbal. Ghurbal was recognized as the superior scholar but Shukri demonstrated a special talent for utilizing documents, especially diplomatic correspondence, and setting them in an international context. Personal relations between the two were not close, a state of affairs perhaps not helped by Shukri's criticism of Ghurbal's view of Muhammad 'Ali. Shukri wrote extensively on Egyptian, Arab and European modern history and thus, according to 'Ali Barakat, was the first Egyptian specialist in modern history 'in the strict sense' (*bi'l-ma'nan al-daqiq*).[112] His work, which primarily focused on the nineteenth century political history of Egypt and other countries of the Middle East, was more prolific than Ghurbal's and served as a lasting contribution to the field of an increasingly sophisticated historiography.[113]

In the late 1940s Shukri took leave from the university and became legal and political adviser (*muntadab*) to the Libyan nationalist leader, Bashir al-Sa'dawi.[114] Backed by Egypt and the Arab League, al-Sa'dawi was a key player in the extended negotiations leading to the emergence of an independent Libya. On at least two occasions in 1949 Shukri was part of a Libyan delegation to the United Nations.[115] The basis for Shukri's appointment is unclear. His doctoral thesis had established his reputation as a specialist of Sudanese history but his later work on Libya, which appeared in the 1950s, may have reflected an interest activated by personal experience.[116] Regardless, the choice of Shukri revealed that the Egyptian government had placed a considerable amount of confidence in him. In his account of the Libyan negotiations, the United Nations Commissioner in Libya, Adrian Pelt, described Shukri as 'the paymaster of the Arab League, at least for Libya' and credited him with a very active role in bringing Sa'dawi over to the Egyptian side. In May 1951, perhaps overplaying his hand, the short, bespectacled historian was expelled from Libya by the British administration on the grounds of inciting demonstrations against Amir Idris.[117] He resumed academic life later the same year, becoming professor of modern history at Cairo University following the retirement of Ghurbal.

By contrast, Ibrahim 'Abduh (b. 1913) provided an example of the academic historian who took on the role of government critic, though significantly only after he had been dismissed from his university post. A student of Ghurbal, 'Abduh graduated with a Bachelor of Arts in 1935, and followed this with a Master of Arts in 1940 before taking up a position in the Institute of Journalism at the Egyptian University. This was the beginning of a long and conspicuous career in which he wrote, among other things, the basic reference work for a study of the history of the press in Egypt.[118] In early 1952 he was appointed Censor but not long after the assumption of power by the Free Officers, 'Abduh was expelled from his university position. Thereafter, he continued to write history at the same time as proving a persistent advocate of democratic values and a source of caustic political comment on the Nasser then the Sadat regime.[119]

The careers of Rif'at, Ghurbal, Sabri and those that followed demonstrate that these pioneering academic historians far from being disinterested, remote scholars were engaged and implicated in the contemporary political scene. For this reason, the emergence of an academic tradition was not simply a scholarly or institutional development but part of the contest of national politics that emphasized the centrality of a national state even if it represented different currents within that tradition. In his introduction to Ghurbal's *Beginnings of the Egyptian Question*, Arnold Toynbee had projected a scholarly image, '[Ghurbal] is so thoroughly detached from the passions and prejudices that enter into his field of study that...it would be difficult to guess from internal evidence whether the author were an Englishman, a Frenchman, or an Egyptian, or none of these.'[120] Yet Ghurbal himself had acknowledged a sense of national mission when he wrote, 'my writing is that of an Egyptian citizen who aspires to be a better one, capable of evaluation and discrimination.'[121] It was this sense of national purpose that characterized the first generation of academic historians in Egypt.

By 1952 the foundations of a local tradition of academic historiography in modern Egyptian history had been laid and played a part in making the university the home of a liberal school of interpretation. Its main slogan was the 'Egyptianization' (*tamsir*) of history – a call echoed elsewhere in the fields of politics, labour law and industry. In the context of historical scholarship it signified two objectives. The first was the end of the dominance of European historians and language in modern Egyptian scholarship and their replacement by Egyptian scholars and Arabic. In this process, Ghurbal and others, although educated in part abroad, were successful in forging the basis of an indigenous tradition that flourished with the succeeding generation of history students. The second objective was to write history from a national perspective rather than from the viewpoint of the palace. In this they achieved mixed success since at times the distinction between the 'royalist' and first academic historians was not entirely clear. Ghurbal's prefatory note to his first book, for instance, specifically recognized the 'munificence' of King Fu'ad.[122] Further, his favourable view of Muhammad 'Ali placed him as in some way connected with, if not part of, the royalist school fostered by the Egyptian monarch. Given Ghurbal's political connections, political inclination may have been one reason for this ambivalence. There may also have been political pressure. In the case of Muhammad Sabri, on at least one occasion Fu'ad had personally intervened and demanded he alter some of his criticisms of Isma'il.[123] Nevertheless, the academic arm of the liberal school did create a broader vision of the nation and a wider interpretation of its identity and interests than the royalist school. By virtue of his position and influence at Cairo University, Shafiq Ghurbal could be claimed, before anyone else, as 'the founder of the Egyptian school' (*mu'assis al-madrasa al-misriyya*) since 'he began moving the centre of gravity of [historical] studies gradually, and without clamour, from the offices of the palace to the university and from the hands of foreigners to the hands of the Egyptians.'[124] Ultimately the liberal school was seriously challenged, and asked to defend itself, not by the royalist school, which lost its *raison d'être* and patron after 1952, but by the revolutionary, materialist streams of thought.

A CHANGING OF THE GUARD

The coming to power of the Free Officers in July 1952 began the process of a radical rearrangement of Egyptian political life which saw the monarchy abolished, the parliament dissolved and political parties banned. As the confidence and purpose of the military regime grew, its revolutionary rhetoric and nationalist tone appealed to the close relationship between history and politics. It was not long before some commentators were attacking established historians for their biased historical perspective and lack of vision.[125] The new climate met with mixed reactions from academic historians: some began to fade from prominence; others adeptly accommodated themselves to or at least did not stand in the way of the political demands of nationalism, Arabism and socialism; yet others warmly embraced them.

Ghurbal's own connections with the Sa'dists and his sympathy for the monarchy would not have endeared him to the new Revolutionary Command Council (RCC). Still, he had substantial administrative expertise to offer and his standing as one of Egypt's pre-eminent historians meant his achievements could hardly be dismissed. In 1952, as undersecretary in the Ministry of Education, he was appointed as a member of a special committee to report on the state of higher education but his retirement from Cairo University, then from the Ministry in 1954, reduced his influence as a public figure.[126] Yet if Ghurbal's views on domestic politics might have become unfashionable in official circles after 1952, his acceptance of Arabism as a theory of historical analysis still meant he had a public role to play.[127] This was recognized with his appointment in 1956 as successor to Sati' al-Husri in the directorship of the recently established Institute of Arabic Studies (Ma'had al-dirasat al-'arabiyya).

By now the undisputed elder statesman of modern Egyptian history, Ghurbal continued to be active well into the 1950s, supervising students and writing occasional articles, including a set of radio lectures broadcast on the broad panorama of the history of Egypt. He remained at the head of the Egyptian Association for Historical Studies and maintained his participation in a large number of other scholarly and cultural organizations. When he died in October 1961 the widespread praise and large number of written tributes were testament to Ghurbal's status amongst his colleagues.[128] The recognition extended beyond academia. In the dedication of what must have been Ghurbal's last published work, Tharwat 'Ukasha, the Minister of Culture and National Guidance, announced Ghurbal's recent death and wrote of his regret at the loss of 'our great historian' (mu'arrikhna al-kabir).[129]

Always less of a public figure than Ghurbal, Muhammad Sabri did not fare well under the July Revolution. In December 1952 after being accused of tampering with examination results he was purged from Cairo University.[130] Without the security of an institutional base and being personally aloof, he became progressively marginalized.[131] The political reasons are not clear. Sabri had shown himself to be sympathetic to progressive causes, being active in the debate on the Sudanese question after the Second World War and prominent in the peace movement in the early 1950s.[132] In 1958, he even wrote a history of the Suez Canal which he dedicated to Nasser and publicly expressed support for his policies on the Suez question.[133] Perhaps his former connections with the Wafd and contemporaneity with the ancien régime, even if he himself was disenchanted with it, explained at least a certain indifference if not official disfavour towards him.[134] His standing amongst historians continued to be recognized but his work from the late 1950s witnessed a retreat to remote historical periods and less controversial subjects, such as literary criticism.[135] Yet, while the careers of Ghurbal and Sabri were on the wane, two younger historians, Ahmad 'Izzat 'Abd al-Karim and Muhammad Anis, were to frame the academic scene during the Nasser years.

AHMAD 'IZZAT 'ABD AL-KARIM:
A HOME-GROWN HISTORIAN

Ahmad 'Izzat 'Abd al-Karim (1909–80) was one of Shafiq Ghurbal's most distinguished pupils and the first Egyptian to earn a doctorate in modern history in Egypt.[136] Beginning his studies at the Egyptian University in 1926, 'Abd al-Karim obtained his doctorate in 1941 for a thesis on the history of Egyptian education from Muhammad 'Ali to Tawfiq. Three years previously 'Abd al-Karim had begun teaching at the university but it was his appointment as associate professor at the new 'Ain Shams University (then the University of Ibrahim Pasha al-Kabir) in 1950 that proved decisive. From there, he nurtured a historical school not only of Egyptian historians but of scholars throughout the Arab world for more than a generation.

'Abd al-Karim was much less a public figure than Shafiq Ghurbal. His public life was almost entirely confined to the university campus and his career as an academic and university administrator more according to the model of a detached intellectual and educator. His steady, if unspectacular, rise through the ranks at 'Ain Shams, from his initial appointment, then subsequently to professor, dean, vice-rector and finally, rector, suggests a career advanced more on the basis of professional and personal merit than any political connections.[137] Surprisingly, in these years he appears to have taken no conspicuous part in the great political debates concerning the relations between the state and the universities.[138] Nevertheless, 'Abd al-Karim proved himself a skilled reader of political winds, supporting the principles of the July Revolution and championing the view of Egypt as part of the Arab World rather than of the Near East, which had been the older view.[139] Before the pan-Arab rhetoric of the regime hit full pitch, he had already authored a number of works consistent with this perspective including a popular high school text on the history of the Arab world.[140] 'Abd al-Karim was also alert to the academic opportunities afforded by the political milieu and he encouraged his students to research the history of Arab countries. In this way he groomed a broad range of regional specialists on the history of the Gulf (Jamal Zakariyya), Iraq ('Abd al-'Aziz Nawwar) and Yemen (Sayyid Mustafa Salim).[141] This strategy meshed comfortably with the pan-Arab project of Nasser but was also grounded in more practical reasons. Egypt, as the cultural centre of the Arab world, was the nursery for its academics. By providing courses and expertise on the Arab world, Egypt not only attracted students from all over the Middle East to its universities, but also benefited by the appointment of many of its graduates to academic positions in universities from Morocco to Iraq and the Gulf.

The history department at 'Ain Shams University also proved itself adept at reflecting the domestic political rhetoric of the Nasser regime. 'Abd al-Karim steered many students towards consideration of social and economic issues in Egyptian history, areas hitherto neglected by the prevailing tradition of political and diplomatic studies. In his own postgraduate theses on Egyptian nineteenth century education 'Abd al-Karim had touched on issues of social history but characteristic of the academic history of the time these had been primarily a study of administration and institutions. By contrast the new approach championed at 'Ain Shams in the 1960s took a more sophisticated view of social and economic processes, putting greater emphasis on their impact across Egyptian society than an institutional and state-centred view. By the early 1970s seminal studies began to appear on issues of landownership, the labour movement, and the development of industry, distinguished by the use of archival material that set new standards for Egyptian historiography.[142]

The fertile ground for much of this work and the forum for many subsequent scholarly discussions was the Seminar of Higher Studies for Modern History (*Siminar al-dirasat al-'ulya li'l-tarikh al-hadith*) first set up by 'Abd al-Karim in the History Department at 'Ain Shams in November 1955.[143] Beginning its first meeting with only six students in attendance (three of whom were studying under Shafiq Ghurbal), it grew to be an influential marketplace of ideas for historical debate, trafficking in the discussion of thesis topics and a wide range of issues relating to modern Egyptian and Arab history. It welcomed attendance by all those working in the field, attracting people from all over Egypt and even scholars abroad. Presided over by 'Abd al-Karim every Thursday evening until his death in 1980, the seminar continues to be held more than 40 years after its establishment.[144]

Despite his image as the father figure of liberal historical scholarship over almost three decades, 'Abd al-Karim was not without his own political predilections. As a historian he took a moderate liberal line – a 'modernist to a certain extent', his long-time colleague and successor at 'Ain Shams, Ahmad 'Abd al-Rahim Mustafa, described him.[145] Amongst younger historians who challenged some of the sacred cows of established Egyptian history, he was well known for his sympathetic view of Sa'd Zaghlul, said to have been the result of a meeting with the Wafd leader when a schoolboy in Upper Egypt.[146] He was particularly unhappy about the critical view of Sa'd Zaghlul taken by 'Abd al-Khaliq Lashin in his doctoral thesis.[147] Moreover, he had little truck with Marxist thought and was uncomfortable

31

with some of the materialist analyses produced by students at 'Ain Shams in the late 1960s.[148]

MUHAMMAD ANIS AND THE SOCIALIST SCHOOL

While 'Abd al-Karim was diligently creating a sober tradition of historical research at 'Ain Shams, Muhammad Anis (1921–86) was urging a full-scale re-examination of Egyptian history at Cairo University. Anis' star had been in the ascendant since the 1950s both as a historian and a public intellectual.[149] Born in Cairo in 1921, he had graduated from Fu'ad I University in 1942 then, like other historians before him, had gone to England for postgraduate study, obtaining his doctorate from the University of Birmingham in 1950.[150] As a young man he had been attracted to the Wafdist Vanguard, the left wing of the party, and taken part in pro-Wafdist demonstrations in 1935. Though this group did include some communist elements, at the time of his departure for England, Anis apparently had no socialist leanings.[151] Upon his return to Egypt, he took up a position at Cairo University where he began to bring a number of national and historical issues before the public eye.[152]

This public, advocatory style became characteristic of Anis. More than any other academic historian of his generation, he became as known for articles in the pages of newspapers such as *al-Masa'*, *al-Ahram* and *al-Jumhuriyya* as for his academic work. Writing in a typically aggressive tone, he canvassed a large number of historical issues in a way quite different from the moderate and measured tones of Shafiq Ghurbal and 'Abd al-Karim. Following the publication of the National Charter, Anis resolutely called for a programme of historiographical renewal based on the theory of historical materialism, or the socialist or so-called 'third school' (*al-madrasa al-thalitha*).[153] From his position as an editor of *al-Katib* and elsewhere, he trumpeted its virtues as the natural successor of the earlier royalist and liberal schools of historical thought and throughout the 1960s remained its most articulate and public exponent.[154]

Anis was more than just a publicly engaged historian. He was fully immersed in Egyptian politics and many of the important ideological debates of the 1960s and early 1970s. A prominent figure in the general secretariat of the Arab Socialist Union (ASU), the mass political organization set up in 1962, he served for a time as undersecretary to Kamal Rif'at in the Secretariat of Ideology and Propaganda.[155] As a member of the Vanguard Organization (al-Tali'a), Anis was part of a secret and elite group that 'was to embody Nasser's conception of the revolution and establish the means for his political ideals to be passed on to future generations'.[156] Since the Vanguard was based on personal contacts and the branches of the ASU were marked by a 'strict personalism', these posts indicate important political connections.[157] As part of the government's effort to woo academics over to its side, Anis was active in taking his fellow historians to task for avoiding their proper political role in promoting the ideas of the Revolution and creating a socialist society.[158] Scarcely daunted by the defeat in 1967, he later warned of the dangers of passing power to the technocrats; attacked Muhammad Hasanayn Haykal's attitude to the Palestinian conflict in 1970; and took an active, if unsuccessful, part in the discussions on the fate of the ASU chaired by Sayyid Mar'i – surely the type of technocrat about whom he had warned.[159] From 1967 onwards, Anis began to spend increasing amounts of time outside of the country, teaching at various universities in the Arab world, such as Algeria, Baghdad and San'a. Yet, he continued to maintain a public profile in Egypt throughout the 1970s even if after the death of Nasser he felt progressively at odds with the changing tenor of the Sadat regime.

Anis' very active public and political career brought history into the daily newspapers and the political debates of the time but it inevitably took him away from the normal routine of university life. While Anis supervised many students, and particularly encouraged Palestinians, his frequent absences from Cairo University meant his influence on the academic front was less than it might have been. He appeared little concerned with placing his students in university positions, a fact which may explain why relatively few of his Egyptian students went on to become academic historians.[160] Nevertheless, the influence he exercised through his published work and political activities should not be underrated and his strident advocacy of a new approach to history inspired many historians well beyond the limits of Cairo University.[161] Yet it was his older contemporary, 'Abd al-Karim, who would become the *shaykh* among Egyptian modern historians. The continuity of his long tenure at 'Ain Shams and his concern to place his students in suitable positions meant that the vibrant and heterogeneous school of modern historical research at 'Ain Shams was the seedbed for many future academic careers in Egypt and the Arab world.

Muhammad Anis and Ahmad 'Izzat 'Abd al-Karim stand as the dominant figures of contemporary Egyptian historiography during the Nasser period. Building on the foundations of the liberal school this increasingly mature historiographical tradition incorporated a more sophisticated analysis of social and economic factors within a broader political framework. More restrained than the socialist school (*madrasa al-ishtirakiyya*) originally envisaged by Anis, it was a social school (*madrasa ijtima'iyya*), embracing many of the tools if not always the theory of historical materialism, that came to be the dominant school of historical thought in the universities from the late 1960s.[162]

The roles played by Anis and 'Abd al-Karim were complementary. Anis was a larger, more flamboyant, intensely political, public figure; 'Abd al-Karim was personally less dynamic and styled himself as a sedate, studious scholar.

Despite their very different personal styles and approaches, mutual relations appear to have been cordial. Yet there was one important issue of history on which they did publicly disagree. In 1961, Professor Hasan 'Uthman of the Institute of African Studies at Cairo University ruled that no postgraduate history thesis would be accepted dealing with events occurring within the last 50 years.[163] It is unclear what lay behind the move at this time but it effectively excluded consideration of the critical period between the revolutions of 1919 and 1952. Incensed, Anis cancelled lectures for a month as a sign of protest, declaring that 1945 was a more acceptable cut-off date.[164] 'Abd al-Karim took the contrary view, supporting 'Uthman's directive on the grounds that the study of a historical event required a certain distance and a proper consideration of documents.[165] Others joined in the debate. Shafiq Ghurbal, by this time retired and withdrawn from public life, stated that any historical event could be studied as long as it was 'complete' (*mutakamil*).[166] Muhammad Sabri, on the other hand, seems to have supported 'Uthman.[167] In any event, 'Uthman's endeavour to restrict the scope of historical studies was unsuccessful. Indeed, 'Abd al-Karim apparently modified his views on the matter since some of his own students would later write on near contemporary historical issues.[168] The matter of when the historian is able to deal with events continues to bedevil the academy. At a conference on the modernization of historical research methods held in Caro in 1992, Sa'id 'Ashur, a pre-modern historian at Cairo University, stated,

> In our study of modern history we should not deal with the past 40 or 50 years because many documents have not yet come to light. A historian is a human being with likes and dislikes, subject to many influences which might affect his recording of contemporary events. His viewpoint may be inaccurate and unobjective. Events we are witnessing at present will in future become part of history. Today they are not history in the real sense.[169]

A MORE DIVERSE ACADEMY: CLASS AND WOMEN

The political and social transformation that occurred during the Nasser years inevitably brought changes to the personnel of history departments in universities. The expansion and reorganization of the public education system after 1952 made a university education more accessible to a greater number of Egyptians. In the period between 1952 and 1972, student numbers in the humanities and social sciences increased more than three-fold.[170] Cairo and 'Ain Shams Universities remained dominant as the main centres of academic research in modern Egyptian history but their courses were supplemented if never seriously challenged by other institutions such as the University of Alexandria, which gave greater attention to the Ottoman period, and the private American University in Cairo (AUC).[171] In the 1970s the steady increase in student numbers brought with it an expansion of the university system. In only 5 years, six new universities offering courses in modern history opened: Asyut (Sohag campus) (1971),[172] Tanta (1972), Mansura (1973), Zagazig (Banha campus) (1974), Minya (1976) and Manufiyya (1976).

Academic positions at the smaller universities were less prestigious than the metropolitan posts but the expansion in academic employment opportunities witnessed an important shift in the social background of Egyptian historians. Prior to 1952, academic historians had tended to come from the middle or upper classes. Shafiq Ghurbal had been from a merchant family; Muhammad Rif'at's origins were in the Turkish aristocracy; Ahmad 'Izzat 'Abd al-Karim's father had worked for the Ministry of Education and his contemporary and colleague at 'Ain Shams, 'Abd al-Hamid Muhammad al-Batriq, hailed from a merchant family in Zagazig.[173] Salah al-'Aqqad (1929–94) a historian of the next generation, came from the *'bourgeoisie moyenne'*.[174] Some historians came from more modest origins. Ahmad 'Abd al-Rahim Mustafa was from a lower-middle class family in Sohag and Muhammad Anis' father had repaired mosques before the family fell on difficult times during the depression in the 1930s.[175] On the whole, however, historians were drawn from the more affluent parts of society. From the early 1970s, students from working and lower-middle class began to feature amongst the new generation of historians. 'Abd al-'Azim Ramadan came from a proletarian background and had even been a worker himself for a time, having come to history relatively late in life; Ra'uf 'Abbas' father worked for the Egyptian Railways; 'Ali Barakat's family is of a fellah origin.[176] Government policy in the 1960s promoted such social mobility. Indeed, 'Abd al-Khaliq Lashin felt that his university education was delayed by the government because he was *not* from a sufficiently humble background.[177] Of the current generation of Egyptian historians, Ra'uf 'Abbas says 'they are all petit bourgeois...express[ing] the ideas, dreams, aims of this category of the middle class'.[178]

Changes in education policy also affected the opportunities of academic training available to history students. Since 1826, when al-Tahtawi had gone to Paris, Egyptian students had been sent to Europe on educational missions. In the period from the arrival of the British in 1882 until the First World War, this policy had been severely limited but the practice was resumed afterwards and continued, particularly in the years when Taha Husayn, himself a graduate of the Sorbonne, was the Minister of Education.[179] With the change of regime in 1952 students were not recalled but the policy of the Egyptian government thereafter gave preference to students in the technical and scientific fields over those in the humanities for study in Europe.[180] Ahmad 'Abd al-Rahim Mustafa, who left for the University of London 2 weeks after the Free Officers seized power, may have been one of the last historians sent abroad for some time. The pattern already set by

Ahmad 'Izzat 'Abd al-Karim, who was the unalloyed product of the Egyptian university system, became the established norm from the 1950s for future academic historians.[181] The availability of a full postgraduate modern history programme in Egypt without the complication and expense of overseas travel may also have made history a more attractive option. Nevertheless, those who completed postgraduate degrees in Europe in the 1940s and early 1950s and returned to teach in Egypt remained influential teachers in the universities well into the 1970s.

Despite the greater accessibility to academic education, university history departments continued to remain a male domain. Since the nineteenth century institutional and social attitudes had been significant barriers to the education and professional advancement of Egyptian women. Some private schools had started to provide for girls education from the middle of the nineteenth century but it was not until 1873, when the Siyufiyya School was opened, that any state school education began to do so. In the following decades schools and colleges for girls were gradually established, notably the Saniyya School (1889), a girls' sections at 'Abbas Primary School in Cairo (1895), and a primary school for girls at Fayum (1909). Women's training colleges were set up in the years before and during the First World War at Mansura, Bulaq in Cairo and Alexandria.[182] These inadequate provisions for the education of women were reflected in the low rates of female literacy. In 1907 only 1 per cent of Egyptian women were estimated to be literate, compared to 13 per cent of men, a figure which improved at glacial pace over the subsequent decades. By 1952 only 14 per cent of Egyptian women were literate, well behind the 39 per cent for men.[183] Given these figures it is unsurprising that the entry of women into academic circles and scholarly forums was very limited.

There were also institutional barriers. At the beginning of the twentieth century neither al-Azhar nor Dar al-'Ulum accepted women and it was not until 1908 with the opening of the private Egyptian University that there was any opportunity of a university education for women.[184] In that year 31 women attended lectures, though perhaps only three of these were Egyptian. In the following year a women's section, attended largely by upper class women, was set up under the direction of Mlle A. Couvreur, where Nabawiyya Musa lectured on the position of women in ancient and modern Egyptian history. The curriculum was expanded but in May 1912 the section was closed down owing to public protests presumably based on religious sensitivities since European and non-Muslim women continued to attend the university.

Notwithstanding the new constitutional arrangements of 1923 and the refoundation of the Egyptian University as a state institution in 1925, Egyptian women were slow to benefit from the reinvigorated political atmosphere in Egypt after the First World War. Indicative of the social obstacles they faced at home was the fact that they were allowed to study abroad before being finally permitted to enrol at the university in Cairo in 1929.[185] Numbers grew steadily. In 1933, the first woman graduated from the Faculties of Arts and Law and within 2 years 173 female students were studying, just over half of them in the Faculty of Arts.[186] In 1937 Suhayr al-Qalamawi became the first Egyptian woman to obtain a Master of Arts degree in Egypt and the first to be awarded a PhD in 1941 for her work in the field of Arabic Literature.[187] Under the post-1952 revolutionary regime the greater educational opportunities in higher education benefited women as well. In 1953, women were admitted to the Dar al-'Ulum and 3 years later the former Women Teachers' Training College became the Women's College at 'Ain Shams University. Finally, following its reorganization and the creation of a separate Women's College, al-Azhar accepted female students in 1962. By 1983, women represented a third of all student enrolments and there had been a significant shift away from the humanities to the sciences (from 32 per cent of women in 1952 to 57 per cent in 1973).[188]

The appointment of women to teaching and academic positions inevitably lagged behind these developments at some considerable distance. Nabawiyya Musa had made some early headway, being the first woman principal of the Girls' School at Fayum in 1909 and lecturing in the women's section at the private Egyptian University but it was not until 1930 with the appointment of Zaynab Hasan to the chemistry department that the university had an Egyptian woman on staff.[189] Gradually women established themselves as credible scholars and educators. In 1937, a number of graduate assistants were taken on in the Faculty of Arts. From 1938 to 1941 Karima al-Sa'id served as the Ministry of Education's inspector of history for girls' schools and much later in the 1960s, as deputy minister of education. Promotion of women was hampered by attitudes amongst administrators, particularly on the matter of the employment of married women. Nevertheless, by the 1950s Suhayr al-Qalamawi at Cairo University, Fatima Salim Sayf at Alexandria and 'A'isha 'Abd al-Rahman at 'Ain Shams held university posts in their respective Faculties of Arts.[190]

Within history departments, opportunity was even more limited. The unwillingness of Ahmad Amin (then dean of Arts at Cairo University) to offer a job to Duriya Shafiq on her return to Egypt at the end of Second World War, may have owed something to a contrast of personalities but it was indicative of the obstacles women faced.[191] Holding a doctorate from the Sorbonne (graduated 1940), Shafiq had to settle for a position as a high school teacher and later as inspector in the Ministry of Education. The first Egyptian woman to hold an academic position as a historian in Egypt was Zayna Ismat Rashid (1919–c. 1995). A student of Shafiq Ghurbal, she had followed the tradition of earlier Egyptian historians by going to the University of Liverpool where she specialized in early modern European history, apparently on Ghurbal's advice.[192] Graduating in 1949 with a doctoral thesis titled 'The Peace of Paris, 1763', she took a position in the department of history at 'Ain Shams University the following year and remained there until 1963 when she accepted the position of dean at the newly-created Women's College at al-Azhar. In 1977 she left al-Azhar to become Director of the Centre of University Studies at the University of Riyadh (1977–80).[193] Another of this first generation of woman academic historians was Sayyida Isma'il al-Kashaf who held the position of professor of Early Islamic history at the Women's College, 'Ain Shams University.

During the 1960s and the early 1970s both Egyptian and other Arab women enrolled as postgraduate students in increasing numbers in the history departments of Cairo, 'Ain Shams and Alexandria Universities. In the early 1970s a number of women, most of them working on the pre-modern period, graduated with PhDs.[194] The first woman to obtain a doctorate in modern history in Egypt was a Syrian, Layla Sabagh;[195] the first Egyptian woman was Layla 'Abd al-Latif Ahmad at Ain Shams University in 1975 under the supervision of Ahmad Izzat 'Abd al-Karim. She was followed by Latifa Muhammad Salim at Cairo University, working under Muhammad Anis in 1979, Nawal 'Abd al-'Aziz Radi and Amal Kamil Bayumi al-Subki.

This upcoming generation of women were to benefit in some measure from the job opportunities opened up with the expansion of the university system beyond the confines of women's colleges, especially in the provincial institutions. By 1975, Amima Muhammad Sabir al-Baghdadi was assistant lecturer in modern history at Tanta. Since then Latifa Muhammad Salim and Amal Kamil Bayumi al-Subki have been appointed to the history department at Zagazig University (Banha Branch); Layla 'Abd al-Latif Ahmad took a position at the Women's College of al-Azhar, and Nawal 'Abd al-'Aziz Radi, after holding a position at the Khartoum Branch of Cairo University, has been appointed to the Institute of African Studies at Cairo University. Women continue to make inroads into academic history departments even if the senior posts in the metropolitan universities remain a male bastion. Zubayda Muhammad 'Ata is now dean of history at the recently established Faculty of Arts at the University of Hilwan and Fatima 'Alim al-Din, is currently head of the history department at the Women's College, 'Ain Shams University. It is likely that the next generation of women will make slow rather than steady progress.[196]

Another smaller group of women historians took an alternative academic route to the state system by attending the private AUC. The first female student was Eva Habib al-Masri, admitted in 1928 and later a prominent feminist activist and editor of *al-Misriyya*. Much later another AUC graduate, 'Afaf al-Sayyid Marsot, pursued postgraduate studies in the US and completed a doctorate at Oxford in 1963. She subsequently held an academic position at UCLA in the United States for many years and published widely.[197] Other graduates of AUC, Nelly Hanna, a medieval and Ottoman historian, and Amira Sonbol al-Azhari, a modern historian now at Georgetown, also obtained postgraduate degrees abroad.[198] All three have since taught at AUC in recent years.

One measure of the profile enjoyed by women historians in Egypt is through an examination of their participation in academic conferences. The evidence from the 1970s suggests that women historians from other parts of the Arab world have had a greater profile than their Egyptian counterparts. At two successive history seminars held at 'Ain Shams University in the 1976 and 1977, only five women out of an overall total of 50 participants took part, four of them non-Egyptian Arabs.[199] The pamphlet commemorating the 20th anniversary of the Seminar of Higher Studies for Modern History at 'Ain Shams (1975) confirmed the limited impact made by women historians, listing only one woman out of 32 academic historians and one from 26 PhD graduates associated with the seminar.[200] In two more recent conferences held in Egypt on modern Egyptian historiography, women again were little in evidence. The 1987 conference featured only two Arab woman presenters, Najwa Khalil and 'Izza Wahba, neither of whom was from a university.[201] In 1995, in a conference which addressed the development of modern and contemporary Egyptian history over the last 25 years, three women presented papers, none of them from the Egyptian state system.[202]

Even if the social background of the academic historian in Egypt changed slowly and the gender profile changed even less, the natural turnover of university staff and the shifting political winds have nevertheless brought new movement. The retirement of 'Abd al-Karim as professor of modern history at 'Ain Shams in 1969 and Muhammad Anis' fall from official favour at about the same time marked the end of the dominance of the two commanding historians of the 1960s. They both remained active in the academic field – 'Abd al-Karim maintained his participation in the History Seminar and continued to examine theses, and Anis, peripatetically taught in various universities in the Arab world – but the 1970s heralded the appearance of a number of new talents. At 'Ain Shams Ahmad 'Abd al-Rahim Mustafa, a PhD from the University of London, succeeded to 'Abd al-Karim's position after having served as his deputy for many years. In contrast to the careful if liberal tone of 'Abd al-Karim, Mustafa politically stood more to the Left. During the 1960s he had been a member of the ASU but, disenchanted by the government's deceptive conduct following the 1967 defeat, Mustafa took up a position at the University of Mosul in Iraq soon afterwards. He returned to 'Ain Shams in 1970 to become head of the history department, then vice-dean of the faculty, but his effective tenure proved short-lived. The student unrest in 1972–73 persuaded him to accept a post at the University of Kuwait in 1973 where he stayed until 1987.[203] Though officially Mustafa maintained his position with 'Ain Shams until 1977, 'Abd al-'Aziz Sulayman Nawwar, a specialist of Iraqi history, became the acting head and chairman of the History Seminar.

Like Mustafa, many of the historians and, even more, the students of the Nasser years were genuinely influenced by Marxist thought and identified in varying degrees with the Left. The students of the 1960s who emerged from this milieu became the bright young historians of the 1970s. 'Asim al-Disuqi, a graduate of 'Ain Shams, had taught in the Workers' Cultural Organization (al-Mu'assasa al-thaqafiyya al-'ummaliyya), an organization dedicated to educating the working class, where he gave lectures to workers and sometimes even spoke in the factories.[204] Both he and 'Ali Barakat, a student of Anis at Cairo University, were active in the Socialist Youth Organization, the youth arm of the ASU. During the Sadat years, al-Disuqi and Barakat, with other historians 'Abd al-Khaliq Lashin and Ra'uf 'Abbas (all born in 1938 or 1939), continued their association in varying degrees with Marxist thought, maintaining membership or loose affiliation with the official party of the leftist opposition, al-Tajammu', and writing in publications of the Left.

Other historians took advantage of the more open political environment to move in different directions. Muhammad Anis himself returned to play a part in the establishment of the reconstituted Wafd set up in 1978. Six years later, he resigned in protest after the party entered into an electoral alliance with the Ikhwan which he felt fatally compromised its secular ideals.[205] Salah al-'Aqqad, professor of modern history at the Women's College (Kulliyat al-Banat), 'Ain Shams, also joined the revived Wafd, sitting on the party's committee for Arab Affairs and contributing a regular column to the party newspaper until his death in 1994.[206] Other historians have eschewed the rough and tumble of party politics and preferred to play a more technocratic role, utilizing their expertise in the service of government. Yunan Labib Rizq (b. 1933) of 'Ain Shams has acted for the government on a number of occasions, notably as a member of the Taba Commission in the resolution of the dispute between Egypt and Israel, and more recently, as a representative at the Madrid Conference in 1991.[207]

'Abd al-'Azim Ramadan (b. 1925), a prominent student of Anis, has charted his own mercurial political course. In the 1970s, Ramadan had been a founding member of al-Tajammu'. Following Sadat's Camp David initiative when the party effectively split over the issue of relations with Israel, Ramadan found himself in the pro-treaty camp along with Louis 'Awad, 'Abd al-Rahman al-Sharqawi and others. He maintained his party membership but, following strong criticism by Salah 'Isa, resigned with some fanfare in 1985.[208] Since then he has steered a course between the policies of the revived Wafd and the government enjoying extensive if not excessive access to the media.[209] One example from a lengthy list is a long-running column on the history of the Wafd that appeared in the party newspaper. Ramadan has also written regular contributions in a number of government-owned journals and newspapers, such as Uktubir and al-Jumhuriyya, which have unremittingly been collected and republished in book form.[210] Since 1986, he has served as editor-in-chief of the *Tarikh al-misriyyin* historical series and been appointed to a number of scholarly and press committees. In 1989, he became a member of the Majlis al-Shura, an appointment that has no doubt facilitated widespread dissemination of his work.

Today, the pages of such popular news and cultural magazines as *Ruz al-Yusuf, al-Hilal, al-Musawwar* and *Uktubir*, continue to feature regular contributions from academic historians. Many of these have been provoked by contemporary political issues of the day: Egyptian foreign debt, the pattern of industrial development and electoral issues.[211] Sadat's decision to fly to Jerusalem and the subsequent signing of the Camp David treaty generated considerable debate in which historians themselves took part. Salah al-'Aqqad and 'Abd al-'Azim Ramadan came out in favour of the move while others, particularly those on the Left, were opposed. More recently, outbreaks of civil strife between Copts and Muslims have attracted similar commentary, though here the academic voice has been more muted.[212] This general phenomenon is indicative of the fact that academic historians, while perhaps not enjoying the high profile of someone like Anis in the 1960s, remain active, public intellectuals engaged not only in specific historical controversies but in many political issues of the day.

AN ORGANIZED PROFESSION

Part of the maturation of the professional standing of the academic historian was the establishment of an association specifically dedicated to historical discussion and research. Shafiq Ghurbal had seen the need for this even when Cairo and Alexandria were the only modern universities in Egypt. In July 1945, he was the founding spirit behind the Egyptian Association for Historical Studies (*al-Jam'iyya al-misriyya li'l-dirasat al-tarikhiyya*) set up under the auspices of the Ministry of Education.[213] The number of academic historians in Egypt at this time cannot have been more than a handful but by drawing together specialists from related fields, as well as interested amateurs, the Association marked an important step in the recognition of the status of the profession and discipline. Originally named the Royal Association for Historical Studies (*al-Jam'iyya al-malakiyya li'l-dirasat al-tarikhiyya*), a title which itself suggests a careful, conservative tone, the Association was dedicated inter alia to the collection of documents, memoirs and archives relevant to Egyptian history; the publication of historical writing and research; and the organization of conferences and lectures.

The Association's membership featured a cross section of established scholars and public figures. Among its office holders, the pairing of Muhammad Tahir Pasha, member of the Majlis al-Shuyukh, as president and Shafiq Ghurbal as vice-president characterized this partnership. Members of early administrative councils included Egyptian academics such as Ibrahim Nushi

Qasim, professor of Greek and Roman history, and Mustafa ʿAmr Bey, vice-rector (both of Cairo University), Muhammad Rifʿat and ʿAziz Suriyal ʿAtiyya of Alexandria University, and resident foreign scholars, Gaston Wiet and archaeologist Etienne Drioton.[214] Among political figures were Muhammad Husayn Haykal, then president of the Majlis al-Shuyukh and leader of the Liberal Constitutionalist Party and also a distinguished writer, and Muhammad Hilmi ʿIsa Pasha, a senior non-Wafdist politician and royalist, who had served as Education Minister under Ismaʿil Sidqi. The Association thus resembled in part the membership and tenor of the well-established learned societies of the time, such as the Institut d'Égypte, but differed in having a relatively more Egyptian and less elitist structure. Membership grew quickly. In 1949, 140 members were listed; by 1951 this had increased to 350.[215] Like other scholarly bodies, after 1952 the Association developed a more Egyptian and less socially eminent membership.[216] By the 1990s there were over 3000 members.

By 1948 the Association had amassed a respectable library of 4000 books and in the following year its own journal, the *Royal Egyptian Historical Review*, appeared initially in English and Arabic. The Association also published historical monographs that reflected the preoccupations of the royalist school.[217] After 1952 the journal was changed to a more appropriate *al-Majalla al-tarikhiyya al-misriyya* (Egyptian Historical Journal) and Shafiq Ghurbal subsequently moved to the position of association president which he held until his death. Later, ʿAbd al-Karim, as the natural heir apparent, served in the position for more than a decade. For many years the Association's modest premises and library off Bustan St near Midan Talʿat Harb served as the symbolic heart of the profession. It was here, for example, that many historians gathered in 1965 for discussions on the significance of the National Charter for the study of Egyptian history. Although the association always enjoyed a healthy membership it was in dire financial straits by the mid-1990s, prompting the Ministry of Culture to increase its annual grant five-fold to LE 10,000.[218] Unexpected assistance came from the ruler of Sharjah, Shaykh Sultan, a history graduate of Exeter and Durham, who financed a new building for the association in Madinat Nasr which opened in May 2001.[219] While it still suffers from some chronic financial problems the Association continues to provide the focus for scholarly interaction. In addition to maintaining a small number of salaried staff, and a library of some 8000 books, it holds weekly seminars, regular lectures and an annual conference. The journal of the Association has, in recent years, been joined by two other academic history journals: *al-Muʾarrikh al-misri* ('The Egyptian Historian') published by the History Department of Cairo University since 1988; and *Qadaya tarikhiyya*, initially edited by Mahmud Mitwalli at the University of Minya, and subsequently moved to the University of the Suez Canal (Port Said).[220]

In contrast to the moderate means and restrained style of the Egyptian association, the international Arab Historians' Union (*Ittihad al-muʾarrikhin*

42

al-'arab) has presented a different profile. Set up following a conference in Baghdad in May 1974 it came to exemplify an uneasy mixture of scholarship and overt political influence. From the beginning the organization was very much an Iraqi project. Its first president was Husayn Amin, then president of the Iraqi Historical Society, but more significant was the financial support given to the Union by the Iraqi government, which provided 40,000 dinars to assist in its establishment.[221] The Union's ostensible aim was 'to move historical research from the captivity of the narrow regional (*qutriyya*) view to a comprehensive national (*qawmiyya*) view'.[222] On the face of it, this meshed comfortably with the pan-Arabist principles of Nasser but more ominously, it was also consistent with Ba'thist ideology. In the course of many trips around the Arab world, Amin canvassed support for the organization while the Iraqi government continued to provide generous assistance in the staging of lavish conferences as well as bankrolling a programme of research. Under Amin's successor, Mustafa 'Abd al-Qadir al-Najjar, an Iraqi and graduate of 'Ain Shams University, the Union became even more active, and if not more respected then better known.[223]

The reaction amongst Egyptian historians was lukewarm. The grand figure of Egyptian historiography, Ahmad 'Izzat 'Abd al-Karim, rejected the idea of the Union as being too political in character, believing that such a Union should be based on cooperation between national historical societies rather than on an individual basis. For some the Union seemed little more than an offshoot of the Ba'thist regime in Iraq.[224] One prominent Egyptian historian felt one of the aims of the society was simply to bolster the legitimacy of the Iraqi regime and its territorial claims in the Gulf, an impression not dimmed by the attendance of President Saddam Husayn at one conference, where he was awarded a medal by the Union.[225] These views must have had some influence since no Egyptians are represented in the list of office bearers – a startling omission considering Egypt's cultural importance in the Arab world at the time.[226] Nevertheless, individual Egyptian historians did become members. Following the conclusion of the Gulf War in 1991, a Cold War of historical societies broke out with the founding of a rival International Union in Cairo by the Gulf and other states hostile to Iraqi ambitions. Two Egyptians were elected director and assistant director, Sa'id 'Ashur of Cairo University, and 'Abd al-'Aziz Nawwar of 'Ain Shams, respectively.[227] To facilitate matters, the Egyptian government quietly asked Ahmad 'Abd al-Rahim Mustafa, who had supervised Mustafa al-Najjar as a student and maintained warm relations with him in the years afterwards, to break off contact with the Iraqi.[228] At the time of writing the two Unions continue to exist side by side.

In the decades after the Second World War, Cairo and 'Ain Shams Universities became the powerhouses of modern Egyptian historiography. The increasing volume of published work testified to a scholarship that no serious academic study of Egypt in the West could ignore. Accompanying this

2

HISTORY, INSTITUTIONS
AND THE STATE

The university might be an autonomous entity with a mandate
to provide cadres for private and public enterprise, but it is
embedded within a larger articulated whole. In most postcolo-
nial societies, university autonomy is a fiction. The police are
located right within the campus.

Arnold Temu and Bonaventure Swai[1]

Since the time of Muhammad 'Ali, the state has actively sought to
cultivate a politically cooperative and acceptable scholarship through its
support of institutions and educational programmes. The manner and
orientation of this authority has changed over time, from the autocratic
demeanour of the palace in the nineteenth century to the more diffuse
character of the state between 1923 and 1952 and the return to an
authoritarian regime after 1952. Institutions such as learned societies,
the universities and other academic centres have served as important
sites for scholarship that has been answerable to, if not controlled by,
state authority. Complementing this strategy has been the use of state
power to constrain historical research through the use of censorship and
the control of archives, something that has profoundly influenced the
pattern and limits of historical research in Egypt particularly in the post-
1952 period. While its attempts to dictate the output of historical writing
have not always prevailed, the state has played a central role in moulding the
intellectual climate and setting the parameters of legitimate historical
discourse.

LEARNED SOCIETIES

During the nineteenth century, learned societies served as the main centres
for credible historical research in Egypt. Broad in their interests, these societies
provided a scholarly environment that attracted interested members of the
elite classes, professional men, government officials, individual savants
and amateur scholars. Regular meetings and social events presented the

45

opportunity for lectures, discussions and debates conducted over a wide range of subjects which nurtured an embryonic scholarship. The active commitment of these societies to the publication of research offered the prospect of an audience beyond the numbers of their select membership. While many of the writings so produced, particularly the scientific papers, held little obvious political significance, the character of historical studies was consistent with the exclusive nature and the royal patronage of these organizations, and invariably expressed a politically conservative and pro-monarchist tone.

The modern tradition of the learned society had been brought to Egypt with the French invasion of 1798. Among his forces Napoleon had included a large number of French scholars whose task was to promote the spread of knowledge both in Egypt and about Egypt, through research, study and publication of a wide range of subjects related to Egyptian nature, industry and history.[2] This array of talent constituted the original Institut d'Égypte and from 1809 until the late 1820s the results of its work were published in the monumental *Description de l'Égypte*. Though the scientific mission itself was terminated with the end of the French campaign in 1801, it was to provide the model and inspiration for a number of scientific societies that followed, intellectually, in its desire to catalogue and describe, and politically, in its relationship to the ruling authority.

The first of these was the Société orientale (later called the Société d'Égypte), formed in Alexandria in 1836 by a group of British, French and German residents. Given personal encouragement and generous financial support by Muhammad 'Ali, its principal aim was to establish a library of works which 'ont traité des questions qui se rattachent à l'Égypte et aux peuples qui sont venus, aux différentes époques de l'histoire, s'y fixer à côté des indigènes ou bien à côté des conquérants plus anciens'.[3] However, by 1859 the Société had become inactive and was replaced in that year by a new society, the Institut Égyptien, founded at the initiative of Sa'id Pasha, now Viceroy of Egypt, who continued the pattern of royal patronage. The institute moved from Alexandria to Cairo in 1880 and its sponsorship was assumed by Sultan Ahmad Fu'ad (later King Fu'ad) in 1917. In the following year it was reorganized by royal decree and renamed l'Institut d'Égypte (*al-Mujtama' al-'ilmi al-misri*).[4]

The principal aim of the Institut was to continue the work and orientalist traditions of the original Napoleonic body. This mission spanned a wide range of disciplines and interests divided into four formal sections: Letters, Fine Arts and Archaeology; Morals and Political Science; Physical and Mathematical Sciences and Medicine; Agronomy and Natural History.[5] The body attracted many notable men of letters to its membership who met regularly to attend lectures delivered by fellow members or distinguished visitors. From its foundation the Institut published a regular *Bulletin* which was later supplemented by a series of monographs, the *Mémoires*. Historical

46

research was predominantly concerned with the ancient and Islamic periods but there were occasional pieces on aspects of nineteenth century Egypt by members such as Artin Pasha and René Qattawi, who took a special interest in Muhammad 'Ali.[6] The early membership of the Institut was largely, though not exclusively, made up of resident Europeans and its character was maintained through a conservative structural arrangement. Members were elected by secret ballot with a limitation of 50 in each of the three categories of titular, associate and correspondent members (the latter two being non-resident), which effectively guaranteed a majority foreign membership. Moreover, the potential readership of its publications in Egypt was limited since French was the Institut's working language in this period, even if some concession was given to Arabic in the publication of administrative accounts and in occasional articles, with infrequent pieces in English. The relative absence of Egyptians among the titular membership was especially true of the Letters, Fine Arts and Archaeology section; in mathematics and science Egyptians made greater inroads.

Nevertheless, there were prominent Egyptian members from the earliest years. Rifaʿah al-Tahtawi was a founding member as was Mahmud al-Falaki, an astronomer and historian, who served as vice-president from 1869 to 1881.[7] Yaʿqub Artin Pasha was especially active filling the post of president for 17 years and being a prolific contributor to the *Bulletin* on a great variety of historical matters. During the first half of the twentieth century, membership became increasingly Egyptian but it was a slow process. By the early 1920s, 'Ali Bahjat (elected 1900), archaeologist Ahmad Kamal (elected 1903), Ahmad Lutfi al-Sayyid (elected 1915) and Taha Husayn (elected 1924) – all with claims to respectable historical work – had become members. Prince 'Umar Tusun, a second cousin to the King and a historian himself, was also active in the Institut. The Institut's close association with royalist interests was reinforced by the elections of the 1930s. The historians cultivated by Fuʾad, such as Gaston Wiet (elected 1930) and Angelo Sammarco (elected 1931) and René Qattawi Bey (elected 1941), preceded the rising generation of young academic Egyptian historians as members. Only in 1941 was Sami Jabra, professor of ancient Egyptian history at Cairo University, elected and not until 1947 did Shafiq Ghurbal and Sulayman Huzzayin, a geographer of prehistoric Egypt, and later rector of Asyut University, join Institut ranks.[8] Indeed, right up until 1952, the Institut continued to maintain a cosmopolitan and socially rather than academically prominent membership.

The orientalist origins of the Institut's scholarship and its conservative political complexion assured generous royal patronage. Upon becoming its patron, Fuʾad had offered a prize of LE 100 to the author of the best work on the history of Egypt dealing with the reign of his father, Ismaʿil.[9] True to his appellation of 'le mécène royal', Fuʾad maintained support for the Institut throughout his reign, a policy continued by his son Faruq. Medallions of the Institut from this period are testimony to the association:

one features profiles of Fu'ad and Faruq, side by side.[10] The Institut held monthly meetings from November to May in its office in the grounds of the Ministry of Public Works but its reliance on the goodwill of the government extended to more than providing the venue. The Institut's financial existence was overwhelmingly dependent on government support. In 1949–50, the grant from the Ministry of Public Education represented 90 per cent of all income.[11] Publication of the *Mémoires* had only proceeded in that year because Taha Husayn, the relevant Minister and an Institut member himself, had disbursed a subsidy of LE 800.

The other learned society that functioned as a significant centre for historical research was the Khedival (later Royal) Geographical Society (*al-Jam'iyya al-jughrafiyya al-khidiwiyya*).[12] Housed in a building on Qasr al-'Aini street adjacent to the parliament, the Society had been founded by Khedive Isma'il in 1875 to encourage knowledge and exploration of Africa and surrounding countries.[13] As with the Institut d'Égypte, the initial membership of the Society was predominately European with a minority of Egyptians. From the former category were famous names such as Mariette and de Lesseps, and from the latter, various military officers, state and palace officials such as Mahmud al-Falaki (who served as the Society's President from 1884 to 1885), Ahmad Shafiq, philologist Ahmad Zaki, and Ahmad Kamal. Nevertheless, like the Institut d'Égypte, the Society maintained a European character and used French as its working language.[14] Following a period of inactivity, Fu'ad was appointed president of the society by his brother, Sultan Husayn, in 1915 and its fortunes revived. In time, the Geographical Society would become the flagship of the many societies patronized by the king.

At the time of its foundation the Geographical Society had been endowed by Isma'il with an annual grant of LE 400, in addition to a salary for the president.[15] Under Fu'ad's presidency, royal patronage became more generous. In the period from 1925 to 1934 alone, the King personally donated over LE 27,000 to the society.[16] Georges Foucart and Adolphe Qattawi Bey expressed their debt to Fu'ad at a Society celebration in 1921: 'Le souci constant de Sa Hautesse le sultan Fouad Ier a été de nous mettre mieux à même d'exécuter la mission qu'avait tracée quelques années plus tôt le prince président.'[17] Over the next decade the Society sponsored conferences and publications dealing with a large range of historical and other issues dedicated to upholding the vision of the King who subsidized the publications with thousands of pounds.[18] As secretary general, Qattawi oversaw the publication of a series of original documents dealing with the period from the French expedition until the end of the reign of Muhammad 'Ali.[19] Indeed, many of the works of the royalist school written in the 1920s and 1930s by such historians as Angelo Sammarco, Georges Douin, René Qattawi and others were published under the imprint of the Geographical Society.[20]

Although they had neither the influence nor the audience that the universities would later enjoy, learned societies made a significant contribution to Egyptian intellectual life. They played an important role as intellectual forums for presentation, discussion and publication of a wide variety of historical and scientific research as well as providing a point of contact with visiting scholars. As elite associations that counted prominent government officials, administrators and professionals among their membership, they served as a model for later professional organizations.[21] As scholarly organizations, the Institut d'Égypte and the Royal Geographical Society exemplified the political nature of the relationship between state authority and scholarship. Influential and effective players in the construction of a conservative historical tradition, they functioned as the institutional heartland of royalist historiography. Their limitation and weakness was that their academic and social tone was elitist and upheld an elitist view of history. While supported by royal patronage and the prestige of their members they prospered; in the face of the political and social realities of the post-1952 period they soon fell on hard times.[22]

THE EGYPTIAN UNIVERSITY

Although Egypt could claim al-Azhar as one of the oldest universities in the world, it had become clear as early as the time of Muhammad 'Ali that the country required a modern education system and appropriate academic institutions to assist in the process of state development and the training of government officials. In the course of the nineteenth century specialized schools were set up to cater to this need. Some, principally those concerned with law and education, taught history or offered the acquisition of skills useful to a historian. From these centres of learning, many modernist intellectuals, nationalist politicians and historians would emerge. One of the first of these was the School of Languages (*Madrasat al-alsun*) set up in 1835 under the energetic directorship of Rifa'ah al-Tahtawi to teach languages and other subjects, including history.[23] In 1868 the School of Administration and Languages opened and subsequently became the School of Law (*Kulliyat al-huquq al-khidiwiyya*) in which incarnation it could claim such historians and political activists as Muhammad Farid, 'Abd al-Rahman al-Rafi'i and Mustafa Kamil as graduates.[24] In 1871, Dar al-'Ulum was established to train Arabic teachers and taught history, geography, mathematics and science subjects unavailable at al-Azhar. However, despite expectations to provide a more modern education, it failed to break free of many conservative Azhari traditions.[25] The Khedival Teachers' College (*Madrasat al-mu'allimin al-khidiwiyya*), set up in 1880, proved a more innovative institution, offering a 2-year course for secondary school graduates organized according to a European educational model. In time, it would produce graduates who were the part of the first generation of Egyptian academic historians, Muhammad Rif'at, Shafiq Ghurbal and Fu'ad Shukri.[26]

These nineteenth century efforts were only partly successful in producing an educated class of Egyptians. By the beginning of the new century some Egyptian intellectuals were starting to talk of the need for a national university to put higher education on a firmer footing.[27] Early calls from the writings of Ya'qub Artin and Jurji Zaydan came to nothing, in part, because of the consistent opposition of Lord Cromer to any educational reform. However, the demand for a national university found increasing support from a wide spectrum of the modernist Egyptian leadership, from Muhammad 'Abduh and the moderate nationalist voices of Qasim Amin, Sa'd Zaghlul and the Umma Party, to the more radical Mustafa Kamil and the Watanists. 'Abbas Hilmi II and the young Prince Fu'ad came to openly endorse the idea. In October 1906, a public campaign for subscriptions was launched to establish a university. While Sa'd Zaghlul seems to have played an ambiguous role when he became Minister of Education soon after, the departure of Cromer from Egypt in 1907 facilitated matters.[28] In December of the following year the private Egyptian University was established, with Fu'ad serving as its first rector (1908–13).[29]

The university was thus the result of a broad national consensus in which many notable politicians took part. Although its significance was downplayed to assuage British sensitivities at the time, the university would later assume a considerable political role.[30] However, in its early days as a private institution, it had more practical issues to confront. One was the engagement of suitable staff. Egypt itself had few people qualified for university teaching, save for autodidacts such as Ahmad Kamal and Jurji Zaydan.[31] Accordingly, though some staff were recruited locally from the Dar al-'Ulum, the majority of teachers had to be invited from Europe. Over the succeeding decades, the political manoeuvring between the governments of England, France, Italy and Germany and the Egyptian authorities, including the King, gave some university appointments the drama of international negotiations.[32] The other major problem was finance. Although a private institution in name, the University relied initially on government funds. A yearly subsidy of LE 5000 from the Ministry of Waqfs was assigned by order of the Khedive 'Abbas Hilmi II, and, from 1911, the Ministry of Education paid an annual endowment of LE 2000. Together these grants represented about 70 per cent of the university's budget.[33] Even so, this support was not always reliable and during the First World War the university's finances were precarious.

Despite these early difficulties, the university was accounted a success and calls were made to extend its scope. By 1917 even the British were supporting the idea of a national, state-owned university.[34] In that year a commission sat to deliberate over proposals for such an institution. The end of the First World War and the subsequent political unrest first interrupted, then spurred on the project. Another commission was formed in 1923 to reconsider the matter, this time against the background of Egypt's powers of self-government under the new constitution. Members of the new Liberal Constitutionalist Party took the lead. Muhammad Husayn Haykal, and future Prime Ministers Muhammad Mahmud and Isma'il Sidqi, all of whom had been playing an active role in the running of the private university, were prominent in directing the political will for its national successor. The role of the Liberal Constitutionalists was also enhanced by the replacement of the Wafd's leader, Sa'd Zaghlul, with Ahmad Lutfi al-Sayyid as the general secretary of the university council in 1922.

The high profile of the Liberal Constitutionalists in the setting up of the university was not coincidental. More than with any other political current, the Liberal Constitutionalists regarded the university as a primary vehicle for national renewal and progress. Their conservative brand of nationalism regarded Egyptian intellectuals with a Western education, namely themselves, as 'Egypt's natural leaders', a view Fu'ad shared.[35] The Minister of Education, 'Ali Mahir, who was entrusted with the task of setting up the university, explained the link between education and nationalism before a committee formed to deal with education reform:

> You all know the importance of this business [educational reform] and its effect in strengthening nationalism through the preparation of a strong generation with high morals, strong will, lofty aspirations, free thinking, and the efficient activity in all fields of public life ... Our task is to persist in our efforts to develop a firm and liberal educational policy even if it leads us to demolish the antiquated practices of the past, since our purpose is to protect our nationality regardless of any sacrifice which this task might incur upon us.[36]

In 1925, the Egyptian University formally became a state institution, made up of a newly-created Faculty of Science with the existing schools of Law and Medicine, and the private university, which became, in effect, the Faculty of Arts. Other faculties would be added over time. On the basis of the temporary good relations of the time between the Liberal Constitutionalist Party and the king, Ahmad Lutfi al-Sayyid was appointed as the university's first rector.

The new university may have owed much to the initiative of Fu'ad but it was hardly his creature.[37] Indeed, the dynamics of the university administration were to be a microcosm of national politics with battles fought on matters ranging from staff appointments to principles of university autonomy between the Fu'ad and the British on the one hand, and the King and the university administration on the other.[38] While Fu'ad's attempts to exercise control had run aground by the early 1930s, the university came to be drawn increasingly onto the main political stage as the decade progressed.

The rise of organized political activism on campus and the student uprising of 1935–6 made it clear that the university was a breeding ground for activists and a theatre of political contest.[39] That was not only true of students. There was an increasing tendency for academics to proceed to, or oscillate between, the campus and a career in politics.[40] Far from being a haven from the turbulence of national politics, the university was very much an integral part of it.

The emergence of a state system of higher education in Egypt introduced a much more complex relationship between state authority and academic scholarship than existed with the learned societies. During the nineteenth century these moves had been at the initiative of the palace with the consolidation of the interests of the royal family at least as much a consideration as the social benefit of an educational institution. The establishment of the Egyptian University in 1925, as the culmination of a number of attempts to institutionalize an academic tradition, inaugurated a new phase. If the learned societies were royalist in inspiration, the modern university was the fruit of the efforts of a broad nationalist coalition, including the king, which sought to establish it as a focal point for Egyptian intellectual life and a symbol of national independence and revival. Conceived as a national institution and disseminator of a national vision, the university was from the outset 'an important instrument for the realization of national (political) goals'.[41]

In 1925, the specific details of these national goals had not been, to put it mildly, matters of unanimous agreement. The political visions of Fu'ad and the various nationalist parties competed with one another for dominance. The king, as his family had done before him, employed foreign scholars and government officials or used his patronage of learned societies to promote his monarchist vision as his influence on the university weakened. By contrast, the nationalist movement, and particularly its conservative wing, came to effectively use the political space afforded by the university to propagate its own historical vision. It was little surprise then that the university became an arena of political contest and served as a base for a counter to the royalist school of interpretation and the consolidation of a more national discourse. It was ironic that 4 years after Fu'ad's death, when the fortunes of the liberal school were waxing at the expense of the royalist school, that the Egyptian University took the name of Fu'ad I University.

THE REVOLUTION AND THE UNIVERSITY

While the coming to power of the Free Officers in July 1952 brought radical changes to the political landscape, it witnessed elements of both continuity and discontinuity in the government attitude towards historical scholarship. Certainly the regimes before and after 1952 were both aware of the political utility of history. Under the monarchy, King Fu'ad had promoted history that reflected a favourable image of himself and his dynasty, while the national movement had begun to realize the university's potential as a basis for projecting its historical vision. In like fashion, the Nasser regime sought to cultivate scholarship to confer political legitimacy on the revolution and its ideology. Yet, whereas the monarchy had pursued this in a more personalized and relatively limited way through the patronage of learned societies and commissioning of individual authors, the revolutionary regime developed a more explicitly political program that called for the rewriting of Egyptian history as a matter of national priority. Indeed, the overthrow of the constitutional government required a historical justification of the need for political change and substantiation of the Revolution's claim to national leadership.

The revolutionary regime initially had no comprehensive political programme, much less a coherent historical vision, but it did encourage a number of themes from the outset. Foremost amongst these was a negative view of the monarchy. As Marsot notes,

> ...the Nasser regime discouraged study of any period of the Muhammad Ali dynasty, that is, the nineteenth and twentieth centuries, unless it was evaluated negatively. The regime sought to undermine the achievements of the monarchy in order to justify the decision to put an end to it.[42]

The corruption of the monarchy and of the parliamentary regime became a constant refrain. Another well-rehearsed theme was the foreign origin, not just of the Muhammad 'Ali dynasty, but of all Egyptian rulers since the time of the pharaohs.[43] The succession of dynasties, the Ptolemies, the Romans, the various Arab dynasties and the Mamluks, were all deemed foreign occupiers in contrast to Nasser and the Free Officers who were Egyptians ruling Egypt for the first time in centuries. The Revolution thus represented a return of Egypt to rule by her own people and the beginning of the new, modern age. As Tharwat 'Ukasha, Minister of Culture and National Guidance, declared to a group of historians, 'The modern history of Egypt begins on 23 July 1952. It has no modern history before then.'[44]

The regime moved quickly to score historical points. *Tahrir*, a magazine published by the Armed Forces Public Affairs Department which first appeared in September 1952, launched the campaign. Initially edited by Ahmad Hamrush, then Tharwat 'Ukasha, an early issue featured an article on the writings of Ya'qub Sanu' (Abu Naddara), a biting critic of Khedive Isma'il.[45] During the 1950s and 1960s, government newspapers such as *al-Jumhuriyya* (established in 1953), *al-Sha'b* and *al-Masa'* (both established in 1956) were used to propagate the official national vision. Yet, to foster a reputable historiography consistent with or at least sympathetic to its political goals, the government had to do more than just issue pronouncements and rely on press articles. Nasser himself had explicitly recognized the

53

importance of history as a foundation for the success of the revolution. His *Philosophy of the Revolution*, which appeared in 1953, was replete with a strong sense of Egyptian history. While modestly disowning any personal expertise ('I do not pretend to be a professor of history') he stated that, 'the truth is the Philosophy of the Revolution of 23 July should be treated by professors who should search deeply into it for the roots spreading at the very depth of our history.'[46] Many of the leading officers of the regime were educated men but they were not historians.[47] It was thus necessary to win over the historians in the universities.

The Free Officers held a decidedly ambivalent attitude towards Cairo University, regarding it as a stronghold of conservative thought and a product of the educational privilege of the wealthy detached from the harsh social realities of Egyptian society.[48] Nevertheless, the political upheavals on campus and the activism of university students from the late 1930s – something which Nasser and other members of the RCC had experienced at first hand – had already demonstrated the university's potential as a hotbed of radical unrest.[49] For their part, while broadly nationalist in their sympathies, the university authorities were guarded in their attitude towards the aims of the revolution.[50] The resultant tension remained characteristic of the relationship between government and university during the 1950s and 1960s as the Nasser regime sought to alternatively court and control the universities, and to woo and win over academics over to its side.[51]

The strained nature of university-state relations was not unique to the revolutionary regime. Almost since the time of its foundation, there had been matters of conflict between the government and the university administration. Direct confrontation between the new regime and the university was therefore not long in coming. In 1952, a special committee, headed by 'Ali Mahir and including Shafiq Ghurbal and 'Abd al-Razzaq al-Sanhuri, the pre-eminent jurist of the Arab world, was set up to report on the state of higher education.[52] It submitted a series of recommendations to the government the following year that advocated among other things greater autonomy for universities. These recommendations went largely unheeded. Indeed, the new regime's subsequent actions suggested that, far from supporting the idea of an autonomous institution, it believed the universities should actively assist in the process of social transformation. It soon gave notice of its intentions. In March 1954, following his ultimately successful confrontation with Muhammad Najib, Nasser took reprisals against pro-Najib forces. The universities were purged, with over 60 professors, mostly Marxists but also some liberals, dismissed.[53] Later in the year, the government increased its control, nominating new rectors and vice-rectors and appointing faculty deans who had hitherto been elected.[54] The incident sent an unambiguous message to the academic community but the universities were still not willing to toe the line and state–university relations remained tense throughout the 1950s. The government continued to chip away at university independence.

In 1961, the socialist laws created a Ministry of Higher Education, set up to bring universities within the scope and direction of national policy.[55] This was reinforced by the formation of the Higher Council of Universities, chaired by the Minister of Higher Education.[56]

Not content with its efforts to cow the universities, or perhaps even as a sign of its failure to do so, the government moved to create other bodies to provide the ideological direction and intellectual leadership it sought. The appointment of Tharwat 'Ukasha as the new Minister of Culture and President of the Supreme Council for Literature, Art and Social Sciences in 1958 heralded the implementation of an energetic policy of providing institutions with 'ideological guidance'.[57] 'Ukasha, more than most members of the ruling clique, had some qualifications for the task. A graduate of the Institute of Journalism at Cairo University in 1944, he was later to obtain a doctorate in literature from the Sorbonne in 1964. Drawing on the expertise of a range of academics, bureaucrats and political favourites, the government initiated a number of committees dedicated to National Consciousness, Research and National Orientation and National Education to act as overseers of Egyptian intellectual life. The scope of these committees both implied an existing lack of national consensus and pointed to the political priority given to shaping diverse social perspectives into a cohesive national community.

Despite, or perhaps because of these efforts, by the beginning of the 1960s it was clear that intellectuals had not rallied to the support of the revolution to the extent that the regime had hoped. In June 1961, Muhammad Hasanayn Haykal, editor of *al-Ahram* and unofficial spokesman of the regime, published an article in *al-Ahram* titled 'The Crisis of the Intellectuals' in which he took Egyptian intellectuals to task for merely collaborating rather than interacting with the revolutionary regime.[58] The issue was not new but it fuelled a lively debate on the role of intellectuals in the proposed socialist transformation. The failure to win intellectuals over was echoed by setbacks to the government in other political arenas. Domestically, the lacklustre performance of the National Union as a vehicle for popular political participation, and internationally, Syria's secession from the 3-year old United Arab Republic in September 1961, demanded more energetic political initiatives.

THE *MITHAQ* AND THE *MASHRU'*

Haykal's initiative served as a prelude to a more elaborate plan by the regime which would mark the beginning of the so-called 'turn to the left'. In October, Nasser called for the formation of a Preparatory Committee to draw up a programme of political action to be discussed at a national conference.[59] The subsequent National Congress of Popular Forces was convened in June of the following year and resulted in the establishment of the ASU as a national political body and the approval of the text of the Charter of National Action (*Mithaq al-'amal al-watani*).[60] The Charter (*mithaq*) was a manifesto dealing with a range of important issues such as the socialist programme, democracy, Arab unity, economics and foreign policy which marked the formalization of the socialist phase of the Revolution and would serve as a blueprint for the policies and philosophy of the Egyptian government over the next few years.

As part of this projected political vision, the Charter set out the regime's most explicit interpretation of Egyptian history to date. Through the 1950s, the government had sought by various means to encourage, even coax, a politically palatable national history from Egyptian academics but with only limited success. In 1956, it had given notification of its intention to pursue the issue when Fathi Radwan, as the Minister of Culture and National Guidance, announced plans to rewrite Egyptian history.[61] Little, however, seems to have come of it. At the end of 1961, the appearance of *The History of Egyptian Civilization* heralded new movement.[62] Published under the auspices of the Ministry of Culture and graced with a preface by Tharwat 'Ukasha, it covered the pharaonic age and drew on contributions from the cream of Egyptian scholarship. Edited by Shafiq Ghurbal, it was the first volume of a series that proposed to cover the whole of Egyptian history. Ghurbal died soon afterwards and the project seems to have been dropped.

The publication of the Charter put new wind into the government's sails. After an introduction and justification of the necessity of the revolution, it presented a concise account of Egyptian history from pharaonic times until the present.[63] Written from the perspective of the 'people', the Charter's historical vision was set out in two chapters, 'The Roots of the Egyptian Struggle' and 'The Moral of the Setback', which together gave a thumbnail sketch of Egyptian history from the French campaign until the present day. While acknowledging that Muhammad 'Ali had 'laid the foundation for modern Egypt', it regarded him as having betrayed 'the true interests of the people' in favour of his own personal ambition. This betrayal, maintained by the collaboration between the royal family with the power of foreign monopolies, culminated with the defeat of 'Urabi and the beginning of the British occupation in 1882.

The Charter barely mentioned the 1919 Revolution but much space was given over to an explanation for the reasons of its failure, clearly a pointed criticism of the Wafd.[64] These were principally the national leadership's unwillingness to recognize the need for social change, its neglect of the connection between Egyptian patriotism and Arab nationalism, and its manipulation by imperialist forces which had granted Egypt an empty form of independence. The 1936 treaty between Egypt and Britain was 'a document of surrender to the great bluff by which the 1919 Revolution was taken in'. The interwar period also witnessed the surrender of the ideals of the revolution by its leaders to the palace and imperialism whose common concern 'was their opposition to the people's interests and the trend of progress'. Pointedly the Charter noted that a group of intellectuals who could have safeguarded the genuine revolution failed to do so. The struggle of the people was renewed after the Second World War, culminating in January 1952 with the burning of Cairo, fanned by the anger of the people, which led to the July 1952 revolution when the revolutionary vanguard as 'the tool of the popular will' placed the armed forces at 'the service of the people' and 'enlisted all nationalist elements in the struggle'. The Charter went on to emphasize the harm imperialism had inflicted on all Arab peoples through its failure to fulfil its promises after the First World War, its policy of setting up states that divided the Arab world, and its support of a movement in Palestine which was used 'to hold down the Arabs'.

This brief historical survey – barely 20 pages in the official edition – sought to set the agenda for Egyptian historical research, particularly in its insistence on the will of the people as the authentic thread of Egyptian patriotism against the forces of the palace, large landowners and imperialism. The reference to the failure of the intellectuals during the interwar period was pointed, as surely was the allusion to earlier histories of Egypt,

> Successive generations of Egyptian youth were taught that their country was neither fit nor capable of industrialization. In their textbooks, they read their national history in distorted versions. Their national heroes were ascribed as lost in a mist of doubt and uncertainty while those who betrayed the national cause were glorified and venerated.[65]

The message was unmistakable. Intellectuals were expected to play their part in the defence and consolidation of the aims of the revolution; the duty of historians was to portray an accurate picture of the past.

Having laid down the general guidelines in the Charter, the Ministry of Culture announced the formation of a specific project to rewrite modern Egyptian history (Mashru' i'adat kitabat al-tarikh al-qawmi) in June 1963. The project (mashru') was to be overseen by a committee of 20 Egyptian university professors under the direction of the minister, Dr 'Abd al-Qadir Hatim, with financial support from the ministry. It proposed to write modern Egyptian history 'along objective lines' and to purge it of 'all the impurities deliberately introduced into it under imperialism and feudalism'.[66] It would deal specifically with issues such as the history of feudalism, national and foreign capitalism, and the working class, which had been neglected by traditional histories.[67]

The initial reaction from historians to the announcement was mixed. Muhammad Anis came out immediately in favour of the project and became its most enthusiastic supporter within academic ranks. Under the heading 'History in the Service of Socialist Development', he wrote two articles in quick succession for *al-Ahram* on the development of modern Egyptian historiography.[68] In these, Anis recognized the substantial contributions of historians such as al-Rafi'i and Shafiq Ghurbal in laying the foundations of 'the national school' (*al-madrasa al-wataniyya*), but stressed the vital importance of creating a new school of interpretation, the 'socialist school' (*al-madrasa al-ishtirakiyya*), as an appropriate response to the political changes in Egyptian society.

> It is for us in the present stage to raise these [historical] studies from a national to a socialist perspective in setting up the development of Egyptian society during the nineteenth and first half of the twentieth century because this socialist view is the offspring of the current phase upon which our society boldly embarks.[69]

There was some enthusiastic support for this view. Jalal al-Sayyid wrote impatiently of the urgency for such a project, pointing out the faults of 'historians of the romantic school and the great man theory who wrote history or were lost in the academic maze far from reality'.[70] He went on,

> Why do we restrict the socialist understanding of history to this project and not set it as a weapon for the professors in our universities?... If today we are building the core of the socialist school in politics and history and literature, then why doesn't this school begin in our universities in every branch until capitalist views vanish inside university lecture theatres in economics, history, literature and philosophy...

Others were more restrained. Ahmad 'Abd al-Rahim Mustafa of 'Ain Shams agreed with the pressing need for Egyptian historians rather than foreigners to write their own history.[71] Yet others voiced doubts fearing that the project might become an instrument for enforcing a historical orthodoxy. Muhammad al-Sharqawi ventured,

> The study of our modern history, which we appealed for and which we want scholars to take note of, [issuing as it does] from the ministry of culture and national guidance, must have as its basis historical truthfulness and freedom from fanatical enthusiasm for a given viewpoint to which the realities of history would be offensive. Similarly, [we must remain] aloof from the attempt to 'suppress' those who advance a view in which they believe and from which they can draw conclusions; and aloof too from 'narrowmindedness' and 'puritanism' in historical research, having left them more or less behind in religious thought.[72]

The circumspect phrasing contrasted with Anis' zeal. Despite Anis' agitation in political forums and the press, there appears to have been qualified rather than enthusiastic support for the *mashru'* from his colleagues. It was not until more than 2 years later at the end of 1965 that over 20 historians gathered at the office of the Egyptian Association for Historical Studies in Cairo to discuss the project. Those present included the senior historians of Egypt: Anis, Ahmad 'Izzat 'Abd al-Karim and Ahmad 'Abd al-Rahim Mustafa from 'Ain Shams University; medievalists 'Abd al-Rahman Zaki and Muhammad Mustafa Ziyada of Cairo University; the then minister of culture and geographer, Sulayman Huzzayin, as well as other distinguished scholars, such as Rashid al-Barawi, a Marxist economist, and political commentators, such as Salah 'Isa and 'Abd al-Razzaq Hasan. Four meetings were held, dedicated in turn to consideration of political, economic, cultural and social aspects of Egyptian history. Many opinions were aired. At one point Hasan al-Sa'ati asked if a group or an 'intellectual giant' was to write the proposed history. Ultimately the question remained unanswered and nothing concrete resulted from the meetings.[73]

Meanwhile, debate continued within the university regarding its role in the socialist transformation while the government kept up the pressure. In June 1964, Kamal Rif'at, deputy prime minister for higher education and scientific research, addressed the academic staff of Cairo University's Faculty of Arts on the role of the universities in building a socialist society. The minister insistently questioned the performance of universities but was countered with complaints of the limited resources available. Muhammad Anis, by this time well-placed in the secretariat of ideology and propaganda, supported his minister and took his colleagues to task,

> I think it is a crisis of progressive thought; we need the professor who combines science and revolution, academic knowledge and progressive tendencies...Socialism is not a political question to be pursued outside university walls but an intellectual cause bound up with the branches of human knowledge.[74]

Anis continued to promote the Charter in the pages of *al-Katib* but if it ever was a feasible idea by 1967 its time had passed.[75] The ambitious plans of the *mashru'* effectively lapsed, an ill-conceived attempt to produce an official national history based on political imperatives and proof of the inability of a committee to write history.[76] As a text authorized by the government, the Charter was successful inasmuch as it directed historical research and debate towards themes of Arab nationalism, the July Revolution and the evils of the Muhammad 'Ali dynasty. However, its influence was probably as superficial as it was widespread. The government was able to employ the talents of those who were suitably disposed to its programme but university historians as a group were reduced neither to a Procrustean bed nor to a prescribed stereotype. The 'Nasirite historian', if such a creature can be said to have existed, was not a creature in university history departments.[77] The 'socialist school' of Anis, while an influential model, never became de rigueur. By the late 1960s Egyptian universities still had, within certain limits, both their conservative and progressive practitioners. Historical research was circum-scribed rather than prescribed. In retrospect, Dekmejian's view still holds good,

> It seems that the regime will not object to diverse historical inter-pretations of nationalism so long as all Egyptian historians are agreed on the more general ideological maxims, e.g. the pursuit of a Cairo-centred Pan-Arab State. In other words, while an ideologically determined historiography has begun to develop, there is no evidence of placing historical research in a strait-jacket.[78]

The government was more successful in utilizing the talents of individual historians through specific education initiatives. The works of al-Rafi'i that had served more than a generation of modern history students were no longer equal to the task. Changes in high school and university curricula stimulated demand for new histories of Egypt and the July Revolution. The market was flooded with a large number of texts written not just by historians but by members of law, economics and political science faculties.[79] There were opportunities to make considerable profit for those willing to write on subjects from a politically acceptable viewpoint. One such effort by Jad Taha on the July Revolution came to be known as the 'Revolution of LE 3000', reputedly the amount paid to its author.[80] Sa'id 'Ashur, a historian of the Mamluk period, wrote a text on the July Revolution which was prescribed for all students but there were many others.[81]

The quality of some of these textbooks was soon called into question. In the pages of al-Ahram, Louis 'Awad despaired of the state of historical knowledge among students:

> The young men of the present generation have an immunity against history, all history: ancient, medieval and modern! Why? Because history books in our schools are no more books of history. They are rather books of pure politics... The young Egyptians have lost their sense of history and, consequently, their sense of politics... [some] are totally ignorant of the history of land reform, the history of socialist measures, or even the history of the Revolution of 23 July 1952 itself.[82]

Indeed, what the Charter would, with some justification, criticize of history books written prior to 1952 was now being said of the history books of the revolutionary period. 'Awad, himself a leftist, inveighed against the trend.

'We should treat...the history and geography of our country without being obsessed with ancestor cults or personality cults, or claiming that we are superior to others.'[83] Ibrahim 'Abduh weighed in with characteristic invective against the Charter, 'A holy book!, the book of revolutionary thought. More copies were printed than copies of the Qur'an and the Bible in several generations...It was taught at schools and in the universities and became a curriculum to pass or fail...The Qur'an was not honoured in the same manner.'[84]

Ultimately, the Nasser regime's attempts to simultaneously assert its control over the universities and woo them to its side achieved only mixed success. The universities were already expressive of a broad national consensus but they represented neither a single political viewpoint nor were of one mind regarding the role of universities in society. Some of the most articulate and active supporters of a more socialist university system, such as Muhammad Anis, his brother 'Abd al-'Azim Anis and Rushdi Sa'id, were academics themselves.[85] The general lack of consensus meant that the battle between those who staunchly advocated autonomy for the universities and those who believed that universities should contribute substantially to the socialist transformation of society remained unresolved. As the Nasser regime moved to the left in the 1960s it sought to take the universities with it. Confident enough to resist total cooptation, the universities accommodated rather than acceded to government pressure. Egypt's defeat in 1967 and the devastating blow it struck the national psyche ensured the stalemate.

INSTITUTES AND THINK-TANKS

The universities as institutions were not to have a monopoly on academic writing and research. The lack of enthusiasm they showed for state policy and their unwieldiness as educational institutions prompted governments to establish specific institutes and think-tanks dedicated to particular aspects of the national interest as an alternative strategy. The approach may have owed some inspiration to the role the learned societies had played for royal interests but they differed from them in being more focused and incorporated as state institutions. In this fashion, the Nasser regime established or recast institutes and centres to channel, and even coopt, intellectual talents in a more focused and politically efficacious manner. They were not rivals to the universities as such – often the institutes drew on the services of university academics – but they were a way of effectively concentrating the most relevant and sympathetic expertise. Some of the historical and political themes taken up by these institutes in fact straddled the monarchical and revolutionary eras but they were reinvigorated and radicalized after the fall of the monarchy. The most important of these were Arabism and Africanism.

The Arab dimension aspect of Egyptian identity had held little influence in the first third of the twentieth century. During the 1920s, pharaonism, a movement that stressed the glories of ancient Egypt as the basis for modern Egyptian national identity, had been widespread amongst many Egyptian intellectuals.[86] Egypt's relationship to the Arab world was derided by the national elites, an attitude summed up in Sa'd Zaghlul's famous dictum on Arab unity, 'If you add a zero to a zero, then to another zero, what will you get?'[87] However, from the early 1930s, a greater acknowledgement of the Arab element of Egyptian heritage became evident. Extolled first by expatriate Arabs in Egypt, it was also driven by a move away from pharaonic ideas to an increasing public commitment to Islam among some leading intellectuals.[88] In 1944 the Egyptian government formally recognized this common cultural heritage and mutual political interest among Arab countries by supporting the establishment and providing the leadership of the Arab League.

During the 1950s, when this embrace became more intimate, Arabism began to make its influence felt on scholarship. In 1953 the Institute of Higher Arabic Studies (*Ma'had al-dirasat al-'arabiyya al-'ulya*) was set up by the League to provide a base for academic research in a number of important fields, including history, to support its vision.[89] Its first director was Sati' al-Husri, a great advocate of Arab secular nationalism, who had already served as an adviser to the League's Cultural Committee and lectured on nationalism and education at Cairo University. In his inaugural lecture at the Institute, al-Husri stated that beyond its general educational aims, he expected the Institute would lead to 'the stimulation of the nationalist awakening of the Arab world by spreading matters concerned with the Arab nation and by increasing the hopes for its future'.[90] He was succeeded 3 years later by Shafiq Ghurbal, now retired from the Cairo University, who did much to raise the profile of the Institute through his lectures and supervision of students.[91]

The principal aim of the Institute of Arabic Studies was to study the history of the modern Arab world and provide analysis of its contemporary situation.[92] Its programme of studies offered a diploma in Arabic Studies to be completed over 2 years as a prerequisite for a masters degree in one of the areas offered by the Institute, namely Arab Studies and History, Geography, Economy, Political Science or Literature. This was the strong suit of the Institute since its specialized courses in Arabic history and Arabic nationalism were not available at the universities.[93] Teaching staff was provided by universities, particularly 'Ain Shams and Cairo. Since its foundation, the Institute has produced a large number of postgraduate theses dealing with various aspects of modern Arab history,[94] and sponsored various research projects on topics such as Arab–Turkish relations, Arab–Iranian relations, Mauretania, Somalia, Bahrain, immigrant Palestinians, and urbanization in the Arab world.[95] Today, it continues under the auspices of the Arab

League and is affiliated to the Arab League Educational, Cultural and Scientific Organization (ALECSO).[96]

The promotion of pan-Arabism was not restricted to the organizational structure of the Arab League. Egyptian foreign policy from the mid-1950s projected the country as the head of the Arab world and one of the leaders of the non-aligned movement. Indeed, the regime's ideological commitment to pan-Arabism was made most stark with its adoption of the name of the United Arab Republic (and the disappearance altogether of the word Egypt from its official name), following the announcement of the union of Egypt and Syria in 1958. In October of that year the Minister of Education decreed the establishment of university chairs in the 'History of the Arab Nation'.[97] There followed a number of changes in the national curriculum. Courses on Arab Socialism, Arab Society and the July 23 Revolution were made compulsory for all university students.[98] When the government reorganized al-Azhar in 1961, it took the opportunity to add Arab Studies as one of the new faculties.[99]

This proliferation of courses in Arab history and politics, reinforced in 1962 by the dictates of the Charter and the consequent demand for relevant textbooks, spurred many, both qualified and unqualified, to publication. One of the earliest efforts had been a history of the Arab world by Ahmad Izzat ʿAbd al-Karim of ʿAin Shams, with two other colleagues, ʿAbd al-Hamid al-Batriq and Abu al-Futuh Radwan, which appeared in 1960.[100] Like the flurry of studies on the July Revolution – in fact the two streams became part of the same current – a great outpouring of historical, political, legal and sociological studies followed. One was a prescribed text on Arab society which featured a chapter on the historical origins of Arab nationalism by Muhammad Anis.[101] Historians of other periods weighed in. Jamal al-Din al-Shayyal of Alexandria University in collaboration with Muhammad Saʿid al-ʿAryan wrote an account of the struggle between the Arabs and imperialism; ʿAli Husni al-Kharbutli, a professor of Islamic history, authored a history of the Arab nation. The list went on.[102]

Yet, despite the government's stentorian rhetoric on the close historical relationship between Egypt and the Arab world and the Arab identity of Egypt, there was never any firm agreement as to what this Arab element actually *was*. As one scholar noted, 'there seems to be no official (governmental) attempt to uphold a single orthodox view on the subject [of Arab nationalism] to the exclusion of all others.'[103] This was both a strength and a weakness.[104] Arabism had many incarnations, many different emphases. The lack of precision was multiplied when hybridized with concepts of socialism and Islam. Secular, cultural and political interpretations of Arab socialism gave the concept of Arabism so many different shades that it came to mean almost everything and nothing.[105] Not long before Nasser's death, the courses on Arab socialism were dropped from the university curriculum.[106]

While the call to the Arab world was the major rallying cry coming out of Cairo from the late 1950s and early 1960s, Nasser was also busy asserting Egyptian claims to an African identity. Egypt had long been conscious of her unique position in Africa. In the nineteenth century, the Khedival Geographical Society had been created to foster research of the region. This interest was maintained into the twentieth century and took on a particular urgency at the end of the Second World War, when the political arrangements regarding the future of Sudan, an Anglo-Egyptian condominium since 1899, became a pressing political issue. In 1946 during discussions conducted in Cairo and London, the Sidqi government called for Egypt and Sudan to be united under a common monarchy. Following Sidqi's resignation, the new prime minister, al-Nuqrashi, took the issue to the United Nations Security Council in 1947.[107] In the same year, as a response to and expression of Egypt's vital concern with the fate of the Sudan, the Institute of Sudanese Studies was established in the Faculty of Arts at Cairo University.[108] Muhammad 'Awad, a geographer and rector of Alexandria University (and later minister of education), and historian Shafiq Ghurbal, were key figures in designing the courses for the new institute.

The diplomatic battle to maintain the political unity of the Nile Valley was lost when Sudan was granted independence in 1956. However, the institute endured, having changed its name to the Institute of African Studies in 1955 in recognition of the modification of Egyptian aspirations.[109] Nasser persevered with his vision of an Egyptian role in Africa,

> I will continue to dream of the day when I will find in Cairo a great African institute dedicated to unveiling to our view the dark reaches of the continent, to creating in our minds an enlightened African consciousness, and to sharing with others from all over the world the work of advancing the welfare of the peoples of this continent.[110]

Despite the Sudanese setback, Egypt's determination to play a role in African affairs continued through the 1950s and 1960s, though never with the same fervour as its pan-Arabist rhetoric. In 1957, Cairo hosted the Afro-Asian Peoples' Solidarity Conference and a Centre for Arab, African and Asian Political Studies was established at Cairo University in 1961.[111] Radio programmes such as Voice of Free Africa were beamed out of Cairo and educational missions further strengthened the bond. By the early 1960s, a large number of Egyptian professors were teaching in Africa, most of them in the Sudan.[112] In 1970, the Institute of African Studies became an independent research centre within Cairo University and 2 years later began to publish its own journal, *The African Studies Review* (*Majallat al-dirasat al-ifriqiyya*).[113] Its programme of studies was developed to include history, politics, economics, languages and anthropology but by the 1980s it appeared to have lost momentum.[114]

THE HIGHER INSTITUTE OF SOCIALIST STUDIES

Unlike the continuities of Arabism and Africanism, socialism took on an entirely new significance in Egyptian political life under the revolutionary regime. With the universities reluctant to embrace the ideological principles of the Revolution and history professors unwilling to follow its prescription for a national history, the government created the Higher Institute of Socialist Studies (*Ma'had al-'ala li'l-dirasat al-ishtirakiyya*) to promote the political and historical vision of the Charter.[115] Established under the auspices of the ASU and put under the personal supervision of Sha'rawi Jum'a and Kamal Rif'at, both prominent members of the Left and the Vanguard Organization, its purpose was 'to train professional party cadres in organization and ideology'.[116]

The staff chosen for the task were academics of high standing with ideological credentials appropriate to the orientation of the Institute.[117] Its director was Ibrahim Sa'd al-Din, a Marxist economist, who believed the socialist transformation of the Egyptian masses would be achieved by 'influencing them, giving them a socialist education, and rooting out old concepts from their minds and hearts'.[118] One means of achieving this was by presenting a new interpretation of Arab and Egyptian history. Accordingly, the curriculum featured courses dedicated to the modern history of Egypt and the evolution of Egyptian society from 1952 to the present.[119] The ubiquitous Muhammad Anis, as a founding member of staff, led the attempt to prepare a social history of Egypt in the light of socialist theory.[120] In 1965, in two lectures given at the Institute, he presented the first ever academic study on the development of Egyptian society from feudalism to socialism.[121] Another historian on staff, Amin 'Izz al-Din, was later to write an important history on the Egyptian working class.

The Institute of Socialist Studies, like the Charter itself, was part of the regime's move to the left under the broad banner of Arab socialism. Nasser's personal support was the critical factor in setting its ideological tone but its aims were regarded with suspicion by conservative elements within the government, principally those inside the military and clustered around the leadership of 'Abd al-Hakim 'Amr. In October 1966, the security services moved against the Institute arresting Ibrahim Sa'd al-Din and others on charges of conspiring to form a political organization. After some investigation, they were released and reinstated to their posts.[122] The incident was a brief hiccup compared to Egypt's spectacular military defeat by the Israelis in the following year when the revolutionary thrust of the socialist agenda was, if not stopped in its tracks, severely blunted. The setback effectively shelved the long-running campaign of the Egyptian government to coopt the universities and provided the opportunity for the opponents of socialist transformation to prepare for a return to power. Although the Institute continued its activities after 1967, it lost its momentum as a centre of radical thought.[123]

THE CENTRE FOR POLITICAL
AND STRATEGIC STUDIES

From his position as editor-in-chief of *al-Ahram* and éminence grise of the Nasser regime, Muhammad Hasanayn Haykal moved to rally and reform the intellectual forces of the country. From the early 1960s he had already made al-Ahram a refuge for leftist intellectuals, such as Lutfi al-Khuli, who had negotiated a truce with the regime. In the wake of the 1967 defeat Haykal proposed the establishment of the Centre for Political and Strategic Studies (*Markaz al-dirasat al-siyasiyya wa'l-istratijiyya*) with aims quite different from the radical tone of the Higher Institute of Socialist Studies. Its main role was to conduct research on political issues and conduct analyses on matters of foreign policy, particularly in relation to Israel. Rather than train cadres for a socialist vanguard, the Centre was set up to utilize the talents of intellectuals in the policy making process.[124]

Though part of the al-Ahram conglomerate, the Centre was relatively independent, operating under its own president and director, who were responsible in turn to a council of advisers and experts. In its capacity as a government think-tank, the Centre took direction from the president of the republic and presented reports on various issues, many of them unpublished. In this role Sadat used the Centre less than Nasser, and Mubarak less again.[125] Some analyses have been critical of aspects of the administration particularly the critique of Sadat's initiative towards Israel in 1977. The appointment of al-Sayyid Yassin to the directorship in 1975 signalled a change of emphasis. Although still concerned with the formulation of public policy, Yassin actively encouraged the Centre to take up the role of educating the general public. Nevertheless, the Centre's orientation has consistently been focused on matters of national interest and towards fulfilling the 'strategic' role envisaged for it.

One of the Centre's special areas of activity has been contemporary history with a history unit (*Markaz al-watha'iq wa'l-buhuth al-tarikhiyya li-misr al-mu'asira*), initially headed by Yusuf Hasan, former grand chamberlain under the monarchy, especially set up for the purpose.[126] One of its earliest publications, an annotated edition and translation of relevant documents from the British archives, marked the occasion of the 50th anniversary of the 1919 Revolution.[127] Prepared by 'Izzat 'Abd al-Karim, then on the point of retiring from a distinguished career, with the help of a student 'Abd al-Khaliq Lashin, the appearance of the book afforded Haykal a public opportunity to signal a change of attitude by the regime. In the preface Haykal acknowledged the disaster of 1967 and recognized the need to remind Egyptians of a more glorious time. The National Revolution of 1919, a dramatic demonstration of the unity and strength of the Egyptian nation, was such an event. For this reason, Haykal stressed that the publication of the documents in an accessible form was so critical. This reassessment was a substantial climb down from the earlier view of the regime that Egyptian modern history did not begin until 1952. It also represented a significant departure from the dismissive attitude of the Charter towards the 1919 Revolution (which Haykal himself was said to have written) and a clear symptom of the political trauma and uncertainty that prevailed in Egypt at the end of the 1960s.

From the mid-1970s onwards a large number of historical studies on modern and contemporary Egypt appeared under the imprint of the Centre. These included monographs by academic historians: Yunan Labib Rizq on political parties, 'Ali Barakat on agricultural landownership and Muhammad 'Abd al-Rahman Burg on 'Aziz al-Misri and the national movement. The Centre began issuing a journal, *al-Siyasa al-dawliyya*, edited for a time by its president Butrus Butrus Ghali, which featured articles on various historical and political issues and carried book reviews of local and foreign language works. Like the edited documents of the 1919 Revolution, other publications more manifestly reflected its national focus. In 1977, the Centre marked the occasion of the 25th anniversary of the 1952 Revolution with a collection of articles edited by its director, al-Sayyid Yassin.[128] More recently, Ra'uf 'Abbas edited a volume to commemorate the 40th anniversary of the 1952 Revolution with contributions from eight other historians.[129] Yet another collection, *One People and One Nation*, published in 1982 with a foreword by Butrus Ghali, reinforced one of the planks of government policy, the national unity between Copts and Muslims. In fact, Butrus Ghali's concurrent appointment for a time as president of the Centre and Acting Secretary of State made explicit the Centre's close relationship with the interests of the state and reflected its role as 'a patriotic brains trust'.[130]

HISTORY BY GOVERNMENT COMMITTEE

While it had been Fu'ad's custom to commission individual historians to write histories sympathetic to the Egyptian royal family, it was more consistent with the ideology of the post-1952 regime that government committees should undertake specific historical projects. The *mashru'*, which was inspired by the Charter of 1962, has already been discussed but there have been more recent attempts to fashion an official history. In 1982, for example, in order to mark the centenary of the 'Urabi Revolution, the Supreme Council of Culture commissioned the secretary-general of the National Historical Documents Centre to prepare a bibliography of relevant documents. The result was a mammoth volume of over 600 pages.[131] However, far more significant as an instance of the government endeavouring to produce its own version of national history was the committee set up by Sadat to write a history of the 23 July Revolution in 1975.

The project arose from a desire by Sadat to both co-opt and contain discussion of the Revolution. Ever conscious of his image – two autobiographies testify to his flair for self-promotion – Sadat became even more so after his elevation to the presidency.[132] In 1975 concerned about how former colleagues from amongst the Free Officers might portray him in their memoirs, Sadat issued two presidential decrees: one which restricted writing about the July Revolution to a specially constituted committee and another which made it difficult for historians to use documents less than 50 years old.[133] Both were aimed at blocking any independent historical analysis of the 1952 Revolution and sought to pre-empt any hostile interpretation of Sadat's personal role in the coup and the revolutionary regime.

The members of the special committee were announced in the press in October 1975.[134] It was a measure of the importance Sadat attached to the committee that Vice President Husni Mubarak was appointed as chairman. Apart from Mubarak, there were 19 members drawn from academic, political and military circles who offered expertise as varied as it was diffuse. As originally announced they were Sayyid 'Ali al-Sayyid,[135] Badawi 'Abd al Latif,[136] Ahmad 'Izzat 'Abd al-Karim,[137] Muhammad Najib Abu al-Lail, Ta'ima al-Gurf,[138] Butrus Butrus Ghali,[139] Jamal al-Din Zakariyya Qasim,[140] Jamal Hamdan,[141] Sayyida Isma'il al-Kashaf,[142] Muhammad Tal'at Ghanima,[143] Mustafa 'Abd al-Hamid al-'Abadi,[144] Fikhri Abaza,[145] Sayyid Zaki 'Abd al-Hadi, Layla Takla,[146] Muhammad Rashwan[147] and 'Abd al-'Aziz 'Abd al-Haq.[148] In addition, members were appointed from the three arms of the military forces: Major-General Muhammad Hasan al-Ghanima, Rear Admiral Muhammad 'Ali Muhammad and Air Force Major-General Muhammad Lutfi Shibana.[149] Even before the appointments were announced one historian had gone into print to emphasize the importance of including academic historians on the committee.[150] When made public the committee's composition did not immediately inspire confidence. It was a hotchpotch of old and new conservatives, Sadatists and a sprinkling of academics. Another historian, 'Abd al-'Azim Ramadan, praised the aims of the project but wondered why of the 19 committee members there were only two modern historians: Ahmad 'Izzat 'Abd al-Karim, by this time retired, but bringing a great deal of prestige with him, and Jamal Zakariyya, a younger man but best known as a Gulf specialist.[151]

The first meeting of the committee set forth the aims of the project and discussed its proposed programme. Sayyid Zaki 'Abd al-Hadi was chosen as secretary-general and civil and military subcommittees were set up. With eight more subcommittees organized to collect documents from the RCC (*Majlis al-thawra*), the cabinet (*Majlis al-wizara'*), the parliament, government ministries, political and scholarly organizations, the breadth of the committee's task was nothing if not ambitious.[152] Linking the formulation of the past with the government's present and future political program, Vice President Mubarak explained that,

The task of the committee is not only to record what was accomplished in relation to the aims of the revolution but to record the efforts which it accomplished and continues to accomplish until now ... and also the efforts which the continuation of the struggle of the past achieved and the resumption of the future struggle [will achieve] ... [153]

Two matters of great importance were stressed: first, the desire of the committee to 'establish the proven facts' and the need to provide a clear account of events. Encouragingly, Sadat was reported to have agreed that the committee be given the right to examine secret and prohibited documents since the study was 'factual'.[154] This announcement was regarded as particularly important. As one academic historian noted, dealing with the post-1952 period had hitherto been 'forbidden ground'.[155] Ahmad 'Izzat 'Abd al-Karim, himself a member of the Committee, emphasized above all the importance of collecting documents.[156] Sayyid Ahmad al-Nasiri of Cairo University concurred, stating, '... it is the mission of the committee to publish the documents of the revolution and not to write [its history]'.[157] Plans were made for the publication of the material, to be issued in a projected three volumes.[158]

Over the following months (and years) the committee went about the collection of material and recording of interviews with considerable fanfare in the media, even attracting the attention of the cartoonist at al-Ahram.[159] The manner of proceeding, however, attracted some suspicions about the motives behind the project. In response to questions in a press interview, Mubarak denied that the existence of the committee stopped anybody else from writing about the Revolution.[160] Yet, for a committee set up to investigate the history of the 1952 Revolution, it was strange that one of its first actions was to commission the military committee to look at the events of the 1967 War. General Muhammad Fawzi, chief of staff in 1967, and General 'Abd al-Muhsin Kamil Murtaji, commander of the Sinai front, were called to give testimony.[161] This has led at least one historian to suggest that the whole aim of the exercise was simply to discredit Nasser.[162]

The hopes of 'Abd al-Karim and many others were not to be realized. After some time 'Abd al-Karim became dissatisfied with proceedings and withdrew from the committee, without officially resigning. Jamal Zakariyya did the same.[163] In August 1978, Husni Mubarak relinquished the chairmanship of the committee and Subhi 'Abd al-Hakim, a geographer and dean of the Faculty of Arts at Cairo University (and later speaker of the Majlis al-Shura) was appointed as his successor. Some time after the activities of the committee ceased and it was formally dissolved in 1985.[164] Despite the large quantity of material collected over almost 10 years, hardly anything was published.[165] It is difficult to disagree with Ra'uf 'Abbas who believes that the committee '... was set up to prevent people from writing on the Revolution unless this was done through the governmental channel, which was the committee. It was for a political reason, not an academic reason'.[166]

ACCEPTABLE LIMITS

If the carrot in the Egyptian government's attempt to influence historical research was the establishment and funding of research centres and the formation of committees with the prospect of publication of documents, the stick was simply to clamp down and repress dissident views. Under both the monarchy and the revolutionary regime, censorship and political pressure played a significant role in shaping the limits of acceptable historical discourse. More often it was the work of non-academic historians (a class of historians discussed in the next chapter) who were targets for state harassment and censorship rather than the more cautious academic historians. Nevertheless, there were occasions when even the latter incurred the ire of the authorities. Ibrahim 'Abduh had been dismissed from his academic post not long after the RCC came to power and the purging of the universities in September 1954 showed the lengths to which the regime would resort. The case of 'Abd al-'Aziz Shinawi was more pointed. Shinawi had written his doctoral thesis on the Suez Canal in the reign of Isma'il and, while in charge of the archives in 'Abdin Palace, was accused of concealing documents that supported the case for the nationalization of the canal in 1956. He was arrested, tortured and imprisoned for 2 years, while continuing to maintain his ignorance of any such documents.[167] Subsequently released he was rehabilitated and appointed professor of modern history at al-Azhar after its reorganization.[168] More recently in the final months of the Sadat presidency, 'Abd al-Khaliq Lashin, then professor of history at 'Ain Shams University, was informed that he would be arrested because of certain comments he had made in his lectures. He fled to Qatar where he taught for the next 4 years.[169]

These incidents relate more to political circumstances than the consequences of historical interpretation. It is much more difficult to ascertain how much censorship has been a factor in curbing expression in scholarship.[170] The causes célèbres in Egypt have most often been related to religious sensitivities, such as 'Ali 'Abd al-Raziq's *al-Islam wa usul al-hukm*, Taha Husayn's work on pre-Islamic poetry, *Fi al-shi'r al-jahili*, and *Awlad haratina* by Najib Mahfuz.[171] It is less clear to what extent historians of the modern period were actually *prevented* from publishing. Certainly, during the monarchy there were certain boundaries to be observed. One factor was the sensitivities of the king. Fu'ad had personally intervened to put pressure on Muhammad Sabri to modify some of his views of Isma'il.[172] Similarly, al-Rafi'i suffered some bureaucratic harassment from the Ministry of

Education who thought his assessment of Isma'il unacceptable.[173] Issues of national unity were also a delicate matter. Two books dealing with the fragile state of communal relations between Muslims and Copts published in the dying days of the parliamentary regime were banned.[174]

Under the Nasser regime the acceptable limits of historical critique became more restrictive and the manner of dealing with recalcitrants markedly more heavy-handed. The banning of political parties in 1953 and the widespread detention of political dissidents throughout the 1950s and 1960s clearly indicated that freedom of expression was hardly to be taken for granted. The mood of the censor reflected the changing political circumstances. Apart from a period in the late 1950s, left wing analyses were granted little indulgence and, even after the regime adopted socialism in the early 1960s, it was always on a conditional basis.[175] Studies on the history of the Ikhwan were banned. An academic work on the Muslim Brothers written by a Palestinian Ishaq al-Husayni at an American university in 1955 was not officially allowed into Egypt and had to be circulated in secret; another study of the Ikhwan written by Muhammad Shawqi Zaki disappeared.[176]

Even if the Nasser regime encouraged negative views of the monarchical period, there was still some latitude allowed for historical interpretation of the pre-1952 period and a Zhdanovist policy was never more than moderately applied.[177] The case of 'Abd al-'Azim Ramadan's master's dissertation published in 1968 is illustrative. An analysis of the development of the national movement between 1918 and 1936, Ramadan's treatment was innovative in presenting a positive assessment of the Wafd and in acknowledging the role of the communists. This view challenged the orthodox rhetoric of the regime, which had principally blamed the Wafd for squandering the gains of the 1919 Revolution. Ramadan gives credit for its publication to the enthusiastic support of Mahmud Amin al-'Alim, a 'former' communist, who was head of the publishing house. However, his second volume, which carried the narrative into the 1940s, met with more obstacles and Ramadan was forced to seek a publisher in Beirut.[178] However, the 1952 revolution and its aftermath as a subject of critical historical study remained largely off-limits. Salah al-'Aqqad's work on the Palestinian question, which held that Egyptian propaganda had transformed the Egyptian defeat of 1956 into victory, was questioned but ultimately approved in 1968.[179] In general, academics knew the limits of what was acceptable. As one Egyptian historian has stated, 'There is no one I know who submitted a book and they refused to publish it. Those kinds of people did not submit in the first place ... if they wanted to publish their writings, they published outside.'[180] It would seem, then, that amongst academic historians the main form of censorship was self-censorship.[181]

With the death of Nasser and the succession of Anwar al-Sadat to the presidency in 1970 there was increasing freedom to discuss and publish historical work. The *infitah* that was the major plank of Sadat's economic policy in the 1970s was accompanied in part by a corresponding historio-graphical opening. There was still some delicacy in dealing with post-1952 history. Al-'Aqqad's book on the June War, *Masa' Yuniu 1967*, which was somewhat critical of the Egyptian government, was delayed for 2 months but subsequently published without alteration in 1975.[182] However, more sensitive matters such as the historical role of Sadat himself still remained beyond the pale. Nor did the new freedom apply equally across the pol-itical spectrum. While in the 1960s under Nasser there may have been more leniency granted to Marxist analyses, when Sadat took power, and this was true of his politics generally, freedom was more conspicuously allowed for conservative and Islamic interpretations.[183] Even so, work sympathetic to the communist movement did appear from the mid-1970s. Rif'at al-Sa'id (b. 1932), a communist and for many years an inmate of Nasser's gaols, was particularly prolific. During the 1970s he embarked upon an extended series on the history of the Egyptian Left, while in the opposition press he presented a careful mixture of political commentary and history.[184]

The institutional and state influences on historical scholarship have not been confined to Egypt. International factors have also come into play. The sudden wealth brought about by the oil price increases of 1973–4 had both positive and negative ramifications for Egyptian historians. One clear advantage was that well-paid academic positions in the oil-rich Arab states became an increasingly attractive option. Henceforth, it became common-place for Egyptian historians to take up positions especially in the Gulf and Saudi Arabia, Iraq, Algeria and Libya, where they could receive salaries ten times as much as they were paid in Egypt.[185] However, the generous educa-tion budgets in the oil-rich countries also meant more of their students could afford to attend European and American universities rather than go to Egypt. In addition, changes in international politics caused a diminution of Egypt's importance. Whereas during the 1960s it had attracted many of the best and brightest students the Arab world had to offer, after the death of Nasser and the decline in pan-Arab sentiment, Egypt no longer held the same appeal. This decline became more dramatically obvious with Egypt's expulsion from the Arab League after the Camp David agreement, though this did not affect individual Egyptian scholars who continued to take up academic positions throughout the Arab world.

The attractive salaries available in the oil-exporting countries did more than expand employment opportunities for Egyptian historians. It also had an arguably deleterious effect on the quality of historical research. Gov-ernments in the Gulf, as elsewhere, sought to use history to legitimate their rule and defend their historical record. Accordingly, they engaged historians on projects designed to further their political interests, often publishing the results in lavish fashion. They may also have promoted a more Islamic perspective. Haddad remarks,

The writing of texts from a specifically Muslim perspective, of course, is in part due to the competition among faculty at Egyptian universities for the highly remunerative teaching positions at the many new institutions of higher learning in the Arabian peninsula. Also influential are the academic conferences on Islamic subjects sponsored by these Arabian universities and by the Muslim World League. By focusing on Islamic topics, they have directed historical and social science research into specific channels, and have fostered a network of authors and professors committed to the pursuit of such research.[186]

Rif'at al-Sa'id supports this view.

Petrodollars are playing an important role in this. Firstly because Saudi Arabia is financing a lot of institutions just to write the Islamic history – not the history of the Islamic period, this is different – to Islamise the history and to glorify the period of Islamic ruling including the Ottoman period... A lot of students preparing for their thesis find it difficult to find places in Egyptian universities, so they look abroad... They used to prepare doctoral theses on subjects that may please the Saudis and others... And of course if you are writing for this purpose, you should write what may please those who will pay your salary later.[187]

Ra'uf 'Abbas of Cairo University concurs: 'It is a time for compromise with the oil producing countries, so some historians act like salesmen and they offer whatever is demanded by the market.'[188]

It is possible to overstate this. Many modern Egyptian historians who have taught in Saudi Arabia and the Gulf have impeccable secular credentials. Nevertheless, the furore in 1995 regarding editorial changes to works of Egyptian literature amidst accusations that 'the expurgations and interpolations were made to accommodate the tastes of Gulf conservatives, as well as local Islamist extremists', suggests that the widespread suspicion of political forces interested in cultivating an Islamic perspective in historiography are not to be lightly dismissed.[189] There are even concerns in some quarters that the circumstances in the oil-rich countries, where an often conservative and insular type of Islamic culture prevails, may adversely influence the representation of non-Muslim minorities in the historical record and seek to impose a hegemonic Muslim culture on the whole of the region.[190]

In recent years the special status of Egyptian historians working in the Gulf has declined compared to the situation of previous decades. Egyptians have now to deal with much more competition from Syrians, Jordanians and Maghribis. In Qatar in the early 1970s, Egyptians were in the great majority; by the end of the century there was only one Egyptian historian employed. In Oman, Jordanians, Sudanese and Moroccans are preferred and more generally there seems to be a policy of not employing Egyptians even when they have held better qualifications. The availability of qualified local staff has also contributed to less employment opportunities for Egyptians. One estimate is that currently in Saudi Arabia about 90 per cent of staff are local and in Kuwait, about 75 per cent.[191]

A DEARTH OF DOCUMENTS

More effective and insidious than censorship in constraining historical research has been the lack of access to state archives and official records. Often overlooked as an element in the control of public scholarship, the state's possession of documents has been critical in determining the pattern and parameters of historical research. Access to state archives and official papers in Egypt has never been routine. At times permission has been granted selectively according to personal or political connections, as occurred most often under the monarchy. More recently the lack of access to official documents of the post-1952 period has been almost total. The result has been a historiography that has had to rely almost entirely on foreign archives, the press, interviews and personal memoirs as the basis for research.

Control of the state archives has been employed as an important political tool by Egyptian governments since the time of Muhammad 'Ali.[192] In the 1920s and 1930s Fu'ad most effectively used access to Palace archives and other official papers to cultivate a sympathetic scholarship. The same access was not always granted to other, often Egyptian, historians regarded as less reliable. Al-Rafi'i, for instance, was sometimes denied access to records while others complained of restrictions.[193] In one of his early works Muhammad Sabri, after thanking a number of specific people, went on to acknowledge the anonymous help of '...deux hauts fonctionnaires...qui ont eu l'obligeance de nous communiquer des documents qui constituent l'une des meilleures contributions á l'histoire de cette époque'.[194] There was no mention of Fu'ad. By 1933, Sabri had come to heel, praising the king for '...l'ombre tutelaire s'étend sur tous les domaines et qui prodigue les encouragements á tous les travailleurs intellectuals', and expressing his gratitude to the monarch for facilitating access to palace archives.[195]

The revolutionary regime has exercised its control of official archives in a far more rigid way such that scholars at least since the early 1960s have consistently lamented the unavailability of material. In the summer of 1962, historians Muhammad Anis and Ahmad 'Abd al-Rahim Mustafa took up the issue, personally lobbying the minister of culture on the matter of the poor state of the national archives and the ownership of the private papers of former Egyptian leaders.[196] They expressed concern over the government policy which granted access only to documents up to the reign of Isma'il, and even then only to material relevant to Egypt and not the Arab world.[197] The archives that were available lacked any order and some documents had even been sent to Turkey in 1952.[198] The meeting achieved some limited results. In August it was announced that a committee would be formed of professors of modern history and postgraduate students from Cairo and 'Ain Shams Universities, headed by Anis and Mustafa, to obtain and publish memoirs relating to the 1919 Revolution, with expenses to be paid by the ministry of culture. In a press interview Anis singled out the correspondence between Sa'd Zaghlul and 'Abd al-Rahman Fahmi as a particular priority.[199]

Early the following year, when the plans of the AUC to collect the private memoirs and papers of such Egyptian leaders as Sa'd Zaghlul and Muhammad Farid became public, Anis saw red. He believed foreign control of such valuable primary material as reminiscent of Fu'ad's deliverance of Egyptian historiography into the hands of foreign historians and a threat to Egypt's ideological heritage. Ownership of a country's historical heritage was, he stressed, a matter of national importance.

> If political independence means that power is transferred from foreign to Egyptian hands, and if economic independence means the transfer of our economic resources to us, then intellectual independence definitely means transferring our intellectual heritage to our own hands.[200]

Anis called on the ministry to intervene, 'The ministry of culture and national guidance bears proper responsibility and [should] move to protect this great heritage and take immediate steps to put an end to the destruction of this heritage.'

Anis' campaign, no doubt assisted by his contacts within the government, bore fruit with the establishment of the Centre of Documents and Contemporary History of Egypt (*Markaz watha'iq wa tarikh misr al-mu'asir*) dedicated to the preparation of historical documents for publication, as well as encouraging research opportunities for graduates.[201] Ultimately, however, it fell short of Anis' hopes of an independent academic centre.[202] Set up originally as a separate unit under the umbrella of the ministry of culture, it soon became part of the Dar al-Kutub and was financially hampered as a result.[203] Nevertheless, the Centre continues to function, now with Yunan Labib Rizq at its head, and publishes original materials with commentary on matters of pre-1952 history as well as historical studies in the *Misr al-nahda* series.

In 1969 there was quasi-official recognition of the problem of government archives. In that year in his preface to the published collection of documents of the 1919 Revolution, Haykal publicly acknowledged that this lack of access was part of the crisis facing Egyptian historiography.[204] In fact, the documents he was introducing were translations of British records but Haykal felt it necessary to at least address the issue of the unavailability of Egyptian records for the period after 1952. He drew on a standard state defence: the events were too recent to make release of the documents appropriate. There was a particular irony that Haykal should write these words. He, himself, possessed a vast personal archive of official documents amassed during his years in favour, which he has since selectively published over time.[205] In truth, it was hardly a question of time; more than 20 years later, the situation had scarcely improved. In his introduction to an edited collection of essays on the occasion of the 40th anniversary of the July Revolution, Ra'uf 'Abbas pointed out that the contributors were unable to gain access to unpublished documents of the revolution,

> The research team was not able to examine the unpublished documents of the Revolution because these documents are unavailable to researchers. We cannot find them where they should be in the National Historical Documents Centre. We do not know, for example, the whereabouts of the papers of the Majlis al-Thawra or the private papers of 'Abd al-Nasir; nor are the archives of the republican palace available to researchers. For this reason the research team relied for the greater part on published documents, in spite of their scarcity, in addition to political memoirs published by some who participated in the revolution.[206]

He voiced the hope that the appearance of the essays might 'encourage the appropriate authorities to adopt a national, comprehensive plan to collect documents of the Revolution'. Over 10 years later there has been little indication of such a move.[207]

While academic historians have ritually bewailed the unavailability of official documents, or the selective way in which they have been made available, others have been more forthright in their criticism. An unflagging gadfly of the regime, Ibrahim 'Abduh remonstrated in his book, pointedly titled *Tarikh bila watha'iq* ('History without Documents'), of his inability to write a history of the Nasser period because of the lack of official documents. He went further and criticized apologists and polemicists of the Nasser regime who used their private stock of documents and official papers for their own political purpose – surely an illusion to Haykal.[208]

Historical research continues to be dogged by the dearth of documents which has been singly detrimental to work on the post-1952 period. Whether he was referring to real or metaphorical dangers, the assessment of Muhammad Anis more than 30 years ago still holds true,

> As far as the documents which speak about the history of revolutions and national movements, they are available in a place for documents

belonging to the republican presidency...completely locked up under the pretext of those responsible for them that they are full of snakes and scorpions and they fear accidents.[209]

Faced with a brick wall on the part of the Egyptian government, historians of Egypt have been forced to rely on three main alternatives. The first has been foreign archives, particularly British records. These had formed the basis of diplomatic histories in the heyday of the royalist school and have continued to be utilized so extensively that they almost form a sub-genre among historical studies.[210] The second source is the Egyptian press, which has provided a rich mine of historical material whose vitality and quantity in the first half of the twentieth century is impressive on any scale.[211] However, following its nationalization in 1961, the press becomes less valuable as a source for critical commentary. Finally, the personal memoirs (*mudhakkirat*) of politicians and other public figures, whose reliability, while often problematic because of their self-justificatory tone, are important historical resources. This is particularly so for the Nasser period. From amongst the members of the RCC alone, 'Abd al-Latif al-Baghdadi, Muhammad Najib (two versions), Anwar Sadat (two versions), Kamal al-Din Ibrahim, Jamal Salim and, most recently, Khalid Muhyi al-Din, have provided invaluable, if often idiosyncratic, accounts of the Nasser years.[212]

Since the nineteenth century the development of educational and research institutions has been an important element in a policy of fostering historical research consistent with state political interests. Either through the patronage of learned societies or through the establishment of academic institutes and think-tanks dedicated to a specific political vision, the state has sought to forge an official historiography. These initiatives have a mixed record, being influential in directing mainstream historical scholarship but less successful in dictating a specific historical line. More effective, even if in a wholly negative way, has been the prospect and reality of censorship and the restricted access to state archives. The dynamics of the relations that have operated between the universities and the state have been more complex. The state's attempts to assert direct control over the universities represent one of the significant domestic political struggles of the period. Since its foundation in 1925 the state university system has been the flagship of academic institutions and the sine qua non of academic history. While in its early years Fu'ad exercised some influence, the university thereafter became absorbed into the fabric of national politics, first as a stronghold of nationalist, then increasingly but not exclusively of progressive and socialist thought. Ultimately, neither those who fought for the absolute autonomy of the universities nor those who sought their control by government prevailed. While a state institution, the university was neither a simple extension of government, though some elements within it have acted so, nor a citadel of independent thought insulated from the political environment, even if some may have wished it thus. Government policy has strongly influenced but never quite tamed academic history. Nevertheless, the university system was founded on a broad national basis and has continued to address national, and generally state-centred, perspectives and concerns. Despite their occasional strained relations, university and state have both been instrumental in establishing the parameters of national historiography.

3

HISTORY IN THE STREET
The non-academic historian

> The principal difficulty that hinders the writing of the true
> history of Egypt since the beginning of the twentieth century
> until now can be summarized in two related points: first, it is
> represented in bias and partisanship due to membership of
> a specific intellectual or party current [which] forces the histo-
> rian to choose what he likes from events after editing to suit his
> views. And secondly...he chooses a framework (*qalab*) logically
> to explain events that agree with this [and] then endeavours to
> cut and paste all events to suit the logical framework established
> beforehand.
>
> Mustafa Tiba[1]

Complementing the academic historian and the university system in the
development of Egyptian historiography has been the phenomenon of the
non-academic historian. Emerging at the end of the nineteenth century
from the new professional classes, particularly legal and journalistic circles,
these historians became and have continued to be a consistent feature in
Egyptian intellectual life. Often stigmatized as amateur and second-rate
scholars, or simply branded as partisan, they have played a seminal role
in pioneering new historical frameworks that have later become influential in academic circles.[2] Less restrained by both the scholarly and
political limitations of the academy, non-academic historians have been
the source of a vigorous, contested and more representative national
historiography.

The term 'non-academic historian' requires some elucidation. Employed
here as an umbrella term rather than one of precise definition, it refers to those
who write history, such as journalists, political commentators, lawyers and
other intellectuals without a professional affiliation to a university or formal
academic institution. Motivated by a range of personal or political reasons,
the category includes political figures, government officials and dissident
writers, ranging from those who are part of the establishment to liberal
commentators and radical critics of the state. The heterogeneous character
of this genre of history is reflected in the very diverse quality, scope and
purpose of its work. Its richness lies in its representation of a great range of

perspectives, from nationalist to communitarian, secular to religious, and pro-government to opposition views. Notwithstanding this wide spectrum, it is possible to make certain observations about this broad class, its association with its academic counterpart and its relationship to political power.

As a form of political expression non-academic historiography differs from academic work in at least two important ways. First, it is not restricted by the limitations and conventions of academic writing. Unencumbered by the demands of the academic profession, which impose certain standards of technique and presentation, and the years of training necessary to acquire these skills, the genre has been more accessible to a greater number of writers. Second, because of its diffuse and non-institutional character, it is more flexible and potentially less compromised by the institutional and political constraints of its academic equivalent. As has been argued elsewhere, academic historiography has been complicit with the state and has had to engage with, if not be subject to, its political interests. By contrast, non-academic historiography is a more vibrant and unrestrained genre that allows its practitioners to tackle more sensitive historiographical issues. What it may lose through its sometimes strident partisan tone or lack of technical sophistication, non-academic history gains in dynamism and breadth of representation. If academic history is the historiographic mainstream, the work of non-academics is the turbulent fringe. This freedom can have disadvantages. While non-academic historians may have support on a small scale from political parties, cultural associations or community bodies, they do not have the resources that university historians can draw on. Nor do they enjoy the protection that a university can offer: non-academics have suffered noticeably more from censorship and political harassment than have their academic counterparts.

Despite these important differences, academic and non-academic historians share the common enterprise of representing a historical vision of Egypt. It is this common purpose that is the basis of the extensive cross-fertilization of ideas between the two groups. What underlines the critical significance of non-academic writers is that new schools of historical thought have consistently been pioneered by non-academics and only been adopted over time by history departments in universities. This chapter discusses several streams of non-academic historiography: the liberal, materialist, Islamic and feminist schools that have played an innovative role in the development of the discipline. It traces the rise and development of each school, closely linking this with the fortunes of a political movement and charting the dynamics of its changing pattern of association with state authority.

BEYOND THE PALACE: THE LIBERAL SCHOOL AND THE NATIONAL MOVEMENT

In the nineteenth century bureaucrats like Rifa'ah al-Tahtawi and 'Ali Mubarak represented the mainstream of historical scholarship in Egypt through their personal and professional association with the palace. Towards the end of the century a new type of historian drawn from a different milieu heralded the beginnings of an alternative historical school. The liberal school (al-madrasa al-wataniyya)[3] emerged from beyond the shadow of state authority and presented the basis of a viable and ultimately successful challenge to the palace historians. Drawn from the emergent professional classes, these historians made use of their independence from the palace to construct a more national interpretation of Egyptian history that included a broader conception of Egyptian society beyond the sphere of the ruler and state institutions. In this way, the increasing sophistication of Egyptian civil society provided the basis for the articulation of an alternative perspective with a more diffuse view of political power and a more inclusive construction of the nation.

In 1882 the establishment of the School of Law (formerly the School of Law and Administration) recognized the increasing importance of a profession that offered an avenue of social advancement. From this time on Egyptian lawyers began to leave the service of the government prosecution office (the Parquet) and enter private practice. The independence and opportunities this brought, subsequently produced a breeding ground for many political activists, writers and historians.[4] Legal training was one way of developing research and analytical skills for middle-class Egyptians and it was common to many of the amateur historians of this and the next generation including Ahmad Shafiq (1860–1940), politician and journalist Muhammad Husayn Haykal (1888–1956), 'Aziz Khanki, 'the tireless chronicler of Egyptian legal history',[5] and Mikha'il Sharubim (1861–1920). The expanding newspaper industry and popular writing also offered opportunities to talented historical writers. In this respect, the contribution of the resident Syrian community to Egyptian intellectual life was remarkable. During the late nineteenth and early twentieth centuries Syrians resident in Egypt produced a distinguished number of eminent intellectuals, journalists, feminist pioneers and newspaper editors. Among historians, Salim al-Naqqash (d. 1884), an actor and journalist, stands out as the author of Misr li'l-misriyyin ('Egypt for the Egyptians'), a detailed and well-documented history of the period from the accession of Tawfiq in 1879 until the defeat of the 'Urabi revolt and the trial of its leaders in 1884.[6]

The impetus of the liberal school did not simply derive from social and economic changes. Its political inspiration came from the failure of the uprising in 1882, the subsequent occupation of Egypt by British forces and the weakened position of the Egyptian government. As it regrouped and reorganized, the national movement sought to project an effective political programme. Part of this was the articulation of an alternative historiography which moved the focus of Egyptian history away from the palace and its fixation with the deeds of the ruler to a broader, more inclusive, popular notion of the nation. The outstanding figure of this movement was the dynamic Mustafa Kamil (1874–1908), whose stirring speeches calling for

81

an independent Egypt, the evacuation of the British and the maintenance of certain, albeit vague, links with the Ottoman Empire, attracted huge crowds in the first years of the twentieth century. In establishing a case for Egyptian independence Kamil also recognized the value of history as an integral part of his political programme. Already in the 1890s, while young men, he and his colleague, Muhammad Farid (1868–1919), had written histories which projected an early version of their political vision of Egypt. Kamil's study, a diplomatic history of relations between the European powers, the Ottoman Empire and Egypt, took a strong anti-European line and expressed the ambiguous nationalist-Ottomanist perspective characteristic of his politics.[7] Farid wrote a history of the reign of Muhammad 'Ali and followed this with a more extensive history of the Ottoman Empire.[8] The views found in these works are more expressive of their youth when both men enjoyed warm relations with the palace. For a number of years Kamil had close links with 'Abbas Hilmi II and the Khedive may even have paid for some of his education in France.[9] Similarly, Farid's work, written while he was still working in the Department of the Public Domain and before his resignation under a cloud in 1896, was very supportive of the royal family.[10] Kamil and Farid therefore represent a transitional phase from the palace-centred perspective of the bureaucrat-historians. Their work, and even more their strong nationalist politics of the following decade, paved the way for an alternative historical interpretation that would blossom with their political heirs.

The establishment of the Higher Schools Club (*Nadi al-madaris al-'ulya*) in 1905 gave Kamil's radical brand of nationalism an organized forum in which to propagate the ideas of the movement. As the venue for many speeches and lectures the club provided an important meeting place for the education of Egyptian nationalists and the promotion of nationalist aims. It attracted many young men from the middle and lower-middle classes who were to provide the basis of the Watani Party, formed in 1907.[11] One contemporary witness described it,

> It was our meeting with the graduates that enriched our scholarly and intellectual maturity, and the lectures and meetings increased in number in the club. It seemed to us like a higher learned institute and we continued our study and enriched our knowledge. I benefited from it greatly. There was a library full with books, newspapers and magazines that helped me become more open-minded and improve my thinking, and I did not miss a lecture.[12]

Eager both to spread knowledge and to broaden its political support, by 1909 the party had also established a system of popular night schools (*madaris al-sha'b*) in poor areas of Cairo which taught modern and Islamic history along with other subjects.[13] From such efforts the liberal school developed and propagated a new interpretation of Egyptian history.

The political spirit, even logic, of this new historiography was to create its own definitions of nation and society. More than 20 years earlier Salim al-Naqqash's history of the 'Urabi revolution presented a more moderate tone and critical account of events than native Egyptian writers, '...rather like the typical product of a Syrian Christian émigré writer, aloof from the nationalistic currents of the time because of their invariably Islamic undertones'.[14] When the nationalist movement gathered strength, under the fiery rhetoric of Mustafa Kamil, the perceived detachment of the Syrians became a political handicap, provoking charges of their lack of enthusiasm for the cause of independence. Thereafter Syrians kept, or appeared to keep, their distance from the mainstream Egyptian nationalism. The parting of company was also no doubt fuelled by religious difference. Kamil's brand of nationalism appealed to the Ottoman Empire and Islam in a way which may have discomforted the Christian population. The situation was exacerbated by the aggressive style of 'Abd al-'Aziz Jawish and by 1911 relations between Muslim and Copts were in a state of crisis. The conspicuous absence of Copts from the ranks of historians suggests that Christians generally, and not just Syrians, may have drawn back from some of the definitional dilemmas writing a national history might have involved.[15]

The career of Jurji Zaydan (1861–1914), a pillar of Syrian–Egyptian historiography, embodies some of these changing attitudes.[16] Zaydan had come to Egypt as a young man and, by dint of hard work, had established himself as a journalist and came to play an important role in publishing, founding the famous publishing house, Dar al-Hilal, in 1892. As a writer of histories and historical novels, he justified his departure from the more traditional preoccupations of historians stating, 'the true history of the nation is the history of its civilization and culture, not the history of its wars and conquests in the manner of the earlier Arab historians of Islam'.[17] He ranged widely in his choice of themes from the pre-Islamic period to modern times, though his *Tarikh misr al-jadid min al-fath al-islami ila alan*, stands out as his major achievement.[18] Written in a popular style, Zaydan owed much to the work of European scholars but his breadth of knowledge was impressive and his output prolific. In 1910, his standing was such that Zaydan was invited to give a course of lectures on Islamic history at the newly-established private Egyptian University. When this became publicly known, the invitation provoked objections in some Muslim quarters on the grounds that a Greek Orthodox Syrian such as Zaydan was unqualified for such a task. The university council gave way under pressure and Zaydan withdrew.[19]

The culturalist writings of the Syrians aside, the histories which appeared beyond the royal sphere of influence in the early twentieth century reflected the ideals and programme of the embryonic nationalist movement.[20] These new historians were often graduates of the Khedival Law School and, though not trained professionals, their writings were to have considerable influence on later academic historians.[21] They included men such as Muhammad

Fahmi, a law graduate and later president of the Committee of Nationalist Egyptians in Geneva, who wrote *La Vérité sur la question d'Égypte*, and Ahmad Lutfi al-Sayyid, the founder of the Umma Party and first rector of the Egyptian University.[22] One historian, above all, came forth from this milieu whose name must be added alongside if not placed before his professional contemporaries as one of the pioneers of modern Egyptian history. This was 'Abd al-Rahman al-Rafi'i.

'ABD AL-RAHMAN AL-RAFI'I

Al-Rafi'i (1889–1966) was born to a middle class family in Cairo, the son of a *qadi* of the shari'a courts.[23] In 1904 he enrolled at the Law School where he met the charismatic Mustafa Kamil. When Kamil established the Watani Party in 1907, al-Rafi'i became a member and embarked on a life-long commitment to political activity. While still a student he had begun writing for the party's newspaper, *al-Liwa'*. Following his graduation in 1908, al-Rafi'i chose journalism over government service in order to allow himself the freedom to participate in the national struggle.[24] Following Kamil's death in the same year, al-Rafi'i worked for his successor, Muhammad Farid, accompanying him on at least one trip to Brussels. During the First World War he immersed himself in party work, serving time in gaol for his political activities and taking an active part in the 1919 Revolution.

Al-Rafi'i's commitment to political activism and the cause of the Watani Party would continue undimmed over the next three decades. With the limited independence granted to Egypt by the British under the 1923 constitution, he was first elected to parliament as a member of the Watani Party in 1924 and again in 1925. Consistent with its policy, the party continued to insist on immediate British withdrawal before any negotiations and the political unity of the Nile Valley, shorthand for Egyptian control of the Sudan – a position hostile to the Wafd's compromise on the principle of Egyptian sovereignty and the Sudanese question. From 1939 to 1951 al-Rafi'i sat in the Majlis al-Shuyukh as an elected member for Kafr Badawi al-Qadim (Daqahliyya), and for a brief period in 1949 served as Minister of Supply in a coalition cabinet. In addition to these parliamentary duties, al-Rafi'i held the post of secretary of the Watani Party from 1932 to 1946.

Throughout this period al-Rafi'i was also a practising lawyer and took advantage of the opportunity to immerse himself in the politics of the National Bar Association. As one of the oldest professional organizations in Egypt, the association was a microcosm of many of the political conflicts fought out on the national stage. This was particularly the case during the annual election of the association's officers.[25] In the period prior to and during the First World War, members of the Watani Party had been prominent among office bearers but its political eclipse after 1919 saw the Wafd dominate the Association until the fall of the monarchy. However, during a time of Wafd weakness, al-Rafi'i was elected as vice-president of the Association in 1940.[26]

While the 1952 Revolution heralded a steep decline in the public career of Muhammad Sabri and a reorientation in the case of Shafiq Ghurbal, al-Rafi'i fared rather differently, accepting a government appointment and being publicly honoured for his writing. His contrasting fortunes might be explained in two ways. First, although the Watani Party had become increasingly marginal in Egyptian politics from the early 1920s, al-Rafi'i's membership of the party meant he had impeccable anti-imperialist and radical, if not revolutionary, credentials. More important, however, was the popular esteem he enjoyed as a historian. By the early 1950s al-Rafi'i had become a pillar of contemporary Egyptian history. More prolific than most academic historians, his work was well known to the public and, since at least the late 1930s, had been on the reading list for cadets at the Military Academy, where he was read by the young Nasser.[27]

Even so, al-Rafi'i's political attitude towards the military regime was marked by a certain ambivalence. In the 1940s he had voiced support for a constitutional, representative system even if at the same time he found fault with the corruption prevalent within it.[28] As late as the crisis between Nasser and Najib in early 1954, al-Rafi'i was quoted in the press as supporting a parliamentary regime and the reintroduction of political parties (banned since January 1953), a position that corresponded with Najib's position. At the same time the Wafd-controlled National Bar Association was making statements backing Najib, calling for parliamentary elections and the dissolution of the RCC. Towards the end of 1954, with Nasser now firmly in control and Najib marginalized, the government squared accounts with the Association, dismissing its officers and suspending procedural rules.[29] Al-Rafi'i, for his part, appears to have quelled his own doubts. Notwithstanding his earlier views on the virtues of parliamentary government, he accepted the government appointment as president of the Bar Association for the next 4 years.[30] In this position, he embraced the government's pro-Arab policy, organizing the second pan-Arab lawyers' conference in Cairo in 1956 and the third in the following year in Damascus, as well as taking up pan-Arab themes in his writing.[31] When he came to write his account of the 1950s, which appeared in 1959, he judged the 1952 Revolution as the crowning achievement of all national efforts.[32] The accommodation was complete. In 1960 al-Rafi'i was publicly and officially celebrated, being awarded the State Prize for the Social Sciences (*Ja'izat al-dawla*) for his lifetime of historical writings. The official commendation noted,

> One of his unique qualities is the pride of his patriotism and his zeal
> for its reputation and honour and that he was enthusiastic towards
> conspicuous historical events and the stand that the Arab nation

took against the imperialists and their supporters. What makes his writing precious is that the national movement was the main aspect discussed in this series [of histories] which was unique among modern writers because it covered political, economic and social history.[33]

Despite his lifelong political activism the award confirmed that it was as a historian that al-Rafi'i made his greatest mark in public life.

Al-Rafi'i had first begun writing before the First World War, when he authored a book on constitutional law, and followed it with another, at the urging of Muhammad Farid, on agricultural cooperative associations.[34] It was not until 1929 that al-Rafi'i turned specifically to Egyptian history, a task to which he would dedicate himself for the next 30 years. In that year his history of the Egyptian national movement in two volumes from the Mamluks until the rise of Muhammad 'Ali, *Tarikh al-haraka al-qawmiyya*, appeared. Following its success, al-Rafi'i embarked upon a more ambitious project: a systematic and much more detailed account of history of Egypt in the nineteenth and twentieth centuries. Over the next decade he produced, in succession, separate monographs on Muhammad 'Ali, Isma'il, the 'Urabi Revolution, Mustafa Kamil and Muhammad Farid, which took the national narrative up to 1919, as well as a work on late nineteenth century Egypt and Sudan. In 1946, he resumed the task with a two volume account of the 1919 Revolution and followed this with *Fi 'aqab al-thawra al-misriyya*, published in three parts (1947–51) which examined the interrevolutionary period from 1921 to 1951. In due course, accounts of the 1952 Revolution and its aftermath appeared.[35] Al-Rafi'i returned to history on a grander scale with a six-part series commissioned, presumably by the Ministry of Education, for high school students dealing with the national struggle from the time of the French campaign until 1952.[36] Throughout the 1950s he continued to be productive, contributing regularly to historical debate with articles in *al-Hilal*.

Al-Rafi'i's extensive contribution to contemporary Egyptian history places him in the first rank of Egyptian historians. As the self-appointed chronicler of the evolution of the national movement, he embraced *the* powerful political theme of the modern period. His choice had been quite deliberate, as he explained,

> I liked it [history] more because from experience I saw in it a successful way for educating minds and raising the level of their patriotism and national consciousness. With time I discovered a lot of short-comings in our society, our behaviour and culture. I noticed from much evidence a weakness in our patriotism and a decline in our national consciousness. I thought of a way to treat this weakness and correct the decline. I found that history is the way that most advanced countries use for educating the behaviour and culture of

people and implanting a national spirit in them. From here came my attachment to history. I wanted to make from it a school to advance society. I found that the minds of the young and old would not accept the advice and would not know the truth unless national consciousness increased and the citizens knew the situations in their countries and how it developed in different stages. Using history they would more accept sound ideas and understand the truth in public affairs. And if the story is the best way to spread good principles, fine thoughts and noble feelings, then history was the perfect way – since it is a real story – to revive ideas, mature talents and refine the behaviour of the generation and direct citizens to the highest ideals in national life.[37]

Given this aim, it was only natural that al-Rafi'i chose to write exclusively in Arabic, a fact which set him apart not only from most of the historians of the royalist school but also from the early academic historians–Muhammad Sabri and Shafiq Ghurbal.[38] Moreover, al-Rafi'i was distinctive in his decision to concentrate on the contemporary history. Again with the exception of Sabri's early work, academic historians of the modern period were more comfortable dealing with the nineteenth century and generally eschewed the post-1919 period until at least the 1960s.[39]

These features of al-Rafi'i's work are central to his status as a non-academic historian. He was writing for an Arab and principally Egyptian readership and not for the limited, educated audience of the academic world. Unlike the historians commissioned by the palace or at least dependent on its goodwill for access to documents, al-Rafi'i by dint of his political activities and connections had his own store of documentary material. Moreover, since he had an independent livelihood as a lawyer he was not financially dependent on his writings. This granted him the freedom to address the politically sensitive area of contemporary history and the ability to weather the times when he came under pressure from the Ministry of Education and the purchase of his books was suspended by the government.[40]

Yet even if al-Rafi'i was relatively free from the shadow of the palace and the discipline of academic scholarship, his longstanding commitment to the cause of the Watani Party has long drawn criticism from academic quarters to such an extent that he is routinely invoked as the archetypal 'amateur' and politically partisan historian.[41] The principal grounds for this reproach derive from al-Rafi'i's favourable portrayal of the Watani Party's role in the national movement and his correspondingly hostile attitude towards Sa'd Zaghlul and the Wafd. Al-Rafi'i himself was not unaware of the potential for personal or political views distorting his analysis. In his memoirs he acknowledged that writing about events in which he and his political colleagues were personally involved did present a certain dilemma even at the same time as he asserted that the truth was his ultimate priority.[42]

Certainly, there is no doubt about al-Rafi'i's political perspective. His narrative grants to the Watani Party, particularly after 1919, an importance that it scarcely warrants. Moreover, his harsh judgement of Zaghlul may have been fuelled by the clashes he had in parliament with the Wafd leader over the handling of the negotiations with the British on the Sudan.[43] Nevertheless, given his view of the Wafd as compromised on the principle of national independence and the unity of the Nile Valley, his analysis if pointed is not unreasonable.

These criticisms aside, al-Rafi'i's work occupies a central place as one of the pillars of the liberal school of historiography. Indeed, his standing in Egyptian historical scholarship was publicly acknowledged by two of his academic contemporaries. In a press interview in 1961, when asked to name the historians who had done the most to spread knowledge of the history of Egypt, Muhammad Sabri had named al-Rafi'i among a group of four Egyptians.[44] Shafiq Ghurbal also publicly defended al-Rafi'i against the charge that he merely recorded historical events and failed to analyze them.[45] As a historian of confirmed political views, al-Rafi'i presented a focused and informed account of the modern history of Egypt that differed from the prevailing works of the royalist school. In his preparedness to write the history of the post-1919 period he differed from the practice of the academic historians of the time but when the academy finally did take up the subject, they relied substantially on al-Rafi'i's work. While those that followed him were not often convinced of the importance he ascribed to the Watani Party, preferring more often to give priority to the Wafd, they did embrace his central theme of the popular role of the national movement. His writing thus remains a standard reference and point of departure for any discussion of the contemporary period.[46]

THE RISE OF THE MATERIALIST SCHOOL

At the time that the liberal school pioneered by al-Rafi'i was establishing itself as the academic orthodoxy in the late 1940s and 1950s, the materialist school began to present its own challenge. Just as the liberal school was associated with the rise of bourgeois nationalism and the political fortunes of the Watani Party and the Wafd, so the development of the materialist school in Egypt was allied to the rise of socialist thought, communist activity and the labour movement. Grounded in the doctrines of Marxism, it sought to articulate an alternative political vision for the nation through the theory of class struggle and its applied analysis of feudalism, imperialism and capitalism. An integral part of this political programme was the development of a materialist interpretation of Egyptian history. By the early 1960s, its relative success in this project was evident when many of its principles and insights, if not the practitioners themselves, were embraced by the regime.

Like the liberal school, the materialist trend was linked to a broad political movement but the political environment in which each worked contrasted markedly with each other in the interwar period. The liberal school's prime political objective had been national independence and the end of the British occupation. In the years before and immediately after 1919 this position had provoked a hostile response from British authorities that saw many nationalists serving time in prison or being exiled. However, with the declaration of 1922, full national independence was recognized as a legitimate aspiration by both the Egyptians and the British, even if they had different views on how and when it might be implemented. In effect, the liberal national movement had become accepted as part of the political mainstream. By contrast, socialist thought and, more concretely, the communist movement was perceived as a dangerous threat by both British and Egyptian authorities. For much of its existence it suffered extensive repression, being declared illegal and having its members subjected to systematic campaigns of harassment. Even during the 1960s, at the height of socialist influence on government policy, communist and labour activists were afforded little political latitude. Nevertheless, despite these obstacles, it was from this milieu that materialist thought came to exert a significant influence on Egyptian historical scholarship.

Marxist and anarcho-syndicalist thought first gained currency in Egypt among certain circles within the resident Greek and Italian communities at the end of the nineteenth century.[47] Just before the First World War Egyptian writers such as Salama Musa began to introduce socialist ideas to an Arabic-reading public.[48] Soon after, in 1915, with the appearance of a booklet by a primary school principal, Mustafa Hasanayn al-Mansuri, Marxist ideas were first applied to an analysis of Egyptian conditions in Arabic.[49] In 1921, the Egyptian Socialist Party was formed in Alexandria, drawing on elements from the labour movement and socialist discussion groups, and attracting a considerable following from Egyptians and resident foreigners.[50] Among its leaders were Joseph Rosenthal and Mahmud Husni al-'Urabi, both trade unionists, and Salama Musa. In late 1922, the party established contact with the Comintern and, after agreeing to certain conditions – one of which was the expulsion of Rosenthal – adopted the name of the Egyptian Communist Party. In the following years the party attempted to broaden its political support especially amongst trade unions but a campaign of systematic harassment by the state authorities, particularly under the first Wafd government, saw the organization infiltrated by government agents and declared illegal. By the late 1920s the party, for all practical purposes, had ceased to function and contact with Moscow was reduced and ultimately broken off altogether.

Although small groups of communists continued to be active underground in the years that followed it was not until the mid-1930s that a second generation of activists, roused both by the continuing poor economic situation in Egypt and the international rise of fascism, revived the movement. Forming a variety of study or 'cultural' centres, such as the Ligue Pacifiste (*Ittihad ansar al-salam*), the Democratic Union (*al-Ittihad al-dimuqrati*) and Groupe d'Études (*Jama'at al-buhuth*), these groups discussed a wide range of political, economic and historical issues within the framework of socialist theory. From the outset, cosmopolitan Jews and members of resident foreign communities were particularly conspicuous in these circles but Egyptians were also involved. With the infiltrations and betrayals of the 1920s still fresh, Moscow declined to officially recognize the claims of any one group, despite repeated requests from various factions. The Egyptian communist movement owed much to the inspiration of the Soviet Union, particularly in the names employed by these groups – Iskra, New Dawn and 'Scientific Research' – all of which belonged to the Soviet Marxist glossary. Nevertheless, it was French and British streams of communist thought rather than Russian that would have greater influence on the Egyptian movement over the next two decades, being facilitated by the well-established prestige of French culture in the country, the political reality of Egypt's occupation by British forces, and by the regular practice of Egyptian students going to Britain and France for study.[51]

During the Second World War the communist movement became more organized and sophisticated, setting up a number of front organizations which recruited members and promoted its political programme. It was well recognized that part of this process required a reformulation and reinterpretation of Egyptian history. In developing this strategy, one group, Iskra, organized by Hillel Schwartz, deserves special attention.[52] More than most left wing groups, its membership comprised a high percentage of intellectuals and students and it emphasized the importance of studying Marxism and applying it to an Egyptian context.[53] Its study centre, the House of Scientific Research (*Dar al-abhath al-'ilmiyya*), was established in 1944 and through a programme of lectures and discussions provided a training ground for communist intellectuals and activists, as well as publishing research. In addition, Iskra was behind the setting up of the National Popular University at the end of 1945 which provided courses in politics, history, philosophy and other subjects for working class leaders.[54]

The *al-Fajr al-jadid* (New Dawn) group was another communist organization that produced important and innovative work. In 1945, one of its leading members, Ahmad Sadiq Sa'd, wrote a study on the Egyptian peasant, which began to explore some of the economic and social issues hitherto unaddressed in mainstream analyses.[55] One of its legal fronts, Dar al-qarn al-'ishrin, published an Arabic translation of *British Imperialism in Egypt*, a work originally published in 1928 by an organization with close links to the Communist Party of Great Britain.[56] This probably represented the first Marxist analysis of contemporary Egyptian history. The mid-1940s, in fact, was a time of relative freedom that witnessed a plethora of leftist periodicals addressing many political, cultural and historical issues of the day.[57] Notable amongst these was *al-Fajr al-jadid*, produced in 1945–46 by the group of the same name and edited by Ahmad Rushdi Salih,[58] and *al-Jamahir*, which appeared from 1947 to 1948, first as an organ of Iskra, and then of the Democratic Movement for National Liberation (HADITU).[59]

The relative openness of wartime Egypt was soon followed by a hardening in the attitude of the Egyptian government in the postwar period. A number of severe clampdowns, most energetically applied by the Sidqi regime in July 1946, and the declaration of martial law in 1948 and again in 1950, saw the closing down of leftist publications, the imprisonment of many cadres and the deportation of leaders such as Schwartz and Henri Curiel. With the seizure of power by the Free Officers in 1952 there was an uneasy stand-off between the Left and the new regime. Communists themselves were split on their attitude towards the coup. The regime suffered fewer doubts, banning political parties in early 1953 and, in the following year, purging the universities of leftists and any others perceived as a threat. Despite these setbacks, leftist writings of the 1940s had effectively employed historical materialism and class analysis to elucidate many of the important social and economic issues of the day that had received little attention from mainstream scholars up to that time. This literature did not primarily address historical issues – so we cannot yet talk of a fully-fledged materialist histori-ography – but its articulation of certain themes laid the foundation for the more extended analyses that would follow.

A WINDOW OF OPPORTUNITY

The opportunity to build on this beginning soon came. In the wake of the diplomatic triumph of Suez in 1956, Nasser set up a newspaper, *al-Masa'*, under the editorship of Khalid Muhyi al-Din, a former member of the RCC who had fallen out with the regime over his left wing views. For the next 2½ years its pages served as 'the ideological workshop of the new Egypt' providing '...the Left, if possible the non-Communist Left, with a legal platform duly confined within the general framework of state policy'.[60] The comparative tolerance of the period allowed the establishment of a number of publishing houses, such as Dar al-dimuqratiyya al-jadida headed by Raymond Duwayk and Lutfallah Sulayman's Dar al-nadim and al-Dar al-misriyya, which gave voice to this progressive tendency.[61]

It was Sulayman who was to publish the first sustained materialist analyses of modern Egyptian history.[62] Over the next 2½ years, Shuhdi 'Atiyya al-Shafi'i, Ibrahim 'Amr and Fawzi Jirjis, three writers all active in the communist movement, took advantage of the window of opportunity to address Egyptian political, economic and social development. Of the three, al-Shafi'i enjoyed the highest profile as an intellectual and activist. Armed with a Master of Arts degree from Exeter College in England, al-Shafi'i had returned to Egypt by 1942 and taken up a position in the Ministry of Education as an English-language supervisor.[63] He soon became prominent in Iskra, serving at one time as the director of the House of Scientific Research, where he co-authored an important pamphlet on the national aims of the organization, and later as editor of the organization's newspaper, al-Jamahir.[64] When serious internal conflicts within HADITU broke out at the end of 1947, al-Shafi'i was one of the leaders calling for greater integration of the communist movement with the national struggle, a view he continued to espouse following the formation of the United Egyptian Communist Party in 1955. In 1957 al-Shafi'i's history of the Egyptian national movement appeared,[65] establishing a materialist interpretation of Egyptian history which 'initiated the reinterpretation of his country's history as one of its peasants and workers propelling from below the struggle for social as well as national liberation'.[66]

Ibrahim 'Amr, a worker by background, was also a member of HADITU, and later Wahdat al-shuyu'in. In barely 2 years 'Amr produced three pioneering works of the materialist school. The first, in the wake of Nasser's announcement of the nationalization in 1956, discussed the Suez Canal.[67] In January of the following year, his study of the national movement, Thawrat misr al-qawmiyya appeared, and in 1958 an analysis of Egyptian agriculture, al-Ard wa'l-fallah, regarded by one commentator as 'the first complete study...of the history of the agrarian question'.[68] The last of this troika of materialist historians was Fawzi Jirjis, an active communist since the 1940s and who, for a time, worked as a journalist.[69] In 1958, his Dirasat fi tarikh misr al-siyasi appeared, applying a materialist interpretation on a grander scale than al-Shafi'i or 'Amr in his examination of Egyptian history from the Mamluk period until the present.[70]

The relative freedom afforded the left in the years after Suez was not to last. In January 1959, Nasser moved against the communists, arresting and imprisoning many of the leadership and cadres. Two months later Khalid Muhyi al-Din and other editors of al-Masa' were removed from their posts. The effect on leftist intellectual life was traumatic. Al-Shafi'i himself was beaten to death in Abu Za'bal prison camp in 1960. Others, such as Anouar Abdel-Malek and Lutfallah Sulayman, preferred to go into exile rather than risk staying in the country.[71] Despite the significant progress made in the materialist conception of Egyptian history, as Abdel-Malek noted later, '...the repressions cut down the Marxist Left in full flight, at the very time when it was labouring to develop a close theoretical analysis of Egyptian society...'.[72] In many ways Nasser's move against the communists was more tactical than ideological since he wanted socialism but without an independent communist organization. Indeed, in 1962, the publication of the Charter embraced many of the principles of socialist ideology and foreshadowed a period of cooperation between government and the Left. In

1965, after extended negotiations, the communist movement, now united, agreed to dissolve itself in exchange for a role for individual activists within the regime. Leading communists and leftists were subsequently appointed to influential positions as editors, writers and publishers in the nationalized press to promote the regime's new vision of Arab socialism.

Among the most important forums of materialist thought were two journals, *al-Katib* and *al-Tali'a*. *Al-Katib* had been an organ of the Peace Partisans' Movement in the early 1950s but by the 1960s was being reissued by the Egyptian Book Organization as the informal mouthpiece of the ASU.[73] *Al-Tali'a* was a new journal, which appeared in January 1965, under the editorship of Lutfi al-Khuli, a communist who had been released from prison some years before.[74] Though housed in the al-Ahram building, it was for practical purposes, an independent publication. Over time its editorial board would boast the considerable talents of Michel Kamil, Ibrahim Sa'd al-Din and Rif'at al-Sa'id, while its pages contained the analyses of historians, political and literary commentators.[75] The work of academic historians also featured in these journals – Muhammad Anis was on the editorial committee of *al-Katib* – but more significantly it provided a forum for historians from outside the universities.[76] It was in the pages of *al-Katib* and *al-Tali'a* that many non-academics, such as Ghali Shukri, Tariq al-Bishri, Abu Sayf Yusuf, Wilyum Sulayman Qilada, Salah 'Isa, Muhammad Sid Ahmad, Jalal al-Sayyid and Khayri 'Aziz – intellectuals of the Left or at least acceptable to it – first presented materialist analyses and commentary to a national audience.[77]

The negotiated settlement between the Left and the Nasser regime may have given the former little freedom of action but it granted a freedom of expression that allowed the further development of a materialist critique and access to a greater readership than ever before. The collaborative spirit of the time was typified by the al-Ahram empire which, under the enlightened if patriarchal editorship of Muhammad Hasanayn Haykal, provided a haven for progressive thought. For this reason, Marxist intellectual Louis 'Awad dedicated his book on universities to Haykal 'because he made *al-Ahram* a university for the people'.[78] The comment was both an implied criticism of the failure of the universities to play a sufficiently progressive role in public education and perhaps also an allusion to the government's purge of the universities in 1954, something 'Awad had himself suffered at first hand.

DIVERSITY ON THE LEFT

If the death of Nasser in 1970 heralded a more open atmosphere for some, it was not the left that was the chief beneficiary. On the contrary, in order to cement his position as the new president, Anwar Sadat purged many left wing intellectuals and Nasserists from their positions in government and the media. While he rarely resorted to Nasserist methods of imprisonment or torture, Sadat took steps to deprive his critics on the Left of a public voice. Once again this precipitated a flight of intellectuals from the country. Literary critic Ghali Shukri fled to Paris in 1973, where he wrote a contemporary history of the 1970s and its scathing indictment of Sadat's rule.[79] Tahir 'Abd al-Hakim, a communist and journalist for *al-Jumhuriyya*, went first to Iraq, then to Paris from where he edited a journal, *Fikr*, which featured important discussions on matters of Egyptian history and historiographical methods.[80] Most leftist or Nasserist critics, however, remained in Egypt where they were periodically harassed or constrained by the authorities. In 1977, following the bread riots, Salah 'Isa, a prominent journalist, was dismissed from *al-Jumhuriyya* as part of another crackdown.[81] Even Haykal fell from favour.

Despite these occasional fits of pique, Sadat's orchestrated attempt to introduce pluralism by establishing political platforms (*manabir*) in 1975 in effect gave the Left a valuable if limited political space within which to work. Following the recognition of al-Tajammu' as the official party of the Left in 1977, *al-Ahali*, the party newspaper, provided an important avenue of expression. Under the energetic editorship of Salah 'Isa, it served as a forum for political, cultural and historical expression during much of the 1980s.[82] A regular column, *Safha min tarikh misr* ('A Page from Egyptian History') by Rif'at al-Sa'id used episodes from Egyptian history as a means of commenting on the contemporary political situation.[83]

Al-Sa'id stands out as a significant figure of materialist historiography of this period in his focus on the communist movement. An active militant himself since the late 1940s, al-Sa'id spent many years in prison during the Nasser years. Following his release, he obtained a doctorate in science from Karl Marx University in Leipzig. During the 1970s, as a result of Sadat's hostility towards leftist journalists which disallowed many from working, al-Sa'id devoted considerable time to writing an account of twentieth century Egyptian history through a series of political biographies on figures such as Sa'd Zaghlul, Hasan al-Banna, Mustafa al-Nahhas and Ahmad Husayn.[84] More significantly, he dedicated himself to the task of mapping out the complex history of the Left in Egypt. In a multi-volume series, he recorded the establishment and development of the communist movement from the turn of the century until the 1980s, relying heavily on the leftist press and scarce source material, as well as his own personal experience and contacts.[85]

Today al-Sa'id is the most published of Egyptian Marxist historians and certainly the most prolific chronicler of the communist movement in Egypt.[86] Yet his work is not simply a scholarly attempt to recover the ideological and institutional memory of a vibrant if fragmented political movement but a project consistent with his position as secretary-general of al-Tajammu', which claims its political legacy. Accordingly, his discourse stresses the centrality of the party organization as the focus of the class struggle and as a former member of HADITU, by 1947 the largest communist faction, al-Sa'id's perspective has positioned this group as, in effect, the communist mainstream.[87] Other smaller communist groups, such as the Workers' Vanguard (a development from al-Fajr al-Jadid), whose strategy focused on raising the consciousness of the workers, though not ignored in the historical record, have not had as prominent a voice in this historiographical school. This state of affairs has been recently challenged by the publication of work by Abu Sayf Yusuf, a leading member of Workers' Vanguard.[88]

Another strand within the materialist tradition has sought to promote the organized trade union movement as the authentic voice of the proletariat. This trend, with its roots in the labour struggles of the mid-1940s, includes a number of veteran trade union leaders among its ranks. The more open political climate of the 1970s saw the proponents of this tradition putting their views of history into print. In their memoirs labour leaders such as Taha Sa'd 'Uthman and Mahmud al-'Askari gave accounts of the struggles of the 1940s which offered a different perspective on events to the interpretations focused on the communist movement.[89] *Sawt al-'amil* ('Voice of the Worker'), a journal edited by 'Uthman and others, also presented a more workerist viewpoint than that sponsored by al-Tajammu' as it sought to 'assert the continuous historic existence of a working-class political subject independent of any other social force, including the Nasserist state'.[90]

Two organizations that grew out of this particular political tendency have assisted and substantially supplemented these efforts. The Centre for Trade Union and Workers Services (*Dar al-khidamat al-niqabiyya wa'l-'ummaliyya*) was established in 1990 dedicated to the defence of workers' interests. One of the strategic objectives of the Centre is to 'revive and preserve the history of the working class struggle and disseminate it among various social classes...'.[91] An important element in this task is the promotion of the historical voice of the labour movement and the collection of sources relevant to its study. Consistent with this aim, it has republished Mahmud al-'Askari's memoirs, issued a study by Taha 'Uthman on the trial and execution of two trade union leaders following the strike at Kafr al-Dawwar in 1952, and brought out an Arabic translation of the pioneering study on the condition of workers in Egypt by Jean Vallet.[92] The Arab Research Centre (*Markaz al-buhuth al-'arabiyya*) has also an active publication programme dealing with the working class and the theoretical perspective of the subaltern.[93] From 1998, in cooperation with the Committee for the Documentation of the History of the Egyptian Communist Movement until 1965, the Centre began publishing a series of personal memoirs from the history of the communist movement in Egypt.[94] By mid-2001 the fifth volume had appeared.

The growing freedom of political expression during the 1980s and 1990s has invigorated contemporary materialist historiography. Publishing houses such as Dar al-thaqafa al-jadida continue to disseminate the work of many writers on the Left. In the mid-1980s it launched an occasional periodical, *Qadaya fikriyya*, under the editorship of Mahmud Amin al-'Alim, which has served as an important forum for materialist historiography and analysis, dedicating individual issues to capitalism in Egypt, the Egyptian working class and political Islam.[95] One issue marked the 70th anniversary of the communist movement and brought together contributions from a wide range of materialist perspectives, both by non-academics such as Rif'at al-Sa'id, Taha Sa'd 'Uthman, Nabil al-Hilali, Sayyid Abu Zayid, and professors of history, 'Asim al-Disuqi and 'Ali Barakat.[96]

In pioneering an examination of the social and economic dimensions of modern Egyptian history within a framework of class analysis, materialist Egyptian historiography has played a very significant role in the intellectual and political development of Egypt. The extent of its influence in scholarship has mirrored the political fortunes of the left. Initially articulated by small but energetic groups from the mid-1940s, historical materialism became more acceptable from the late 1950s and its cooptation, even compromise, within a nationalist framework mirrored the position of communists themselves within the regime in the mid-1960s. Fortunes fluctuated under Sadat but by the mid-1970s, materialist ideas, particularly historical analyses of economic and social issues, were more generally acceptable to the academic mainstream. Even so, it would be difficult to say that there is any explicitly Marxist historian in an Egyptian university today and the real centre of materialist historiography continues to be located in journalistic and other intellectual circles outside the universities.

CONTEMPORARY ISLAMIC HISTORY: RELIGIOUS-CULTURAL RADICALISM

Although it has its roots in the interwar period, the Islamic current represents the most recent and challenging school of non-academic historiography. The status of Islam as the majority faith and the resultant cultural resonance has meant that it has always been an important element in modern Egyptian life. However, its articulation within the context of modern historical discourse has been a function of the more recent rise of political Islam. A broad current of interpretation, the Islamic trend sites Islam as its central motif and reference point. In contrast to the primacy given by the liberal and materialist schools to secularism and modernization as key driving forces to national independence, the Islamic current holds Islam to be an integral element of the national character and the basis of cultural authenticity as well as an explanation for the dynamics operating within society.[97]

Those who have contributed to this Islamic rewriting of modern Egyptian history might be categorized into three broad groups. The first are the cultural historians of the 1930s and 1940s, who emerged as a reaction to the pharaonism espoused in the 1920s and sought to promote a reassessment of Egyptian history that gave greater force to the significance of early Islam as a religious-cultural basis for Egyptian national identity. This reorientation, conducted largely by repentant modernist intellectuals, coincided with the emergence of the second group, the Muslim Brotherhood (Ikhwan), as an organization and incipient political force. It was principally from these ranks that Islamic historiography would be brought into contemporary scholarship. From the mid-1940s its writers began to explicate, in concert with the Brotherhood's own political platform, a reinterpretation of Egyptian modern history and, in time, a defence of the Ikhwan's historical role in Egyptian politics. Finally, the third group is a more recent phenomenon made up of intellectuals, some former secularists, who have sought to incorporate Islam into their interpretation. In short, the first group provided the basis for a reorientation of national identity; the second created a political entity that embodied and empowered this realignment; and the third proposed a refined and more sophisticated Islamic perspective.

BRINGING ISLAM BACK

The emergence of Islamic modernism is generally linked with two late nineteenth-century thinkers, Jamal al-Din al-Afghani and Muhammad 'Abduh, who sought to reform Islam in order to make it more able to respond to the challenges of the modern world. While not primarily historians themselves, their political philosophies provided the inspiration for later historical studies.[98] In Egypt, 'Abduh (1849–1905) was to influence a whole generation of intellectuals in undertaking a reassessment of Islam in the light of a wide range of political, social, theological and historical issues. His legacy has been a heterogeneous one, with many, ranging from those who advocated a liberal interpretation to others who offered a more traditionalist view of Islam, claiming him as a spiritual antecedent. These different strands of Islamic discourse were to increasingly invigorate the political debate of the interwar period.

The aftermath of the 1919 revolution and the primary role played by the Wafd in the nationalist struggle during the 1920s witnessed the ascendancy of its vision of a modern, secular and independent state. The limited but nevertheless significant step of self-government granted under the terms of the constitution of 1923 instituted an idiom of progress and modernization advocated by the broad nationalist front as the dominant discourse of the period. Culturally the period was characterized by a revived pharaonism, a view that promoted a national identity on the basis of ancient Egyptian traditions. Many leading Egyptian intellectuals of the time wrote of the singularity of Egyptian culture, stressing its pharaonic origins and downplaying its Muslim and Arabic aspects.[99]

Yet like the Wafd itself, the movement achieved only limited success. By the 1930s there was a shift away from pharaonism to a greater concern with the Islamic element of Egyptian identity. Its advocates were often the very writers that had been champions of the pharaonic line in the 1920s.[100] Muhammad Husayn Haykal, one of the leaders of the Liberal Constitutionalist Party and chief editor of its weekly *al-Siyasa*, had been a prominent voice of an Egyptian territorialism based on pharaonic culture. By the late 1930s he was having second thoughts. He wrote later, 'I realized that it is in our Islamic history alone that the seed which can bud, grow and bear fruit is embedded.'[101] 'Abbas Mahmud al-'Aqqad travelled over similar ground. An ideologue of the Wafd and prominent journalist for its newspaper, *al-Balagh*, he left the party in 1938 to join the Sa'dist group and write for its organ, *al-Asas*.[102] In 1936 his laudatory account of Sa'd Zaghlul, subtitled 'biography and tribute' appeared; by the early 1940s he was writing biographies of Muhammad and early Islamic leaders.[103] These second thoughts were symptomatic of a greater movement, a so-called 'crisis of orientation',[104] that included many other writers, such as Tawfiq al-Hakim and Ibrahim Jum'a, who shared a profound disappointment with the promise of Western civilization. In response they turned to an Islamic and Arabic discourse as a source of national renewal and presented these elements of Egyptian culture as a counterweight and alternative voice to pharaonism and Western-inspired secular nationalism.[105] The message was clear: 'Only with the advent of Islam did Egypt attain full national maturity as an independent entity.'[106]

THE MUSLIM BROTHERHOOD

The reinvigoration of Islam as an integral element of the Egyptian nation upheld by prominent intellectuals was echoed by developments in the political arena. The Society of the Muslim Brotherhood (Ikhwan), founded by Hasan al-Banna in 1928, began to articulate Islam as a contemporary political idiom during the 1930s.[107] By the early 1940s it had become a significant if still minor player in Egyptian national politics while its writers and intellectuals contributed to the process of revitalizing and incorporating an Islamic discourse into a contemporary context. Consonant with its aim of a profound spiritual renewal, the Ikhwan regarded itself not simply as a political party (*hizb*) but as a society (*jama'a*) presiding over an extensive range of activities that sought to promote an Islamic programme in all aspects of public life. From the beginning it recognized the importance of history in projecting this agenda. In regular weekly meetings at headquarters in Cairo and in regional centres throughout the country, the Society held lectures and discussions on various historical, political and economic matters aimed at articulating an Islamic reinterpretation of Egyptian history.[108] It also diffused its views to a wider audience through a series of newspapers and journals. The first significant publication was *Majallat al-ikhwan al-muslimin*, which appeared in May 1933, subsequently succeeded by *al-Manar*, a title taken over after the death of Rashid Rida. This was to serve as a voice of the Ikhwan until the government revoked its licence in 1941. Others followed in due course: a daily newspaper, *al-Ikhwan al-muslimin* (1946–8), a weekly news magazine, *al-Mabahith* (1950–1) and *al-Da'wa*, which was issued between 1951 and 1956.[109]

The propagation of Ikhwanist material was not confined to periodicals.[110] From the middle of the 1940s, as the Society's support grew, a flurry of books by prominent members appeared. Salih 'Ashmawi, a prolific contributor to the pages of *al-Ikhwan al-muslimin*, authored a book on communism in Egypt, which accused the Jews of using leftist ideology and freemasonry against Islam and as a means to establish a Jewish state. Another of Ashmawi's works charged the Wafd with hostility towards Islam.[111] Shaykh Muhammad al-Ghazzali (1917–96), 'one of the most prolific authors of the Islamic renaissance' produced a long series of works on economic and political questions.[112] Other writers included 'Abd al-Qadir 'Awda, later implicated in the assassination attempt on Nasser and hanged, and the prolific Anwar al-Jundi.[113] In February 1949, the assassination of the Supreme Guide, Hasan al-Banna, precipitated a string of biographies of the leader.[114] Over time, these studies established a substantial body of literature that articulated the ideological perspective of the organization and put forward an alternative view of the historical development of Egypt and, indeed, the Muslim world.

These Ikhwanist writers straddled a world that spoke of traditional values and yet profited from the opportunities of the emerging modern state and society. Though most would have received some traditional education, their orientation to militant political activism represented a break from the established culture of al-Azhar. They favoured attending modernizing institutions like Dar al-'Ulum and took employment in state service. Hasan al-Banna himself had graduated from the Dar al-'Ulum in 1927 and worked as a schoolteacher for almost 20 years. Sayyid Qutb, after attending the *kuttab* in his village and later the Dar al-'Ulum, subsequently worked as a journalist before joining the Ministry of Education, where he took the position of education inspector in Qina. 'Umar al-Tilmisani (1904–86) also received a *kuttab* education and attended an Islamic Benevolent Society Elementary School before studying law and joining the Financial Ministry in 1933.[115] Al-Ghazzali had attended al-Azhar and graduated with a diploma from the Faculty of Religion in 1941, then had taken up employment in the Ministry of Waqfs, first as a preacher, then as a mosque inspector, and ultimately as undersecretary of the Ministry.[116] This hybrid background, founded on traditional discourse and empowered by new forms of organization, was characteristic of the Islamic current.

The Ikhwan took pains to present a consistent and disciplined public message. This was especially so after 1951 when its press and translation committee, which supervised periodicals, was headed by Sayyid Qutb. The committee attempted to exercise similar control over the increasing number of books written by individual members, since work written by Brothers did not always take the same view.[117] There were different historical assessments, for example, of the role of Muhammad 'Ali. While in the pages of *al-Ikhwan al-muslimin* he was described as a 'great man who had rejuvenated a great people', al-Ghazzali saw him as an instrument of Western penetration acting to the detriment of Islam.[118] There was more agreement on King Faruq, at least after his departure from the country. As Mitchell notes, 'The 1952 Revolution freed the movement's writers from earlier restraints and launched the great campaign to discredit Faruq as the source of all corruption in the country.'[119]

As with the materialist writings of the communist movement, the output of published Ikhwanist writings mirrored the political fortunes of the organization. Periods of repression were interleaved with periods of relative tolerance. The flow of publications from the mid-1940s was stanched during the disturbances of 1948 and 1949 but resumed thereafter. Following the coming to power of the military in July 1952, the Ikhwan was untouched by the regime's decision to ban all political parties in January of the next year, not least because it had some important connections within the RCC. Thereafter as the regime asserted itself, the relationship between the government and the Ikhwan became increasingly uneasy, exacerbated by leadership difficulties within the Society itself. In October 1954, following an assassination attempt on Nasser in Alexandria, the organization was ruthlessly suppressed. Several members were tried and executed and many militants imprisoned.[120]

The repression proved an effective way of silencing the Brotherhood as an organization but individual members who remained at liberty continued to espouse an Islamic cause. Towards the end of the 1950s, evidence of renewed activity appeared with the issuing of a whole range of works in the field of philosophy, history, politics and theology by publishing houses such as Dar al-'uruba.[121] Qutb reinvigorated the movement with his writings. Greatly influenced by 'Abbas al-'Aqqad before he joined the Ikhwan in 1951, over the next decade and a half, and often while in prison, he wrote widely on ideological and political questions. Although not a historian himself, Qutb considered history as an important field of study and recognized the need for a historical revision of the period from the birth of Islam until the present day. A committee was formed for such a purpose although apparently nothing came of this.[122] Following another assassination attempt against him in 1965, Nasser again moved against the Ikhwan setting in train another wave of arrests and further repression. Qutb was executed the following year.

A REVIVED FORCE

During the 1970s, as the political fortunes of the Left waned under Sadat's presidency, they waxed for the Islamic movement. Pandering to the growing religious idiom in politics, the new president allowed the Ikhwan to operate in a semi-official capacity and act as a counterweight against the Left.[123] This latitude gave the Society the opportunity to rejoin the political and historical debate.[124] In 1976 al-Da'wa, which had been silent for two decades, resumed publication now under the editorship of the Supreme Guide, 'Umar al-Tilmisani.[125] Over the next 6 years it served as the official organ for the Society, featuring a wide range of discussions on political, religious and cultural issues, and reaching a reported monthly circulation of 80,000.[126]

In the pages of al-Da'wa and elsewhere the Ikhwan addressed issues of Islamic and Egyptian history on two main levels. First, it attacked the way Islam was taught in history classes in government schools, deploring, for example, how the birth of Islam and the role of the Prophet were analyzed like ordinary political events and not accorded their proper status. The state curriculum was also attacked for ascribing a 'racist and nationalist spirit' to Islam.[127] 'Umar al-Tilmisani, now the leader of the Society, was virulent in his criticism of Nasser's policies,

> He [Nasser] falsified Egyptian history in a way no one would believe. He erased the history of Islam in Egypt and removed the history of Egypt in recent centuries. This falsification which 'Abd al-Nasir inflicted on Egyptian history is in urgent need of thousands of studies and works of research in order to correct the falsification which he caused.[128]

Second, al-Da'wa provided a forum not just for the rewriting of national history on a grand scale but for the justification of the historical role of the Ikhwan itself. A special column, 'The Muslim Brethren in the Pages of the Past', took this as its central task.[129] Muhammad 'Abd al-Quddus, described as 'one of the most astute political analysts writing for the Islamic press' presented a version of the Nasser years from the Ikhwan's perspective.[130] Queried as to the attention devoted to the history of the movement in its own press, al-Tilmisani replied that 'Brothers had the right to respond to the lies that were told about them in recent years.'[131] Sadat thought otherwise. As part of the widespread repression of all political opposition, al-Da'wa was again banned in 1981. Other avenues served as the public voice of the Ikhwan. An expanding number of publishing houses specialized in work associated with or sympathetic to its programme. The inevitable memoirs began to appear: those of al-Tilmisani himself, Zaynab al-Ghazzali, the leader of the Society of Muslim Women, 'Abd al-Halim Khafaji and others.[132] Jabir Rizq established a reputation as the historian of the Ikhwan during the repression of the Nasser years.[133]

With the increasing political influence of the Islamic current, advocates from beyond Ikhwanist circles adopted an Islamic discourse in their commentaries and analyses. This was not simply due to the political tactics

of Sadat which tolerated, even encouraged, the Islamic movement as a counterweight to the left but was a reaction to Egypt's comprehensive defeat by
the Israelis in 1967. To many this stunning reverse seemed to demonstrate the
bankruptcy of the revolutionary nationalist regime and the failure of Arab
socialism. Another crisis of orientation, not unlike the movement of liberal
intellectuals towards Islam during the 1930s, followed but this time the
move was from the left wing of politics. The need for an alternative, and
one that was more convincingly part of the culture of the region, gave the
Islamic current a new lease of life. One prominent voice in this movement
was *al-Sha'b*, a newspaper first established by Nasser in 1956 but which
by the 1980s had been commandeered as the organ of the Socialist Labour
Party (*Hizb al-'amal al-ishtiraki*). The party's platform combines elements
of nationalist, Islamic and socialist thought consistent with its claims to the
political legacy of Misr al-Fatat – an impression reinforced by the fact that
editors of *al-Sha'b's* have included 'Adil and Majdi Husayn, half-brother
and son respectively of Ahmad Husayn. This Islamic tone was further
reinforced when the Ikhwan turned to the Labour Party as a more natural
political partner, following the failure of its electoral alliance with the Wafd
in 1984. From that time *al-Sha'b* served as the principal legal mouthpiece
for political Islam and a significant forum for historical commentary until
its closure by the government in May 2000.[134] In 1993, it published a richly
illustrated special issue marking the 60th anniversary of Misr al-Fatat's
foundation with extracts from the writings of party members, such as Ahmad
Husayn, Nur al-Din Taraf and Ibrahim Shukri, as well as from the panoply
of heroes from the broad Islamic current, including 'Umar Tilmisani, Sayyid
Qutb and 'Abbas al-'Aqqad.[135]

By the beginning of the 1980s contemporary Islamic historiography had
permeated beyond the boundaries of party press and ideological tracts. In
this context the work of Tariq al-Bishri (b. 1931) stands out as the leading
exemplar of the new Islamic discourse in contemporary Egyptian historiography. Like al-Rafi'i and the early historians of the liberal school, al-Bishri
came from a legal background. After graduation, he took a teaching position
in the Faculty of Law, before becoming a judge (*mustashar*) and later deputy
head of the Majlis al-Dawla. Although he has no professional training in
history, he believes the techniques and demands of legal work which have
contributed so substantially to his research skills, may be more exacting
than a formal historical education.[136]

As early as the mid-1960s, al-Bishri had begun to publish historical articles
in *al-Tali'a* on issues of twentieth century Egyptian history. His views were
nationalist and of a leftist orientation, rather than specifically Marxist, but
he was influenced by Marxism in his understanding of economic processes
and the classification of the national struggle.[137] His history of the critical
period following the Second World War, *al-Haraka al-siyasiyya fi misr,
1945–52*, based upon material already published in *al-Tali'a*, appeared in

1972.[138] Described as 'one of the best examples of left wing historiography', it effectively made his reputation as a significant historian.[139] In the course of the 1970s al-Bishri, like some others, began to rethink his position. Dating the impetus for this to the defeat of Egypt in 1967 he began to move towards the view that Egypt should adopt a new framework of 'civilizational independence' (*istiqlal hadari*) that drew on Islam and popular culture and not on Western notions of progress.[140] It was some time before he incorporated these views into his historical analysis. These were first set out in the lengthy introduction to the second edition of *al-Haraka al-siyasiyya* in 1981, where he proposed his fundamental division between authentic Egyptian tradition and alien, largely Western, influences in his historical interpretation. His book on the history of Muslim and Copt relations, *al-Muslimun wa'l-aqbat fi atar al-jama'a al-wataniyya*, published in 1982, represented another major contribution to contemporary historiography.[141] Since this time al-Bishri has been a celebrated voice in the Islamic current and a regular participant in the public debate on contemporary historical issues, contributing regular articles in newspapers like *al-Sha'b* and short studies on issues dealing with legal questions and matters of national unity.[142]

One of the central aims of al-Bishri's analysis is to restore Islam to its status as a fundamental element of the Egyptian national identity. Rejecting modernist views that had dismissed Islam as a traditional and conservative force, al-Bishri has sought to reassess its role in Egypt's historical development. In an interview he commented,

> The Islamic approach to history...does not mean a new criterion for judging the objectivity of facts at hand. When we carry out historical research, and set up criteria to evaluate events, we should simply keep in mind the weight and influence of Islam, as a concept and as a culture, in shaping historical events.[143]

One means of achieving this was to elevate the role of those political forces that embodied Islamic values. This stands out as the most obvious innovation of al-Bishri's reappraisal of the pre-1952 period. Hitherto, liberal and left wing historiography had regarded the Ikhwan as ideologically obscurantist and politically subservient to the minor parties, and Misr al-Fatat as fascist in character. In al-Bishri's re-evaluation the two parties were now resituated as authentic elements within the nationalist mainstream movement. Yet, far from being a simple apologist for the Ikhwan and Misr al-Fatat, al-Bishri's work has received wide praise from many parts of the political spectrum, including the Coptic Church.

Although one of its most prominent exponents, al-Bishri is by no means alone in his espousal of the centrality of Islam in historical interpretation. Other writers, and not only Muslims, incorporated Islamic values into their analyses.[144] Abdel-Malek, a Copt and former communist, has more recently extended his view of Islam beyond its status as a religion to that of a cultural entity and the product of a historical experience which can be used for cultural and political liberation.[145] 'Adil Husayn, another erstwhile Marxist, took a similar position, 'Islam is not only the religion of the majority... it is the common history of the nation.'[146]

From its first appearance as narrow partisan scholarship in the 1940s to a more sophisticated perspective in the hands of practitioners like Tariq al-Bishri, the Islamic current of contemporary historiography now poses as a considerable rival to other schools of historical discourse. Like these other historical schools, its influence has corresponded to a certain extent with the fortunes of its political counterpart, principally in this case, the Ikhwan, but also embodied by other more radical Islamic groups, such as the Jama'at Islamiyya. More than this, however, its use of a familiar religious idiom and invocation of cultural authenticity has guaranteed it a wide appeal among the Egyptian public.

FEMALE VOICES

The emergence of a female voice in historical scholarship brings together some of the themes found in the earlier discussion: royal patronage, the pioneering and continuing role of the press, the prominence of Syrians, diverse political trends and the centrality of the national movement. However, the special nature of the position of women in Egyptian society involves other factors that not only explain the different (and later) trajectory of scholarship by women but also its role as both supplementary and antagonistic to the male mainstream.

In the last quarter of the nineteenth century, women began to make a small but significant impact as journalists and writers of literature. Initially, they were almost wholly from an upper class background and predominantly from Syrian families. Perhaps the first work of a historical nature was a biographical dictionary of women by Maryam al-Nahhas, published in 1879 and dedicated to (and sponsored by) Princess Cheshmat Hanim, the third wife of Khedive Isma'il.[147] Al-Nahhas died before she could complete the next volume but the biographical theme was continued by Zaynab Fawwaz (c. 1860–1914) whose dictionary, *al-Dur al-manthur fi tabaqat rabat al-khudur*, which dealt with both Eastern and Western women, appeared in 1894. The biography was a traditional form but Fawwaz had a revolutionary intent declaring, 'History, which is the best of all sciences, is largely dominated by men. Not a single one of those male historians has dedicated a single chapter in which to discuss women who represent half of humankind.'[148] This literary-historical genre, on a grander scale, was taken up by other women writers, notably by May Ziyada (1886–1941), who wrote biographies in the 1920s on two of the early women of Egyptian letters,

'A'isha al-Taymuriyya and Bahithat al-Badiya (Malak Hifni Nasif).[149] Like al-Nahhas and Fawwaz, Ziyada was born outside of Egypt (in her case, Nazareth) and exemplified the prominent place those from a greater Syrian background occupied in Egyptian cultural life at this time.

The increasing literary visibility of women was part of the broader social transformation occurring across the ranks of educated society at this time. It was the burgeoning field of journalism, and particularly in magazines and journals owned by women and directed towards a female audience, that offered the greatest opportunities to gifted women writers in the period before First World War. The first of these was *al-Fatah* edited by Hind Nafwal (*c.* 1860–1920), daughter of Maryam al-Nahhas, which appeared in November 1892. Dedicated to a wide variety of literary and social matters, *al-Fatah* was also keenly aware of the importance of addressing the historical aspect of women's role in society. In its first issue, it announced its intention to discuss '...the condition of woman and her natural place in ancient times, the middle ages and this period, a period of civilization and culture'.[150] Almost another 20 women's magazines would appear before 1914, in which again Syrian Christian women were most prominent among the founders and editors but which also included Egyptian Copt, Muslim, Jewish and Greek women.[151] Even if the general lack of access of women to education and their low level of literacy limited the readership and influence of these journals, they nevertheless served an important role in bringing different issues to the public eye. Further, they offered a means of legitimation to women writers as contributors to Egyptian intellectual life and opened avenues for them in the mainstream Arabic and foreign language press.[152]

The demand for a female public voice gathered momentum after the First World War with the reinvigoration of the nationalist movement. Women had played a significant part in the nationalist demonstrations of 1919–21 and the formation of women's organizations was evidence of their determination to maintain a role in public life. The establishment of the Egyptian Feminist Union in 1923 under the leadership of Huda Sha'rawi and the subsequent launch of its monthly journal in the French language, *L'Égyptienne* in 1925, under the editorship of Saiza Nabarawi, provided a forum for the discussion of a large range of political, social and historical pieces of particular interest to women.[153] (Its Arabic language sister publication, *al-Misriyya*, would not appear until 1937.) In 1925 Munira Thabit founded *L'Espoir* which propounded a more openly political Wafdist line.[154] By 1936, the year of the establishment of the Association of Women Journalists under the presidency of Fatima Nim'at Rashid, the status of the woman journalist and commentator had received formal recognition.

The lack of opportunities for education of women continued to hamper an effective base for the propagation of a feminist voice and the emergence of a historiography that dealt with the role of women. The brief period when the private Egyptian University had held classes for women may have facilitated the making of connections – this is where May Ziyada met Huda Sha'rawi, Nabawiyya Musa and Malak Hifni Nasif – but the spaces in which women could develop their own views and scholarship were limited to magazines, organizations and cultural salons. The writings of Bahithat al-Badiya and the biographies of Ziyada had pointed the way to an appreci-ation of the role of women in Egyptian history but it was not until 1940 that a historical study of Egyptian women appeared. Significantly, it came from an Egyptian studying abroad. In the late 1920s Duriya Shafiq had gone to study at the Sorbonne with the financial support of Huda Sha'rawi. In 1940 she graduated with a doctoral thesis at the Sorbonne, subsequently pub-lished in French and dedicated to her mentor, that dealt with the position of the Muslim woman in contemporary Egypt in its religious, legal and historical aspects.[155] Refused a position at Cairo University on her return to Egypt, she took up employment with the Ministry of Education. In the following years, Shafiq became increasingly active, editing a number of journals and conducting an increasingly aggressive political programme. In 1945 Shafiq collaborated with Ibrahim 'Abduh of Cairo University to write a more focused history of Egyptian women, this time in Arabic.[156] The book provided an overview of the 'feminist awakening' (al-nahda al-nisa'iyya) from the time of Muhammad 'Ali onwards that paralleled the broader national awaken-ing. Ten years later Shafiq and 'Abduh collaborated again, this time addressing the position of Egyptian women from the pharaonic period until the present day.[157] It was almost 30 years later before the first works dealing with women in modern Egyptian history appeared from within the academic mainstream.

The lack of enthusiasm for women's history in Egyptian universities, abetted by the paucity of women historians on staff, encouraged its histor-ical elucidation to be taken up elsewhere. This happened in two arenas. The first has been by scholars, first Egyptian, then others, based abroad. Inspired by personal experience or feminist thought and activism or both, they lay an important foundation for a historical understanding of the development of the Egyptian feminist movement. Afaf Marsot's work on the 'revolutionary gentlewomen' who established philanthropic bodies such as Mubarra and used their social entrée and influence to gain favours from the male ruling class relied on her own knowledge of these organizations.[158] Though not strictly speaking historical, the writings of Nawal Sa'dawi were important in laying the basis for a genuine feminist discourse. During the late 1980s and 1990s there was an explosion of interest among other scholars working in the West. Margot Badran, Miriam Cooke, Beth Baron, Nikki Keddie and Cynthia Nelson (AUC) all addressed various aspects of the lives and activities of Egyptian women to articulate what has been a latent and ignored voice in Egyptian history.[159]

In Egypt, the main source of new feminist historiography has been as much from non-academics working in the press as from non-historian academics associated with non-governmental organizations specifically dedicated to women's concerns.[160] The one most engaged in the articulation of women's historical experience has been the Women and Memory Forum, established in 1996 by a number of Egyptian women, mostly of an academic background but not drawn from the Egyptian historical establishment. Headed by Huda al-Shadda, professor of English literature at Cairo University, the Forum aims to remedy the marginalization of women in history and offer a rereading of Egyptian and Arab culture and history.[161] Using a multidisciplinary approach, the group has conducted workshops dedicated to the articulation of new theoretical frameworks and methodologies. It has also sponsored the publication of a series of works dedicated to the pioneers of the Egyptian women's movement. The first of these was *al-Nisa'iyyat* a republication of some of the writings of Malak Hifni Nasif to commemorate the 80th anniversary of her death.[162] In the same year, a collection of essays was published by members of the Forum which examined the question of women's history in the Muslim and Arab world in different historical periods, critiquing the hegemonic male perspective and the male nature of the source material.[163]

NON-ACADEMIC HISTORY AND
THE UNIVERSITY

Despite the different dynamics operating within non-academic and academic historiography the common enterprise shared by the two genres of representing various aspects of the national history has guaranteed an exchange in ideas, methods and materials. This has been reciprocal. Yet, the claims of academic historians to superior technique and historical judgement notwithstanding, it has been non-academic historians who have pioneered influential currents of thought in contemporary Egyptian historiography. The interaction between the university and those outside has not simply been the result of a free market of ideas but has been conditioned by the political climate, particularly the attitude of the state, the academic culture and, to a limited extent, personal initiative. The academy has been careful to stay within the constraints of acceptable national discourse, mindful of the institutional relationship it has with the state and the political challenge that an alternative historiography may entail. When these constraints have been relaxed new ideas from the outside have been more readily taken up by the academy.

The liberal school, which had its germination at the beginning of the twentieth century, found full flower in the works of 'Abd al-Rahman al-Rafi'i during the 1930s and 1940s. Assisted by the post-First World War political environment and the needs of the national movement, the liberal school became dominant outside of the university, particularly in the press, and

107

from the late 1940s it had begun to exercise considerable influence inside the academy, establishing itself as the academic orthodoxy after 1952. Even if the ideological bent of the July Revolution limited its impact on the interpretation of the contemporary period, the work of historians such as 'Abd al-'Azim Ramadan in the second half of the 1960s, and the later studies of Muhammad Anis, which revived the role of the Wafd in the national movement, saw it set on a more secure footing.

Despite the growing influence of the communist movement and socialist ideas during and in the years after the Second World War, the materialist school of interpretation took a longer time to make inroads into the academy. In 1948, Rashid al-Barawi, an economics professor at Cairo University, was criticizing the way history was being taught in Egyptian universities,

> I found out from my historical studies, over the years when the teaching of the discipline became available, a clear pattern in most cases, and I mean by this that most of the writers when they analysed historical development did not recognize the materialist or economic factor as the driving force in the progress of society, and the foundation on which all diverse developments depend.[164]

The reluctance on the part of the Egyptian academy to embrace these ideas is in some ways puzzling. Immediately after the Second World War, if not before, academic historians were well aware of the insights offered by historical materialism. As early as 1945, Fu'ad Shukri was teaching socialist thought in classes on European history at Cairo University, and applied this framework in his later work on the French Revolution. Significantly, however, he refrained from employing it to an Egyptian context.[165] Students, such as Muhammad Anis and 'Abd al-Razzaq Hasan, who were sent for postgraduate studies to England by the Egyptian government in this period, were directly exposed to socialist ideas and the reality of a Labour Government in London. Yet, 10 years later there was little evidence that this had influenced the way Egyptian history was taught in universities. Privately Muhammad Anis recognized the importance of the materialist works of al-Shafi'i and 'Amr soon after their publication in the late 1950s,[166] but it was not until the early 1960s that he seized the opportune moment to publicly espouse their ideas with any conviction in his own analysis of Egyptian history. In 1962, before the ink of the National Charter was dry, Anis began invoking its principles to call for a rewriting of Egyptian history and the need for a 'socialist school' of interpretation to succeed the 'national school' [i.e. liberal school]. Although the government's plan to produce an official history based on socialist theory failed to take root, partly, it would seem, because of resistance from the academics themselves, Anis with al-Sayyid Rajab Haraz set out a new framework for modern Egyptian history along Marxist lines which relied substantially on the works of 'Amr, al-Shafi'i and Jirjis.[167]

Despite Anis' efforts, Marxist historiography never successfully stormed the academic citadel. However, under state patronage, historical materialism and class analysis of Egyptian society became increasingly influential in social, economic and even political histories during the mid-1960s. Elements were taken up by students of Anis, such as 'Abd al-'Azim Ramadan and 'Ali Barakat, and the generation of scholars that graduated from 'Ain Shams University in the early 1970s. While not doctrinaire Marxists themselves, they freely acknowledged the influence of Marxism on their work.[168] The materialist school enjoyed almost official endorsement during the height of Anis' influence – symbolized by the establishment of the Higher Institute for Socialist Studies – but it continued to find its strongest advocates more in the ranks of the press than in the history departments of universities. Ultimately its tenets were to be modified by the academy to the more moderate approach of the 'social school' (al-madrasa al-ijtima'iyya).[169]

No credible historian in Egypt has been able to totally ignore the importance of Islam in Egyptian national life. Mustafa Kamil's historical writings at the turn of the century had emphasized the religious component in the Egyptian identity, even if this had been associated with the idea of Ottoman imperial authority. The prominence of Islam as a political discourse receded during the period after the First World War, but there was never any doubt about its religious and cultural significance. Even the doyen of Western-educated academic historians, Shafiq Ghurbal, showed evidence of its increasing influence in his Arabic language account of Muhammad 'Ali in the 1940s.[170] Nevertheless, the implicit political threat within Islamic historiography meant there were certain limits and, particularly under Nasser, the repression of the Ikhwan brought with it a corresponding constraint on Islamic discourse.

The case of Ahmad Shalabi illustrates some of the political pressures at work. Born in Zagazig, Shalabi attended a kuttab and was educated at a provincial institute of al-Azhar, before entering the Dar al-'Ulum, where he took a degree in 1943. After the Second World War he went to England for further study and graduated with a PhD from Cambridge University in 1950. On his return to Egypt he took a position at the Dar al-'Ulum '… fervently committed to Islam, playing down national identities and stressing the undivided Islamic umma'.[171] A victim of the purge of September 1954, he was reduced to teaching in a private school in Zamalik but in the following year was permitted to leave the country to teach at the Islamic University in Indonesia where he stayed until 1963. He returned to the Dar al-'Ulum but later took time out to set up the Department of History and Islamic Civilization in the Islamic University of Omdurman in the Sudan in 1966.[172]

Despite the early difficulties of Shalabi and others, an Islamic tendency could not be excluded entirely from the academy and it made its first substantial inroads through its natural gateway, al-Azhar, with the appointment of 'Abd al-'Aziz al-Shinawi as professor of modern history there in 1964.[173]

A student of both Shafiq Ghurbal at Cairo and Muhammad Tharwat at Alexandria, al-Shinawi's early academic work had been based on Western traditions of scholarship. However, from the time he moved to al-Azhar he was drawn to Azhari thought and took a strong interest in the place of the university in Egyptian history. In 1969 he presented two papers for the conference commemorating the 1000th year of the city of Cairo which dealt with the role of al-Azhar in the Ottoman period and during the French campaign.[174] He followed this with two books, *al-Dawla al-'uthmaniyya dawla islamiyya muftari 'alaha'* [1971] and *al-Azhar jami'an wa jami'a*, which were informed with the same spirit and maintained this perspective until his death. It was also at al-Azhar in 1973 that Mustafa Ramadan completed his doctoral thesis on the role of al-Azhar and Azharites during the popular resistance to the French and the rise of Muhammad 'Ali.[175]

The studies of al-Shinawi and Mustafa Ramadan were written at a traditional university and dealt with the beginning of the modern period. Nevertheless, they put forward analyses that emphasized a positive and constructive interpretation of the role of Islam and its institutions in the national narrative. With the work of Zakariyya Sulayman Bayumi, Islamic historiography breached both the contemporary period and the walls of the modern university. A graduate of 'Ain Shams University and later professor of history at the University of Mansura, Bayumi has, since the late 1970s, written extensively on the role and influence of 'the Islamic tendency' (*al-ittijah al-islami*). Challenging the prevailing academic picture of the Ikhwan as a reactionary organization, he has presented a radical reassessment of its role in Egyptian political life.[176] Drawing on the Society's own writings, he presented the Ikhwan in a more sympathetic light, defending it against accusations of being a creature of the palace and lukewarm in the struggle against the British. Bayumi's analysis may not have attracted much positive support from within academia but it has provoked considerable response.[177]

During the course of the 1980s and 1990s, Islamic discourse has continued to make inroads into many Egyptian public institutions – government departments, professional associations and political parties. Universities have by no means been exempt from this trend but, apart from provoking a strong response, its influence appears to have made less impression in history departments. Despite the recognition given to the works of Tariq al-Bishri, Islamic historiography of the contemporary period has been regarded by the academic establishment with uneasiness and attacked as ideologically driven.[178] Its claims to a comprehensive framework notwithstanding, one reason for this failure may be because, according to some historians, it offers little in the way of a distinctive historical methodology.[179] As least as significant, however, is that just as the Islamic movement has posed a political threat to the Egyptian state so Islamic historiography has challenged the secular, national historiography that is the broad consensus of the universities and the state. It is therefore not surprising that most historians writing from an Islamic perspective, as indeed the pioneering analyses of the liberal and materialist schools, have emerged from quarters beyond the academy, and enjoyed more influence in the wider Muslim society than in government institutions.

The emergence of a feminist approach to historical study has had very limited impact on universities in Egypt. The start made by Shafiq and 'Abduh in the 1940s and 1950s was not taken up by the academy until the mid-1980s when two junior women professors of history in provincial universities, Latifa Muhammad Salim and Amal Kamil Bayumi al-Subki produced books on the position of women in Egyptian society.[180] While there has been a general acknowledgment of the symbolic importance of the women's movement and its contribution to the national movement, the academy has not embraced an active agenda of research on the historical role of women, much less a radical programme of alternative history. Neither of the two conferences dedicated to modern Egyptian historiography held in 1987 and 1995 featured any paper dealing with women on its programme. For the foreseeable future Egyptian history departments will remain a bastion of male culture and reflect its concerns.

Despite its politically disparate sources of inspiration, non-academic historiography has continued to play a vibrant and vital role in contemporary Egyptian historiography. Drawn from different parts of civil society and inspired by diverse outlooks and ideologies, its wide range of interpretations has served as a source of fresh ideas, perspectives and approaches. As a counter to the rigours of academic orthodoxy, it has invigorated the historical debate by questioning standard assumptions about Egyptian identity and development. In being a radical force of innovation, it has challenged state authority, questioning its claims and legitimacy and often incurring savage repression as a result. Accordingly, it offers a scholarship less compromised by the authority of the state and a forum more expressive of the heterogeneous and complex character of Egyptian society often disguised by a homogeneous nationalist discourse.

4

EGYPT FOR WHICH EGYPTIANS?

> Nationalism is the difference between the reality and your
> opinion as informed by your social or communal status, not
> your individual opinion...Nationalism is a kind of veil, a veil
> that does not enable you to see the reality as it is.
>
> Abdallah Laroui[1]

The unity of Egypt and the country's paramount struggle for national
liberation and independence provide the conceptual bedrock of mainstream
contemporary Egyptian historiography.[2] Even if the characterization of
Egyptian society and the dynamics of the political struggle may vary,
contesting historiographical currents share the common enterprise of
constructing a cogent and coherent narrative of the national history. This
chapter examines the contest by comparing the interpretations of the
liberal, materialist, Islamic and feminist schools, of the period from 1919
until the death of Nasser. Based on contrasting evaluations and configurations of party, political, economic and cultural forces they offer an
illuminating divergence in the definition of national identity and the classification of the constituent elements of Egyptian society that constitutes
the contestation of the nation.

Contemporary Egyptian political history is most readily divided into two
periods. The first, the period from 1919 until 1952, is characterized by
great political volatility in which a shifting pattern of alliances and struggle
between competing interests, a strong, intrusive monarchy and an interfer-
ing British High Commissioner, serve as the centre stage of Egyptian political
life. The dynamism of public life, manifest in the diversity of political parties
and the heterogeneous character of Egyptian society, are fertile ground for
a complex and contested articulation of Egyptian political life. The period
after 1952 takes on a different complexion. In place of the vibrant if volatile
character of the prerevolutionary era, the Nasser regime appropriated, then
monopolized, the field of legitimate political activity. The abolition of the
monarchy and parliament and the banning of political parties, recast the
political landscape and muted oppositional forces as the July Revolution
occupied the public space and sought to reconfigure political institutions
and the economic, social and cultural order. With the nationalization of
political life the regime arrogated to itself what had previously been spheres

and expressions of political plurality within civil society. For the historian this has meant that political trends which provide the most obvious points of reference in an analysis of the parliamentary era give way to a preoccupation with the character of the state, the nature and programme of the regime, and an evaluation of its strengths and weaknesses in forging a new national society in the post-1952 period.

THE LIBERAL SCHOOL: FROM PALACE TO PEOPLE

The liberal school developed as a reaction to the narrow conception of Egypt of the palace-centred narrative upheld by the royalist school. While it retained the elements of the statist discourse of its predecessor, it propagated a broader view of the nation that included the Egyptian people in some sense. Its exemplars were principally concerned with the struggle for national independence and its analysis of the domestic political scene was dominated by the conflicts and coalitions between political parties and individual politicians and, more abstractly, in the struggle between the forces of freedom and those of autocracy. In this analysis the Egyptian population itself was given little individuality or autonomy of political expression; rather, it was the political parties, such as the Watani Party and the Wafd, who secured its support and embodied the national will.

The important transition of historical thought from the royalist to the liberal school is represented by the work of Shafiq Ghurbal. The product of an English postgraduate education imbued with moderate nationalist views, Ghurbal presided over the relocation of scholarship from the palace to the university and a redefinition of the nation, or what has been termed, the Egyptianization (*tamsir*) of modern Egyptian history.[3] Ghurbal's conception of Egypt as a modern nation was strongly influenced by his views on the development of Egyptian civilization. This was most clearly presented in a series of radio lectures broadcast in English in the 1950s in which he adapted the famous aphorism of Herodotus that 'Egypt is the gift of the Nile', and proposed instead that, 'Egypt is the gift of the Egyptians' (*Misr hibat al-misriyyin*).[4] The formulation prompted the question: to which Egyptians or what vision of Egypt was Ghurbal referring?

Although he wrote little on twentieth century Egyptian history until late in his professional life, Ghurbal's first book, *The Beginnings of the Egyptian Question and the Rise of Mehemet Ali*, stands out as his most substantial historical work and provides a clear statement of his conception of the Egyptian nation at this time.[5] A history of the period from the arrival of the French in Egypt in 1798 until 1812, *The Beginnings of the Egyptian Question* casts Muhammad 'Ali as its central character and the driving force behind the stabilization of Egypt as an independent state and the initiator of its subsequent modernization. Ghurbal's account of the founder of the modern Egyptian dynasty reads as a testimony to the political skills of an active and resourceful leader. By its conclusion, Muhammad 'Ali is firmly in control of the country and Ghurbal's conclusion is one of unalloyed admiration, 'Mehemet Ali made modern Egypt.'[6] This positive assessment is based on the achievements of Muhammad 'Ali in consolidating the power of the nation and his successful embarkation on a programme of state-building. In this process, Ghurbal portrays the Egyptian population as monolithic and passive,

> They became homogeneous in serving one master, they were drilled into soldiers and sailors and marched to victory against the Sultan, they were forced into schools and the production of wealth, and they were governed and taught to expect and find security.[7]

The Beginnings of the Egyptian Question is essentially a work of high politics, concerned with diplomatic relations, military actions and affairs of state. Its discourse is one of the motives and actions of individual rulers, military officers and diplomats; its theatre is the battlefield, the palace and high political councils; its primary source material is substantially the foreign archives in Britain and Europe. In short, it portrays the grand actions of a political elite against the background of a compliant, malleable population.

While this early praise of Muhammad 'Ali differed little from the judgement of the royalist historians, Ghurbal's later work shifted emphasis in its view of the national community. His history of the negotiations between Egypt and Britain over the 1882–1936 period, which appeared almost 25 years later, was another diplomatic study but it gave greater recognition to the active role of the Egyptian population.[8] In his description of the 1919 uprising, Ghurbal acknowledges the Egyptian people as a historical agent,

> The "Revolution" is an angry outburst for honour; its story is a story of bravery which cannot be measured, its beauty a beauty of clear, pure sacrifice; it was carried out without fear by boys, girls, youths, men and women, they all forgot their religious and social differences and cared only for Egypt and asked for nothing other than its freedom and independence.[9]

Here Ghurbal proposes an almost transcendental unity as the motivation for political action and, despite some token recognition of the diversity within Egyptian society, presents the people en masse as clamouring for independence without reference to material or everyday concerns.[10] This rather one dimensional characterization of the Egyptian nation was consistent with Ghurbal's notion of its civilizational unity. Though not unaware of the importance of social and economic factors, Ghurbal granted them little political meaning or force. Rather he favoured the role of the individual and the class of the notability as the agents of the Egyptian nation.[11] His later explanation for the ultimate disappointment of 1919 was represented in terms of the moral failure of a patrician class:

> ...the hopes for a national rebirth were not fulfilled. We did not have the courage of our professions. We paid the people in words. We were selfish and we were cynics. We had less excuse than our fathers at the debacle of 1882, because we built on what they left and we could have learnt from their mistakes.[12]

By the early 1960s these views left Ghurbal open to charges of being 'aristocratic and reactionary'.[13] His analysis of 1919 was attacked as an 'obscure characterization' (al-ta'rif al-ghamid) and an 'improbable explanation' (al-tafsir al-ba'id) since it failed to recognize the factors within Egyptian society that generated the clamour for economic as well as political changes.[14] Ghurbal's focus on the actions of the ruler and the state, and reliance on the 'great man theory of history' (nazariyya al-rajul al-'azim) has prompted Choueiri to deem Ghurbal as a 'manager of legitimation'.[15] The 'great man' approach was soon out of step with more fashionable historical methodologies but Ghurbal was not alone in this. Other historians, such as Fu'ad Shukri and Muhammad Rif'at, who had been trained in the same tradition of diplomatic history, continued to write on the foreign relations and policy of the Egyptian and other states.[16] Their discourse focused on the motives of the elite class who formulated and enacted state policy and reinforced the centrality and legitimacy of the state.

PARTY AND NATION: SABRI, AL-RAFI'I AND RAMADAN

While Ghurbal cast Egyptians as the basic constituents of a civilizational entity and as compliant subjects of the ruler within an idiom of state building, his contemporaries Muhammad Sabri and 'Abd al-Rahman al-Rafi'i proposed an alternative framework that became the keynote of the liberal school. Instead of the world of diplomacy and foreign policy, they conceived of Egyptian history as the emergence of the popular national movement which was em-bodied by a particular political party, or group of parties. The liberal school constructed a narrative around two themes: first, the political struggle between the Egyptian national movement and the British; and second, the conflict amongst Egyptian political parties in their struggle to take command of the national movement.

Muhammad Sabri's two volume work *La Révolution égyptienne* is an account of the turbulent period of 1919 to 1921. The first account of the 1919 revolution written from a national viewpoint interpreted the events as a 'general national revolution' (*thawra wataniyya 'ama*) and not simply as the 'unrest' (*shaghab*) described by British sources. In being critical of the future King Fu'ad and emphasizing his unpopularity amongst Egyptians, it dissociated the people from the traditional authority of the Egyptian state.[17] Clear evidence of his conception of the historical role of revolutions as central to the mechanics of historical change, Sabri's analysis portrayed the revolution as a united front made up of all sections of the Egyptian populace, from city and country, the fellahin and worker, men and women, Muslim and Christian, brought together by their collective patriotism.

> C'est l'amour de la Patrie qui a effacé toutes traces de discorde et harmonisé les coeurs. C'est l'amour de la Patrie qui a poussé la femme, le paysan, l'étudiant, le théologien, le prince, l'ouvrier et le fonctionnaire à se dresser en bloc en face du Protectorat. C'est l'amour de la Patrie qui a fait que les Égyptiens se sentent membres d'une même famille, et créé entre eux ce miraculeux et bienfaisant lien de solidarité. Cette solidarité est sans précédent dans l'histoire. Notre Révolution est la seule qui n'ait pas connu la défection de minorités.[18]

This image of a united Egypt demanding independence from the British occupier, first put forward by Sabri, has been an influential and enduring one in nationalist historiography. However, his analysis shed little light on the nature of this national solidarity nor made much attempt to distinguish the different elements among Egyptians.

> Cette union est d'autant plus admirable qu'elle n'est pas le résultat d'une discipline plus ou moins imposeé comme dans des en guerre ...Cette union est maintenant indéfectible, parce qu'elle a pris racine dans le coeur même de tout un peuple. Elle est devenue comme une seconde nature.[19]

While this romantic characterization of the basis of national unity, 'as second nature', borders on mystification, Sabri is more specific in his conception of the leadership of revolution. As he explained '...individuals of the people do not undertake revolutions and national agitation unless they have a leader that has a strong influence on them.'[20] Accordingly, his narrative focuses on the activities of the Wafd and its leader Sa'd Zaghlul in its struggle with the British, on the one hand, and with its domestic contest with 'Adli Yakan and the non-Wafdist forces on the other. Zaghlul is the popular leader and hero, distinguished by his own special qualities, yet at the same time typifying the Egyptian fellah.

> Zagloul possède au plus haut point les qualités d'un chef d'opposition et d'un leader populaire. Au physique, une haute stature qui impose et une physionomie représentative du vrai type égyptien autochtone qu'est le Fellah; au moral, un caractère ferme et tenace, une intelligence toujours vivace, une finesse pénétrante, et un esprit pondéré.[21]

Sabri's description of the unanimity of action in the momentous revolutionary struggle is a powerful image in conveying the strong sense of national unity and desire for independence. At the same time the emphasis given to Zaghlul is a clear statement of the role of the great leader as the embodiment of the national movement and the Wafd as the repository of the national will.

Perhaps more than any other modern Egyptian historian, 'Abd al-Rahman al-Rafi'i dedicated himself to the development of the Egyptian national movement as a historical theme. Following its course from the indigenous resistance during the French campaign in 1798 through to the revolution of 1952 and beyond, he presented a celebrated and seminal account of great scope and force that dwarfs Sabri's narrative of the events of 1919–21. While it accords with the centrality of party politics found in Sabri's account, it differs in regarding the Watani Party and not the Wafd as the truer expression of the Egyptian national movement and the embodiment of its aspirations. From its formal establishment in 1907 until the end of the monarchical period, the party forms the central reference point in his narrative. Indeed, so much so that his history of the period from 1892 until the 1919 Revolution is written explicitly as the biographies of the two outstanding Watanist leaders, Mustafa Kamil and Muhammad Farid.[22]

For al-Rafi'i, the Watani Party ('National Party') represented the radical voice of nationalism whose clarion call was the unconditional withdrawal of British forces from Egypt. Supported by the petite bourgeoisie, the party stood in contrast to the more moderate Umma Party (literally 'party of the nation'), led by Ahmad Lutfi al-Sayyid, which attracted the support of landowners and some intellectuals. Recognizing the benefits of British rule, the latter advocated a more gradualist, negotiated schedule for independence. The names of both parties made clear their claims to represent the movement for Egyptian independence but consistent with his party loyalties, al-Rafi'i gave the Watani Party the greater part of the credit for laying the groundwork for the 1919 Revolution.

> The principles of President Wilson had an influence in the introduction of the revolution inasmuch as he announced the right of people to self determination, just as the *jihad* of the Watani Party

[was] a great benefit in the preparation of the country for it; and through the propagation in the succeeding years of the spirit of genuine nationalism, which Mustafa Kamil and Muhammad Farid and their supporters and pupils had planted in the hearts of the generation the greatest examples, so the *umma* followed in their footsteps in the pure *jihad* of god and country when it moved in 1919 to a willingness to offer every great sacrifice which it glorified in the cause of independence.[23]

After 1919, with the emergence of the Wafd as the mass-supported nationalist party from the remnants of the Umma Party, the Watani Party without Kamil or Farid became increasingly marginalized as a popular party even if it remained active as a party of cadres consistently resolute in its opposition to the British occupation. Nevertheless, al-Rafi'i continued to cast the Watani Party as a leading player in the national movement during the 1920s and 1930s. The disproportionate importance given to the Watani Party in the postwar years had its corollary in the negative attitude shown towards the Wafd, of which al-Rafi'i was consistently critical, especially towards its leader, Sa'd Zaghlul. The Wafd's popularity and influence was impossible to ignore – indeed al-Rafi'i framed his first volume account of the period after 1919 around the life of Zaghlul – but his attitude to the great national leader was frequently antipathetic and dismissive of his political role.[24] He had already found fault with Sa'd's actions before the First World War, particularly in relation to his withdrawal of support for the Egyptian University, and his close relationship with Lord Cromer.[25] In the aftermath of the 1919 Revolution, al-Rafi'i held Zaghlul completely responsible for the national divisions which resulted in much damage to the Egyptian cause.[26] Further, he disapproved of Zaghlul's policy in conceding a settlement with the British on the Sudan.[27] Indeed, the first volume of *Fi 'aqab al-thawra al-misriyya* includes a chapter on the personality of Sa'd Zaghlul and a final section on 'the faults of Sa'd' (*al-ma'akhidh 'ala Sa'd*).

After Zaghlul's death, al-Rafi'is maintained this critical line, censuring the terms of the 1936 Anglo-Egyptian treaty negotiated with the British Government by the Wafd government of al-Nahhas. The treaty recognized Egyptian independence, set limits on the deployment of British troops, formalized defence arrangements in case of external aggression and included undertakings by the British to sponsor the abolition of the Capitulations. Yet, for al-Rafi'i it represented the formalization of a 'harsh protectorate' (*himayya qasiya*).[28] His hostility towards the Wafd was unremitting: he found fault with its support for the establishment of the Arab League in 1944, since it had been set up with British backing, and again reprimanded the party for its slowness in rescinding the treaty of 1936 in 1951.[29]

Al-Rafi'i's conception and description of the national movement in the post-1919 period is of party manoeuvring, pronouncements and negotiations.

118

The Watani Party is the radical party, the exponent of Egypt's natural right to national independence. The Wafd represents an imperfect incarnation of the national will, prepared to compromise on fundamental matters of national sovereignty and the unity of the Nile Valley. Yet like Ghurbal and Sabri, al-Rafi'i's historical method continued to be influenced by the 'great man' school of history.[30] His dedicated attention to the careers of Mustafa Kamil and Muhammad Farid, as much as his critical assessment of Zaghlul, indicated a preoccupation with the role of individual leaders. Nevertheless, his account of the 1919 Revolution and its aftermath presented a broader, more popular (*sha'bi*) perspective of the period than had been offered before.[31] His skilful use of a wide range of party documents, unpublished memoirs and court records, his personal contacts with many participants in the events, as well as his own personal involvement, represent an important shift of emphasis from diplomatic analyses based on foreign language sources to a richer and more grassroots portrayal of Egyptian political life.

That said, al-Rafi'i gives comparatively little attention to the complexity of the domestic political scene with no recognition of any aspect of class struggle nor a conception of the class significance of political alliances. There seems to be little awareness of or an indifference to the emergence of new political movements, such as the working class and its role in the national struggle.[32] Nor is there any mention of communism or the socialist movement – agents that al-Rafi'i considered criminal since they were illegal and opposed to the national government.[33] In the conference at the Egyptian Historical Society in 1965, Muhammad Anis singled him out for criticism,

> In his writings al-Rafi'i did not see the existence of the relations of production or the forces of production at all. The history of the Egyptian people as a social force was not written. What was written lacked the social background or what is sometimes known as the materialist background that gives political movement its meaning.[34]

The comment was testament as much to the changing political climate as it was to the stature of al-Rafi'i as the pre-eminent historian of the national movement.

Muhammad Sabri's pro-Wafdist interpretation of the 1919 Revolution in the wake of the events themselves – the second volume of *La Révolution égyptienne* had been published in 1921 – perforce lacked the advantage of historical hindsight and extensive documentation. Published some years later, al-Rafi'i's account of 1919 and its aftermath, despite its overstatement of the Watani Party's role, stood as the dominant interpretation of the period. Over time, even if its picture of the role of the Watani Party looked increasingly unconvincing, it maintained its standing abetted by the advent of the July Revolution in 1952 which precluded the Wafd, the symbol of the decadent parliamentary regime, from receiving a more sympathetic historical treatment. It was not until almost 40 years after the death of Sa'd Zaghlul that an academic historian in a systematic and detailed study would seek to establish the claims of the Wafd to the pre-eminent role in the Egyptian national movement.

'Abd al-'Azim Ramadan's *Tatawwur al-haraka al-wataniyya fi misr min 1918–36*, appeared in 1968 and reinstated the party of Sa'd Zaghlul and Mustafa al-Nahhas as the principal representative of the will of the Egyptian nation.[35] Writing towards the end of the Nasser period which had consistently denigrated the Wafd as the perpetrators of a failed revolution, Ramadan's aim was to restore the party to its rightful place in history.[36] The central dynamic in his narrative was the struggle between the forces of democracy, led by the Wafd, and those of autocracy, embodied by the King, the minor parties and the British government. As Ramadan saw it, the Wafd was the great secular, national party, that combined the virtues of the secularism and political realism of the Umma Party with the radicalism and popular support of the Watani Party before First World War. Its mass support and commitment to democratic nationalism elevated it above all other parties as the representative of the nation.[37] Ramadan, therefore, rejected criticism made by some leftist historians that the Wafd was just another party of large landowners led by the bourgeoisie and serving its own narrow class interest. As Meijer accurately notes, 'More than any other historian, Ramadan identifies the Wafd with the Umma.'[38]

The centrality Ramadan grants the Wafd accords in part with the image the party held of itself as the true representative, the delegation (*al-wafd*) of the nation, not simply a political party. Its autocratic leadership, particularly in the time of Sa'd Zaghlul but also under his successor, Mustafa al-Nahhas, continually emphasized that it enjoyed the full confidence of the people. Concepts such as 'mandate of the people' (*tawkil al-sha'b*) and 'consensus of the nation' (*ijma' al-umma*), were employed to bolster the Wafd's claims to political legitimacy.[39] Zaghlul set the tone,

> Anyone who says we are a party demanding independence is a criminal for this implies that there are other parties which do not want independence. The whole nation wants independence, we are the spokesmen of the nation demanding it, we are the trustees of the nation.[40]

It was therefore only appropriate that Zaghlul's house in Cairo was known as the House of the People. This arrogation of the voice of the nation took on semi-religious tones even after the death of Zaghlul. The leader of the party, Mustafa al-Nahhas, styled himself as the 'leader of the nation' (*za'im al-umma*), entrusted with its 'sacred leadership' (*al-za'ama al-muqaddasa*). These overreaching, almost mystical claims, while rallying mass support to the Wafd, were arguably responsible for the alienation of much political talent and may in part explain the long series of splits from the party, from the early departures of Isma'il Sidqi and Ahmad Lutfi al-Sayyid, to those of al-Nuqrashi and Ahmad Mahir in 1937, and Makram 'Ubayd in the 1940s.[41]

Ramadan's narrative resolutely maintained its pro-Wafd perspective into the 1930s and beyond. The 1936 treaty with Britain was 'part of the world-wide struggle against fascism'.[42] Ramadan's explanation of the events of 4 February 1942, when British tanks surrounded 'Abdin Palace and forced Faruq to agree to the appointment of al-Nahhas as Prime Minister, painted the Wafd in the best possible light. The source of considerable criticism of the Wafd ever since, even from those with Wafdist sympathies, the incident provoked accusations that al-Nahhas acted as a willing accomplice of the British and seriously compromised Egyptian national sovereignty.[43] Ramadan absolved the Wafd of the charge of intriguing with either the British or the king, stressing the forces of autocracy and the reactionary allies of imperialism ranged against it.[44] According to Ramadan, the substantial powers enjoyed by the King under the 1923 constitution and his persistent plotting with the minority parties, particularly with Isma'il Sidqi in the early 1930s, constantly thwarted the Wafd and successfully kept it out of office for long periods of time. In this political struggle, both the Ikhwan and Misr al-Fatat collaborated with the palace against the Wafd and the will of the nation.[45]

The other if lesser innovative feature of Ramadan's analysis was his recognition of the communist contribution in the national movement, crediting them particularly with the promotion of progressive policies during the 1940s. While he found fault with the fragmented and sectarian character of the movement, Ramadan singled out al-Fajr al-Jadid for praise, since he regarded this group as having most consciously projected a national character and shown a better understanding of the Egyptian situation. Significantly, al-Fajr al-Jadid also maintained regular links with the Wafdist Vanguard, the progressive wing of the Wafd. By contrast, Ramadan was less impressed with the other larger communist groups. He branded HAMITU as petit bourgeois, and Iskra, as autocratic, and was critical of the problems that troubled both organizations concerning the diverse character of their membership, especially the position of Jews in the movement, and factional debates over political strategy and tactics.[46]

The liberal school focuses on the struggle of the Egyptian people (sha'b) for political independence, in the first instance from the British occupation, then from the domestic enemies of democracy opposed to the will of the masses, such as the King, minority parties and conservative politicians. The ideological leadership of the national movement, whether the Watani Party, as proposed by al-Rafi'i, or the Wafd, as put forward by Sabri and Ramadan, represents the unqualified desire of the Egyptian people for national sovereignty and the main force for historical change. This discourse continues to be influential and popular, particularly in the memoirs of ancien régime politicians and Wafdist writers such as Jamal Badawi who emphasize the unity and heroism of 1919 in the national struggle. Rarely, however, does it question the social basis of the nationalist front or the nature or motives of the constituent elements of the movement.

THE MATERIALIST SCHOOL: NATION, CAPITAL AND CLASS

The materialist school of historiography extended the parameters of political history as they had been traditionally understood and represented a more complex picture of the nation that traded in the currency of class struggle, the dynamics of imperialism and the nature of international capitalism. Its explanation of historical change as arising from contradictions in the economic structure of society widened the scope of historical inquiry beyond the domain of leaders and political parties to include economic and social factors. As Shuhdi ʿAtiyya al-Shafiʿi, a pioneering materialist historian, explained

> Its basis is that the history of social development is firstly and above all the history of peoples (shuʿub), and that history cannot be truly scientific if it confines itself to the study of the activities of kings and commanders of armies, the reports of invasions, the details of negotiations and treaties...and with the existence of the role of leaders in history, except that they are not able to play this role except to the extent that they represent the interests of their people and their comprehension of the laws of the development of society.[47]

This effectively challenged the conceptual basis of Egyptian national unity and the monolithic characterization of Egyptian society held by historians of the liberal school.

A central pillar of materialist historiography is the belief that the laws of social development are a product of the economic structure of society. It was therefore the task of the historian to ascertain the historical basis of the economic structure, or more precisely the forces and relations of production, in order to determine the configuration of classes and political power within the society and nation. In the Egyptian context materialist analysis articulated the dynamics of class exploitation and its relationship with imperialism by proposing a political divide between those allied to the colonial power and the interests of the ruling class and those who opposed them in the name of the national movement. This was particularly characteristic of the materialist works of the 1950s.[48] Ibrahim ʿAmr proposed a division of pre-1952 Egyptian society into three groups: the 'allies of colonialism' (hulafaʿ al-istimʿar), comprised of large landowners and finance capitalists, personified by notables such as Ismaʿil Sidqi and embodied in the Egyptian

Federation of Industries, who formed business partnerships with foreign companies controlled by foreign residents; the nationalists (*al-qawmiyyun*), a coalition of commercial capitalists, wealthy agricultural businessmen and the middle class throughout the country; and the popular forces (*al-quwan al-sha'biyya*), made up of the popular masses and working class.[49]

Fawzi Jirjis put forward a division amongst the capitalist class into two wings. The national wing (*al-janah al-watani*) was represented by the Wafd and included some large landowners, the rural rich, small producers in the city and intellectuals. This national bourgeoisie was manifested in the Bank Misr group, a coalition of Egyptian businessmen who supported the bank established in 1920 to pursue a policy of using native capital for the financing of industrial projects. The other group was the industrial wing (*al-janah al-sina'i*), comprador capitalists who maintained relations with foreign capital and economic agencies connected to colonialist interests. This second coalition invested in banks, industry, trade, mortgage, real estate and in other activities that were characterized by monopolistic practices and imposed economic authority over small producers.[50] This division of the capitalist class into two groups, a 'non-native bourgeoisie' supportive of colonial authority; and the other, a progressive national bourgeoisie, became a consistent feature of materialist historiography.[51] The latter were progressive not only because of their nationalist programme but because they were regarded as the most effective agents of industrialization and thus the best means to accelerate Egyptian economic development and increase the size of the proletariat, a precondition for socialist revolution.

FROM REVOLUTION TO REVOLUTION

Like the liberal school, the materialist school acknowledged the critical importance of the 1919 Revolution as a symbol of national unity and an expression of the desire of Egyptians for independence but differed in its explanation of the basis and motivation of the event. One interpretation regarded 1919 as a convergence rather than a unanimity of interests and a coalition of forces rather than a case of metaphysical national harmony. In their analysis of the 1919 revolution, Ahmad 'Abd al-Hamid and Rashid al-Barawi described the tension between the different actors and the ultimately contradictory class interests.

> The real truth is concealed in that the movement was set up by the leadership of the upper bourgeoisie class in a special kind of way supported by the petite bourgeoisie, and the agricultural aristocracy joined so that the final gain for them was to protect their situation so that everything would stay in their hands...and the revolutionary

movement was joined by groups of labourers, small farmers and hired agricultural workers.[52]

The agreement between the Egyptian leadership and the British following the declaration of February 1922, which expanded the political and economic power of the bourgeoisie by providing for a system of direct elections to representative bodies and made positions available in government administration, revealed the political priorities of the national leadership. The conclusion of 'Abd al-Hamid and al-Barawi on the 1919 revolution is explicit: one class, the bourgeoisie, appropriated a 'national' event for its own aims and benefit.

> A group of the bourgeoisie organized the revolution and used the public and the workers in the country and city, and when it achieved its aims discarded these groups and the overwhelming majority of the people and left them a diet of poverty, ignorance and unemployment.[53]

Al-Shafi'i's analysis by contrast emphasized the positive elements of the 1919 Revolution, considering it a success in bringing the British protectorate to an end and providing a system of constitutional and representative government, as well as setting in motion a commercial, social and cultural awakening (*nahda*). However, he conceded that it had failed to liberate Egypt from the power of imperialism, feudalism and its domination by the king and the large landowners.[54] Muhammad Anis also regarded 1919 as an incomplete bourgeois revolution through its failure to resolve the conflict of interest between large landowners and the indigenous industrial class.[55] The indecisive outcome of the conflicting interests between the reactionary large landowning class and the industrial bourgeoisie provided the basis of the main contest in domestic politics in the period leading up to the Second World War. The former, represented before the First World War by the Umma Party and elements from within the Royal family and after 1919 by the Liberal Constitutionalists and other minor parties, compromised with the British because of its mutual economic interests and therefore, acquiesced in, if not actively encouraged, continued foreign investment in Egypt. The latter, in its incarnation as Bank Misr, operated in competition with the foreign banks and commercial interests supported by the power of the large landowning class.

In this equation, the political weakness of the Watani Party, representing the petite bourgeoisie, and the Wafd, which came to be dominated by moderate elements, contributed to the inability of national capital to gain the ascendancy over foreign investment. In effect, the compromise with the British in 1923 had already impeded the path of national industrialization and indigenous economic growth. By the late 1930s, Bank Misr's inability to go at it alone became evident. It was left with little option and signalled its failure to develop an Egyptian-owned industrial base by entering into joint ventures with foreign investment banks. Indeed, al-Shafi'i viewed the 1936 treaty between the Wafd government and the British as more than a political compromise but tantamount to a deathblow to the national capitalists.[56] By the end of Second World War the lines had been redrawn: the interests of landholding and industrial bourgeoisie, including the Bank Misr group, had effectively merged and stood opposed to the camp of petite bourgeoisie intellectuals, workers and fellahin.[57]

These pioneering materialist analyses of the pre-1952 period were later regarded as mechanistic and were criticized for inappropriately employing concepts, such as feudalism and bourgeoisie, since they were grounded in a European historical experience.[58] Even so, they provided an important foundation for the more empirical research of later scholars who critically examined, refined and sometimes even overturned the thrust of these early studies. To take one particular issue, the doctoral theses of Ra'uf 'Abbas, 'Asim al-Disuqi and 'Ali Barakat on aspects of private landownership, all published in the 1970s, undermined both the concept of a national and non-national bourgeoisie and the idea of the conflicting interests between local and foreign landowners.[59] It was therefore becoming increasingly difficult to argue that there was a struggle between a national and non-national bourgeoisie within the capitalist class.

In 1981, 'Asim al-Disuqi published an important reassessment of the early materialist interpretations of Egyptian economic development and put forward a more complex description and model of the national economy, grounded in the specificity of Egyptian conditions.[60] One of his targets was the distinction maintained between large landowners and the industrial class. Al-Disuqi's examination of company registers revealed that many of the individuals and families that had large landholdings were also prominent in industry. Indeed, the profits of agricultural surplus were often the source of industrial and commercial capital investment. Conversely those who profited from trade and business regularly invested in land.[61] This seriously undermined, if not fatally wounded, the notion of a reactionary landowning class and progressive national industrialists. Nevertheless, al-Disuqi continued to maintain that the agricultural landowners allied with the industrial and trade finance capitalists, despite the evidence of clashes and agreements between them, comprised the ruling class. Further, he argued for recognition of the peculiar conditions operating inside Egypt. The clearest case was the system of Capitulations (al-imtiyazat al-ajnabiyya) and the Mixed Courts (al-mahakim al-mukhtilafa), which conferred economic privileges on foreign businessmen and gave them advantages over their Egyptian competitors and thus distorted the path of Egyptian economic development. The efforts of Bank Misr notwithstanding, the majority of banks remained in the hands of foreigners and continued to maintain the advantage of foreign capitalists over their Egyptian counterparts. According to al-Disuqi, it is therefore not possible to date 'the real beginning of the role of Egyptian capitalism' until after the abolition of the Capitulations in 1937, and the end of the Mixed Courts in 1949. 'Then the 1952 revolution arrived and hampered the growth of Egyptian capitalism in a way that allowed the establishment of the capitalist system in the technical sense.'[62]

The lack of evidence for a genuine distinction between the national and non-national capitalists had important implications for the analysis of domestic political forces but it was not the only difficulty. It had long been recognized that large landowners were prominent in all the major parties but the prevailing view of the liberal school had placed the Wafd at the head of the progressive national bourgeoisie and their domestic opponents, the Liberal Constitutionalists and other minor parties, as representative of the interests of reactionary large landowners.[63] But if the leadership of the Wafd was drawn from the same social and economic class as the leadership of other parties, were their interests ultimately in conflict? Ramadan and even Anis, both confident of the Wafd's bona fide nationalist credentials, had explained the party's political failure to transform its mass support into solid political outcomes on its being outmanoeuvred by the British, the King and the minor parties. Materialist views suggested an alternative explanation, pointing to the social character of the Wafdist leadership and questioning its genuine commitment to political and economic reform. It suggested the increasingly conservative Wafdist policies and the moderate, legalistic approach of the party in negotiations with the British were the consequence of an unwillingness to embrace the masses politically since such a policy might have threatened the social position of its own leadership.[64] Al-Bishri explained the discrepancy between the rhetoric and achievements of the Wafd in terms of competing interests within the party.[65] In the period after 1945, he identified three wings who wrestled for control of the organization: the conservatives, who controlled the leadership and Central Committee; the liberal wing, which maintained a minority on the Central Committee and sought to uphold the party's ideals; and the left wing, or Wafdist Vanguard, which was popular among youth and students and closest to the masses. These contradictions and the effect on the viability of the Wafd became particularly evident during its last ineffectual ministry of 1950–2.

However the failure of the Wafd might be explained, the inability of the political system to deal with the economic and political crisis that developed after the Second World War set the scene for the events of 1952. Ibrahim 'Amr regarded the July Revolution as a result of the growth of the national revolutionary forces, and especially the increasing economic demands of the popular forces, fuelled by the deep economic crisis brought about by the struggle between large landowners and the capitalists.[66] Al-Shafi'i emphasized the troika of internal and external forces of imperialism (*isti'mar*), monopoly (*ihtikar*) and feudalism (*iqta'*) as the major factors hampering the development of the Egyptian economy after the Second World War.[67] These insurmountable obstacles caused the onset of a profound economic crisis. According to al-Shafi'i, it became 'necessary for the development of Egyptian industry and the Egyptian economy to wreck the shackles which connected it with imperialism, and subjected it to monopolism and feudalism'.[68] While neither the consciousness nor the organization of the working class was sufficient to lead the masses in such a struggle, the existing traditional political parties, beholden to the wealthy classes and large landowners, were unable to provide the political leadership to develop industry.[69]

VANGUARD OF THE NATION

Materialist historiography was not only concerned with the dialectic of class struggle and the dynamics of the national liberation movement but with the identification of those progressive elements in society which would ultimately pave the way for the socialist revolution. As the liberal school put the Watani Party and the Wafd forward, so running through the materialist narrative is a thread predicated on the notion of the vanguard (al-tali'a) as the leaders of the political transformation. With the radical rearrangement of the political landscape after 1952, divergent streams of the materialist school presented the army, the communist movement and the labour movement as the vanguard of the nation.

The army

One stream of materialist thought embraced the army as the embodiment of the progressive cause. This was characteristic of the first materialist analyses of the late 1950s, such as that of al-Shafi'i, and had the virtue of recognizing the political realities of the time: a military regime bathing in the foreign policy successes of Suez and Bandung that had effectively outmanoeuvred the domestic opposition. This interpretation subordinated the class struggle to the national movement led by the Free Officers and took pains to emphasize the compatibility of class and national aims in the political struggle. In al-Shafi'i's narrative, the course of events from the public demonstrations of February 1946 until the Fire of Cairo in January 1952 proved that new leadership was required to represent the 'interests of the national economy' (masalih al-iqtisad al-watani).[70] In July 1952, the Free Officers took up this role by championing the development of national capitalism against imperialist interests and precipitating the collapse of the monarchy and the feudal order. As the culmination of the efforts of earlier national movements and the realization of the unfulfilled promise of the 1919 Revolution, the Nasser regime stood as the representative of the national middle class and a vehicle for the invigoration of a genuinely Egyptian-controlled economy.

Though a prominent leader in the United Egyptian Communist Party, Shuhdi 'Atiyya al-Shafi'i gave no role to the communist movement in his account of the national and class struggles in Egypt between the time of 'Urabi and Suez. Instead, he credited the army with the collapse of the feudal system which thereafter became 'the inheritor of popular national consciousness and the new leadership of the nationalist movement'.[71] The role ascribed to the army by al-Shafi'i remained influential, being taken up in the National Charter and adopted into the academic mainstream by Muhammad Anis.[72] Always more a Nasserist than a radical socialist, Anis wholeheartedly endorsed the revolutionary role of the army in the process of socialist transformation as it gathered steam during the 1960s. In his account of the July Revolution written with Rajab Haraz, Anis, like al-Shafi'i, gave no explicit recognition to the role of the communist movement in the events leading up to the coup.[73] His analysis of Egyptian society prior to 1952 described the popular revolutionary camp (*mu'askar al-thawra al-sha'biyya*) as comprising workers, peasants and the 'revolutionary intellectuals' (*al-muthaqafun al-thawriyyun*). The last, he explained, included a class that emerged from the universities, the army and the petite bourgeoisie but he made no mention of communists.[74] This failure to acknowledge the contribution of the communist movement by al-Shafi'i or Anis is very likely a function of political circumstances. The case of the former, a materialist historian and communist militant, is likely to be explained either by censorship or a sign of the political compromise required of communists to stay within the broad national front.[75] Similarly, Anis was writing just at the time when the communist party was dissolving itself at the behest of the regime and when its own independent political significance was being downplayed.

From a leftist perspective Nasser's government could certainly claim great political successes both domestically and internationally. The land reform proved a relatively effective measure against the power base of 'the feudalists'. The confiscations of foreign-owned companies during the 1950s and the nationalizations of 1961 struck a further blow against the power of the capitalist class. Internationally, Egypt's leading role in the non-aligned movement and the successful nationalization of the Suez Canal, with the final withdrawal of British troops, were great successes. The regime was particularly praised for its pro-Arab and anti-imperialist stance by some writers.[76] Others on the left, however, showed a more equivocal or ultimately hostile attitude towards the revolutionary credentials of the military regime.[77] The execution of two trade unionists following demonstrations at Kafr al-Dawwar in August 1952 had not been a good omen. The periodic repression of communist cadres that followed throughout the 1950s and early 1960s seemed to confirm the impression of an authoritarian wolf in anti-imperialist sheep's clothing. By the early 1960s, Anouar Abdel-Malek, now exiled in Paris, was describing the army as 'the instrument of the monopolist upper middle class'.[78] Writing some years later, he was unequivocal: 'The pretension of the army, as a corporate force, to occupy a hegemonic position in Egyptian politics is now profoundly rejected by all popular classes and groups.'[79]

The communist movement

It was not until the 1970s, when Sadat's 'corrective revolution' was moving the country to the right that the contribution of the Egyptian communist movement to the national movement was discussed in historical scholarship in any great detail. 'Abd al-'Azim Ramadan's Wafdist history had introduced the issue; the works of Rif'at al-Sa'id and Tariq al-Bishri provided sustained left wing analyses, fuelled and supplemented by the personal memoirs and accounts of those who had been active in the movement.[80] Though an accurate assessment of the role and significance of the communist movement was made difficult by the underground nature of its activity and its highly fragmented structure, from the mid-1970s the second wave of materialist historiography upheld its position as the central actor in the political life of the nation.

In the work of al-Sa'id, the communist movement is the political organization most in touch with the feelings of the masses and thus represents the genuine agent of revolutionary change.[81] This role is exemplified in his analysis of the political turbulence of early 1946. Al-Sa'id maintains that the communist students were the main force behind the Executive Committee of Students which led the protests against the imperialist domination of the Egyptian economy and culture.[82] This group had joined with the workers' committees to form the National Committee of Workers and Students, which proclaimed a national strike and a 'day of evacuation' (yawm al-jala') on 21 February 1946. The coalition, according to al-Sa'id, was 'an excellent example of alliances between communists and other national forces in a revolutionary and progressive framework.'[83] Tariq al-Bishri's analysis is more critical of the communist movement and less wholehearted in his support of its claims to represent the masses (al-jamahir), the vital force in Egyptian politics.[84] Nevertheless, at least in his original analysis of the period 1945–52, he still considers the communist movement as the political organization most in touch with the aspirations of the Egyptian people.[85]

The plausibility of the claim that the communists were the vanguard of a broad national front was based on its ideological position and not its political support since it could hardly pretend to the mass following of the Wafd.[86] However, there were serious difficulties within the movement itself that hampered its impact. Its splintered nature, compounded by disagreements in political strategy, tactics and ideology, further weakened its claims to represent the vanguard of the nation. Debilitating also were the problems arising from the large proportion of Jews amongst the leadership of some communist groups in the 1940s. Al-Sa'id believed this 'foreign' leadership to be an advantage to the movement but other leftists have held the prominence of Jews hampered its understanding of the Egyptian situation and may have diminished its influence in Egypt.[87]

Workers

The third stream of materialist historiography has taken a more workerist perspective and emphasized the claims of labour as the progressive cause in the national movement. Characteristic of this trend is the work of Mahmoud Hussein dedicated to Mustafa Khamis, the striker hung by the RCC in the early months of the July Revolution, which presented a virulent indictment of the Nasser regime.[88] Citing the ideological inspiration of the Cultural Revolution, it asserted that 'the Egyptian masses are the only depositories of the national dignity', and employed 'a proletarian, revolutionary conceptual framework' in its critique of the 'bourgeois conceptual apparatus which Nasserism has used ... to protect itself against growing consciousness on the part of the labouring masses concerning the class nature of this regime'.[89] More recently the work of Taha 'Uthman's, a veteran trade unionist, has proposed an analysis of the history of the labour movement that seeks to establish its autonomy from the Nasserite state.[90] These works meshed in part with the history of the working class by Amin 'Izz al-Din published in the early 1970s which employed a more mechanistic Marxist analysis. They contrasted with other, mainly academic, studies of labour that employed a nationalist or Nasserist framework, which viewed the union movement as being manipulated by larger political forces, principally by the Wafd in the 1920s and later by the Nasser regime.[91]

Materialist historiography has sought to present a sophisticated picture of Egyptian national politics through its analysis of class struggle. By articulating political interest in terms of the economic structure, it moved away from the monolithic characterization of Egyptian society upheld by the liberal school and presented a more complex and intricate analysis of national and class politics. The concept of class struggle and the idea that political action and public institutions were expressive of class interests within society asserted a society of diverse and conflicting interests. In this way the materialist school posed a more heterogeneous model of Egyptian society even as it offered a more determinate explanation of its development. This less personalized view of the national leadership questioned the claims of political organizations, such as the palace and the Wafd, to represent the voice of the nation. Drawing its inspiration from Marxist thought and allied to a considerable extent to the ideology of the communist movement, the materialist school tended to locate the progressive cause less in the hands of a specific political organization, since there was no hegemonic party of the left, and more in the principles of anti-imperialism, economic independence, and the liberation of the masses.

Nevertheless, for both practical and conceptual reasons the materialist school did not cast aside the tenets of the liberal school entirely. The hostile often repressive political environment in Egypt meant that materialist historiography had to accommodate political realities or face circumscription if not censorship by the authorities. Marxist historians were under pressure to stay within or were kept to the acceptable limits of national discourse. The tension in Marxist theory between class and national interests, which it arguably never resolved, also mitigated the thrust of the materialist school. In Egypt the relationship between these two frames of reference was made even more complicated because of the complex matrix of British imperialism, the Capitulatory regime and the courts of mixed jurisdiction. Further, grounded in European historical experience, the materialist conception of history provoked much debate regarding the compatibility of terms such as feudalism and capitalism in an Egyptian context and offered no clear direction in divining the political role of the army.[92]

THE ISLAMIC CURRENT: AN 'AUTHENTIC' NATION

The Islamic current sites its national discourse within a religious-cultural framework, employing the concept of the Islamic community as an integral element of the national identity and the foundation of a discourse of cultural authenticity. As a framework for historical interpretation it appraises all political, economic and social phenomena with reference to Islam employing an idiom of cultural legitimacy, tradition and religious authority. Like the other schools of interpretation discussed, the Islamic current adopts an anti-imperialist position but principally aims its denunciation at the influence of the Western ideas of modernization and secularism, attacking them as instruments of 'internal imperialism' (al-isti'mar al-dakhili) or simply as foreign elements (wafid).[93] In a fundamental way, therefore, it questions the basic relationship between secularization, nationalism and progress propagated by both the liberal and materialist schools.

History has been an important element in Islamic thought since its beginning in the seventh century AD.[94] While often, perhaps principally, focused on the time of the Prophet and the early centuries, i.e. the Islamic period, an Islamic historiographical perspective has developed more recently with the emergence of the contemporary Islamic movement. Given that Islam lays claim to being a universal faith, it is important here to clarify the position of the Islamic current, and specifically of the Ikhwan, towards the concept of the nation and nationalism.[95] Critical of the Western variety of nationalism that is based on secular and materialist ideologies and worships the modern state, the Ikhwan has regarded the defence of the nation (watan), properly defined by divine principles, as a religious duty. This was not for territorial or political reasons but because it was a Muslim land: 'Nationalism (qawmiyya) in our minds attains the status of sacredness.' This marriage of ideas between Islam and nationalism, in which the nation became a place of 'religious self-respect' and a base for the promotion of the word of God, in effect, an Islamic state, underpins the historical discourse of the Islamic trend.

Like the other streams so far discussed, the Islamic current regards the period prior to First World War as the critical stage in the formation and configuration of national forces.[96] Bayumi describes the Egyptian political landscape as comprising two blocs: the progressive forces, led by the Islamic camp and including the Watani Party, which supported a radical national policy, and the reactionary forces, headed by the Umma Party, that adopted a moderate and accommodationist position towards the British occupation.[97] This division into two camps differed from Muhammad Anis' analysis which had regarded the Watani Party as a radical petit bourgeois party and al-Azhar as the voice of the Islamic movement, and even that of al-Rafi'i who had stressed above all else the Watani Party's commitment to British evacuation.[98] Yet, Bayumi's identification of the Watani Party as part of an Islamic current was not entirely new. 'Abd al-'Azim Ramadan had described the party in the same terms and, indeed, the political aims of Mustafa Kamil and the specific nature of his declared allegiance to the Ottoman Empire had long been the subject of debate among historians.[99] However, Bayumi's characterization of the policy of the Watani Party *was* different. Ramadan believed that the party's refusal to negotiate with the British until they had evacuated the country to be an uncompromising and ultimately futile position. Bayumi held it to be a principled attitude.[100] In effect, Bayumi's interpretation challenged the widespread assumption that secular, national forces represented the vehicle of progress, while Islamic tradition posed as a reactionary or traditionalist force.

Bayumi's analysis of the 1919 Revolution similarly criticized some of the basic assumptions of secular historiography and found fault with its failure to understand the public role of religion.[101] Invoking the *shari'a* and its recognition of equal legal rights for non-Muslim minorities as the basis for national unity, Bayumi held that religious factors formed the basis of the revolution and the source of the motivation for all classes, including the fellahin, to support it. The participation of the Copts in the revolution and the various pronouncements of Coptic leaders were proof that there was a complete merger of national and Islamic elements within the Islamic totality (*kul islami*). Accordingly, Bayumi censured secular historians for misrepresenting the events and aftermath of 1919 as a secular phenomenon and neglecting its religious dimension. While conceding that other elements did play a role, he insisted that the religious aspect was the most important: 'The political, economic and social factors were important in the language of establishing the revolution except that the religious factors came in the forefront of these.'[102]

In the aftermath of the 1919 Revolution, the Islamic current suffered a period of weakness both in Egypt and abroad. The mass support for the Wafd and the decline in the fortunes of the Watani Party, combined with the defeat of the Ottoman Empire and the abolition of the caliphate in 1924, meant that with the exception of al-Azhar the Islamic community had little formalized political voice. Bayumi blames Sa'd Zaghlul and his supporters for taking advantage of this weakness and moving the national movement away from its rightful place within an Islamic society towards the limited concept of Egyptian nationalism.[103] It was in reaction to these setbacks that the Ikhwan was founded by Hasan al-Banna in 1928 and formed an authentic part of the nationalist movement and the heir to the political legacy of the Watani Party (notwithstanding the fact that both parties existed side by side).[104] Bayumi emphasizes its strong and principled opposition to British imperialism and its commitment to the cause of national liberation and rejects the charge that the Ikhwan was a creature of the minority parties, an accusation refuted by its suppression by the government of al-Nuqrashi in 1948.

Tariq al-Bishri's revised analysis of the critical period between the end of the Second World War and the July Revolution consolidated and expanded this Islamic rereading.[105] In the first edition of *al-Haraka al-siyasiyya fi misr, 1945–52*, al-Bishri's narrative identified the Egyptian 'masses' (*al-jamahir*) as the central actor of the national movement and the communist movement as the political organization that best represented its aspirations.[106] When the study appeared in a second edition in 1983, the author retracted significant elements of this interpretation in a lengthy introduction (the main narrative remained unchanged). While his principle of the centrality of the masses was unmodified, al-Bishri had radically revised his views of the nature of the national struggle and the ideological and cultural values of Egyptian political parties. He explained,

> I only now begin to understand what I have [sic] not been able to understand during the 1960s when I was preparing this book, that is, there exists a general and important principle in the delimitation of the social and political map of Egypt during the past century. This principle is that the course of the Egyptian history and the social movement in whatever period are not only determined by the struggle between the nationalist movement and imperialism, nor are they only determined by the social struggle between classes with different interests, but they are also determined by the ideological struggle between *al-wafid* and *al-mawruth*.[107]

These two concepts, *al-wafid*, literally, that which comes from outside, and *al-mawruth*, that which 'consists of values, organizations, ideas, customs, morals and culture which have been bequeathed to the present society by previous generations',[108] provide the basis for distinguishing those elements of foreign and specifically Western origin from those part of the authentic Egyptian *turath* (heritage). According to al-Bishri, the struggle between *al-wafid* and *al-mawruth* during the nineteenth century resulted in the growing influence of Western concepts of secularism, socialism and modernity and the increasing abandonment of the *shari'a*, one of the principal sources of the *turath*. It was therefore part of the anti-imperialism struggle to retrieve the *turath* and resist any further encroachment of alien ideas. Al-Bishri applied this cultural, indeed, civilizational polarity, not only to the political struggle against the British but to his analysis of the Egyptian political scene. Accordingly, political parties and class interests are evaluated according to the degree in which they manifested the *turath* or foreign values and correspondingly rated as legitimate expressions or representatives of the national will.

In his discussion of the period before the First World War, like Bayumi al-Bishri regards the Watani Party as expressive of the authentic Egyptian national movement and the Umma Party as a product of Western cultural tradition and political ideas.[109] However, in the post-1919 period he recognizes a broader range of political forces – the Wafd, the Ikhwan and Misr al-Fatat – as representative of the nation. This bracketing of three apparently dissimilar forces may seem odd but for al-Bishri they each actualize, if imperfectly, different elements of the *turath*. As the party that led the nationalist movement after 1919, the Wafd is worthy of both praise and blame.[110] Its commitment to national unity and the extent of its popularity were unquestionable, and therefore sufficient proof of its authenticity, but its support of secular nationalism was Western in inspiration and contrary to the *turath*. However, its great failure was its unwillingness to embrace the cause of the masses for fear of disrupting the social order. In this way a great political opportunity was lost. Contrary to the liberal school, then, al-Bishri regarded the link between secularism, nationalism and progress, propagated by the Wafd during the 1920s, as an aberration and not a golden age of national unity.[111]

The most dramatic change in al-Bishri's reassessment is his attitude towards the Ikhwan. It had been a standard charge common to both the liberal and materialist schools to regard an Islamic political program as either traditional or reactionary. The latter charge was particularly aimed at the Muslim Brotherhood and Misr al-Fatat, who were branded as fascist organizations, hostile to the secular nationalism of the Wafd, and employed as tools of the king to further his autocratic ambition. The Muslim Brotherhood, particularly, was accused of obscurantism (*ghumud*) in its profession of Islam as a political program.[112] Al-Bishri rejects all these charges. Indeed, as the political organization that most openly embraced Islam, the Ikhwan is an authentic element of Egyptian culture.[113] He thus locates the Society within the political mainstream as the party and genuine agent of the Egyptian masses because it best understood the dangers of cultural imperialism and the dynamics of the struggle to be waged against secularization and Western ideas. Indeed, al-Bishri explains the development of support for the Muslim Brotherhood as a result of growing popular disenchantment with the Wafd.[114] Refuting the longstanding charge that the Muslim Brotherhood collaborated with the minor parties and the British occupier, al-Bishri argues that the Ikhwan's primary aim was not the struggle for political independence but for cultural and ideological values, exemplified in its advocacy of the implementation of the *shari'a*.[115] However, he finds fault with some aspects of the Ikhwan's political judgement, charging it with inflexibility (*jumud*) in failing to adapt the *shari'a* through *ijtihad* to the requirements of modern times. Moreover, its leader, Hasan al-Banna, failed to reassure Copts of their place within Islamic society and thereby threatened national unity.

Complementing al-Bishri's volte-face on the Ikhwan is his relegation of the communists to the status of agents of an alien ideology.[116] As an ideology that failed to give due recognition to Egyptian culture, al-Bishri rejects communism and its emphasis on class and international solidarity as contrary to the basic principles of an Islamic community. More recently, he has become particularly critical of the prominent role played by Jews within the movement, regarding this as motivated by a reaction against the increasing strength of the Islamic movement and an attempt to maintain the privileged position of Jews in Egyptian society. The policies employed within HADITU for the 'Egyptianization' (*tamsir*) and 'workerization' (*ta'mil*) of the movement were, for al-Bishri, simply tactics designed to conceal their real intentions.[117] This revisionist assessment of the communist movement, and especially the leadership of Henri Curiel, a quintessential figure in communist circles in the 1940s, was brought to the fore with the publication of Curiel's memoirs in the late 1980s, which provoked comment from al-Bishri, historians and former communists.[118]

Al-Bishri's view of Misr al-Fatat as the party whose ideology expressed an authentic Egyptian nationalism and exalted both its Islamic and pharaonic elements is also unusually sympathetic.[119] While acknowledging that the party initially supported the royalist program, he points to its change of slogan (in which the king was replaced with the people) as an important sign of its ideological reassessment. Further, he praises Young Egypt's awareness of the importance of the economic dimension of the national struggle, exemplified in the Piastre Plan and its forthright rejection of the foreign domination of industry. By putting forward a policy of land reform and economic liberation, Young Egypt laid claim to being a revolutionary organization. Its main failure, however, was its unwillingness to cooperate with the Wafd and the poor strategy of its leadership.[120]

NASSER IN ISLAMIC DISCOURSE

Al-Bishri's narrative in *al-Haraka al-siyasiyya* ends with the revolution in 1952 but elsewhere he has offered an interpretation of the Nasser regime.[121] Here his analysis distinguishes between different spheres of activity: foreign affairs, economic policy and the political process. Al-Bishri is most supportive of the foreign policy of the Nasser regime, particularly in its anti-imperialist and pan-Arab outlook, and its realization of the threat posed by Zionism. In economic affairs, he lauds the regime's recognition of the principle of economic independence, expressed in the implementation of the land reform and the nationalization of large parts of the economy, which paved the way for economic development and social justice. However, he is very critical of the authoritarian culture of the regime. Its abolition of political parties, the repression of opposition and the increase in the power of the executive, resulted in the alienation of the masses from political power. In addition, the reliance on trusted elements in the administration tended to strongly favour Muslims over Copts and thus endangered the cause of national unity.[122] The socialist phase of the revolutionary regime represents the high point of Western influence since its concepts of political and economic independence were adopted from the West and not adapted from the historical consciousness of Egypt.[123]

In his study of the period after 1952, Bayumi employs the theme of the corrupting foreign influence and stresses that the Ikhwan never knew the 'stain' (*ghadada*) of Western civilization.[124] While acknowledging the close connections between the Free Officers and the Ikhwan at the time of the coup in 1952, he explains that the basis for the disagreement between the two was the Ikhwan's refusal to join the 'communist camp' (*al-mu'askar al-shuyu'i*). In the same way the Ikhwan's conflict with Sadat came when he allied himself with the 'Western camp' (*al-mu'askar al-gharbi*).[125] For Bayumi, ultimately, the failure of the Nasser regime (and other nationalist regimes in Muslim countries) was its misguided attempt to impose a secular ideology on an Islamic society.

> We can say that the failure of the intellectual and political elite to introduce secular ideologies in an Islamic milieu, such as the attempts of Ataturk, 'Abd al-Nasir, Burgiba or the Ba'th Party, cannot be justified by political ignorance – keeping in mind that it was different from one to another – for which they are responsible. Rather, it is to be found in the incompetence of the elite governments who could not introduce an ideology for economic development that could lead to social justice and help in consolidating the basic elements of political legitimacy. Therefore most of the Muslim nations that suffer from economic crisis have no choice but to go back to an ideology that reinforces this legitimacy in themselves, and that is the Islamic ideology.[126]

While the historical interpretation of al-Bishri is grounded in a sober contemplation of the principles operating in Egyptian history, and Bayumi's work is presented in an orthodox academic format, some Islamist writers have criticized the conduct of the Nasser regime in a more unrestrained manner. In the pages of *al-Da'wa*, Muhammad 'Abd al-Quddus took advantage of the tenth anniversary of Nasser's death to present a broadside against the regime and its policies, listing a long catalogue of crimes committed against Egypt and the Egyptian people. Of the five general categories, the first significantly was the Islamic field (*al-majal al-islami*) in which 'Abd al-Quddus condemned the government for its massacre and imprisonment of those who called for the rule of Islamic law, denounced its misuse of *waqfs*, the abolition of the *shari'a* courts, the nomination of the shaykhs of al-Azhar for its own purposes, and its association with communism and Moscow. He went on to attack Nasser's performance on human rights, economic policy and in foreign affairs – the last which he regarded as being conspicuously hostile to Islam. He summed up the record,

> There is no doubt that the regime of 'Abd al-Nasir was absolutely the most evil of the ages [through] which Egypt has passed. It is not possible to compare this era to the current one or any other. The disasters of the age of 'Abd al-Nasir exceeded all imagination and resulted in the single result of the destruction of the Egyptian people in its worth, faith, character and nationalism and rubbed the name of Egypt in the dust by repeated defeats in every particular battle.[127]

'Umar Tilmisani, the head of the Ikhwan during the 1970s, reinforced the point. His book on the Nasser period provided another lengthy inventory, this time listing 81 sins of the regime.[128] He was particularly critical of Nasser's education policies.

> If the imperialists implemented an education system that had been suitable only for reproducing labourers, [then] Jamal 'Abd al-Nasir put barriers in the education curriculum that destroyed all Islamic meaning in the souls of the students, so that they graduated knowing nothing about their religion, that is, if it did not make them look at their religion with disrespect and resist holding onto its beliefs.[129]

These interpretations are neither comprehensive nor balanced assessments although their central preoccupation with the regime's consistent denigration of Islam and its promotion of Western and communist ideas are themes shared with the more refined works of al-Bishri and Bayumi.

The unwavering reference to the precepts of Islam as a source of religious authority and a standard of cultural authenticity and political thought and action is the primary characteristic of the Islamic school. Islam, or better a certain construction of Islam, provides the foundation for an understanding of the character of Egyptian nation and the principles of its history that eclipses all other cultural influences. As Bayumi states,

> Islam as a creed and culture managed to influence greatly every cultural aspect in Egypt, that is, its social, economic and cultural aspects. Nothing of the previous Pharaonic, Greek or Roman culture remained. Egyptian history before Islam therefore was limited to what we find in temples and museums. Thus, the thousands of minarets across the Nile Valley do not only represent the religious aspect that is restricted to religious practices, they show how deeply they influence the cultural and social life across the long periods in the history of Egypt. And in the same way that Islam influenced Egyptian culture, this culture with its ancient elements and the changes which took place in Egypt during the time of Islam, managed by its Islamic beliefs to become a unique Islamic nation and influence its Muslim neighbours, even those who preceded Egypt in embracing Islam.[130]

Yet, by positing Islam as the unifying concept of Egyptian history, the Islamic school suggests Egypt be characterized by a homogeneous and discrete cultural identity. While al-Bishri is broad in his definition of the *turath* – he includes both the Coptic Church and the secularist Wafd – the relationship between national identity and Islam as the essential quality of its authenticity effectively throws a cultural blanket over the whole of Egypt. It claims that, 'Egyptian history is the legacy of every Egyptian, whether he likes it or not.'[131]

WOMEN AND NATION: SYMBOLIC SUPPLEMENT OR DISSONANT DISTAFF?

In the liberal, materialist and Islamic schools of interpretation, women have been regarded as an integral part of the nation even if they are cast in different roles to express the values and interests of each discourse. While this can offer a certain depth to the analysis, women are neither a central concern nor agent in the narrative but rather function as a supplement, performing a symbolic or metaphorical role within the parameters of an essentially male construction. For this reason, women in these historical interpretations have often been a disjointed presence in which, when they appear, it is in a supporting, secondary and fleeting context. Only in more recent interpretations generated outside of the national mainstream, have women come to take on a more dissonant role which seeks to articulate an organic and relatively autonomous character.

In the interpretation of the liberal school, women are cast as symbols of the national awakening and contributors to the development of the national movement. In the former category the writings of Qasim Amin, *Tahrir al-mar'a* (1899) and *al-Mar'a al-jadida* (1900), stand as key milestones for a re-evaluation of the position of women in Egyptian society.[132] In this narrative the pioneering generation of women writers, such as 'A'isha al-Taymuriyya and Bahithat al-Badiya, serve as the symbols and manifestation of the social transformation of the late nineteenth century. In the political sphere, the participation of women in the upheavals after the First World War most dramatically announce the presence of women in the liberal narrative as they formed action committees, took part in nationalist demonstrations, and even provided martyrs to the sacred cause.[133] The establishment of the Wafdist Women's Central Committee in 1920 and of the Egyptian Feminist Union (EFU) in 1923, both under the presidency of Huda Sha'rawi, and the Sa'dist Committee for Women in 1925 under Sharifa Riyadh, gave increasing organizational expression to the contribution of women in the national struggle. Consistent with the political culture of the Wafd, Safiya Zaghlul, the wife of Sa'd Zaghlul, became *Umm al-misriyyin* ('Mother of Egyptians'), the embodiment of this ideal.

Within this stream of liberal nationalism there were different and opposing elements. At the beginning of the twentieth century the progressive ideas of Qasim Amin had been opposed by the traditional views of Tal'at Harb and Mustafa Kamil, themselves icons of the national movement. In the 1920s the moderate political program of the EFU concentrated on social issues and refrained from calling for equal political rights until 1935 while others associated with the Wafd, like Munira Thabit, took a more radical and aggressive tone calling for female suffrage in the mid-1920s. Nevertheless, at least during the lifetime of Sha'rawi, the EFU remained the dominant women's organization in agitating for recognition of the rights of Egyptian women. It also took up foreign policy issues supporting the Palestinian cause and a broader Arab agenda, symbolized by the foundation of the Arab Feminist Union in Cairo in 1944.[134] Even if the EFU lost vitality after Sha'rawi's death, the activism of bourgeois feminism reached its zenith in the years after the Second World War. The participation of women in the demonstrations of 1946, the emergence of the National Feminist Party and of Bint al-Nil under Fatima Ni'mat Rashid and Duriya Shafiq respectively signalled increasing enthusiasm for an active part in political life. Its militancy was most dramatically demonstrated with an occupation of the Egyptian parliament in 1951 and the hunger strike of Duriya Shafiq in 1954. The irony was that not until 1956, 3 years after political parties had been banned, did women finally gain the vote in Egypt.

While the materialist school offered a radical critique of liberal discourse in its understanding of economic forces and its use of class struggle as an analytical tool this did not lead to a radical reconception of the political or social role of women. In the hierarchy of the materialist school, class and nation came before gender or feminist issues. Nevertheless, women were active participants in the broad leftist movement. Particularly in the period after the Second World War, women joined the communist movement, belonged to progressive organizations such as the League of Young Women of Universities and Institutes and took part in the popular demonstrations of the 1940s and early 1950s.[135] In the labour movement the Association of Egyptian Working Women under Hikmat al-Ghazzali was formed after the Second World War.[136]

Nevertheless, the definitions of political and economic activity employed by materialist analyses had the effect of largely excluding women. The communist movement did call for recognition of women's rights in its program but it was predominantly male in character and the existence of a separate section for women in HADITU suggests a secondary status.[137] The focus of the materialist school on the working class likewise favoured the waged, urban and organized worker, a sector in which male workers were overwhelmingly the majority, and the great number of women who worked in domestic or unpaid employment were left outside of the frame of reference. Later specialized materialist works inspired by Arab socialism shifted emphasis and examined the participation of women in the workforce as the main measure of the liberation of women and social equality.[138] However, this analysis offered little breadth and was criticized for its definition of categories such as 'labour force' and the unemployed.[139] The Nasserist stream of the materialist school aligned with progressive statism could point to the benefits for women under the regime: grant of the franchise in 1956, the election of the first women to parliament in the same year and the appointment of the first woman, Hikmat Abu Zayd, to the cabinet in 1962. Ultimately, however, in the materialist school gender concerns have laboured behind the priority given to class and national discourse.

Wedded to the maintenance of religious and traditional values, the Islamic trend casts women in a different role to the liberal and materialist schools. Couched in a discourse of resistance to the forces of political secularization, social transformation and the impact of Western cultural influence, it offers a critique that both modifies and challenges secular interpretations. Bayumi's discussion of the Ikhwan's position on the issue of women in Egyptian society offers a good example of a revisionist reading of the standard liberal narrative.[140] Far from a call for the liberation of women Bayumi sees in the writings of Qasim Amin the alien hand of Western influence. He contrasts Amin's views with those of Mustafa Kamil and Mustafa Sadiq al-Rafi'i, both of whom opposed the changes that were transforming the social role of women: greater educational opportunities, unveiling (*sufur*), and mixing (*ikhtilat*) of the sexes. Rather than a voice for women, Huda Sha'rawi is regarded as a conduit of Western penetration and an instrument of the undermining of Egyptian cultural values. As confirmation of the alien origin of her ideas, Bayumi points to her study trips to Paris and America and her use of material so collected in the statements and illustrations found in EFU publications. In contrast, Bayumi discusses approvingly the feminist activism of organizations that promoted Islamic values, particularly the Society of the Muslim Sisters, as the embodiment of the authentic women's movement.[141] Consistent with their view of the position of women in society, the Muslim Sisters confined themselves to issues of social welfare and matters such as women-only tram carriages and remained firm in their opposition to unveiling and mixed education. The negative attitude of not only the Ikhwan but also al-Azhar to voting rights for women and women members in parliament on religious grounds confirmed their opposition to female participation in public life.

In the three schools of interpretation discussed here women have been incorporated into each discourse in a supplementary and secondary role which gives priority to certain social elements and political activities. In the liberal school women are mostly upper or middle class attached, either by marriage or through other connections, to the male political class. The materialist analysis, in so far as it is concerned with women's issues, highlights the contribution of women as cadres in the movement and in the workforce while the Islamic trend casts women as a repository and defender of traditional values consistent with religious belief and cultural practice. Nevertheless, as national discourses they share some common ground, most clearly in their opposition to the British. Thus, in 1952 Saiza Nabarawi of the EFU, communist activist Inji Aflatun, and Zaynab al-Ghazzali of the Muslim Sisters and other feminist activists could come together to establish the Women's Committee for Popular Resistance and demonstrate against the occupation.[142]

The move to a historical discourse in which women are subjects rather than objects or constituents has been the impetus behind a different historical approach. On a personal level this has been evident in the memoirs published by women. The personal histories of Nabawiyya Musa, Nawal al-Sa'dawi and Leila Ahmed offer insights into aspects of women's life less alloyed and even counter to the male discourse of the public space. Even those women whose writing is embedded with national political values such as Huda Sha'rawi, Inji Aflatun, and Zaynab al-Ghazzali present elements that speak of a level of historical experience beyond the boundaries of the liberal, materialist and Islamic constructs. Most recently, the Women and Memory Forum has sought to promote a systematic and radical re-evaluation of the historical role of women in Egypt. This is being done through a number of strategies. First, there has been a program of republication of the writings of pioneer Egyptian feminists to recall and highlight their role and contribution to Egyptian life. Second, it has encouraged a critical evaluation of the male origin of historical sources and the impact this has had on the construction of scholarship.[143] Above all, the Forum seeks to restore the historical consciousness of women as active participants and calls for 'gender-conscious historical accounts and legacies'.[144] The project is still in its early days and it remains to be seen how this approach might deal and interact with the other markers of social identity such as nationality, ethnicity, class, and religion.[145]

As politically influential streams of thought, each of the mainstream schools of historical interpretation has incorporated, co-opted and constrained women within their discourse with little autonomous voice. While they can point to a record of the participation of women in 'national' events, organizations and describe (or prescribe) their place in Egyptian society more generally, there are many historical issues relevant to women that do not sit comfortably within the existing national frameworks. The development and political impact of issues of education, social welfare, social attitudes towards the veil, polygamy, divorce, prostitution, personal status, and mixing between the sexes, add a complexity that the national discourses cannot easily contain. Recent work on hitherto neglected aspects of Egyptian society, such as prostitution, suggest that there may be more interest in these issues but it remains to be seen if this work merely supplements the existing national narratives or challenges them.[146]

As national discourses the liberal, materialist and Islamic currents share the central theme of the national liberation of Egypt and the struggle against imperialism. However, each school offers its own variation according to its conception of the arena of the political contest and the configuration of national identity within Egyptian society. These different conceptions bring conflicting attitudes towards different phases of the contemporary period. For the liberal school, the period after the 1919 Revolution represents the golden age of liberal democracy in which united support of the national movement provided the most pristine expression of the national will, subsequently to be undermined by the machinations of the British and the King. By contrast, the materialist school regards this period as one of lost opportunities characterized by social inequality and class conflict. It is under the progressive if authoritarian hand of the revolutionary regime that substantial political successes were achieved. For the Islamic current as represented by al-Bishri, both the misguided secularism of the parliamentary period and the repression of the Nasser period, are gloomy political times and it is by drawing on the traditions of the past that a more authentic polity might be achieved in the future. Feminist interpretations both reinforce and multiply these perspectives as well as offer the potential for a radical reassessment of the construction of the national history.

The conflicting interpretations and hierarchy of political actors posed by these historical schools are a reflection of the main political contest and evidence of the contested definition of the nation in contemporary Egyptian historiography. Paradoxically, as national discourses, each of these interpretations is based on the implicit assumption of an essentially homogeneous society (even if some elements are seen as marginal or foreign) and a common national identity. Yet the contested nature of national politics and the heterogeneity of Egyptian society suggest that the claims to speak for 'all Egyptians' are illusory. This is the central dilemma for the historian of contemporary Egyptian history: if Egypt constitutes a collective entity, how does the historian deal with the diversity of class, religion, gender, culture and political ideology?

Part II

NATIONAL DISSONANCE

One of the greatest achievements of Sa'ad Zaghlul was that he
made it possible for Moslems and Copts to work together for
the good of Egypt regardless of their differences. Someday, if
the ideals of the revolution prevail, it will be possible for the
Greeks, Jews, Armenians, Syrians, Lebanese, and other minorities to follow in the footsteps of the Copts ... [and] we shall
all be Egyptians together in what I hope will be the modern
equivalent of the cosmopolitan society that flourished under
the Umayad dynasty in Spain

Muhammad Najib[1]

The words of Muhammad Najib, written in the aftermath of the July Revolution, both recognized the existing heterogeneity of Egyptian society and
projected a pluralist vision of national unity. Despite Najib's intention, the
Revolution, in fact, presided over a narrowing of the national identity and
not the evolution of the multi-ethnic society he envisioned. Over time, even
the much prized unity between Muslims and Copts has come under strain.
This process of the contraction of Egyptian national identity towards a more
narrow, chauvinist nationalism was a product of political and ideological
forces that are also manifest in contemporary historiography.[2]

Earlier discussion has been concerned with the political development and
discourse of contemporary historical interpretation within a national framework. Each interpretation, I have argued, is founded on a particular characterization of the Egyptian nation which seeks to aggregate the disparate
elements of Egyptian society and orientate them around a core political value
(or group representing such a value) in a national narrative. As discourses, each
has asserted a national vision that has marginalized, obscured, even silenced
from the historical record the role of certain actors in Egyptian society
regarded as unimportant, irrelevant or even hostile to the national vision.

The following two chapters discuss the historiographical fortunes of two
subaltern groups in Egyptian society who have in different degress been
historiographical casualties. The first group are the Copts, who have a

continuous but understated profile in Egyptian public life; the second are the *mutamassirun*, the resident communities of Greeks, Italians, Armenians and Jews, who maintained a considerable presence in Egypt from the middle of the nineteenth century until the early 1960s. The discussion examines the portrayal of these two non-national entities in the discourse of the liberal, materialist and Islamic schools focusing on their different characterizations and contrasting these representations with accounts written from Coptic and *mutamassir* perspectives. In different ways, these two examples illustrate some of the boundaries and conceptual limitations of national discourse.

5

THE COPTS

The public status of Copts is perhaps *the* sensitive issue in contemporary Egyptian historiography. As a substantial Christian population in the midst of a Muslim majority, Copts are a unique case of a group with uncontestable claims to being Egyptian and yet which occupy an ambiguous status in the national body politic. Even if the basis of this ambiguity was rarely articulated, the recent re-emergence of *ta'ifiyya* (sectarianism) after the tranquility of the Nasser years has provoked a historiographical reassessment from a number of quarters, not least from members of the Coptic community itself. An examination of twentieth century Coptic historiography therefore raises questions regarding the character of the national culture and the relationship between religion and state. In short, it has significant implications for the talisman of modern politics, the national secular state.

As the physical and cultural descendants of the pre-Islamic Egyptian population, Copts represent an enduring element in Egypt's society. While their fortunes varied under the authority of the late Roman and Byzantine era, Coptic culture entered a long period of steady decline following the arrival of Islam in 641 and Egypt's incorporation into the Umayyad Empire. Under Islamic law, Copts were relegated to the protected if second-class status of *ahl al-dhimma* which exempted them from military service in return for the payment of a poll tax. Over the succeeding centuries, as a succession of Islamic dynasties consolidated the position of Islam as the majority faith, the proportion of Copts in the total population decreased, doubtless abetted by the civic advantages gained from converting to Islam. Religious observance was maintained but Coptic as a language gradually fell into disuse. By the nineteenth century, the Coptic population had stabilized and a pattern of social equilibrium had been established between Coptic and Muslim communities.

Today, despite a recent trend of emigration to Australia, the United States and Canada, the Coptic presence in Egypt is undeniable if politically muted. A precise estimate of its size is difficult to ascertain, principally, as will become clear, because of political sensitivities. Estimates have varied widely from 3 per cent to as much as 20 per cent of the total population. In 1977,

147

President Carter caused a flurry by stating publicly that there were 7 million Copts out of a population of 41 million, i.e. about 17 per cent.[3] This percentage is often reported privately though the official government figure stands at about 6 per cent, the Church itself claims around 15 per cent and immigrant groups have gone as high as 20 per cent.[4] A figure of about 10 per cent of the population, i.e. about 6 million, is probably not wildly inaccurate.[5]

The distinction between Copt and Muslim is, strictly speaking, one of religious affiliation, with no clear geographical, linguistic or class correspondence. Copts form neither a distinct socio-economical category nor are they a regionally based population. They are represented throughout all levels of Egyptian society, amongst the fellahin, the landowning class and in business circles. Though present in relatively greater numbers in Upper Egypt, Copts live throughout the settled Egypt, both in urban and rural settings. On the face of it, therefore, Cromer's famous remark has some validity, '... the only difference between the Copt and the Moslem is that the former is an Egyptian who worships in a Christian Church, whilst the latter is an Egyptian who worships in a Mohammedan mosque'.[6] Yet while the Ottoman millet system had guaranteed the status of non-Muslim minorities, it also meant that religious affiliation itself *had* legal implications. Excluded from high political office Copts were prominent in senior administrative positions and, for example, were conspicuous as tax farmers due to the Muslim antipathy towards usury. Thus there was a difference between the two groups because religious status had a public and therefore political meaning.

Given this tradition, it is not surprising that since at least the time of Cromer there has been a persistent undercurrent of Coptic activity in the political arena. Periodically political parties or social movements have emerged seeking to articulate a Coptic voice, usually at times of difficult communal relations. This most notably occurred in the early years of the twentieth century and again during the last years of the monarchy.[7] Since that time, the constitutional prohibition on political organizations based on religious affiliation may have masked similar projects.[8] Nevertheless, the national Coptic press has testified to a vibrant public presence, reporting on issues of general importance and at times maintaining a high profile in national politics.[9] Since 1958, the only national Coptic newspaper has been *Watani* ('My Nation'), a weekly established by a group of Coptic notables. In 1981, it attracted Sadat's ire and was suspended, not resuming publication until 1984. Following this clash with state authority, *Watani* has maintained a rather conservative, measured Coptic voice dealing with national, community and church issues.[10]

One matter that has fuelled a Coptic voice in public debate has been the issue of government employment. Since at least the beginning of the twentieth century there have been claims of persistent discrimination against Copts in government service. At this time, Copts were favoured occupying 45 per cent of all government posts; by 1927 this had dropped dramatically to a mere 9 per cent.[11] There have been more specific charges of a policy of exclusion of Copts from particular ministries. Prominent in the Departments of Communications, Public Works, Health, Finance and Justice, Copts have been noticeably fewer in the 'sensitive' ministries of Education, Defence and Foreign Affairs. Rarely were Copts appointed to senior government positions, and never did they serve as governors. A similar phenomenon was found in the armed forces, where Copts served but almost never in the upper ranks.[12]

The political events of recent years have, if any proof was needed, demonstrated that communal difficulties between Copts and Muslims were neither a hangover of an earlier era nor, as often claimed, simply the result of imperialist manipulation. One more immediate explanation was the policy of President Sadat of clamping down on the left and using Islamic groups, particularly the Ikhwan, as a counterbalance to consolidate his political position. Sadat's tactic of pre-empting the Islamists by styling himself as the 'Pious President' and employing a religious idiom in his political rhetoric injected a dangerous element into national politics that released social tensions that had been repressed during the Nasser years. The Coptic Church had been energized by the appointment of the young and vigorous Pope Shinuda III in 1971, who became a vocal defender of Coptic interests and took on a more active role in public affairs in a way that contrasted with its traditionally quietist approach. In January 1977 at a Coptic Congress in Alexandria, Shinuda voiced a number of concerns and called on Copts to fast in protest at moves to apply Islamic legislation to non-Muslims.[13] Seemingly heedless, Sadat pressed on, introducing the referendum of 1980 which made the *shari'a* the basic source for the national legal code. This strategy, in concert with the consequences of the *infitah* (economic liberalization) unleashed an explosive mix. For the first time in many years outbreaks of violent *ta'ifiyya* became increasingly common. Khanka in 1972, Asyut, Alexandria in 1980 and notoriously at al-Zawiyya al-Hamra in June 1981 were the scenes of violent sectarian clashes.

At the beginning of the 1980s the situation was beginning to get out of hand. While castigating the Islamists for their rising militancy, Sadat at the same time lashed out at the Copts, accusing them publicly of wanting to set up their own state in Upper Egypt.[14] In September 1981, the President moved against his critics, arresting many prominent figures, including Shinuda, and dissolving a number of Coptic and Muslim associations.[15] Following his assassination in October 1981, the country entered a period of relative calm but, since the second half of the 1980s, increasing incidents of *ta'ifiyya* have again become a regular occurrence.[16] Indeed, the revival of a religious idiom in politics has continued to be a feature of the Egyptian political scene. For these reasons, despite the undoubted integration between Muslim and Copts on many levels of Egyptian society, the continuing pattern of tension in communal relations provides ample justification for considering

Copts as a specific cultural-religious group and, at a some level, a distinct socio-political identity.

A QUIETIST ACADEMY

In Chapter 3 it was proposed that non-academic historians expressed a greater range of historical interpretation and a closer engagement with contemporary political issues than has generally been the case with academic historians. This is no more marked than in the field of contemporary Coptic historiography where historians of the political street, journalists, lawyers, political commentators and intellectuals, both Coptic and Muslim, have been prominent in addressing the issue of intercommunal relations. The diffidence shown by the academy on Coptic contemporary issues is, on some counts, quite surprising. One might have expected the changing tenor of Egyptian nationalism from the 1930s, the rise of the Ikhwan, and the re-emergence of Islam as a political force from the 1970s to have provoked a corresponding historical reassessment of the place of Copts in Egyptian society. The appearance of *ta'ifiyya* in the late 1940s and again from the 1970s onwards alone has provided sufficient grounds for a fuller consideration of the historical dimensions of the issue. And yet, relatively little reaction has appeared from university history departments. At an international academic conference dedicated to Egyptian historiography of the 1919–52 period in Cairo in 1987, which was attended by a large number of Egyptian academics, writers and intellectuals, not one paper dealt with the issue of Muslim and Coptic relations in the national community.[17]

This apparent lack of interest on the part of academic historians may be explained in a number of ways: the small number of Copts who are modern historians, the institutional culture of the public education system and considerations of political strategy. The relative absence of Coptic modern historians seems odd, given the prominence of the Coptic middle class in government bureaucracy and their reputed talent for foreign languages and administration at the beginning of the century. However, the culture of the education system has tended to steer Coptic students away from the humanities.[18] Salama Musa, a Copt and one of the exceptional Egyptian men of letters, pointed to the obstacles of non-Muslim students studying the humanities as late as the 1950s:

> ... it might be noted that specialization in Arabic language and literature is confined to Mohammedan students not only at the Azhar, but also at Dar el-Ulum, a college which has been in existence about half a century. Christian and Jewish students can specialize in Arabic language and literature in the faculty of literature at Fuad University, but since they know they will never be accepted as

teachers, they do not study under this faculty...The teaching of literature and language has always been the best way for a man of letters to begin his career, and it explains why Christians have not been conspicuous in Egypt's literary life. This does not mean that there are no Christian literary figures, but in proportion to their number, which is about two million, and to their higher educational standards, there are very few.[19]

The observation as far as it applies to historians holds true. In the late nineteenth century Mikha'il Sharubim (1861–1920) was probably the first modern historian of any note with a Coptic background. Sharubim had the advantage of coming from a notable family, playing a leading part in community affairs as well as holding a number of government posts including being a judge of the State Court of al-Mansura in 1884.[20] His history in four volumes, a survey of Egyptian history from ancient times until the end of the reign of the Tawfiq, has received praise for its judicious use of sources and balanced presentation.[21] Thereafter, apart from an exceptional case such as Salama Musa himself, it is difficult to find any Copt writing on modern history, and certainly not in the university system, until the 1960s.[22]

Musa was writing on the eve of the July Revolution which was subsequently to improve access to education for all Egyptians. There are now a considerable number of Coptic intellectuals and yet few are found amongst the ranks of modern historians within the academy.[23] A recent case in the Ministry of Education demonstrates that this institutional bias is not a thing of the past. When asked by a ministry official to supervise the history exam for *al-thanawiyya al-'amma*,[24] Ra'uf 'Abbas, a (Muslim) professor of modern history at Cairo University, declined, citing pressures of work but suggested a (Coptic) colleague in his place. On being told that appointing a Copt would be contrary to the security regulations, 'Abbas went public on the matter in protest, only to be reproved by the minister for not privately bringing the issue to his attention and further was accused of damaging the cause of national unity.[25] Such institutional attitudes in part explain why Copts have generally preferred or been steered towards studies in medicine, engineering and pharmacy – disciplines which provide employment opportunities outside the public sector, or applied their talents in business.[26] Where there *are* Coptic historians they most often specialize in earlier periods, particularly the ancient and Coptic eras.[27] Even those Copts that *are* modern historians feel constrained in writing on relations between Copts and Muslims, preferring to avoid the subject and to leave it to others. One of the few Coptic modern historians professed the view that religious affiliation had nothing to do with politics despite having published something on recent outbreaks of *ta'ifiyya*.[28] Another acknowledged that the sensitivity of the issue and the prevailing political atmosphere meant it was difficult for

Copts to publish certain material: Copts had to be cautious and rely on Western scholars to research and publish on these matters.[29]

Of course, it is not only Copts who can write on issues of Coptic–Muslim relations. Yet the seeming reluctance of Muslim academics to engage with this issue in a contemporary setting may stem from the complicity between the university and the state in establishing the acceptable parameters of national discourse. Since the establishment of the Egyptian University, the concept of national unity has been a central pillar of academic historiography of the post-1919 period. Discussion of the Copts as a separate entity in any political sense might be seen as, if not deliberately undermining the cause of national unity, then at least an encouragement to others to do so. A Coptic discourse, perhaps even more than an Islamic discourse, potentially affronts this sacred cow of academic historiography. By querying the secular basis of national politics, so the argument goes, one is lending aid and reinforcement to the legitimacy of a religious political idiom and implicitly assisting an Islamic discourse. At heart, the issues raised by modern Coptic historiography are thought to question, and perhaps threaten, the unity of Egyptian society and the stability of the secular state. Similar concerns were voiced long ago by Ahmad Lutfi al-Sayyid in 1908 during a time of tense communal relations,

> Those who set out to arouse the religious sensibilities of either the Copts or the Muslims by way of speeches or articles, however praiseworthy their purpose or however honorable their aim, reap from the whirlwind they stir up only the destruction of the [existing] solidarity among the individuals of the nation, and widen the distance between the two brothers. The Muslims and the Copts are far enough apart as it is – considering that they comprise the body of a single nation – neither praying together nor intermarrying. Why should we go out of our way to exaggerate these differences which are [as yet] harmless, and add to them other differences which would destroy our national community.[30]

This apprehension of exacerbating Muslim–Copt relations by publicly discussing them still seems influential amongst academic historians. With some limited exceptions, academic studies have tended to confine treatment of the theme to the pre-First World War period, when it could hardly be disregarded. Thereafter, there is little reference made to Copts in the analysis of the contemporary period. In the preface to her book on the 'liberal period' of 1922–36, Afaf Marsot (niece of Lutfi al-Sayyid) felt it important enough to state, 'I want to point out that any general reference in this book to Egyptians includes both Copts and Muslims who share the same characteristics and traits that make up the Sons of the Nile'. Thereafter she made scant reference to the two religions.[31] Even with the outbreak of incidents of *ta'ifiyya* from the 1970s, the reaction amongst academic historians in terms of exploring the historical roots of the phenomenon has been remarkably muted.

Finally, there is a tendency in academia to marginalize Coptic history as peripheral or irrelevant to the national narrative. When Muhammad 'Afifi, a young historian at Cairo University, published his doctorate on Copts in the Ottoman period, he was asked by many Muslims, 'Why are you studying *Coptic* [i.e. their] history?', and by some Copts, 'Why are you studying *our* history?'[32] Ghali Shukri, a Coptic intellectual, pointed to the systematic and institutionalized pattern of discrimination and devaluation of aspects of Coptic culture and history.

> It's amazing that the departments of philosophy and history in our universities take an interest in Christian history and the history of the church in Europe, but Coptic Egypt has completely dropped out of sight, except for the Coptic Museum and the Coptic religious institutions. Our school systems, our national broadcasting, our literature and newspapers, our national holidays – and one hears only about Pharaonic Egypt, Greek-Roman Egypt, Islamic Egypt. It is astonishing that we do not recognize a Coptic Egypt, that is, a Christian Egypt, an Egyptian Egypt. This is even more astonishing in light of the fact that...what has survived [from] Coptic Egypt ...are people who live among us like an authentic scarlet thread in the weave of the Egyptian nation...As if the Islamic conquest was the beginning of the history of Egypt, and the non-Muslims are the uninvited guests of this history.[33]

Public discussion, even in an academic context, continues to be a political minefield. In 1994 when the Ibn Khaldun Centre for Developmental Studies sought to stage a conference on the issue of minorities, it was denounced for applying such a label to the Copts. Still, there are some signs that the climate may be slowly changing. Following a sustained press campaign, the Ministry of Education announced the formation of a committee of historians in April 1999 to revise school history textbooks. Chaired by 'Abd al-'Azim Ramadan and including historians Yunan Labib Rizq and Ra'uf 'Abbas amongst others, it aims to introduce the hitherto neglected Coptic era into the curriculum. Nevertheless, sensitivities remain high. Already a member of the committee has criticized the Ibn Khaldun Centre for wanting 'a Coptic history and an Islamic history' rather than 'a history for all Egyptians'.[34]

COPTIC INSTITUTIONS

The apparent neglect of a Coptic perspective in state academic institutions has prompted a reaction from within the community itself to promote cultural and historical scholarship both as a means of reviving Coptic culture and to maintain a presence in national affairs. Such efforts began as early as 1908 with the establishment of the Sunday School Movement by Habib Jirjis aimed at reviving a traditional and stagnant church.[35] Since 1947 the Movement has published a journal, *Majallat Madaris al-Ahad*, which has served as a forum for scholarly works on community history. Another project was the formation of a Committee of Coptic History in 1919 to promote Coptic history in community schools.[36] Other more ambitious moves have sought to set up institutions that might speak to a national audience. The creation of the Coptic Museum in 1908 by Murqus Sumayka and the establishment of the Society for Coptic Archaeology by Mirrit Butrus Ghali in 1934 gave the Christian element of Egyptian culture greater visibility.[37] However, it was not until 1954 that an institution of higher education dedicated to the study of Coptic history and culture was founded. In that year, with the support of the Coptic Church, the Higher Institute of Coptic Studies (*Ma'had al-dirasat al-qibtiyya*) was established in Cairo under the presidency of 'Aziz 'Atiyya to address the urgent need to revive Coptic studies.[38] Enrolment was non-denominational but students were required to hold a university degree or a diploma from the Clerical College. Despite limited resources, since then the Institute has continued to provide an environment for research across a broad range of subjects of Coptic culture including history, law, music and art.

It was characteristic of the cautious attitude of the time that the Higher Institute of Coptic Studies confined itself to the study of Coptic culture and history in the Coptic era, i.e. the centuries between the Roman period and the arrival of Islam. Modern history and politics were avoided. Others, however, saw the need to raise an appreciation of the Coptic contribution in the contemporary period. In 1951 there had been a call for the formation of a Committee of Historical Studies to remind Egyptians of the role played by Copts in the national movement but it appears to have come to nothing.[39] From the late 1950s *Watani* went some way to filling this need, particularly with the launching of its historical page some years later. This latter feature, however, has been conservative in tone, restricting itself primarily to the events of the 1919 Revolution and ecclesiastical matters and, according to one Coptic intellectual, is 'a page of dead people'.[40] More recently, the Coptic Centre for Social Studies and Cultural Promotion (*al-Markaz al-qibti li'l-dirasat al-ijtima'iyya wa'l-tanmiyya al-thaqafiyya*), based at the Centre of St Mark for Social Services in Madinat Nasr, has made a more public effort. With church support, it has sought to engage in issues of contemporary history and politics by sponsoring activities such as inviting notable Egyptian intellectuals from a wide range of political views to speak on matters of national interest.[41] Following the lifting of restrictions on the establishment of private universities in June 1996, the idea of a Coptic University has been canvassed by a group of Coptic businessmen, although the Church has opposed this.[42] Finally the Coptic diaspora, well established in the United States, Canada and Australia by the 1970s, has come to play a role in promoting academic work. *The Coptic Encycloedia*, represents the fruits of a collaboration that brought together the work of both Egyptian and international scholars with the financial support of the Egyptian government, the National Endowment for the Humanities in the USA, the Coptic Church and Coptic communities throughout the world. Sweeping and ambitious in scope this multi-volume work, produced under the energetic editorship of 'Aziz 'Atiyya, provides a comprehensive coverage of Coptic history and culture from the Coptic era up until modern times.[43]

COPTS IN CONTEMPORARY HISTORICAL DISCOURSE

This record of continuing efforts to raise the historical profile of Copts and promote the study and dissemination of Coptic culture has been a reaction to the relative pattern of neglect of Copts as a distinct presence in contemporary historical discourse. National historiography, predicated on the unity and indivisibility of the nation, has shown little inclination to draw attention to the Muslim–Copt dimension of Egyptian society unless the poor state of intercommunal relations has made it unavoidable. Even then, the reaction, certainly from the academy, has been restrained. Nevertheless, the manner of representation of the Coptic presence in the national community employed by different national currents of historiography, such as the liberal, materialist and Islamic schools, provides an interesting basis for comparison with histories written from a Coptic perspective.

THE LIBERAL SCHOOL: UNDER THE PROTECTION OF THE WAFD

The liberal school is based on a secular view of the Egyptian nation and characterizes Copts as an integrated element in political life. With the emergence of the national movement as its principal focus, it stressed the motif of national harmony between Muslim and Copt during the Revolution of 1919 when crescent and cross were united. It is, therefore, little inclined to discuss Copts as a distinct public entity or the actions of individual Copts unless it contributes to this image. Further, it gives little prominence to incidents of difficult intercommunal relations or violent sectarianism save to deplore it and invoke the spirit of 1919 as epitomizing the true embodiment of the national identity and spirit of the Egyptian nation.

Despite the disinclination to focus on the sectarian aspect of Egyptian society, even the liberal school cannot ignore the poor state of communal relations prior to the First World War. The Coptic Congress held to air certain grievances in Asyut in March 1911 was a clear indication of a high state of political tension and level of dissatisfaction felt by some Copts regarding their status in the Egyptian national community. In response, the Egyptian Conference at Heliopolis was convened, attended by the leaders of both the Umma and Watani Parties, Ahmad Lutfi al-Sayyid and 'Abd al-'Aziz Jawish respectively. It urged tolerant coexistence and passed resolutions asserting that political rights should not be based on religious affiliation and that Copts as a community should not be entitled to any special financial aid. In its assessment of these communal problems, the liberal school generally lays the blame on the manipulation and divisive policies of British rule.[44] The assassination of Coptic Prime Minister, Butrus Ghali, by a member of the Watani Party in 1910 is therefore an action motivated by hostility towards Ghali's pro-British policies rather than for any religious reason. By contrast, the liberal school has tended to underplay the ambiguous pro-Ottoman rhetoric of Mustafa Kamil and instead highlighted his role as a strong nationalist leader.[45]

The 1919 Revolution swept away the communal tension of prewar Egypt with a great display of national unity and secular consensus, immortalized in the slogan, 'Religion is for God and the nation for all' (al-din li'allah wa'l-watan li'l-jami'an).[46] The spirit of this unanimity of purpose and basis for collective identity among Egyptians was institutionalized in the Wafd, whose leadership included prominent Copts, the so-called 'Coptic pillars' of the party, such as Makram 'Ubayd, Wasif Ghali and Wisa Wasif. Its great victory in 1923, which represented a triumph for secularism and national unity, was the rejection by the Constitutional Commission of the idea of proportional representation for Copts, even if the Wafdist leadership was not actively involved in this decision.[47] Under the new constitution, Copts were to stand before the electorate without any special consideration. Thereafter, in the liberal narrative of the period up until the 1952 Revolution, the Wafd embodies the national, secular ideal and acts as guarantor to Copts of their inclusion within the national community. In short, the Wafd was the 'political home of the Copts' (bayt al-aqbat al-siyasi).[48]

It is characteristic of the liberal school that it should emphasize the political platform of the Wafd and the significance of its large Coptic membership as the foundation for this concept of secular unity. Just as Sa'd Zaghlul embodied the will of the nation, so the presence of Copts and especially of Makram 'Ubayd amongst the Wafd leadership, symbolized the participation of the Coptic community in the national movement. This approach is typified in Mustafa al-Fiqi's study of the post-1919 period which takes Ubayd's career as the long-time secretary-general of the Wafd as the personal manifestation of this political ideal.[49] Al-Fiqi explains the reasons for his focus on 'Ubayd:

Both as a personality and in his political career, Makram Ebeid was the very embodiment of the thought, feelings and ambitions of an individual coming from a minority community...[which was] to enable him to act as the main representative of the Copts in the modern National Movement.[50]

Accordingly, al-Fiqi charts the fortunes of Copts within the national community by following the career of 'Ubayd as the second most important figure of the Wafd during the 1930s until his break with al-Nahhas and the party in 1942. More than many historians, al-Fiqi records the communal tensions of the late 1940s and early 1950s though his assessment that the situation would have been better managed if 'Ubayd had remained in the Wafd seems superficial.[51]

The Nasser period has provoked a more ambiguous response from the liberal school. The banning of political parties and the absence of any significant number of Copts in the military – now, in effect, the political class – meant there was little opportunity for their participation in public life.[52] Nevertheless, Nasser's policies were inspired by a strong secular nationalism and, especially in the field of education, proved an important avenue of social mobility for many Copts. Further, despite a number of prominent Free Officers being close to circles within the Ikhwan, the regime maintained a strong hostility towards the Brotherhood and politically militant forms of Islam. Indeed, Nasser himself made a personal point of maintaining good relations with the Coptic Church.

There were always a few difficulties with the liberal portrayal of 1919 as a victory for secular nationalism and the crystallization of national unity between Muslims and Copts. The 1923 constitution, despite claims for its secularism, had recognized Islam as the official religion of state.[53] While the Wafd, as the self-proclaimed representative of the nation, was regarded as the natural party for Copts and the most effective guarantee of their rights, throughout much of the interwar period other political forces were less supportive of this position. The increasing profile of the Ikhwan and Misr al-Fatat in the 1930s highlighted internal tensions in the Egyptian community and reintroduced an overtly religious tone into national politics. The Liberal Constitutionalist Party, itself secular in principal, criticized the Wafd for being controlled by Copts.[54] Throughout his public life 'Ubayd had to defend himself against attacks based on his religious affiliation and despite his status as the outstanding Coptic politician of the period, his political rhetoric which employed religious references caused disquiet amongst some Copts. His stock political phrase that if he was 'a Copt by religion, he was a Muslim by fatherland' left some of his coreligionists cold.[55] Moreover, the claims of the Wafd to be the 'political home of the Copts' had only relative force. The Wafd had neither a monopoly on Coptic support nor cabinet appointments – indeed during the mid-1940s, more than one anti-Wafdist cabinet included two Coptic Ministers.[56] Wafdist claims to being political guarantor of the Copts were diminished by 'Ubayd's departure from the party in 1942 which saw many but not all Copts follow him to form the Wafdist Bloc (al-Kutla al-wafdiyya).[57] Others, such as Ibrahim Faraj and Sa'd Fakhri 'Abd al-Nur, stayed with the Wafd holding prominent positions in the party (both later served as secretaries-general). By this time it was clear that the Wafd itself was changing and realigning itself according to religious considerations as sectarian tensions increased.[58]

While the prominence it ascribed to the Wafd banished the liberal school to the margins of acceptable historical scholarship during the Nasser years, it has come to enjoy a revived popularity in more recent years. The work of Jamal Badawi, long-time editor of the Wafd newspaper, is very much in this tradition.[59] Indeed, the publication of a book dedicated to the idea of national unity titled al-Sha'b al-wahid wa'l-watan al-wahid ('One People and One Homeland') by the Centre for Political and Strategic Studies at al-Ahram in 1982 suggests the government itself had moved towards such a position.[60] With a preface written by Butrus Butrus Ghali, then Minister of State for Foreign Affairs and the grandson of the assassinated Prime Minister Butrus Ghali, the book brought together the work of three historians in a statement of national unity: a prominent judge and Coptic intellectual, Wilyum Sulayman Qilada, Tariq al-Bishri, and Mustafa al-Fiqi, then a young government official.[61] Each praised the ideals of the Wafd and the 1919 Revolution from different perspectives. The Egyptian Committee for National Unity (ECNU) (al-Lajna al-misriyya li'l-wahda al-wataniyya) took a similar stand. Formed in the early 1990s and made up of a large group of intellectuals, political activists, artists, writers, politicians, journalists and thinkers and historians from both government and opposition circles, it issued a joint statement condemning the phenomenon of ta'ifiyya and invoked the historical unity of Muslims and Copts by quoting the Wafdist slogans of the 1919 Revolution approvingly.[62]

THE MATERIALIST SCHOOL: CLASS AND TA'IFIYYA

While the liberal school gazed back longingly to the golden age of 1919 and the vision of national unity upheld by the Wafd, materialist historiography has sought to provide a more creative response to the phenomenon of ta'ifiyya in the contemporary period. Not a social class in any Marxist sense, Copts did not represent a natural subject of ideological interest for the materialist school. However, the continuing deterioration in communal relations during the 1970s has prompted a series of studies that demonstrated a greater interest and awareness of the dynamics of sectarian conflict and the implications of religious discourse in the domestic political arena.

The official party of the Left, al-Tajammu', has taken a leading role in addressing the phenomenon of ta'ifiyya from the late 1970s. With the publication of a collection of articles in 1980 edited by its president, Khalid Muhyi al-Din, the party drew on the talents of a number of writers, both Muslim and Copt, including Salah 'Isa, Muhammad 'Awda, Ghali Shukri, Milad Hanna and Wilyum Sulayman Qilada.[63] Another volume, this time under the name of the Committee in Defence of National Culture (Lajna al-difa' 'an al-thaqafa al-qawmiyya) appeared in 1988 and addressed various aspects of the problem from a historical, political, economic and social perspective. Again it drew on contributions from figures associated with or sympathetic to the Left: Ahmad Sadiq Sa'd, Latifa al-Zayyat, 'Abd al-'Azim Anis, Fu'ad Mursi and historian 'Asim al-Disuqi.[64] In addition, in his weekly column in al-Ahali, party secretary-general, Rif'at al-Sa'id, regularly took up the issue of ta'ifiyya during the early 1990s.[65]

In the modest academic works that emerged from this milieu, analyses laid the responsibility for ta'ifiyya at the feet of imperialism and the autocratic tendencies in domestic Egyptian politics. Ra'uf 'Abbas' study on the pre-First World War period pointed particularly to the meddling policies of the British.[66] According to 'Abbas, with the majority of Copts hostile to the British occupation, the Watani Party of Mustafa Kamil enjoyed the support of Egyptians across society in its call for national independence. To support his view, 'Abbas quotes from a speech of Wisa Wasif, one of the prominent Copts of the party, 'the National [i.e. Watani] Party accepts the membership of Copts, Jews and Muslims'. However, he acknowledges that some wealthy Copts, particularly the young, intellectual elite, were drawn to the party of Akhnukh Fanus, which called for Coptic autonomy under British control and were supported in this by newspapers, Misr and al-Watan. 'Abbas lays the blame for the antagonism between Copt and Muslim at the feet of the British who supported communal claims on both sides, using both pan-Islamists, 'Abd al-'Aziz Jawish and 'Ali Yusuf and the editor of al-Watan, Ibrahim Jundi, as a way to weaken the national movement. The proof of the perfidy of these communal leaders was their lack of support for the 1919 Revolution.[67]

'Asim al-Disuqi takes up this theme of the British strategy of encouraging division as one of the primary reasons for intercommunal conflict in his analysis of the post-1919 period.[68] He regards the British declaration of February 1922, which granted Egypt self-government but reserved the right to protect minorities, as motivated by a desire to maintain its imperial interests within Egypt and to hinder the national movement.[69] However, despite this attempt to split the national consensus, the Egyptian drafters of the constitution of 1923 accepted equality for all Egyptians regardless of religion, race or language and rejected the idea of minority representation. According to al-Disuqi, however, a number of other factors soon emerged to undermine this brief moment of national unity. In 1924 the abolition of the caliphate by Kemal Ataturk ignited a debate regarding the relevance of traditional Islamic institutions and brought back religion as a force into the mainstream political arena. King Fu'ad's own aspirations to the position of caliph aggravated the situation. This change in atmosphere prompted the formation of the Young Muslims' Association (*Jam'iyyat al-shaban al-muslimin*) in 1927 and the Muslim Brotherhood (*al-Ikhwan al-muslimun*) in the following year, both dedicated to bringing Islam back into national politics. The appearance of Misr al-Fatat in 1933 reinforced the trend. Though it initially attracted both Copts and Muslims to its ranks, with the accession of Faruq to the throne in 1936, it began to take on a more Islamic orientation, changing its name to the Islamic National Party in 1940. These forces, in loose alliance with the palace and the minority parties, arrayed themselves against the Wafd and undermined its principle of 'unity of the nation, democracy and full citizenship' (*wahda al-umma wa'l-dimuqratiyya wa'l-muwatana al-tama*).[70]

In the late 1940s demands for the implementation of the *shari'a* by the Ikhwan and Misr al-Fatat, and the use of provocative slogans such as 'Islam, poll tax or the sword' (*al-Islam aw al-jizya aw al-sayf*) and 'today is Zionism's day, tomorrow is Christianity's' (*al-yawm yawm al-sahyuniyya wa ghadan yawm al-nasraniyya*), prompted a defensive reaction from elements in the Coptic community. In the pages of *Misr* there were calls for the protection of Coptic language and heritage; one organization, the Society of the Coptic Nation (*Jama'at al-umma al-qibtiyya*) called for self-government for Copts. In the elections of 1950 religion emerged as a prominent factor in the campaign and Coptic membership in the Majlis al-Umma fell appreciably. Al-Disuqi ends his description of the parliamentary period with a wistful quote from a Copt writing in 1950, who bewailed the retreat from the national unity of 1919 and the failure of Egypt to live up to its proclamation of, 'Long live the cross with the crescent'.[71]

In contrast to his portrayal of the last years of the constitutional monarchy as a descent into social chaos, al-Disuqi praises the 1952 Revolution for its abolition of the monarchy, which had polarized Islamic elements in the country, and its liberation of Egypt from the control of the British, who had roused the 'fire of sectarianism' (*nar al-ta'ifiyya*).[72] The revolutionary regime is praised for its implementation of a program of political and administrative reform (*islah*) that was designed to provide equality of opportunity in education and work, and restore the basis of national unity. The religious courts were abolished and a single system of courts established; the hitherto heterogeneous education system was brought more under the supervision of the state, and the public service opened up to all university graduates regardless of religion. Nasser personally relaxed the restrictions applying to the building of churches through a personal agreement with Patriarch Kyrillos. Finally, al-Disuqi notes that the regime instituted the constitutional practice of nominating ten members to the

Majlis al-Umma in order to insure some Coptic representation in the chamber.

More than the liberal school, the materialist school has shown itself willing to engage with *ta'ifiyya* as a historical and contemporary phenomenon. Though it shares the idea of British imperial policy as a cause for inter-communal friction in the early part of the century, the materialist school has not been content with merely invoking Wafdist rhetoric or the liberal pronouncements of secular nationalism in the post-1919 period. Instead, it has shown a greater awareness of the difficulties facing Copts in the national community and sought to explain the historical existence of sectarianism by reference to a more complex model of Egyptian social and political forces.

THE ISLAMIC CURRENT: *AHL AL-DHIMMA* OR A FIFTH COLUMN?

The Islamic current challenges the notion of secular nationalism and opposes the separation of religion and state. Its national perspective would seem then to pose a significant barrier between the two groups since it is grounded in Islam – the very thing that distinguishes Copts from the Muslim majority. On the face of it, it presents the most aggressive challenge to national unity and for that reason has incurred the charge in some quarters of fuelling *ta'ifiyya*. Certainly, in its more extreme form, the Islamic current has challenged the political rights and cultural attachment of Copts in Egypt. Even so, to a greater extent than the other national schools of thought discussed here, the Islamic current does not represent a homogeneous interpretative framework and, particularly in the work of Tariq al-Bishri, has attempted a more complex and sympathetic account of the Coptic presence in Egypt.

In the late 1940s and early 1950s Ikhwanist views on the historical relations between Copts and Muslims were strongly influenced by the concept of the Copts as *dhimmi* or 'people of the book' (*ahl al-kitab*) who enjoyed a protected if inferior status under Islamic law. At the same time, there were also more belligerent analyses accusing Copts of hostility to Islam and impugning their genuine attachment to Egypt. Some writers emphasized the different cultural orientation of Copts, citing the ideas of writers, such as Salama Musa, who had stressed the pharaonic or African elements of Egyptian identity, as proof of the Coptic desire to detach Egypt from the Islamic world.[73] Musa's call for the abolition of the *shari'a* courts, and his stated preference for European laws, was invoked as further confirmation of a difference in national identity. One recurrent claim was that Copts sought to make Islam a stranger in Egypt, an idea usually linked to accusations of some sort of Coptic alliance with Western interests. The charge has a considerable lineage, being levelled prior to First World War at Prime Minister 'Butrus Ghali by 'Abd al-'Aziz Jawish and 'Ali Yusuf when the government's pro-British policies and the existence of groups such as the Egyptian Party gave it at least superficial plausibility.[74] Even after 1919 doubts expressed about the loyalty of Copts were not uncommon and were assisted by the British government's arrogation to itself of the protection of minorities. Moreover, the religious discourse of the Ikhwan led it to make a certain equation between the political and economic domination of the foreigner with that of the local Copt and Jew.[75] With communal tensions rising again in the 1970s, similar sentiments began to reappear in the pages of the Ikhwan's organ, *al-Da'wa*: 'Everything was for the best until Shenouda became patriarch of the Copts in Egypt. Then phenomena appeared the like of which had never before been seen: we heard it said that Egypt was Coptic and there was no place for Muslims…'[76] Comparisons were made between Copts and the Crusaders. There were accusations that 'foreign influences were attempting to make the Copts a fifth column in Egypt'.[77] The Jama'at Islamiyya accused the Church of aiming at a 'dictatorship of the minority under the slogan of preserving national unity' and seeking to 'take over the country and expel the Muslims'.[78]

The academic work of Zakariyya Bayumi presents a more moderate 'Islamic' reading than this aggressive sectarian tone. Rather than excluding Copts from the national community, Bayumi subsumes them within an Islamic conception of the national identity. His rereading of the 1919 Revolution as a national unity based on Islam is a case in point. Quoting approvingly the words of Salama Musa, that Islam was the religion of the nation (*watan*), and the statement of Makram 'Ubayd that he was 'Christian by religion but Muslim by nationality' (*masihi dinan wa lakinna muslim watanan*), Bayumi concludes that Egyptian Christians had become absorbed within the framework of the Islamic community.[79] Tariq al-Bishri's book, *al-Muslimun wa'l-aqbat fi atar al-jama'a al-wataniyya*, is a more ambitious attempt at confronting one of the most daunting issues of contemporary Egyptian history head-on.[80] Covering the period from the time of Muhammad 'Ali until the 1952 Revolution, it offers a comprehensive discussion of relations between Muslims and Copts in Egypt viewed through the prism of al-Bishri's conception of authentic Egyptian tradition (*turath*). Although principally based on Islam within the framework of the *shari'a*, the *turath* incorporates elements of Arab and Egyptian tradition, including the Coptic Church, grounded on the principle of national unity. Copts are therefore an integral element of the national community and al-Bishri is an insistent advocate for the national rights of Copts within the modern Egyptian state. He stresses, however, that this conception of the Copts is not on the basis of outmoded traditional practices, such as the *jizya* (poll tax) or the status of *dhimmi*, but through a reinterpreted *shari'a*.[81] In the words of one scholar, al-Bishri's historical interpretation is driven by 'his insistence that Islamic legal specialists find a religious formula granting equal political rights to Copts in an Egyptian nation-state which is also an Islamic state in some sense'.[82]

Al-Bishri's assessment of political forces is in part based on the extent to which they contributed to national unity. He is therefore sympathetic to the Wafd because of its stand on political equality between Copts and Muslims, even if this was based on a secular ideal. However, he views the domestic repercussions brought about by the abolition of the caliphate in 1924 as undermining this concept of national unity. This was further destabilized by the continued activity of Christian missionaries in the country, one of the factors that led to the establishment of the Ikhwan in 1928.[83] Thereafter, al-Bishri regards the Ikhwan and, after 1933, Misr al-Fatat as being authentic national movements because of their recognition of the importance of Islam in Egyptian national identity. Nevertheless, he finds fault with the political strategies and tactics of both parties: criticizing Hasan al-Banna for risking the cause of national unity by failing to integrate the Copts into his vision of the Islamic society, and faulting the leadership of Ahmad Husayn for his unwillingness to make common national cause with the Wafd.[84] Despite this criticism, al-Bishri lays the principal blame for the Muslim–Copt division in Egyptian society in the pre-1952 period not at the feet of Islamic groups but with autocracy and imperialism, the two political forces with an inherent interest in spreading division.[85] Al-Bishri also finds fault with the Nasser regime for failing to incorporate Copts into the national community. Since Copts were rarely represented in the upper echelons of the armed forces, the practice of relying on the military in administration meant that the ruling elite was not sensitive to the special circumstances of Copts. Copts suffered disproportionately from the nationalizations because they were represented in business in a proportion greater than their numbers. Indeed, the proof of Nasser's failure to integrate the Copts into political life was their absence among those elected to parliament.[86]

Al-Bishri's interpretation has left some unconvinced of the validity of concepts such as an authentic past and the plausibility of a synthesis that seeks to be simultaneously national, democratic and Islamic.[87] Nevertheless, his position has been widely applauded by both state and church authorities since he attempts to articulate the basis for political equality of Copts and Muslims in a national community albeit within Islamic law.[88] This view is a far cry from the sectarian Islamic interpretations of the Ikhwan or the more militant Islamic currents. At their most chauvinist, these have used a common religion, Christianity, as the grounds for alleging a link between Copts and Western powers and generalized this to a statement regarding the political loyalty and national allegiance of the Coptic community as a whole. The political loyalty of Muslim Egyptians or their membership of the national community has never been called into question in the same way since there is a fundamental equation between Islam and the nation.

COPTIC RESPONSES

As might be expected, the issue of relations between Copts and Muslims and the periodic difficulties that have erupted between the two communities have provoked a response from Coptic writers themselves. While there is no distinctive 'Coptic' view or interpretation – some writing has much in common with attitudes expressed within the liberal and materialist currents – there is a body of work that exhibits a greater willingness and concern than the currents already discussed to address the historical relationship between Muslims and Copts and its implications for Egyptian public life. Generally speaking, they have sought to discuss communal differences and difficulties at the same time as appealing to the ideal of a secular national unity.

One of the earliest examples of this is a book particularly critical of the British written for a foreign audience by Kyriakos Mikhail before First World War during a time of poor Muslim–Copt relations.[89] The Revolution of 1919 and its immediate aftermath may have provided some respite but by the late 1940s sectarian clashes were provoking some to reassessment. In 1950 Zaghib Mikha'il, director of the National Hospital in Abu Qarqas, a town in Upper Egypt, authored a book pointedly titled, *Divide and Rule, National Unity and National Character*, which discussed how the national dream of a united crescent and cross upheld in 1919 had failed to materialize and how Copts continued to be discriminated against in government positions with allegations of favouritism and bribery surrounding many appointments.[90] In the following year another book on the history of Copts and Muslims written by a Christian of Syrian background, Jacques Tagher, appeared.[91] By this time communal relations, and indeed, the national political scene was becoming increasingly unstable, and it was presumably fear of provoking a hostile reaction in this environment that led the government to ban both works.[92] Following the burning of a Coptic church in January 1952, an article signed 'Egyptian Historian' (*mu'arrikh misri*) appeared in *Misr* putting forward a potted national history which stressed the good historical relations between Muslims and Copts.[93] Again a revolution, this time led by the military, submerged communal tensions.

The return of sectarian clashes in Egypt during the 1970s and 1980s aroused a more pronounced response and a reassessment of the achievements of the national movement after 1919 on a scale not seen before. The phenomenon marked a significant departure on the part of some Copts from the traditional attitude of the Coptic establishment that shied away from public debate on Coptic–Muslim relations, probably for the same reasons advocated by Lutfi al-Sayyid decades before. An older, more circumspect Pope Shinuda summed up this philosophy of political quietism: 'There are Muslims and Christians in Egypt. We want them to remain united. If there is any problem, it should be addressed privately, by us and the state; it should not be the subject of public discussion.'[94] This approach preferred to assert the common national identity of Copt and Muslim and rejected the concept of the minority status for Copts.[95]

From the early 1980s, these Coptic writers began to increasingly address the matter of communal relations publicly. They did not represent a single view: some, such as Father Bulus Basili, took an ecclesiastical viewpoint;[96] others, such as Samira Bahr and Zaki Shinuda, adopted a communal perspective;[97] yet others, particularly those of leftist inclination, like Milad Hanna, Ghali Shukri and Wilyum Sulayman Qilada, took a more national position, or even an Arab viewpoint, as Abu Sayf Yusuf.[98] In some ways the movement that had seen some (Muslim) leftists of the Nasser period move towards Islam for political inspiration in the years after 1967 was mirrored in a move of Coptic leftists towards issues concerning the Coptic community, if not the Church itself.[99] With the apparent failure of secular ideology, religious faith and culture had taken on a new political significance.

By this time also there were elements in the sizeable Coptic diaspora who contributed to the debate but some of these voices were much less measured. The American Coptic Association, headed by Shawqi Karas, was vocal in complaining through pamphlets and other published literature about the situation and discrimination against its co-religionists in Egypt.[100] Coptic protests were held in the United States and were particularly embarrassing during at least one visit to the White House by President Sadat. However, if *any* public discussion of the Coptic issue was a departure from the Church's traditional position, these relatively militant actions were even less appreciated by many Copts in Egypt. Some felt that a comfortable Coptic middle class in America was not in a position to appreciate the delicacy of the Egyptian situation.[101]

COPTIC INTERPRETATIONS

Coptic interpretations, like the national currents already discussed, view the rise of the national movement at the beginning of the century as a significant period in the formation of Egyptian national politics even if they take a somewhat different attitude towards the actors involved. While the figure of Mustafa Kamil and the Watani Party stand out heroically in the writings of the liberal and materialist schools as symbols of national unity, Coptic assessments have been less convinced. Indeed, the rhetoric of the Mustafa Kamil, replete with allusions to the Ottoman Empire and the Muslim *'umma*, were cause for ambivalence among Copts.[102] This was intensified after Kamil's death by the provocative rhetoric of 'Abd al-'Aziz Jawish, whose reference to 'black-skinned Copts' and his increasing use of Islamic language, did little to assuage these doubts. Copts withdrew from the Watani Party and some, disappointed with the lack of support from the Umma Party, formed the Egyptian Party under the leadership of Akhnukh Fanus.[103]

There followed the assassination of Butrus Ghali in 1910 and the spectacle in the following year of a Coptic Congress being held at Asyut while a rival 'Egyptian Conference' convened at Heliopolis.

Samira Bahr's study of Copts in Egyptian political life stands as a significant example of modern Coptic historiography.[104] After a discussion of the poor state of communal relations in the period before First World War, her narrative devotes considerable attention to the 1919 revolution as the high point of national unity. An entire section is dedicated to the deliberations of the constitutional committee and the drafting of the 1923 constitution, where the idea of specific representation for Copts in the national parliament was defeated. Bahr characterizes this debate as a struggle between the ideals of the Wafd, who opposed the idea of minority representation as anathema to its political ideology, and those in favour, described by Bahr as Muslims hostile to the Wafd and political allies of Liberal Constitutionalist leaders, 'Adli Yakan and 'Abd al-Khaliq Tharwat.[105] The defeat of the proposal for minority representation was therefore a victory for the Wafd and secularism.[106] She concludes her discussion on the Wafd's vision of national unity with a quote from a speech of Sa'd Zaghlul during the electoral campaign in September 1923,

> The recent revival (*nahda*) was better than the one before it because it created this sacred unity between cross and crescent...Our enemies say that they protect the minorities because you are racist and that's why they have to enforce equality. This pretense collapsed in the face of your unity...there are only Egyptians. And those who are called Copts were and still are supporters of the *nahda*. They sacrificed themselves as much as you did, they worked as much as you, there are a lot of good people amongst them upon whom we can depend. If it were not for the Copts' patriotism and great loyalty they would have accepted the invitation of the foreigners to protect them. And they would have gained status and good positions instead of being gaoled and exiled. But they preferred to be Egyptian sufferers deprived of the status of positions and interests, they experienced death and injustice and they were protected by their enemies and your enemies. This special thing we have to protect and keep in our hearts and I feel very proud when I see you united supporting each other by protecting your unity.[107]

From this high-water mark, Bahr's narrative of the period up to 1952 is one of the decline of Coptic fortunes and an account of the Wafd's political failure to implement its secular vision of national unity, leading to the re-emergence of sectarian violence in the late 1940s and early 1950s.

The analysis of Abu Sayf Yusuf presents a more complex picture of the period between the two revolutions that takes into account the economic context.[108] He identifies the principal political failure of the period as the inability of the Egyptian state to effectively develop the national economy and sees this and the resulting political disruption as the root cause of the poor state of communal relations after the Second World War. The appearance of Coptic political organizations, such as the Christian Democratic Party and Society of the Coptic Nation are reactions from left and right wing elements within the Coptic community to a wider political malaise. The program of the Christian Democratic Party which called for the separation of religion and state, representation for Copts in representative councils in proportion to their numbers, and promotions for Copts in government positions, the army and police force was thus a sect-based reaction to an increasingly unstable national polity.[109]

If the final years of the monarchical period are a cause for pessimism, Coptic historians have taken an ambivalent view of the situation of Copts under the Nasser regime. As a national leader Nasser is generally praised and his policies, most notably in regard to state education, have been widely acclaimed.[110] Nevertheless, there has been much less agreement about the political culture nurtured by the regime and its conception of Egyptian national identity, particularly in its policy of Arabization and the employment of Islam as a legitimizing discourse. Bahr's assessment of the Nasser period exemplifies this ambivalence. On the positive side, she praises Nasser's policy of granting public education to all Egyptians on a more egalitarian basis and his relegation of al-Azhar to the status of a normal university. Further, state economic policies resulted in 'a type of class equality between citizens' (naw'an min al-musawa al-tabaqiyya ... bayna al-muwatanin). While she notes that various measures, such as the nationalizations, affected sectors where Coptic interests were considerable, such as in the transport industry, she recognizes that these policies did not differentiate between sects.[111] Balanced against these positive achievements is the character and membership of the regime itself. Bahr points out that 'the ruling clique' (al-jama'a al-hakima) consisted only of Muslims: there were no Copts among the Free Officers and the army itself mirrored the traditional division between Muslim and Copt.[112] This bias was compounded by the regime's reliance on 'the civil administration' (al-idara al-madaniyya) whose conservative character reinforced the established division between Muslim and Copt in Egyptian society. This meant that the new political class perceived the state in 'an Islamic framework' (itar islami). Bahr also stresses the dangerous waters being fished by the use of religious idiom to legitimize policies such as the socialist and nationalization laws. According to Bahr, Nasser invoked not Marxist ideas but appealed to Islam and the sayings of the Prophet and his companions on social justice to justify the measures to the Muslim majority whereas Christian spokesmen of the regime defended socialism by reference to the life of Christ and the apostles.

Bahr saves her most severe criticism for the analysis of political institutions. The abolition of political parties in 1953 and the practical bar to the upper echelons of the military meant there was little opportunity for Copts for formal political participation. When elections were held for the Majlis al-Umma in 1957 the failure of any Coptic candidate to win a seat prompted Nasser to adopt the practice of appointing Copts to the Majlis, an expedient he continued to employ throughout the 1960s and is still current practice. Further, he nominated Copts, usually technocrats and university professors, as ministers to marginal ministries.[113] Bahr holds this system of nomination (ta'yin) and specialized appointments as responsible for the perception of Copts as a minority (aqalliyya). Effectively it cast Copts, whatever their individual qualifications and personal talents, as 'sectarian representatives and not as citizens' (al-tamthil al-ta'ifi wa la ka muwatanin). Indeed, Bahr suggests this perception as so pervasive that it was one reason for the emigration of many Copts during this period.[114]

Abu Sayf Yusuf's evaluation of the Nasser period differs markedly from Bahr's interpretation. In his view, far from being alienated by pan-Arabist rhetoric, Copts embraced the move to Arab unity, quoting in support the Coptic Church's pro-integrationist stance and its hostility towards Israel.[115] Against Bahr, he praises Nasser's practice of neither employing a religious idiom in either domestic or foreign politics nor ever using religious affiliation for political purposes. For this reason, the period saw the disappearance of 'acute sectarianism' (ta'ifiyya hadda) from Egyptian politics.

Finally, the work of Rafiq Habib presents a more controversial analysis, which highlights the rise of religious activism among Copts. One of the younger generation of Coptic scholars, Habib broke dramatically with the Coptic tradition of quietism.[116] In a comparative study of Muslim and Christian social movements of the 1970s and 1980s, he appeared to label both faiths as equally susceptible to political fundamentalism, albeit in different manifestations.[117] His views, therefore, radically departed not only from the traditional Coptic strategy of not publicly discussing such issues but also from the discourse of Coptic writers such as Milad Hanna and Wilyum Sulayman Qilada, who held that the extremists were only on the Muslim side.[118] Habib's work has received an almost universally hostile reception from Coptic intellectuals who have seen the effect, if not the intent, of his analysis, as legitimating a religious idiom in politics and, by bringing out into the open the bogey of Coptic activism, lending ideological comfort to the Islamists. In a series of three articles Ghali Shukri attacked Habib for effectively upholding political Islam and pointed to the support he had received from 'Adil Husayn and Fahmi Huwaydi, both Islamic writers, as a clear indication of its effect.[119] One Coptic historian felt Habib was 'scorning his own history'.[120] Some other criticism was more temperate. Sulayman Nasim, for example, believed that Habib's analysis was flawed because he had examined a distorted period in the history of the Church.[121]

Almost all pointed to the fact that Habib was a Protestant as an explanation for what they saw as his unacceptable and idiosyncratic views.[122]

SOCIETY OF THE COPTIC NATION
(JAMA'AT AL-UMMA AL-QIBTIYYA)

The sensitivity and diversity of views surrounding the issue of an active even militant Coptic politics is epitomized in the historiographical debate surrounding one of the most controversial Coptic organizations in recent Egyptian political history, the *Jama'at al-umma al-qibtiyya* (JUQ) ('Society of the Coptic Nation'). Despite its brief and ultimately ephemeral role in Egyptian history, its significance as a political association has received widely varying assessments. Regarded as a serious political movement reacting to the rise of Islamic militancy by some writers, others have seen it as part of an internal struggle within the Coptic community or even a frivolous action by some overenthusiastic young men. For the purpose of this discussion, its importance lies less in what JUQ achieved (which was little) and more in the diversity of historical interpretation which this episode has provoked.

The basic facts are as follows. JUQ was formed in 1952 by a young lawyer, Ibrahim Fahmi Hilal, and a group of young Copts with the aim of reviving Coptic culture and reforming the Church. According to Hilal, the impetus for its establishment was the burning of a church in Suez in January of that year, an event that caused widespread alarm amongst the Coptic community at large. The group was active between September 1952 and 1954 though its size is disputed: Hilal himself claimed 92,000 members but others have dismissed these figures as grossly exaggerated.[123] The group collected arms and trained its members though for what purpose is not clear. In March 1954, following a judicial decision, JUQ was dissolved on the grounds of being an unconstitutional organization but its most spectacular action occurred some months afterwards when, one night in July 1954, a number of members, including Hilal himself, kidnapped the Coptic Patriarch, Anba Yusab II, and forced him to sign an instrument of abdication. The leaders were soon arrested and subsequently sentenced to gaol terms for the kidnapping.[124]

The phenomenon and political significance of JUQ was ignored for many years in mainstream Egyptian histories. The group first received attention from an Egyptian writer in Ghali Shukri's anti-Sadat book published in 1978 in which he described the incident in the context of his attack on the way Sadat was stirring up religious tensions.[125] The episode of the Patriarch's kidnapping was taken up soon after by Muhammad Hasanayn Haykal in his analysis of the Sadat years.[126] Since then, it has been a regular reference in historical discussions of Muslim–Copt relations.[127] Shukri himself considered the group as a serious political organization. Although the motivation for the kidnapping of the patriarch related to church issues, he regarded the name of the group as suggestive of more than church reform and possibly indicated grander political designs.[128] The emergence of JUQ begged comparison with the Ikhwan. The former's motto, 'God is our King, Egypt our country, the Gospels our law and the Cross our badge, and death for the sake of Christ our greatest hope', inescapably recalled that of the Ikhwan: 'The Qur'an is our constitution, Arabic our language, and death in the way of God our greatest hope.'

Other historians have agreed that the incident had strong political connotations. Bahr regards JUQ foremost as a religious movement but also sees it as a reaction to the increasing influence of the Ikhwan in Egyptian politics. Bahr also gives an economic justification for its emergence, regarding the large numbers ascribed to the organization as proof of the dissatisfaction felt amongst young Copts with discrimination in government jobs and other systematic disadvantages.[129] Abu Sayf Yusuf's Marxist analysis provided a more complex explanation for sectarian tensions. While recognizing the religious elements of its program, he explains JUQ in the context of the economic and political failures of the late 1940s precipitated by the weakness of the Wafd. For Yusuf, JUQ was a class reaction among the Coptic middle and upper classes to the failure of the bourgeoisie to obtain its independence in a genuine civil society. In this way it was not unlike other Coptic organizations of the same time, the National Democratic Party of Ramsis Jibrawi and the Christian Democratic Party.[130] Rafiq Habib also views JUQ as part of a class-based reaction among Copts to political instability, characterizing it as a modern, conservative Coptic tendency (*al-ittijah al-qibti al-muhafiz al-tahaddithi*).[131] By contrast, others have preferred to downplay the importance of the organization altogether. In Yunan Labib Rizq's study of political parties, JUQ barely rates a mention being described dismissively as 'more a secret society than a political party' (*jama'a sirriyya akthar minha hizban siyasiyyan*).[132] Some reject any political significance at all, denying that JUQ had roots in the political or social life and suggesting the kidnapping of the Pope showed a sense of humour or was little more than a student's prank.[133]

Finally, it is worth comparing accounts of the reaction to the actual incident that provoked the formation of JUQ, namely, the burning of a church in Suez and the murder of a number of Copts in January 1952. Al-Fiqi refers to the strong representations made to the Wafdist government by various Copts at the time and in particular to Ibrahim Faraj, the only Coptic member of cabinet, then wistfully contemplates the absence of Makram 'Ubayd.

> One can imagine that, if the Suez event had taken place while Ebeid was still the second man officially in the Wafd, and the architect of national unity, he would have played the most effective and dynamic role in his political life, because, as a Coptic politician and

170

a Wafd leader, he would have done best to avoid such reactions as did in fact occur.[134]

This analysis, centred on the personality of 'Ubayd and talents of the political elite, explains little of the dynamics at work within the Coptic community. Girgis Guda Girgis' version of the same episode gives a much different impression which sheds light not only on the absence of political leadership but on how out of touch the old Wafdist clique was with the younger generation of Copts. He recounts how a number of members of JUQ, approached Ibrahim Faraj and demanded the government to take some action. Faraj's response was to demand to know 'For whom do you work?' and accused them of 'threatening national unity'.[135]

The increasing incidents of communal clashes between Muslims and Copts and the range of responses within the Coptic community towards them, such as the appearance of the National Christian Party and the JUQ as well as the changing orientation of the Wafd, suggest that such concerns should not be dismissed so lightly. The early 1950s were a time of great political instability and severe national crisis so much so that Muhammad Anis suggested that there was a danger that the Copts might have withdrawn from the national community.[136] The widely varying interpretations amongst Coptic writers of the significance of JUQ is in part to be explained by the fact that it raises a taboo of national politics – separate, or worse separatist, Coptic activism, a charge Sadat had publicly levelled at Copts in 1980.[137] For some commentators, to raise the spectre of Coptic separatism in a historical, as much as a contemporary context, is not only to confirm Muslim suspicions but to encourage a religious and sectarian political discourse and to legitimize the program of Islamic groups that would potentially relegate Copts to a second class status or, in its extreme form, exclude them altogether.

The schools of historical thought discussed here have interpreted the Coptic presence and assessed its fortunes within the national community in different ways. There is relative agreement that between 1882 and the end of the First World War the British were the primary cause of communal tensions.[138] However, there are doubts amongst Coptic historians about the character of the Watani Party under Mustafa Kamil, and even more so after his death. The events of 1919 and its immediate aftermath enjoy a greater consensus. Indeed, it is one of the articles of faith of modern Egyptian historiography that the 1919 Revolution witnessed a united stand by Muslim and Copt against British imperialism that forged the basis of the Egyptian national community. There is less agreement about what that basis actually *was*. For the liberal school the period from 1919 is a celebration of the ideal of national secular unity under the sponsorship of the Wafd. As al-Fiqi notes,

The Zaghloulist era after 1919 represents the golden era of the Coptic involvement in national politics. During that period and the

Wafd's political heyday, the Copts experienced a feeling of security and trust within the greater community, and began to be openly involved without any reservations, playing a positive role, even with many sacrifices. The Wafd pursued the same philosophy after Zaghloul until its power was suppressed in 1952. The Copts thereafter had a limited role in public life and turned their attention increasingly to private pursuits in business and the free professions.[139]

Materialist analyses are less effervescent. While praising the aims of the Wafd, they are more conscious of the continuing pattern of British interference in communal relations, evident as early as 1922 with the British declaration arrogating to itself the protection of minorities. More than this, the materialist school dedicates more attention to the power of a religious idiom in politics, particularly in relation to the emergence of the Islamic movement. Its explanation of the causes of communal tensions in the 1940s and early 1950s recognizes more clearly the failure of the Wafd to implement its vision of national unity. For the materialist school, it is during the Nasser years that a greater equality between Muslim and Copt was achieved.

Islamic and Coptic currents are more heterogeneous in their interpretations and thus more difficult to categorize. In general, both see the period after 1919 as an increasing departure from the ideal of national unity but for different reasons: the Islamic current because of the separation of national politics from its religious roots; and the Coptic current because of the failure of the Wafd to consolidate a secular polity. While there is a virulent anti-Coptic strain within the Islamic current, there is no genuine equivalent among Coptic writers, even if the analysis of Rafiq Habib may point to a more diverse political response than is generally acknowledged. The Nasser period has attracted a more variable response. Hostile analyses of the revolutionary regime, whether Islamic or Coptic, recognize its attempts to forge a national community but are critical of the manner in which this was done. Al-Bishri accuses Nasser of neglecting Egypt's cultural roots and failing to promote any real sense either of the importance of Islam or the Coptic community as elements of the national identity. By contrast, Bahr charges the regime with using traditional institutions and rhetoric – both of which embodied an existing innate discrimination against Copts – to implement its policies in such a way that it undermined its avowed aim of a secular community. In this way, these two historians have more in common in their identification of the revolutionary regime's shortcomings than the analysis of Abu Sayf Yusuf which is closer to the views of the materialist school. This should not be so surprising since, despite their different points of reference, the Islamic and Coptic currents share a recognition of the political and social dimension of religious identity in the national community.

Modern Coptic historiography touches on a number of sensitive issues: relations between Muslims and Copts in Egypt, the quietist tradition of the

Coptic community, the policy of the state to finesse or subsume the Coptic element of Egyptian identity and the accompanying reluctance of academic historians to address and discuss the separate character and distinctiveness of Copts in the modern period. The position of the government towards Copts has also been an ambiguous one with a tension operating between two considerations: one, the political realities of deferring to an unmistakably Muslim majority, and the other, a stated commitment to the principle of a secular national unity. The continuing sensitivity of Muslim–Copt relations and the signs of a greater willingness on the part of some Copts to express communal concerns suggest that in the future Copts may be a less easily ignored presence in modern historiography.

6

THE *MUTAMASSIRUN*

If Copts occupy an ambiguous position in contemporary Egyptian historiography, the *mutamassirun*, or the resident 'Egyptianized' foreigners, suffer no such uncertainty: they have been systematically excluded by mainstream historical scholarship from any legitimate place in the Egyptian national community. This was not always the case. In the 1920s, the royalist school could speak of the positive contribution of foreigners in Egypt and point to the diverse cultural, religious and linguistic society that made up 'cosmopolitan' Egypt. With the rise of the Egyptian national movement after the First World War this perception began to be steadily eroded as national boundaries became more rigid and narrow. Even if Muhammad Najib could express sentiments sympathetic to the presence of some resident foreign communities, the domestic and international rhetoric of the Nasser regime accelerated the emergence of an increasingly exclusive nationalism. Scholarship, as much as political ideology and economic policy, was subjected to a process of Egyptianization (*tamsir*) and Arabization (*isti'rab*) that left little conceptual room for the *mutamassirun*, who came to be portrayed as foreign and parasitic elements, vilified as enemies of the people, allies of imperialism and blood-sucking capitalists. Since then, they have rarely received any positive treatment in Egyptian scholarship. As a presence, therefore, that runs counter to the development of a hegemonic national discourse, the historiography of the *mutamassirun* serves as an important example of shifting national boundaries and the ideological limitations of national discourse.

The establishment of foreign resident communities in Egypt in the early nineteenth century was the result of a complex series of economic, political and social preconditions. While relatively small in numbers, from the early twentieth century onwards resident foreigners came to occupy a significant place in Egyptian society. Routinely characterized in nationalist discourse as a homogeneous collective, there were important differences between and within these different communities. One important distinction was between the nationals of Western colonial powers and other resident foreigners. From the former category, the British were the occupiers of the country, providing military personnel and administrators, and the French and Belgians, were largely represented in the upper bourgeoisie. From the latter, Greeks, Italians, Armenians, Maltese, Jews, and other Levantines, were characterized by a greater socio-economic range that included predominantly middle and working class elements. They enjoyed a wider degree of contact with the larger Egyptian society and were a familiar, if not entirely assimilated, part of it. These latter foreigners were the *mutamassirun*, literally the 'Egyptianized'.

The term *mutamassirun* recognizes both an affinity and conformity with the Egyptian way of life and yet, at the same time, a certain detachment from it: they were not Egyptian, but *Egyptianized*. Other terms have also been applied, each with its own historical and political connotations: Cromer described them as 'Levantines' or 'Orientalised Europeans';[1] Mustafa Kamil employed 'European guests' (*al-nuzala' al-urubbiyun*);[2] amongst Egyptian historians the most frequent usage has been 'foreign minorities' (*al-aqalliyat al-ajnabiyya*) or simply 'foreigners' (*ajanib*), usually with little distinction made between different nationalities or classes. Focusing on their commercial activities, economic historians have employed a variety of formulations: 'foreign resident bourgeoisie', 'local foreign minorities', and 'middleman minorities'.[3] Colloquially, to the ordinary Egyptian, they were the *khawajat*.[4]

As these terms indicate, the *mutamassirun* were far from being a homogeneous group. They included a great number of nationalities and occupations, languages and religious affiliations. Amongst the Jewish population alone there was considerable diversity, from Karaite Jews, who had a long history of residence in Egypt, to Sephardic Jews, who had migrated from Arab and Ottoman lands in more recent centuries, and European Jews, who had moved to Egypt from the nineteenth century to take advantage of the opportunities the country had to offer.[5] Since the *mutamassirun* were not, strictly speaking, a legal but a vague social-cultural category it is difficult to accurately establish their numbers but at the end of the First World War, they were probably at least 200,000.[6] Characteristically, they enjoyed a particular attachment with Egypt being resident there, sometimes for generations, and integrated with Egyptian society in a way not true of the occupying British forces and European haute bourgeoisie. Nevertheless, the *mutamassirun* generally maintained a certain distinct affiliation, cultural and legal, and therefore were separate in some sense from the majority of Egyptians. They normally did not hold Egyptian nationality but the record on this is not entirely clear.[7]

Although foreigners had a long tradition of residence in Egypt, the modern presence of the *mutamassirun* in Egypt began with the policy pursued by Muhammad 'Ali, and continued by his successors, to encourage the migration of those with labour, business and administrative skills to assist in the modernization of the country.[8] Favourable economic terms added to these already attractive prospects, the most significant being the Capitulations (*al-imtiyazat*), the legal and economic concessions granted to foreign nationals resident in Egypt, which derived from a series of agreements made between the Ottoman Empire and European states. By the end of the nineteenth century substantial Greek, Armenian and Italian communities were concentrated in the cities of Alexandria and Cairo but were also found in smaller cities and towns, especially in the case of the Greeks. Some achieved great financial success and entered the ranks of the cosmopolitan elite. The family of a Greek, Constantinos Salvagos, was prominent in the cotton and banking industries, and many of Cairo's department stores, such as Cicurel and Sidnawi, were established by *mutamassir* families.[9] Some even reached high political office. Nubar Pasha and Ya'qub Artin Pasha, both Armenians, served several times as Prime Minister and as under-secretary to the Minister of Education respectively in the late nineteenth century. During the 1920s, Yusuf Qattawi, prominent member of a long-established Jewish family, was finance minister for a time. The great majority of *mutamassirun*, however, were much less well-off. In the middle and lower middle class, they were commonly employed in service industries, working as professionals, entrepreneurs, moneylenders, administrators and shop owners. Greeks were conspicuous in the cotton ginning business and as small shopkeepers – the well-known *baqqal rumi* ('Greek grocer'); Italians dominated the building trades, shoemaking was largely a Greek and Armenian activity, Jews were prominent in tailoring and Syrians pre-eminent in the press.[10] There were also large numbers of working class *mutamassirun*. In Cairo and Alexandria, factory workers in industries such as cigarette and soft drink production, metal workshops and in the transport sector worked alongside unskilled Egyptian labour.[11] In the Canal zone, Greek and Italian port workers were particularly important.

In the course of the 40 years from the end of the First World War until the early sixties, this considerable *mutamassir* presence was effectively eliminated, a casualty of the decolonization process and the rise of Egyptian nationalism. The relation between these two phenomena was exacerbated by British policy. Under the terms of the declaration of February 1922, Britain had reserved to itself the right to protect foreign interests and minorities in Egypt. As predominantly foreign citizens, the *mutamassirun*, willingly or not, continued to enjoy the protection of the British authorities and the compromise which such a position entailed. The legal advantages that this brought, especially under the Capitulatory Regime (in place until 1937) also had negative implications in an international context. During the Second World War, at the insistence of British authorities, adult male Italian citizens were incarcerated as enemy aliens. In 1948, the foundation of Israel made the position of all Jews in Egypt increasingly tenuous, no matter what their nationality, and the position of Greeks was affected by the vicissitudes of the Greek Civil War in the 1940s. Another critical setback came during the Suez crisis in 1956 when all those who held British and French citizenship were deemed enemy aliens and expelled from the country.[12]

Hand in hand with the British retreat from empire came the rise of a strident even chauvinist Arab nationalism, particularly after 1956. Since at least the 1930s the dominance of foreign interests in many parts of the Egyptian economy, had prompted increasing calls for Egyptianization. The initial measures, while slow to take effect, made it progressively difficult for foreign nationals, resident or not, to own and operate business interests or maintain employment. The situation became more difficult following Suez, when a large number of businesses owned by British and French nationals were confiscated. The final blow came in 1961 when, though not aimed specifically at the *mutamassirun*, the nationalization laws effectively deprived many of their livelihoods. The emigration, already well underway, now seemed unstoppable.

THE *MUTAMASSIRUN* AND THE NATION

The historiography of the contemporary period has mirrored the rise and decline of *mutamassir* fortunes in Egypt. In 1869, Rifa'ah al-Tahtawi could write that Egypt was encouraging foreigners to settle the country so that they could pass on skills to Egyptians in return for being treated as Egyptians themselves. In support of the policy he quoted the historical analogy of Psammetichos I, a pharaoh who had welcomed Greek settlers to Egypt in the sixth century BC.[13] Since this policy of foreign migration was most clearly associated with the palace, it was a natural theme to be taken up by the royalist school of historiography fostered under Fu'ad. Indeed, the membership of the learned societies, such as the Institut d'Égypte and the Royal Geographical Society that served as its heartland, was largely foreign and historians such as Angelo Sammarco and Radamanthos Radopoulos wrote exemplary studies of this scholarship.[14]

The emphasis of royalist scholarship on the economic, cultural and social contribution of resident foreigners to the development of modern Egypt was reinforced by reference to the process of social integration. These two elements were both on show in a historical and geographical survey published in 1926. In his contribution to the book, Henein Bey Henein wrote of the positive contribution of the '*colonies étrangères*' which he regarded as the latest in the Egyptian tradition stretching back to at least the time of the Phoenicians of hosting foreign communities. He remarked particularly on the willingness of the colonies to 'participer au développement intellectuel et économique de l'Égypte, apportant à l'oeuvre de progrès général, le génie et les aptitudes de leurs races respectives'. Henein stressed the close relations between the foreign colonies and Egyptian society.

> C'est donc partout, dans les villes comme dans les campagnes,
> que les étrangers, Occidentaux et Orientaux, sont intimement mêlés

à toutes les manifestations de la vie égyptienne et qu'ils travaillent en parfaite harmonie à la prospérité d'une contrée qu'ils aiment et à laquelle ils sont hereux de consacrer leurs forces intellectuelles et morales.[15]

The Greeks and Italians were singled out for special mention,

Ce qui est remarquable chez ces dernières [ie the Greek and Italian colonies], c'est qu'elles sont intégralement représentatives de toutes les classes sociales de leurs mères patries et que, de ce fait, elles sont en rapport direct avec toutes les couches de la population autochtone.[16]

On the whole, however, this theme of a harmonious, integrated society plausible of *mutamassir* communities such as the Greeks and Italians but hardly of the entire foreign presence, played second fiddle to the more emphatic theme of the foreigners' contribution to Egyptian prosperity. At times this took on a patronizing tone that seemed to little acknowledge the efforts, even the presence, of the native population. At a time when the voices of the Egyptian people themselves were barely being expressed in scholarly histories, this smacked of cultural superiority and insensitivity. Thus, even before the decline of the royalist school and fall of the monarchy in 1952, other interpretations of the *mutamassir* presence in Egypt were being articulated that questioned the assumptions of royalist scholarship and conceived of the position of foreigners in quite different terms.

THE LIBERAL SCHOOL: FOREIGN NATIONALS

While multiethnic Egypt was nurtured, though not created, under the British occupation, by the beginning of the twentieth century the emergent Egyptian national movement was beginning to delineate the parameters of a narrower and more defined national community. The focus of the liberal school on the emergence of the national movement under Mustafa Kamil and the importance it ascribed to its struggle saw it embrace and rigidify the conceptual division between Egyptian and resident foreigner. When the significant test came during the upheavals of 1919–21, the *mutamassirun* were regarded as the willing associates of British rule and ultimately hostile to the cause of national independence.

It is surprising in part that one of the first casualties to a broad definition of the Egyptian nation was a group that was culturally most akin to Egyptians. Since at least the time of Muhammad 'Ali, Syrians had prospered in Egypt. Faced with no language barrier, they had come to occupy a prominent place in the intellectual and cultural life of the country by the late nineteenth century. They played an important role in the Arab cultural awakening, being responsible for the establishment of some of its famous publishing houses, such as Dar al-Hilal, and newspapers, such as *al-Muqattam, al-Muqtataf*, as well as producing a number of outstanding intellectuals, among them historians, Jurji Zaydan and Salim al-Naqqash. However, the pro-British sentiments of *al-Muqattam* did little to endear Syrians to the Egyptian nationalist aspirations and their employment in the service of the British administration was a cause for some resentment. As Muhammad Rif'at observed,

> As to the enlightened or educated [Egyptian] classes, they were galled to see practically all responsible and important posts in the Government occupied by foreigners, not necessarily all English and French – but even Greeks and Levantines in whom the English had confided to avail themselves of their knowledge of Arabic and of European languages as well.[17]

More powerful in political rhetoric was the stinging charge of Mustafa Kamil that the Syrians were 'intruders' (*dukhala'*), an accusation made plausible by the overt support of some leading Syrian Egyptians for the British occupation, and possibly reinforced by the fact that many were Christians. The Syrians never seemed to recover from the reproach.

Just as the events of the Revolution of 1919–21 serve as the demonstration of national unity for the liberal school, so do they most emphatically lay down the basis for the division between Egyptians and the *mutamassirun*. The subsequent political settlement and in particular the declaration of the British government concerning the protection of foreign minorities meant that the *mutamassirun* were regarded at best as passive beneficiaries of its authority and at worst active supporters of British imperialism. Thereafter, discussion of foreign residents is determined by this association with imperial protection and, in a concrete way, the legal privileges of foreign nationality. In this latter aspect, the Capitulations stand as both the symbol and substance of the fundamental division between Egyptian and foreign nationals. The extraterritorial immunity from local jurisdiction and taxes they granted to those holding European nationality were complemented by the authority of the locally-based Mixed Courts. Presided over by both foreign and Egyptian judges, these courts provided the judicial machinery for civil cases involving foreign citizens.[18] This legal regime therefore gave European nationals distinct economic and legal advantages over Egyptian citizens and served as an obvious target for anti-imperialist anger and the rising nationalist mood. In accordance with the Anglo-Egyptian treaty signed in 1936, Britain agreed to sponsor negotiations on the status of the Capitulations which resulted in their abolition in the following year under the terms of the Montreux Convention. Finally, on 15 October 1949 – on a day described by al-Rafi'i as 'one of the most memorable days in the history of Egypt' – the Mixed Courts were abolished and all legal administration transferred to the national courts.[19]

Consistent with its focus on the national movement as the central theme of its narrative, the liberal school casts the foreign resident as alien to the Egyptian identity, antithetical to the fulfillment of national independence and an obstacle to its national aims. While this view is sustained by the significant advantages enjoyed by foreigners under the Capitulations and the relationship that the British authorities deliberately cultivated with the foreign communities, it presents a one-dimensional and legalistic position that collapses Egyptian society into a strict dichotomy: Egyptian or foreign. Beyond being the beneficiary or minion of imperialist authority, the *mutamassir* presence is given little account in the face of the dominant theme of Egyptian nationalism. The liberal school's weakness is that it grants little recognition to the organic relations of the *mutamassirun* within Egyptian society and perceives them only through the bipolarity of imperialism and nationalism. Nor does it closely question the specific circumstances for holding foreign nationality, neither addressing the phenomenon of *mutamassirun* obtaining Egyptian citizenship (and the difficulties in doing so) nor discussing the relevance of foreign nationality to everyday life.[20] Instead, it invests foreign nationality with a fundamental and pervasive significance that determines political, social, economic and cultural behaviour.

If Egyptian nationalists regarded the *mutamassirun* as allied with foreign, and particularly British interests, it is interesting to contrast the view taken by the British authorities. Employing his fondness for crass generalization, Lord Cromer offered the following characterization: 'The squirearchy, the Copts, the Syrians, and the Levantines hovered between friendship and hostility, being torn by conflicting sentiments and driven hither and thither by every passing breeze of self-interest.'[21] He further expanded on the question of foreign nationality, which he regarded as being a matter of utility for the Levantine,

> The particular Consulate at which the Levantine is inscribed is a mere accident. He is, above all things, a Levantine, though he dislikes to be designated by that appellation; for, partly because he dislikes to merge his national individuality in a cosmopolitan expression, and partly because he is sensible of the material benefits which he derives from his foreign nationality, the Levantine will often develop a specially ardent degree of patriotism for the country which affords him Consular protection.[22]

While the views of an imperial grandee, Cromer's assessment of the Levantine was to prove influential, being substantially adopted into the liberal tradition by Albert Hourani:

...the Levantine bourgeoisie of the big towns, Syrian, Christian, Armenian, Greek and Jewish...very rich and very powerful in the economic and financial spheres, they were slavishly imitative of Europe, at least on the surface, and more often than not despised the Oriental life around them. Often they had no loyalties at all, certainly no political loyalty to the State in which they were living. They tended to attach themselves to one or other of the foreign Governments with interests in the Middle East, to imitate the French and English way of life and serve foreign Governments with a feverish and brittle devotion.[23]

In short, both the Egyptian national movement *and* the British authorities looked with suspicion upon a diverse group that seemed not to fit readily into a national category and whose political allegiances, therefore, were deemed to be doubtful and unreliable.

THE MATERIALIST SCHOOL: THE NON-NATIONAL BOURGEOISIE

Consonant with the fundamental importance it ascribes to the economic basis of society, the materialist school focuses its analysis on the role of the *mutamassirun* in Egypt and its contribution to national development and prosperity. This had been a theme of the royalist historians but the materialists gave it a decidedly negative twist, emphasizing the deleterious effects of capitalism and the class exploitation of native labour. In the international context, it held the *mutamassirun* responsible for facilitating the penetration of the Egyptian economy by foreign capital, hindering the emergence of a national bourgeoisie, and acting as an obstacle to economic independence.

The equation of the *mutamassirun* with a comprador, non-national bourgeoisie came as a consequence of the dynamics of the national movement after 1919. Prior to the First World War, the economic and indeed political distinction between national and foreign interests had been ill-defined. In his study of large landownership in the period before 1914, Ra'uf 'Abbas could argue that landowners, whether foreign or Egyptian, formed if not a single social class in the Marxist sense, then a unified class which collaborated in order to safeguard its mutual interests.[24] For 'Abbas, the turning point was the 1919 Revolution in which the political agenda of national independence swamped the subtle tissue of social and economic relationships that existed between Egyptians and *mutamassirun*. Thereafter, the *mutamassirun* were increasingly identified as the incarnation of an economic middle class without its commitment to national independence. In short, they were the 'non-national bourgeoisie'.

181

The dynamics of this conflict of capitalist interest is captured in the fortunes of Bank Misr, one of the cherished themes of the materialist narrative of the interwar period. Founded in 1920 and headed by Tal'at Harb, the bank's avowed aim was to develop Egyptian industry financed by local national capital. Its much larger rivals were the foreign-owned banks, such as the National Bank of Egypt (NBE), and the interests of monopoly and imperialist capitalists represented by the Egyptian Federation of Industries (EFI), of whom Isma'il Sidqi was the president, and Isaac Levi, a quintessential *mutamassir*, the secretary-general.[25] The 1920s and 1930s witnessed the battle between Bank Misr, on behalf of national capital, and the EFI and NBE, on behalf of non-national (i.e. Egyptian monopoly capitalists) allied with foreign capital, to assert control over the Egyptian economy.[26] In this narrative, the *mutamassir* are aligned with the interests of non-national capital. The subsequent failure of the Bank Misr project and the aim of national capitalists became evident by the late 1930s and was symptomatic of the economic weakness of the national movement. The period up to 1952 is accordingly one that descends into increasing economic disarray and political chaos. With the July Revolution, the cause of national capitalism, progressively state-controlled, was embraced by the new regime. The *mutamassirun*, as the representatives of foreign capital, were then progressively squeezed out and ultimately vanquished with the nationalization laws in 1961.

The study of Nabil 'Abd al-Hamid on the economic activities of foreigners in the interrevolutionary period provides an illustrative case of a synthesis of elements from both liberal and materialist schools, or, in effect, the social school that has broadly defined the academic mainstream since the early 1970s.[27] In his opening paragraph, 'Abd al-Hamid addresses the definitional problem raised by the term 'foreigner' (*ajnabi*). Acknowledging that the definition of a foreigner is based on a social construction of reality, he nevertheless prefers a legal determination.

> Society's view is [that] the definition of foreigners [is] constructed on the basis of reality. But that basis is not recognized in law and is not enough to prove or recognize the person by nationality or legal membership in the state. However this definition, naturally, has to follow the legal definition when it lays down the rules and regulations which define who is a citizen and consequently who is foreign.[28]

The parameters of the study having been established on the basis of this definition, the author proceeds to discuss the changes in the laws of nationality in Egypt during the 1920s and the legal privileges that the Capitulations conferred on foreign nationals.[29] Restricting his discussion to European foreigners, on the grounds of their economic importance and the fact that most other foreigners were former Ottoman citizens and had taken Egyptian nationality, 'Abd al-Hamid deals with various aspects of the activities of foreigners in agriculture, industry, trade and banks. The exclusive emphasis on economic and capitalist activities makes the equation of the *mutamassirun* with the non-national bourgeoisie, and thus the allies of imperialism, almost inevitable. In his conclusion the author takes up the standard theme of Bank Misr as the prime example of the difficulties faced by national capital in its competition with foreign capitalists.

There is little doubt of 'Abd al-Hamid's estimation of the role of foreigners in the Egyptian economy. In his concluding remarks he states that 'whoever undertakes the study of the economic activities of foreigners in Egypt in this period [i.e. 1922–52] finds in the end that they have studied the economic history of Egypt and vice-versa.'[30] However, there is little positive evaluation of this record nor any acknowledgment of the class or ethnic diversity within the foreign community in Egypt. The existence of a foreign working class is not discussed nor does there appear to be much recognition of social and political differences within different national groups. In a section titled 'Incidents of Attacks on Foreigners' which seeks to illustrate the changes in Egyptian attitudes towards foreigners after 1922, 'Abd al-Hamid only discusses attacks on English nationals and officials, an interpretation that collapses any differentiation between foreign nationals. This dichotomy made between Egyptian and foreigner and the lack of differentiation between foreigners that in effect equates them with the capitalist or imperialist is characteristic of national historiography.

In one area, and even then in a limited way, the materialist school does acknowledge an exception to this monolithic perception. Among Egyptian labour historians there is general agreement on the substantial role played by resident foreign workers in the development of the trade union movement and working class consciousness among Egyptian workers at the beginning of the twentieth century, even if the nature of relations is not discussed in any detail.[31] This was particularly the case with Greek and Italian workers in Alexandria and Cairo and in the ports of the Suez Canal. This solidarity on the left took on stronger political overtones with the emergence of a communist movement in which *mutamassir* elements were conspicuous. In 1921, the Egyptian Socialist Party (later the Egyptian Communist Party) was established with Joseph Rosenthal, a European Jew, Sakellaris Yannakakis, a resident Greek, and Egyptians, such as Salama Musa and Husni al-'Urabi, as prominent members and many resident foreigners, particularly Russian Jews, in the rank and file.[32] Repressed and undermined in the following years by both Wafdist and non-Wafdist governments, the party was effectively broken up by the mid-1920s. It re-emerged in the late 1930s as the so-called second wave, again with middle class *mutamassirun*, and especially Jews, playing a leading part.[33] These interconnections notwithstanding, the materialist like the liberal school regards the National Revolution of 1919 as a watershed in Egyptian politics. It holds that 1919 precipitated a reconfiguration within the labour movement that saw a greater separation between Egyptians and foreigners with the formation of separate unions, working under different wages and conditions, and growing nationalist consciousness among the Egyptian working class.[34] Less an expression of mutual solidarity, the multinational character of the communist movement of the 1940s is here a cause for internal factionalism and political weakness on the national stage.

The materialist school presents a more organic and rounded portrayal of the role of foreign residents in Egypt than is found in the analyses of the liberal school. In discussing the extent of their commercial activities and the pattern of economic relations between Egyptian and local foreign interests, there is some recognition given to connections between the two groups. Further, because of its ideological bent, the materialist school is more open to consideration of the role of foreigners in the development of the labour and communist movements. Nevertheless, consistent with its central position on the importance of national economic independence, the materialist school prioritizes the capitalist above all other classes as the representative member of the foreign resident community. When all is said and done, the *mutamassirun* are little more than the non-national bourgeoisie. Willing to recognize the positive contributions of the Egyptian capitalist, the materialist school is resistant to granting that the *mutamassir* capitalists might have played a similarly constructive role.

THE ISLAMIC CURRENT: 'DOMESTIC IMPERIALISTS'

If the liberal school looks askance at the *mutamassirun* because of their different legal status and the materialist school stressed their exploitative economic role, the Islamic current has emphasized both these evils and added to them the charge of introducing an alien culture into Egyptian society and corrupting its traditional values. In the work of early Ikhwan writers the *mutamassirun* were principally criticized in their role as the economic agents of imperialism. Muhammad al-Ghazzali, Sayyid Qutb and to a lesser extent, Hasan al-Banna himself, inveighed against the moral evils of capitalism and the foreign domination of the Egyptian economy. Foreigners resident in Egypt were guilty of both charges: they were 'domestic imperialists' (*musta'mirun dakhiliyyun*).[35] This applied not only to the British imperialists occupying Egypt nor the resident foreign nationals but even those foreigners who had assumed Egyptian nationality, presumably a reference to some *mutamassirun*. Accordingly, the economic policies of the Ikhwan, developed to counter foreign control of the Egyptian economy by the nationalization of natural resources and the replacement of foreign by local capital, were targeted as much at the local minorities, the internal agents of imperialism, as British imperialism itself.[36]

Characteristic of the Ikhwan's thought, this was not simply an issue of economic exploitation but one which took on religious, moral, even civilizational overtones. As Mitchell notes,

> In no discussion of this matter [i.e. Egyptian capitalism] by Banna or his followers was the economic question of control separable from the cultural, religious, societal, or personal question of inferiority and humiliation – an angry response to the conspicuous contempt of the foreign 'economic overlord' for the Egyptian and to 'Muslim servility' before the foreign master. The importance of this view cannot be overemphasized; strongly felt and widely held, it remained a constant in the movement's dynamic.[37]

The sins of the imperialist order were many: it had presided over the corruption of traditional Muslim values, it had facilitated the decay of Islamic heritage, it had introduced a civil education system and an alien legal code that had undermined the *shari'a*. European civilization was held to be the source of the great vices of materialism, communism and atheism. In this the *khawajat*, were merely the local agents of Western economic and cultural imperialism. Jews, as non-Muslims, who were assumed to both hold foreign nationality and to be crypto-Zionists, received particular censure.[38]

Al-Bishri develops this theme of a corrupting alien cultural presence. He holds 'imperialism and its local European allies' (*al-isti'mar wa hulafa'ha al-mahalliyyun urubiyyun*), a clear reference to the *mutamassirun*, as responsible for the encroachment of Western values and foreign institutions on Egyptian society that began during the reign of Isma'il.[39] If the royalist school had talked in terms of the positive contribution of foreigners, al-Bishri views their economic, religious and cultural activities as divisive and having a corrosive effect on the 'Islamic foundation' (*qa'ida islamiyya*) of Egyptian society. A judge in Egyptian public life, al-Bishri is very conscious of the legal dimension and implications of the *mutamassir* presence, particularly manifest in the Capitulations, the institution of the Mixed Courts and the periodic interventions by the European powers in the political and administrative affairs of Egypt. He therefore regards one of the most important demands of the Egyptian national movement to have been the unity of the legal system.[40] There is a certain irony in this. While predicated on notions of an 'authentic' Egyptian and Islamic identity, al-Bishri's analysis falls back on legal categories derived from agreements made with European powers to determine boundaries rather than by reference to Egyptian traditions of openness to foreign influence, the multiethnic millet system of the Ottoman Empire or the religious sanction of *ahl al-dhimma* (protection of non-Muslims).[41] More generally, the Islamic current shares with the liberal and materialist schools the characteristic homogenization of the *mutamassir* communities, making little or no distinction between different social classes or ethnic groups. More than this, it presents the most hostile position towards the presence of the *mutamassirun*, counting them as outsiders in a political, economic, cultural and, above all, a religious sense.

MUTAMASSIR VOICES

The hegemonic negative image of the *mutamassirun* in contemporary Egyptian historiography is a function of both external and internal political factors. Certainly the increasing nationalist atmosphere of the interwar period driven by anti-imperialist sentiment was the single most important element. Even if official statements made in the wake of the July Revolution were evidence of the fact that the concept of a multiethnic Egypt was not implausible, subsequent developments put this beyond reach. The policies of nationalization and Egyptianization, while not necessarily aimed at *mutamassir* elements *per se*, undercut their economic standing and the viability of their place in the wider Egyptian community. By the mid 1960s, amidst the prevailing anti-capitalist and anti-Western rhetoric and with the individual communities in obvious decline, the negative characterization of the *mutamassirun* far outweighed any positive interpretation of their presence in Egypt. The royalist school, encouraged by the throne for its own political purposes, had offered a raison d'être for the *mutamassir* presence, or at least its well-heeled elements. With the fall of the monarchy this protection, already substantially in decline, was no longer available and, indeed, had become a source of accusation. With little effective political patronage upon which to call and even less formal political power, there was no real refuge left.

The weakness of the *mutamassirun* to project a positive image was not only due to circumstances external to the communities. As has been argued in the discussion on other streams of scholarship, internal cohesion and organizational resources are important aspects in the propagation of a historical voice. The inability of the *mutamassirun* both because of their small numbers and the lack of material means meant that they were unable to compete with national institutions, or even with minor political actors, in propagating a favourable, counter historical interpretation. The sites of cultural production that might have generated this supplementary voice, such as the community press and publishing houses, were largely inaccessible to the majority of Egyptians because of limited circulation and the language barrier. The independence of the community education systems was also significantly undercut when the Egyptian government placed them under greater state supervision in the late 1950s.[42] In the face of this sustained political and historiographical barrage, there was little likelihood that the *mutamassirun*, even while in Egypt in considerable numbers, could turn the nationalist thrust. The continuing decline of the communities, and the tightening political and economic noose of the nationalizations, proved any efforts to generate a wider national vision to be ultimately in vain.[43]

Despite the seemingly irresistible force of nationalism, there were attempts by individuals and organizations from within the *mutamassir* communities to create an alternative, or better, a supplementary discourse. Though they probably had only a limited impact beyond their immediate circle, they signify an important statement of claim for incorporation into a broader, more inclusive sense of the Egyptian nation. These efforts differed from the royalist works of Sammarco and Radopoulos in not being sponsored by palace interests nor simply extolling the contribution of foreigners to Egypt. Rather they sought to present a more organic and integrated portrayal of the country's social diversity that emphasized interrelations and interaction over ethnic, cultural or other differences. They thus offered a dissonant or supplementary perspective on the historical character of Egypt than that put forward by the more narrow national discourses. One such case was the Société d'études historiques juives. Set up in 1925 by prominent Jews, Yusuf Qattawi, Rabbi Haim Nahum and others, it served as a forum for scholarly discussion and published research on the history and literature of the Arab world and Middle Eastern Jewry. Later in the 1930s, the Association de la jeunesse juive égyptienne and an Arabic language Jewish paper, *al-Shams*, both sought to promote an awareness of Jewish heritage as a constituent of Egyptian historical identity.[44] These efforts were ultimately drowned out by the clash between competing ideologies of Zionism, communism and a narrow nationalism that had dire implications for Jewish life in Egypt.

As the largest of the ethnic communities, it was the Greek community of Egypt that was the most active and organized in its intellectual and cultural life. The figures of its published output alone are impressive. In the hundred years from 1862 (the date of the first Greek language newspaper in Egypt) about four hundred different newspaper and periodical titles owned by Greeks were published in the country, mostly in Greek but also in Arabic and French.[45] In the same period, more than three thousand books were published in Greek on a great array of topics.[46] Much of this material reflected community concerns, reported and discussed developments in the Greek state, or was European and especially French in cultural orientation. Nevertheless, there was also a strong focus on the specific manifestation of Greek culture in Egypt, and an awareness of its contribution and place within the broader Egyptian society. In Alexandria, where at one time almost half of the Greeks in Egypt lived, the Greek community supported a particularly active group of intellectuals and historians from the late nineteenth century onwards.

By the mid-1920s, probably prompted by the changing political environment, elements in the community began calling for greater recognition of the importance of research on the Greek presence in Egypt.[47] Over the following decade two periodicals were particularly important in articulating an Egyptian Greek discourse.[48] The first, a progressive weekly journal,

Panegiptia (1926–38), was edited by a well-known liberal, Stephanos Pargas, and dealt with a whole range of political, social, economic and cultural issues. Among its stated aims was the study of the specific problems of Egyptian Greeks and the promotion of intellectual and social connections between Greeks and Egyptians.[49] The second publication was a bilingual monthly newspaper in Arabic and Greek titled *Egiptiotis Ellin–al-Yunani al-muta-massir* ('The Egyptianized-Greek') (1932–40), owned by Angelos Kasigonis and specifically dedicated to the 'strengthening of fraternal links between two peoples' (*taqwiyat al-rawabit al-akhawiyya bayna al-sha'bayn*).[50] In pursuing this aim *Egiptiotis Ellin* featured articles on historical and community links between Egyptians and Greeks, consistently promoted the importance of learning Arabic and tourism in Greece, and drew on the services of a large number of Greek and Egyptian contributors. In addition, Pargas and Kasigonis owned separate publishing houses, Grammata and Erevna respectively, which were active in the publication of Greek language works on Egypt, among them a short history of Egypt by Georgios Arvanitakis and a history of Egypt–Greek relations since 1800 by General Yiannis Petridis, which was also translated into Arabic.[51]

One of the central intellectuals of the Egyptian Greek community was Evgenios Mikhailidis (1885–1975). Born Najib Mikhail Sa'ati in Jerusalem, Mikhailidis was an Arabophone Christian who had graduated with a diploma from the Theological School of the Holy Cross in Jerusalem before obtaining a doctorate in Arabic language and philology at the College of Zahle in Lebanon in 1911.[52] In early 1912 he migrated to Alexandria where he worked as a teacher of religion, history, Greek, Latin and Arabic in the Greek community, patriarchal, private and evening schools. For the next 60 years he would be a prolific contributor on a wide range of historical themes in the Greek language press and periodicals as well as the author of a large number of works on Egyptian Hellenism. One of Mikhailidis' principal goals was to document the intellectual achievement of Egyptian Hellenism and the historical and cultural connections between Egypt and Greeks but he did not restrict himself to these themes. In the pages of *Panegiptia,* his articles on cultural and political aspects regularly addressed aspects of the Egyptian national movement. He also wrote monographs on contemporary issues of Egyptian intellectual life, such as his discussion of the controversies generated by the work of 'Ali 'Abd al-Raziq (in Greek) and the life of Taha Husayn (in Arabic). In *Ekkliastikos Pharos*, a journal of the Alexandrian Patriarchate, Mikhailidis authored a series of eight articles in 1927–8 on the Egyptian intellectual movement as well as an ongoing series of reviews of Arabic language books of history and literature. From 1940 to 1952 he also served as editor of an Arabic language publication of the Patriarchate, *al-Ra'i al-salih* ('The Good Shepherd').

While perhaps the most prolific, Mikhailidis was only one of a number of Greek Arabists active in Egypt in the interwar period who served as important conduits between the Greek and Egyptian communities. In the pages of the press and literary journals such as *O Pharos, Ermis, Panegiptia*, and *Egiptiotis Ellin*, articles and translations on Egyptian culture, society and politics by Panos Patrikios, Odysseas Spanakidis, Xenophon Paskhalidis, Nikitas Kladakis, Sotiris Mikhailidis and others, regularly appeared. Alongside these Arabist scholars stands Khristophoros Nomikos (1883–1951), the pre-eminent Egyptian Greek historian of Islamic history.[53] Born in Athens, Nomikos had gone to Egypt in 1907 to take up a position with the Bank of Athens. Part of the progressive circles in Alexandria, Nomikos first published material on early Islamic history in the pages of the journal *Grammata* and authored a book of essays on the history and art of Muslim Cairo. In the years following his retirement in 1924 he continued to write, publishing a series of lectures *Anatoli ke Islam* ('East and Islam') (1925), and 2 years later, his *Eisagogi stin istoria ton Aravon* ('Introduction to the History of the Arabs'), an examination of the period from the time of the Prophet until the Umayyads. Nomikos' focus on the Arabs was unusual since most pre-modern historical studies by Egyptian Greeks had centred their narratives on the ancient period or the history of the Alexandrian Patriarchate. Perhaps for this reason Nomikos felt obliged to defend his choice of subject in the introduction to his Arabic history by stating that the greatness of the Arabs lay in that they had shown themselves to be the great and cultured rivals of the Byzantine Empire.[54]

The historical subject that received increasing attention from Greek writers was that of the modern Egyptian Greek presence itself. A landmark in this literature is the two-volume work of a Greek diplomat, Athanasios Politis, which was published in Greek and French at the end of the 1920s.[55] Written during his term of service in Egypt, the work owed something both to the royalist school, in its strong confidence in the benefits of European civilization and those that conveyed it, and something to the tradition of diplomatic reports. Nevertheless, its central theme of the historical development of the Greek presence in Egypt since 1798 and its contribution to modern Egypt was a significant departure both from works that had been drawn to more ancient periods to illustrate the close relations between Greek and Egyptian cultures and those who were concerned with developments on the Greek mainland. In effect, Politis reinforced the significance of Egyptian Hellenism as a subject of historical and contemporary study and produced a work that has proved a valuable resource for any study on the subject ever since.

The flow of works that followed in its wake, addressing and in some ways justifying a place for Greeks in Egypt continued throughout the 1930s and beyond. In the years after the Second World War, a number of organizations were set up to serve as a forum for study and research on aspects of the Greek presence in Egypt. In 1950, the Greek–Arabic Association began producing a bilingual periodical. Two years later the Institute of Oriental Studies under the auspices of the Patriarchal Library of Alexandria founded its own journal, *Analekta*, featuring articles on matters of religious and ancient Egyptian history in French, Greek and Arabic. In 1960, Mikhailidis was the leading force behind the establishment of the Centre for Greek Studies, which served as a Egyptian Greek cultural and intellectual voice, this time under the auspices of the Greek Consulate in Alexandria. By the end of the 1960s, with the Greek community in steep decline, the bulletin of the Centre had taken on a stronger focus on Greece and was being published in Athens.

In addition, the tradition of local histories dedicated to individual Greek *koinotites* (official communities) and broad-brush accounts of Egyptian Hellenism have been central in this increasing body of work by Egyptian Greeks.[56] Highly variable in quality, these often modest studies usually gave a brief outline of the Egyptian context and the hospitality of the Egyptian people before they submerged the reader in the minutiae of Greek community affairs. In scope, the trend reached its zenith with the work of Manolis Yalourakis (1921–87) who provided the definitive encyclopedic account of modern Egyptian Hellenism as the curtain was being lowered on a once vibrant community.[57] Published in Athens, Yalourakis' work testified to a new development: the historical presence of the Egyptian Greeks was being given new voice, not by the remnants of the community still resident, much less by Egyptian historians, but from elements of the Egyptian Greek diaspora. This trend was maintained over the following years by various individuals but it was the establishment of a network of Egyptian Greek associations around the world that allowed for the possibility of an institution-alized framework for these endeavours. In 1984 at the first international conference of Egyptian Greeks held in Athens it was suggested that a centre for the research and study of Egyptian Hellenism be set up. Although this specific proposal was not realized, a solution was found by setting up a collection of both published and archival research material, dedicated to the life of the Greeks of Egypt in the Greek Literary and Historical Archive (ELIA) in Athens.[58] The Association of Egyptian Greeks in Athens has itself also been active in propagating historical work through its journal *Panegiptia*, and by lending support to the publication of personal accounts written by individual members.

The project to revive and represent the historical Greek presence in Egypt has not just been community based. From at least the early 1980s, academics like Efthimios Souloyiannis, Christos Hadziiosif, Alexander Kitroeff, Pandelis Glavanis and Ilios Yannakakis, all of Egyptian Greek background, have made important contributions to this growing body of literature.[59] In this trend, the study of Alexander Kitroeff on the Greek community in Egypt in the interwar period stands as a significant milestone. Kitroeff's motivation for the study was in part a reaction to the tendency to ethno-centrism prevalent in earlier studies on the Egyptian Greeks. In the preface he stated,

In trying to reclaim the Greeks in Egypt on behalf of historiography (if I may be permitted to make such a bold statement) my wish was a study with conclusions which have a wider use in the examination of ethnic minorities in the past. I tried my best to avoid a 'Greco-centric' approach by considering the Greek entity in Egypt as an integral part of Egyptian society and conceptualising it in terms of its status as an ethnic group and a socially stratified unit.[60]

Applying this approach, Kitroeff's narrative gives particular emphasis to the class distinctions within an ethnic group during a time of social transformation and challenges, and at least modifies, many of the standard views of the Greek community found in Egyptian nationalist historiography. Thus, in his discussion of the riots which occurred in Egypt during the 1919 revolution, and generally held in nationalist narratives to be an expression of the resentment held against all foreigners, Kitroeff offers a revisionist interpretation, citing an emotional speech of the Greek consul-general in the face of an angry Egyptian crowd that diffused communal tensions and other individual cases of cooperation between Greeks and Egyptians on a local level.[61] Similarly, his discussion of the labour movement in the years after 1919 draws attention to the class-based character of trade union activity, rather than the ethnic-based picture that many historians have preferred.[62] In a departure from the standard view of national categories upheld by most Egyptian and Greek historians, Kitroeff concluded that ethnic feelings were more a feature of the Greek petite bourgeoisie than amongst the Greek working and upper classes.[63]

More recent work has added to this growing *mutamassir* literature. An edited collection titled, *Alexandrie 1860–1960*, brought together articles by a number of Egyptian-born writers dedicated to the discussion of the cosmopolitan city.[64] With chapters dedicated to specific *mutamassir* communities (Jews, Armenians, Greeks and Italians), it does not reintroduce the old Egyptian–European hierarchy but offers a complex analysis of the multi-ethnic culture of which they were part, set within a discussion of everyday life and literature. Its interest lies not only in presenting a more complex historical view of Egyptian society, culture, and politics that would appear at odds with the hegemonic national discourse but in highlighting diversity *within* individual ethnic communities – a subtlety little acknowledged in the writing of Egyptian historians.[65]

These modest but significant inroads into the academic literature have been supplemented by another genre of writing that has illuminated the historical experience of the *mutamassirun*, namely, historical fiction. A form that is more accessible to writers than the rigorous standards of academic scholarship, some of these authors have effectively presented themselves as underground historians whose work challenges the academic mainstream by being located outside of the hegemonic national framework.[66] The trilogy of Stratis Tsirkas, *Akivernites Polities* ('Drifting Cities') stands as a principal example.[67] Tsirkas (1911–80) (real name Yiannis Hatziandreas) was an ethnic Greek and Egyptian national who was born in Egypt and was active in the communist movement from the 1930s until his departure in 1963. The plot of the novel clearly draws much on Tsirkas' own experience, employing many characters based on actual persons against a background which proves itself to be an accurate historical account of the period when checked against other sources.[68] Set in Egypt and the Eastern Mediterranean during the Second World War, *Drifting Cities* portrays a Levantine world of Greeks, Jews, Christians and Muslims, interlocked and yet distinct from one another. Despite the seemingly irresistible tide of different national-isms, Egyptian, Greek and Zionist, the novel vividly conveys the complex conjunction of circumstances that ran both in favour of and counter to these forces, particularly in its representation of the Greek family living in a poor neighbourhood in Cairo. According to one critic, Tsirkas presented a 'world seen from kitchen windows and mean neighbourhoods'.[69] Many other Egyp-tian Greek writers of short stories and full-length works set in Egypt have in similar fashion celebrated their attachment to the country and the people.[70] The genre is not, of course, restricted to Egyptian Greek circles. *Le Tarbouche*, a novel by Robert Solé, a Syrian Egyptian who grew up in Egypt and now lives in France, presents a view of twentieth century Syrian life in Egypt, an area untouched by any academic work of an Egyptian historian.[71] Another autobiographical novel by André Aciman performs a similar service for Jewish life through its vivid depiction of the saga of a Jewish family in Alexandria in the first half of the twentieth century which sheds valuable light on its attitude and response to emergent Egyptian nationalism.[72]

Some of the spirit if not the detail of these works is found in Egyptian (Arabic language) literature. *Miramar* by Najib Mahfuz, the stories of Edward Kharrat and Tawfiq al-Hakim draw on Greek, Jewish and Armenian charac-ters to paint a picture of multi-ethnic Egyptian society.[73] There is also a nostalgic type of non-fictional writing that upholds a favourable view of cosmopolitan Egypt, even if it largely confines itself to the social and cultural elite.[74] The most prominent example of this genre is Samir Raafat. A member of a prominent upper-middle class Egyptian family, Rafaat was educated at Victoria College in Alexandria and graduated with a Bachelor of Arts degree in Economics, a social and educational background unusual for an Egyp-tian historian.[75] Working as a freelance journalist for the *Egyptian Gazette* and *Cairo Times*, Rafaat has written a large number of historical articles since the mid-1990s that present a far more positive view of the resident foreign communities than is generally found in the work of Egyptian his-torians at any time since 1952. One of Raafat's persistent themes is the contribution of the foreign minorities to the economic, social and, indeed, physical construction of Egypt. An occasional ongoing series, 'Adopt a Monu-ment', describes individual buildings and architectural features, often built by *mutamassirun*, which serve as a platform for recounting their contribution to the cosmopolitan splendour of Egypt at the same time as recording and decrying its decline.[76]

While in some aspects Raafat's focus on the micro-history, the role of individuals and their business and personal affairs, is traditional and inspired by a yearning for the belle époque, set beside the hegemonic logjam of nationalist discourse it offers a refreshing alternative approach. His perspective is particularly challenging not only in the way he assesses the contribution of *mutamassir* interests to Egypt's development but also in his commentary on aspects of the standard nationalist narrative. In his discussion on the NBE, a bête noire for nationalists and a symbol of the foreign control of the Egyptian economy, Raafat stresses the bank's positive role in the development of the country and the important part played by *mutamassir* businessmen, Raphael Suares, a Jew of Italian nationality, and Constantinos Salvagos, a Greek. He further subverts this stock nationalist reference by pointing out that Tal'at Harb, founder of Bank Misr and darling of the nationalist cause, received his training in banking while working for Suares.[77]

Raafat's only book to date, *Maadi 1904–62: History and Society in a Cairo Suburb*, brings these themes together in one case study.[78] The choice of Ma'adi as a historical subject is particularly significant. A suburb established in 1904 by foreign business interests, it encapsulated much of the cosmopolitan aspect of Egyptian society in its prime, being a favoured residence for the well-to-do in Jewish, British, French, Greek and American circles. While in his autobiography 'Ali Sabri, a prominent member of the Nasser regime in the 1960s (and ironically a relative of Raafat) had written disparagingly of Ma'adi, the area where he had grown up, with its foreign residents and alien atmosphere, Raafat uses the same suburb to illustrate the complexity and richness of this society as a part of modern Egyptian history.[79]

Raafat's views are partly motivated by his reaction to the hypocrisy of the current regime in continuing its nationalist tirade against the historical role of the *mutamassirun* at the same time as it presides over practices that pale in comparison with the situation before 1952. While acknowledging the advantages that the Capitulations gave to foreign nationals, Raafat considers them as a lesser concession than the privileges currently enjoyed by foreigners working in Egypt under the terms of bilateral agreements between the Egyptian and American governments.[80] It comes as little surprise, then, that Raafat's work has not been well received in the prevailing political atmosphere in Egypt. It is significant that he contributes to two *English* language publications and that his book on Ma'adi was also published in English. Raafat explains,

> My articles have been rejected in Arabic. I suspect had they been presented in a more haphazard way without favourable mention of

the Jewish minority they could have had a better chance. The Maadi book itself was rejected in Arabic.[81]

He comments, 'In view of the political situation I can do without being stigmatized "minority lover" especially when the successors of one of these important minorities is an unwanted neighbour.'[82]

In academic circles where the conceptual limitations of national discourse are even more complicit with the interests of the state the boundaries of 'legitimate' Egyptian scholarship have not strayed far from the ideological constraints of the hegemonic political culture. The history departments of Egyptian universities have yet to show themselves a hospitable environment for a balanced analysis of the foreign resident presence in Egypt and a genuine consideration of its organic relationship with the broader Egyptian society. Despite, for example, the extensive historical work on the communist movement by Egyptian (and Western) scholars, there has been little recognition of the political engagement of *mutamassir* leftists in Egyptian politics, save a brief role in the early 1920s.[83] It is a curious feature of Egyptian historiography that the *mutamassirun* appear in many different contexts as capitalists, entrepreneurs, industrialists, members of the social elite, workers, communists, drug dealers, journalists and intellectuals, but that they are almost always incidental and rarely cast in a central and certainly not a positive role in a mainstream historical issue.[84] Few of the cultural and social interconnections between Egyptian and *mutamassir* communities and individuals have been explored and there has been little distinction made within the foreign communities, between the British colonial official and the Armenian shoemaker, the French businessman and the Greek grocer.[85]

While some may have entertained the prospect of a multi-ethnic and multicultural Egypt, none of the main historiographical currents discussed here, with the exception of the royalist school, has had a place for the *mutamassirun* in their national framework. Nor is there much inclination amongst Egyptian academic historians to recognize their claims to a stake in legitimate Egyptian discourse.[86] The dichotomy constructed between Egyptians and foreigners that emerges with the arrival of the British occupation becomes irresistible after 1919 which, for the liberal and materialist schools, represents a definitive turning point in Egypt. Thereafter, it has been one of the articles of faith of national discourse that the *mutamassir* communities were little more than transplanted colonies of their motherlands, allied with and serving foreign interests and with little organic connection with Egyptian society. Each of the three other schools discussed had characterized them in blanket fashion as disconnected and natural outsiders to the Egyptian community. In the words of one scholar, 'they were resident in Egypt but they were not of Egypt'.[87]

It might be more accurate to state that 'they were of Egypt but they are not now.' The political and ideological process that occurred during the course of the twentieth century that saw a reconstruction of the nation also has substantially distorted the role of the *mutamassirun* in the historical record. Vitalis quotes a concrete example of this process, recounting how after the first Aswan Dam was finished in 1902, a plaque was put up describing the multi-ethnic character of the enterprise:

> This dam was designed and built by British engineers
> Egyptians assisted by Greeks excavated
> To the rock foundations and
> Built the rubble masonry
> Skilled Italian workmen dressed and built
> The granite ashlar

In 1947, in a radically different political atmosphere, the wording of the plaque was deemed unsuitable and it was removed because it did 'not shed a true light of things'. It was then effectively claimed as a wholly Egyptian construction.[88] This rather trivial incident crystallizes the fate of the *mutamassirun* in contemporary Egyptian historiography. Despite their substantial and varied presence in Egyptian history and place in society and culture, they have been erased from the record by the ideological demands of national discourse.

The historiography of the *mutamassirun* demonstrates pointedly the political contingencies of historical scholarship and the conceptual boundaries of national discourse. In the early part of the century, in the discourse of the royalist school, the *mutamassirun* were participants and contributors in the task of national development and state building. Over the following decades, as other schools of interpretation emerged, they were marginalized from any legitimate claim of belonging to Egypt and cast out as political, economic and cultural aliens. They became casualties in the clash between nationalism and empire; their political loyalties were deemed at best as ambiguous, and more often as inimical to the national cause. The power of nationalism, reinforced by the authority of the state, may have made the fate of the *mutamassirun* inevitable. Nevertheless, the subsequent failures of the hegemonic nationalist vision and the *mutamassir* response in academic work, personal memoirs and historical fiction suggest that an understanding of Egypt's historical development may require a reassessment of the 'national' categories upon which it has recently been based and the recognition of a more inclusive definition of Egyptian society.

CONCLUSION

The development of Egyptian historiography in the twentieth century has been the product of a complex interaction of political, social, cultural and intellectual factors. The academy, the state and diverse forces in civil society have each served as significant sites of struggle and important reference points in the contest to establish a hegemonic national historiography. While the authority of the state has clearly been a central factor in this contest, its influence has been moderated by the configuration of other political and social forces. The resulting diversity of historical interpretation is expressive of the conflictual nature of politics, the inherent political enterprise of writing history and the complexity of Egyptian society.

The interaction between scholarship and politics has taken on quite specific forms. During the nineteenth century and especially in the reign of Fu'ad, royal authority was keenly aware of the political utility of cultivating individuals, learned societies and institutions to produce sympathetic history. In the twentieth century, the changing nature of politics and the emergence of the modern university system presented a more complex relationship between the academy and state authority that has nonetheless been complicit in determining the boundaries of national discourse. The academy and the state have not been alone in appreciating the political dimensions of historical scholarship. Since the emergence of an educated middle class at the end of the nineteenth century, non-professional historians have been the agents of a vigorous and innovative scholarship. Often created and sustained by political cliques, they have articulated alternative historical interpretations as part of a broader political programme and social vision. While neither possessing the resources nor enjoying the support of the state, neither were they beholden to its ideology nor to the professional and political constraints of the academy. Indeed, they have been able to produce dissident discourses that have at times complemented, significantly challenged and even overthrown the hegemonic discourse. These three loci, the university, the state and the political street, have operated as the principal sources of historical scholarship and been responsible for producing, sustaining and containing the currents of contemporary discourse.

In constructing a text consonant with its political position the schools of interpretation discussed here have proposed contested conceptions of national identity, alternative configurations of the elements of Egyptian society and competing hierarchies of agents and forces that carry implications for political legitimacy. The royalist school, utilizing an idiom of institutional state-building and benevolent leadership, sited the nation within the confines of the palace. The liberal school, employing the catchcry of political independence, portrayed the will of the Egyptian nation as articulated by leaders such as Mustafa Kamil and Sa'd Zaghlul in the battle against the imperialists. For the materialist school, the national bourgeoisie and the communist movement were at the forefront of the struggle for political and economic independence, while the Islamic current proposed a culture of authentic nationalism based on the values of Islam and embodied by groups such as the Ikhwan. Each of these perspectives, drawing on elements from a heterogeneous Egyptian tradition, sought to construct a national discourse that represented the collective identity of all Egyptians. Thus, in different ways each has been preoccupied with the same 'national' events: the 1919 Revolution, the struggle against the British, the July Revolution and the Nasser regime. This national perspective has been just as true of the materialist and Islamic schools that offered, potentially at least, a more internationalist focus.

In this study I have suggested that historical interpretation is empowered by political forces as a means of defining, reinforcing, justifying and above all contesting what is politically legitimate and feasible. The pattern of future developments in Egyptian historical scholarship will be dominated by this dynamic. Within the matrix of political and social forces, universities will remain the heartland of a broad current of thought where both conservative and liberal wings of a synthesis of elements from the liberal and materialist schools, the 'social school', hold sway. Given sufficient freedom of expression, political forces outside of the academy will continue to sponsor versions and revisions of Egyptian history that are consistent with their ideological antecedents and their political programmes. Historiographical challenges to the national-secular consensus upheld by the academy and the state may come from a number of directions. The first is the broad Islamic current which poses as the most significant political threat to a regime that is secular in principle. A related phenomenon, contemporary Coptic historiography, has already been aroused by the failure of the state to make good on its claim to represent a united nation and citizenry. Given the ongoing struggle between Islamic and secular orientations, it is probable that a Coptic discourse will continue to manifest its voice in historical scholarship. Other, less threatening, voices in civil society are also likely to maintain a dissident voice in proportion to their social and political significance. Feminist historiography has the potential to challenge the hegemonic male orientation of scholarship but without a substantial shift in the position of women in Egyptian society, this is unlikely to exert considerable influence. Some new work on the historical role of the labour and communist movement has presented a more autonomous and nuanced account of the left. Outside of Egypt, the voice of the *mutamassir* diaspora has served to represent a multicultural and pluralist vision of Egypt that acts as an important if politically impotent counter to the dominant national discourse.

At the beginning of the twenty-first century, the Egyptian polity is faced with a number of significant challenges. The tension or resolution of the precarious balance maintained by the state between the calls for a more Islamic society, the demands for a more open and democratic political culture and the outside pressures of global capitalism and international alliances will certainly be reflected in the pattern of historical scholarship. A more robust Islamic trend may bring with it a greater emphasis on the cultural-religious values of Islamic and, by association, Arab society and a corresponding neglect, even rejection, of other elements deemed as foreign. A more pluralist atmosphere, less fixated on the essentialism of the nation may provoke a reassessment and constructive critique of the historical role played by subaltern elements of Egyptian society such as the *mutamassirun*. In turn, this may facilitate a less chauvinist and even celebratory view of the historical and contemporary diversity of Egyptian society rather than the insistence on the programmatic unity that has been the talisman of national historiography.

NOTES

INTRODUCTION

1 From a large body of literature on Middle East historiography which employs this approach, see Bernard Lewis and P.M. Holt (eds), *Historians of the Middle East*, London: Oxford UP, 1962; M. Mustafa Ziyada, 'Modern Egyptian Historiography', *Middle East Affairs* (August–September 1953) 266–71; Salama Musa, 'Intellectual Currents in Egypt', *Middle East Affairs* (August–September 1951) 267–72; Halil Inalcik, 'Some Remarks on the Study of History in Islamic Countries', *Middle East Journal* 7 (1953) 451–5; Nabih Amin Faris, 'The Arabs and Their History', *Middle East Journal* 8 (1954) 155–62; Bernard Lewis, 'History Writing and National Revival in Turkey', *Middle East Affairs* 4 (1953) 218–27; Anwar G. Chejne, 'The Use of History by Arab Writers', *Middle East Journal* 14 (1960) 382–96; Anwar G. Chejne, 'The Concept of History in the Modern Arab World', *Studies in Islam* 4 (1967) 1–31. On Asian and African historiography, Geoffrey Barraclough, *Main Trends in History*, New York and London: Holmes & Meier, 1979, 141–7.

2 These assumptions also underwrite encyclopedic works such as John Cannon (ed.), *The Blackwell Dictionary of Historians*, Oxford: Blackwell, 1988 and Lucian Boia (ed.), *Great Historians of the Modern Age*, New York: Greenwood Press, 1991.

3 Gallagher's series of interviews emphasize this aspect of the historian as an individual and self-aware scholar, Nancy E. Gallagher (ed.), *Approaches to the History of the Middle East: Interviews with Leading Middle East Historians*, Reading: Ithaca, 1994.

4 For example, Jack A. Crabbs Jr, *The Writing of History in Nineteenth-Century Egypt, A Study in National Transformation*, Detroit: Wayne State University & Cairo: AUC Press, 1984; Gamal al-Din al-Shayyal, *A History of Egyptian Historiography in the Nineteenth Century*, Faculty of Arts, no. 15, Alexandria UP, 1962.

5 For such discussions of the 'Arab intellectual', see Samir Khalaf, 'The Growing Pains of Arab Intellectuals', *Diogenes* 54 (1966) 59–80; Hisham Sharabi, 'The Crisis of the Intelligentsia in the Middle East', *Muslim World* 47 no. 3 (July 1957) 187–93. In contrast to this stereotyping, compare Ihsan 'Abd al-Quddus' description of Egyptian intellectuals as 'the most disunited, scattered and mutually-hostile group in the country', in Nissim Rejwan, *Nasserist Ideology, Its Exponents and Critics*, Jerusalem: Israel Universities Press, 1974, 78.

6 George M. Enteen, *The Soviet Scholar-Bureaucrat, M.N. Pokrovskii and the Society of Marxist Historians*, Pennsylvania UP, 1978; Shahram Akbarzadeh, 'Nation-building in Uzbekistan', *Central Asian Survey* 15 no. 1 (1996) 23–32; David Christian, 'Marat Durdyiev and Turkmen Nationalism', 57–81 in Aleksandar Pavkovic *et al.* (eds), *Nationalism and Postcommunism, A Collection of Essays*, Aldershot: Dartmouth, 1995.

7 Bogumil Jewsiewicki and David Newbury (eds), *African Historiographies, What History for Which Africa*, Beverly Hills, CA: Sage, 1986; Arnold Temu and Bonaventure Swai, *Historians and Africanist History: A Critique, Post-Colonial Historiography Examined*, London: Zed Press, 1981.

8 Anthony Reid and David Marr (eds), *Perceptions of the Past in Southeast Asia*, Singapore: Heinemann Educational Books, 1979.

9 Youssef M. Choueiri, *Arab History and the Nation-State, A Study of Modern Arab Historiography*, 1820–1980, London: Routledge, 1989; Lisa Anderson, 'Legitimacy, Identity, and the Writing of History in Libya', 71–91 in Eric Davis and Nicolas Gavrielides (eds), *Statecraft in the Middle East, Oil, Historical Memory, and Popular Culture*, Miami: Florida International UP, 1991; Amatzia Baram, *Culture, History & Ideology in the Formation of Ba'thist Iraq 1968–89*, New York: St Martin's Press, 1991; Speros Vryonis Jr, *The Turkish State and History, Clio Meets the Grey Wolf*, Thessaloniki: Institute for Balkan Studies, 1991; Jack A. Crabbs Jr, 'Politics, History and Culture in Nasser's Egypt', *IJMES* 6 (1975) 386–420; R. Hrair Dekmejian, *Egypt under Nasir, A Study in Political Dynamics*, University of London Press, 1972, 64–81; Thomas Mayer, *The Changing Past, Egyptian Historiography of the Urabi Revolt, 1882–1983*, Gainsville: University of Florida Press, 1988; Ulrike Freitag, 'Writing Arab History: The Search for the Nation', *British Journal of Middle East Studies* 21 no. 1 (1994) 19–37.

10 See, for example, Donald M. Reid, *Cairo University and the Making of Modern Egypt*, Cairo: AUC Press, 1991; 'Abd al-Mun'im Ibrahim al-Disuqi al-Jumay'i, *al-Jam'iyya al-misriyya li'l-dirasat al-tarikhiyya*, Shubra: Matba'at al-jablawi, 1985.

11 Ahmad 'Abd Allah (ed.), *Tarikh misr: bayna al-manahij al-'alimi wa'l-sira' al-hizbi*, Cairo: Dar al-shuhdi li'l-nashr, 1988; 'Ali Barakat, 'al-Tarikh wa'l-qadaya al-manhaj fi misr al-mu'asira', *Qadaya fikriyya* 11–12 (July 1992) 73–90; Roel Meijer, 'Contemporary Egyptian Historiography of the Period 1936–1942: A Study of Its Scientific and Political Character', Amsterdam, 1985; Ulrike Freitag, *Geschichtsschreibung in Syrien 1920–1990, zwischen Wissenschaft und Politik*, Hamburg, 1991.

12 Nadav Safran, *In Search of Political Community, An Analysis of the Intellectual and Political Revolution of Egypt, 1804–1952*, Cambridge, Mass.: Harvard UP, 1961, 128; Israel Gershoni and James P. Jankowski, *Egypt, Islam and the Arabs, The Search for Egyptian Nationhood, 1900–1930*, Oxford UP, 1986; Gudrun Krämer, 'History and Legitimacy: The Use of History in Contemporary Egyptian Party Politics', 2; on Egyptianity, see Vatikiotis, *Arab and Regional Politics*, London: Croom Helm, 1984, 252. For a catalogue of concepts see Shimon Shamir, 'Self-Views in Modern Egyptian Historiography', in Shimon Shamir (ed.), *Self-Views in Historical Perspective in Egypt and Israel*, Tel Aviv University, 1981.

13 See foreword by Edward Said in R. Guha and G.C. Spivak (eds), *Selected Subaltern Studies*, Oxford UP, 1988, vi. The term *subaltern* in the Gramscian sense refers to a non-hegemonic class or classes. For a critical evaluation of the project see Jim Masselos, 'The Dis/appearance of Subalterns: A Reading of a Decade of Subaltern Studies', *South Asia* 15 no. 1 (1992) 105–25.

14 Abdul R. JanMohamed and David Lloyd (eds), *The Nature and Context of Minority Discourse*, New York, Oxford: Oxford UP, 1990, 6.

15 Gallagher, *Approaches to the History of the Middle East*, 26.

16 Abdallah Laroui, *The Crisis of the Arab Intellectual*, University of California Press, 1976, 176.

17 Earl of Cromer, *Modern Egypt*, vol. II, London: Macmillan, 1908, 126–30.

18 For example, Judith E. Tucker, 'Problems in the Historiography of Women in the Middle East: The Case of Nineteenth-Century Egypt', *IJMES* 15 (1983) 321–36.

In her interviews, Gallagher routinely asks about the role of women in history, *Approaches to the History of the Middle East*.

19 Margot Badran and Miriam Cooke (eds), *Opening the Gates, A Century of Arab Feminist Writing*, Indiana UP, 1990, which brings together a large selection of writings by Arab feminists; Nikki R. Keddie and Beth Baron (eds), *Women in Middle Eastern History*, New Haven and London: Yale UP, 1991; Beth Baron, *The Women's Awakening in Egypt*, New Haven & London: Yale UP, 1994; Margot Badran, *Feminists, Islam, and Nation, Gender and the Making of Modern Egypt*, American University in Cairo Press, 1996.

20 Joel Beinin and Zachary Lockman, *Workers on the Nile: Nationalism, Communism, Islam and the Egyptian Working Class, 1882–1954*, London: I.B. Tauris, 1988, 3.

21 Robert Tignor, *State, Private Enterprise and Economic Change in Egypt*, Princeton NJ: Princeton UP, 1984; Robert Vitalis, *When Capitalists Collide, Business Conflict and the End of Empire in Egypt*, Berkeley: University of California Press, 1995.

22 Nathan J. Brown, *Peasant Politics in Modern Egypt, The Struggle Against the State*, New Haven and London: Yale UP, 1990; see also Timothy Mitchell, 'The Invention and Reinvention of the Egyptian Peasant', *IJMES* 22 (1990) 129–50.

23 But see Tomas Hagg (ed.), *Nubian Culture Past and Present*, Stockholm: Almqvist and Wiksell International, 1987; Thomas Phillip, *The Syrians in Egypt 1725–1975*, Stuttgart: Steiner Verlag Wiesbaden GmbH, 1985; Alexander Kitroeff, *The Greeks in Egypt, 1919–1937, Ethnicity and Class*, London: Ithaca, 1989.

24 Crabbs, *WH*, 18.

25 P.J. Vatikiotis, 'State and Class in Egypt: A Review Essay' in C.E. Bosworth *et al.* (eds), *The Islamic World, From Classical to Modern Times, Essays in Honor of Bernard Lewis*, Princeton NJ: Darwin Press 1989, 875–89. See also his hostile review, 'The New Western Historiography of Modern Egypt', *Middle Eastern Studies* 27 (April 1991) 322–8.

26 On the decline of cosmopolitanism in Egypt, see the chapters by Ahmed Abdalla and Mohamed Sayyid Said in Roel Meijer (ed.), *Cosmopolitanism, Identity and Authenticity in the Middle East*, Richmond: Curzon, 1999.

27 Throughout the text I have employed the term 'contemporary history' to refer to the period from the 1919 Revolution until the present. The 'modern' period is used more broadly to refer to the time from the arrival of the French and the establishment of the rule of Muhammad 'Ali at the beginning of the nineteenth century until the present day although some Egyptian historians apply the term from the arrival of the Ottomans in Egypt in 1517.

28 The selection of specific historical texts discussed is perforce limited but has been chosen as representative of the historiographical landscape. Where possible I have consulted the original sources but, on occasion, I have relied on some excellent second-hand discussions both in the Arabic and Western literature.

29 Apart from the royalist school, the names of these historical schools require some explanation. I have used, with some reservation, the term 'the liberal school' for what is known in the Egyptian literature as 'the national school' (*al-madrasa al-watani*). Since, as will become clear from my discussion, each of these schools is national in some sense, this seemed advisable to avoid unnecessary confusion. The 'materialist school' is an umbrella term that brings together historical approaches associated with leftist thought variously described as 'historical materialism' (*al-maddiya al-tarikhiyya*) or the socialist school (*al-madrasa al-ishtirakiyya*) and which has been termed as Marxist-nationalist by some Western

scholars. The 'Islamic current' (*al-ittijah al-islami* or *al-tayyar al-islami*) has been adopted from Egyptian usage, to describe a more heterogeneous stream of interpretation than a *madrasa*. The feminist school refers in the broadest sense to the body of scholarship that is principally concerned with the historical role of women. Each of these terms should be understood as representing a generalized historical school and not be regarded in a strict technical sense.

30 While the emphasis in this study is on the political context and construction of historical scholarship, one aspect that is not explicitly dealt with (and which requires more research) is the question of readership. Clearly not all historical writing has been addressed to the same audience nor been written for the same purpose. Academic works, school textbooks and party political tracts share research, pedagogical and advocatory elements in different measure according to the intentions of the writer. Language, literary standard, distribution and economic considerations are all variables that affect the accessibility of a work and its influence. Throughout this discussion there is an implicit notion of audience but the overriding emphasis is on the diversity of the production of historical scholarship rather than its reception.

1 THE EMERGENCE OF THE ACADEMIC TRADITION

1 *A Personal History*, London: Hamish Hamilton, 1983, 256.

2 See Crabbs, *WH*, 209; 'Abd al-Khaliq Lashin, *Misriyyat fi al-fikr wa'l-siyasa*, Cairo: Sina, 1993, 19; Choueiri, *Arab History and the Nation-State*, uses 1920 as the division between amateur and professional historians in his study.

3 David Ayalon, 'The Historian al-Jabarti', in Lewis and Holt (eds), *Historians of the Middle East*, 392. See also the high opinion held by Muhammad Anis quoted in Crabbs, *WH*, 43.

4 Daniel Crecelius (ed.), *Eighteenth Century Egypt, The Arabic Manuscript Sources*, California: Regina, 1991, especially the article by Jack A. Crabbs, 'Historiography and the Eighteenth Century Milieu', 9–24; Gilbert Delanoue, *Moralistes et politiques musulmans dans l'Égypte du XIXe siècle*, vol. 1, Cairo: IFAO, 1982, 5–13.

5 Crabbs, *WH*, 53 sees al-Jabarti as part of the medieval historical tradition but believes the subject of his work prompted him to greater heights. 'The French experience was so contrary to anything Egyptians had ever known that of its very nature it tended to provoke thought and a re-examination of values.' It did not seem to provoke anybody else.

6 Crabbs, *WH*, 48.

7 al-Jabarti quoted by David Ayalon, 'The Historian al-Jabarti and His Background', *Bulletin of the School of Oriental and African Studies* 23 (1960) 220.

8 Ayalon, 'The Historian al-Jabarti and His Background', 229–30. Al-Jabarti's positive remarks about the French were similarly distinctive although his lesser work, *Mazhar al-taqdis*, is very critical of the French. Crabbs, *WH*, 46–8 cf. Ayalon, 'The Historian al-Jabarti and His Background', 231 no. 1.

9 Crabbs, *WH*, 48.

10 Ibid., 61 no. 4. However, it appears his son *was*, see Ahmad 'Abd al-Rahim Mustafa, 'Muhammad Anis, mu'arrikhan wa munadilan', *al-Hilal* 94 (November 1986) 61.

11 Crabbs, *WH*, 69–73.

12 Cairo: Matba'at shirkat al-ragha'ib, 1912 (originally published 1869).

13 Quoted in Jamal Mohammed Ahmed, *The Intellectual Origins of Egyptian Nationalism*, London: Oxford UP, 1960, 13.

14 See Timothy Mitchell, *Colonising Egypt*, Cairo: AUC Press, 1989, 119, who discusses the idea of the nation as a means of controlling the undisciplined masses.

15 Albert Hourani, *Arabic Thought in the Liberal Age 1798–1939*, Oxford UP, 1970, 73.

16 Ahmed, *Intellectual Origins*, 15.

17 Crabbs, *WH*, 109–19.

18 Gaber Asfour, 'Remembering Ali Mubarak', *al-Ahram Weekly* 25 November 1993. Mubarak also held the posts of undersecretary (*wakil*) to Minister of Education (1867) and minister (*nazir*) of Railways, Education and Public Works (1868), J. Heyworth-Dunne, *An Introduction to the History of Education in Modern Egypt*, London: Frank Cass, 1968, 253–4.

19 'Ali Mubarak, *al-Khitat al-tawfiqiyya al-jadida li-misr al-qahira wa muduniha wa biladiha al-qadima wa'l-mashhura*, 20 vols, Bulaq, 1306 AH (1889–90).

20 Samia Mehrez, *Egyptian Writers Between History and Fiction*, Cairo: AUC Press, 1994, 66.

21 Ibid., 68.

22 Reid, *CU*, 23, 30.

23 *L'Instruction publique en Égypte*, Paris, 1890 (Arabic trans. by 'Ali Bahjat, 1894); *La Propriété foncière en Égypte*, Cairo, 1908 (Arabic trans. by Sa'd 'Ammun), see Crabbs, *WH*, 187. For a listing of Artin's writings, see Jean Ellul, *Index des communications et mémoires publiés par l'Institut d'Égypte (1859–1952)*, Cairo: L'Institut Français d'Archéologie Orientale, 1952, 126–7.

24 Crabbs, *WH*, 186–7.

25 Isma'il Sarhank, *Haqa'iq al-akhbar 'an duwal al-bihar*, 3 vols, Cairo: Matba'at al-amiriyya bi-bulaq, 1896, 1898, 1923; Jirjis Hunayyin, *al-Atyan wa'l-dara'ib fi al-qutr al-misri*, Bulaq: al-Matba'at al-kubra al-amiriyya, 1904.

26 *Taqwim al-nil*, 6 vols, Cairo: Dar al-kutub al-misriyya, 1916–36. Not finally published until 1936, Sami's work merges with that of the later royalist school under Fu'ad.

27 Amin Sami, 'Lamma kuntu mu'alliman', *al-Hilal* 45 (1937) 610–12; Lois A. Aroian, *The Nationalization of Arabic and Islamic Education in Egypt: Dar al-'Ulum and al-Azhar*, Cairo: AUC Press, 1983, 26, 68 no. 4.

28 Crabbs, *WH*, 123.

29 According to Crabbs, *WH*, 136–41, Sarhank was very critical of the excesses of Isma'il's profligacy and generally more circumspect in his approach but compare the less flattering assessment of Salah 'Isa (Mayer, *The Changing Past*, 76 no. 9).

30 Muhammad Anis, 'Shafiq Ghurbal wa madrasa al-tarikh al-misri al-hadith', *al-Majalla* 58 (November 1961) 13.

31 Reid, *CU*, 28–30.

32 For a full discussion of Fu'ad's patronage of the Arts and Sciences see Hanotaux (ed.), *Histoire de la nation égyptienne*, vol. VII, see ii–xxxii.

33 Gabriel Hanotaux, *Histoire de la nation égyptienne*, vol. VII, Paris: Plon 1931–40, xx–xxi.

34 Pierre Crabitès, *Ismail, the Maligned Khedive*, London: Routledge, 1933, ix.

35 Metaxas to Ministry of Foreign Affairs, 15 January 1929, *1929 Politika Zitimata Egiptou β/29*, Archive of the Greek Ministry of Foreign Affairs.

36 Athanase Politis, *Le Conflit turco-égyptien de 1838–1841 et les dernières années du règne de Mohamed Aly, d'après les documents diplomatiques grecs*, IFAO for RGS, 1931; Athanase Politis, *Les Rapports de la Grèce et de l'Égypte pendant le règne de Mohamed-Aly, 1833–1849*, Rome, 1935.

37 For the following, see Ettore Rossi, 'In Memoriam: Angelo Sammarco (1883–1948)', *Oriente Moderno* 28 (October–December 1948) 198–200; I.G. Levi, 'Angelo Sammarco (1883–1948)', *Bulletin de l'Institut d'Égypte* 31 (1949) 205–7.

38 Only the third volume appeared, *Le Règne du Khédive Ismaïl de 1863 à 1875*, Cairo, 1937.

39 For the following and bibliography of Douin's work, see René Qattawi Bey, 'Georges Douin (1884–1944)', *Bulletin de l'Institut d'Égypte* 27 (1946) 89–95.

40 Quoted ibid., 92.

41 Crabitès served as a judge of the Mixed Tribunal in Cairo for 25 years, first as the American representative and later as Chief Judge, see 'P. Crabites Dead; Jurist, Author, 66', *New York Times* 11 October 1943.

42 *Ismail, the Maligned Khedive*, London: Routledge, 1933, vii.

43 P.W. Wilson, 'A Challenging Biography of Egypt's Ismail', *New York Times Book Review*, 24 June 1934.

44 Pierre Crabitès, *Ibrahim of Egypt*, London: Routledge, 1935 (Arabic trans. by Muhammad Badran, 1937).

45 Henry Dodwell, *The Founder of Modern Egypt, A Study of Muhammad 'Ali*, Cambridge, 1931, reprinted New York: AMS Press, 1977. Dodwell had a much lower opinion of Muhammad 'Ali's successors, especially 'Abbas I (p. 267); for his obituary see *The Times* 31 October 1946; for the payment, 'Adil Husayni, 'al-Tarikh kidhab', *Ruz al-Yusuf* no. 1777 (2 July 1962) 31.

46 Gudrun Krämer, *The Jews in Modern Egypt, 1914–1952*, London: I.B. Tauris, 1989, 95.

47 Joseph Cattaui [Qattawi] (ed.) *L'Égypte, Aperçu historique et géographie gouvernement et institutions vie économique et sociale*, Cairo: L'Institut Français, 1926, viii. Qattawi later wrote a grand survey of Egyptian history from pharaonic times until Fu'ad, dedicated to Prince Faruq, *Coup d'oeil sur la chronologie de la nation égyptienne*, 1931; and a work on Isma'il, *Le Khedive Ismail et la dette de l'Égypte*, 1935.

48 Dr Isaac Levi (b. Istanbul, 1878) obtained a doctorate in law, economic sciences and Semitic languages from the University of Naples. He held a wide range of offices, including secretary-general of the Egyptian Federation of Industry, vice-president of the Israelite Community of Cairo, and secretary of the Fu'ad I Society of Political Economy, E.J. Blattner, *Who's Who in Egypt and the Middle East*, Cairo: Minerbo, 1949.

49 Wiet held this position until 1951 and also sat on thesis committees at the Egyptian University, Reid, 'Cairo University and the Orientalists', *IJMES* 19 (1987) 54.

50 'Divers historiens et archèologues', *Précis de l'histoire d'Égypte*, L'Institut Français d'Archéologie Orientale du Caire, vols 1–3, 1932–3; vol. 4 was published in Rome, 1935.

51 Among these were *Mohammad Ali et Napoléon (1807–1814)*, Cairo, 1925 and *La Formation de l'empire de Mohamed-Aly de l'Arabie au Soudan (1814–1823)*, *Correspondance des consuls de France en Égypte*, Cairo, 1927, see *Précis de l'histoire d'Égypte*, vol. 3, 375.

52 *Précis de l'histoire d'Égypte*, vol. 1, ix.

53 *Histoire de la nation égyptienne*, Paris: Plon 1931–40; R. Radopoulos, *O Vasilefs Fouat o protos ke anagennomeni Egiptos*, Alexandria, 1930, 387.

54 Henri Dehérain 'Un Mécène royal, S.M. Fouad 1er, roi d'Égypte', in Gabriel Hanotaux (ed.), *Histoire de la nation égyptienne*, vol. VII, xxxii.

55 Ibid., xxviii.

56 *Who's Who 1949*, 562; Jacques Tagher, *Muhammad Ali jugé par les européens de son temps*, Horus: Cairo, 1942. The volume was dedicated to 'la glorieuse mémoire' of Muhammad 'Ali, 'régénérateur de l'Égypte'.

57 Georges Guindi Bey and Jacques Tagher, *Ismail, d'après les documents officiels*, Cairo, 1946 (Arabic edition, Dar al-kutub al-misriyya, Cairo, 1947).

58 J. Tagher, *Mémoires de A.-B. Clot Bey*, IFAO, Cairo, 1949; *Coptes and musulmans*, Cairo, 1951 (Arabic edn) 1952 (French edn).

59 In the former category were writer Ahmad Rashad and Ibrahim al-Muelhi, chief archivist at the Citadel, and in the latter, H.A.R. Gibb (Oxford), Harold Glidden (Washington), J.H. Kramers (Leiden) and Charles Pouthas (Sorbonne), see *Cahiers d'histoire égyptienne* 1 no. 1.

60 See Tagher's obituary by Gaston Wiet, *Cahiers d'histoire égyptienne* 4 (October 1952) 163–5.

61 See, for example, Muhammad Anis, 'Shafiq Ghurbal wa madrasat al-tarikh al-misri al-hadith', 13.

62 Pierre Crabitès, *Americans in the Egyptian Army*, London: George Routledge, 1938, xi. Crabitès thanks not Fu'ad, but Prince Muhammad 'Ali, for the inspiration for this book.

63 See Radopoulos, *O Vasilefs Fouat*, 385–8 for a listing of Fu'ad's donations to various historical projects.

64 Anwar al-Jundi, 'Tathir al-tarikh', *al-Risala* 1002 (15 September 1952) 1043; Jalal al-Sayyid, 'Tarikhna al-qawmi fi daw' al-ishtirakiyya', *al-Katib* 29 (August 1963) 87–92.

65 A. Sammarco, *Gli Italiani in Egitto: Il contributo italiano nella formazione dell'Egitto moderno*, Alexandria, 1937; *Il contributo degl' Italiani ai progressi scientifici e practici della medicina in Egitto sotto il regno di Mohammed Ali*, Cairo, 1928; Pierre Crabitès, *Americans in the Egyptian Army*, 1938; Athanase G. Politis, *L'Hellenisme et l'Égypte moderne*, 2 vols, Paris: Félix Alcan, 1929–30.

66 'Adil Husayni, 'al-Tarikh kidhab', 30–1; 'Abd al-'Azim Ramadan, *Misr fi 'asr al-Sadat*, vol. 2, Cairo: Madbouli, 1989, 81; Ahmad 'Abd al-Rahim Mustafa, 'Hawla i'adat taqyim tarikhna al-qawmi', *Ruz al-Yusuf* 1830 (8 July 1963) 12.

67 Ahmad Shafiq, *L'Égypte moderne et les influences étrangères*, Cairo, 1931, 3–6.

68 'Abd al-'Azim Ramadan, *Misr fi 'asr al-Sadat*, vol. 2, 81.

69 *L'Égypte moderne et les influences étrangères*, Cairo, 1931. There was also a series of memoirs, *Mudhakkarati fi nisf qarn*, Cairo, 1934–6.

70 Crabbs, *WH*, 123.

71 René Qattawi, *Le Règne de Mohamed-Aly d'après les archives russes en Égypte*, 3 vols, Cairo, 1931–6; *Mohamed-Aly et l'Europe*, Paris, 1950 (Arabic trans. by al-Farid Iluz, 1952).

72 Mayer, *The Changing Past*, 16–17.

73 For example, Dodwell's history of Muhammad 'Ali, the histories of Crabitès on Ibrahim and Isma'il, and the work of René Qattawi were all translated into Arabic.

74 Karim Thabit, *Muhammad 'Ali*, 2nd edn, 1943, 9–12. Thabit also wrote a biography of Fu'ad, *al-Malik Fu'ad, malik al-nahda*, Cairo, 1944.

75 M. Rifaat Bey [Muhammad Rif'at], *The Awakening of Modern Egypt*, London: Longmans, Green, 1947, vi.

76 'Ali Barakat supports Rif'at's claim (*QF*, 75–6); Choueiri (*Arab History and the Nation-State*, 65) prefers Ghurbal; Crabbs, *WH*, 209 and Ramadan, *Misr fi 'asr al-Sadat*, vol. 2, 86, favour Sabri.

77 Ghurbal's first major work was in English and Sabri, apart from one early work in Arabic, wrote for many years in French. Rif'at's well-known *The Awakening of Modern Egypt*, not published until 1947, *was* in English.

78 al-Jumay'i, *Ittijahat al-kitaba al-tarikhiyya*, 75 states that Rif'at was sent by the Ministry of Education though Rif'at himself says that most students at this time were sent overseas at their family's expense, *Awakening of Modern Egypt*, 228.

79 *Tarikh misr al-siyasi fi al-azmina al-haditha*, 2 vols, Cairo, 1920, 1932.

80 Barakat, *QF*, 76.

81 Muhammad Rif'at was also for a time head of the history department at the Institute of Arabic Studies, Interview with Salah al-'Aqqad.

82 Rif'at, *Awakening of Modern Egypt*, v.

83 For discussions on Shafiq Ghurbal's life, see 'Abd al-Mun'im al-Disuqi al-Jumay'i, *al-Jami'a al-misriyya wa'l-mujtama' 1908–1940*, Cairo: Markaz al-dirasat al-siyasiyya wa'l-istratijiyya bi'l-ahram, 1983, 110–12; Muhammad Anis, 'Shafiq Ghurbal wa madrasat al-tarikh al-misri al-hadith', 12–18; Muhammad Rif'at, 'Kalimat al-ustadh Muhammad Rif'at', *MTM* 11 (1963) 7–9; Ahmad 'Izzat 'Abd al-Karim, 'Muhammad Shafiq Ghurbal, ustadh jil wa sahib madrasa', *MTM* 19 (1972), 25–31.

84 Toynbee's ideas strongly influenced Ghurbal and, indeed, the two remained lifelong friends.

85 Shafik Ghorbal, *The Beginnings of the Egyptian Question and the Rise of Mehemet Ali*, London: Routledge, 1928, with a preface by Toynbee.

86 Arthur James Grant (1862–1948) had spent many years as professor of history at Leeds, and only on retirement took up his Egyptian appointment, see his obituary, *The Times* 1 June 1948.

87 When once asked about his writings Ghurbal answered, gesturing to his students, 'These are my most important writings', quoted Anis, 'Shafiq Ghurbal wa madrasat al-tarikh al-misri al-hadith', 13.

88 Barakat, *QF*, 77–8, al-Jumay'i, *Ittijahat al-kitaba al-tarikhiyya*, 161–2; Ahmad al-Hitta completed a Masters dissertation on the Egyptian peasantry in the reign of Muhammad 'Ali (1936) and his doctorate was published, *Tarikh al-zira'a al-misriyya fi 'ahd Muhammad 'Ali al-kabir*, Cairo, 1950; 'Ali al-Jiritli obtained a PhD from the London School of Economics in 1947 on 'The Structure of Modern Industry in Egypt', subsequently published in *L'Égypte contemporaine*, and wrote a history on trade in the nineteenth century and another on banking. As an economist with the National Bank of Egypt, he was appointed to the Permanent Council for Development of National Production in 1952 but later fell out with the Nasser regime (Vitalis, *When Capitalists Collide*, 199–200). 'Afifi wrote an economic study on the Muhammad 'Ali period ('Tijara misr fi 'ahd Muhammad 'Ali'); Abu al-Futuh Radwan wrote an MA on the history of the Bulaq press and went on to obtain a PhD from Columbia University, published the same year as *Old and New Forces in Egyptian Education*, New York: Columbia University, 1951. Ibrahim 'Abduh and 'Abd al-Karim will be considered below.

89 *The Times* 27 October 1961.

90 This aspect of Ghurbal's career has often been overlooked in favour of his 'academic' achievements. See, for example, Boia, *Great Historians of the Modern Age*, 14–15. Ghurbal's political connections have only recently been raised by Barakat and Choueiri, see below.

91 Taha Hussein, *The Future of Culture in Egypt*, New York: Octagon, 1975, 46–7.

92 Choueiri, *Arab History and the Nation-State*, 67; Barakat, *QF*, 77 refers to a 'closeness' (*taqrib*) between Ghurbal and the palace. According to one view, the Sa'dist party was the effendis' party made up of 'technicians and managers'; the Wafd, by contrast, was the pashas' party of 'big landlords and business men', Berque, *Imperialism and Revolution*, 630.

93 Choueiri, *Arab History and the Nation-State*, 69–70, cf. Crabbs, 'Politics, History, and Culture in Nasser's Egypt', 415 who offers a more moderate assessment of Ghurbal's political views.

94 Barakat, *QF*, 77 does not specify the nature of the disagreement.

95 Blattner, *Who's Who in Egypt and the Middle East 1949*, s.v. 'Chafik Ghorbal Bey'.

96 Inter alia, he was a member of the Majma' Arabic Language, Institute d'Égypte, Royal Geographical Society, the Higher Council of Antiquities, and the Society of Coptic Antiquities, al-Jumay'i, *Ittijahat al-kitaba al-tarikhiyya*, 169.

97 There is some dispute about whether Sabri was born in 1890 or 1894. He had certainly published work by 1910, which makes the later date less likely, and perhaps even as early as 1907, which would make it untenable (Irene Gendzier, *The Practical Visions of Ya'qub Sanu'*, 138). For the following, see 'Abd al-'Azim Ramadan, *Misr fi 'asr al-Sadat*, vol. 2, 85–7; Barakat, *QF*, 76–7; Crabbs, 'Politics, History, and Culture in Nasser's Egypt', 389.

98 The prinicipal thesis for his *doctorat d'état* was titled *La Genèse de l'ésprit national égyptien (1863–1882)*; the minor thesis was *Mémoire d'Arabi Pasha et ses avocats*.

99 For his work on Ahmad Shawqi, see 'Hadith ma'a al-duktur Muhammad Sabri', *al-Katib* 9 (1961) 80–8.

100 His first published work was *Shu'ara' al-'asr*, 2 pts, 1910–12.

101 Yunan Labib Rizq, 'Annals of an obscure historian', *al-Ahram Weekly* 19–25 August 1999. Among the French language historians of the nineteenth and early twentieth centuries were Ya'qub Artin Pasha, Mahmud al-Falaki, Ahmad Kamal and Ahmad Shafiq, el-Shayyal in Lewis and Holt, *Historians of the Middle East*, 415–16.

102 Quoted in 'Abd al-'Azim Ramadan, *Misr fi 'asr al-Sadat*, vol. 2, 86.

103 al-Jumay'i, *Ittijahat al-kitaba al-tarikhiyya*, 172–4.

104 al-Jumay'i, *al-Jam'iyya al-misriyya li'l-dirasat al-tarikhiyya*, 171; *Ittijahat al-kitaba al-tarikhiyya*, 172.

105 Gendzier, *The Practical Visions of Ya'qub Sanu'*, 138 quoting from *Abu Naddara* 8 (15 November 1907).

106 M. Sabry, *Le Révolution égyptienne*, 2 vols, Paris: Librairie J. Vrin, 1919–21.

107 Aulard invoked 1789 in the preface he wrote for the second volume of *La Révolution égyptienne*.

108 Barakat, *QF*, 76–7; Choueiri, *Arab History and the Nation-State*, 66 states that Sabri was the secretary of the Egyptian delegation at the Paris Peace Conference of 1919.

109 Crabbs, *WH*, 209.

110 Choueiri, *Arab History and the Nation-State*, 65.

111 For sources on Shukri, see Muhammad Anis, 'al-Mu'arrikh al-rahil Muhammad Fu'ad Shukri', *al-Ahram* 20 December 1963; 'al-duktur Muhammad Fu'ad Shukri, 1904–1963', *MTM* 11 (1963); Barakat, *QF*, 81–3.

112 Barakat, *QF*, 81. Barakat also credits Shukri with being the first Egyptian historian to apply a materialist explanation to academic history. In this way, his ideas look forward to those of Muhammad Anis, with whom he would co-author a number of books.

113 Among Shukri's important works on Egypt were *Bina' dawla misr Muhammad 'Ali*, 1948 and *Misr fi matla' al-qarn al-tasi' 'ashar, 1801–1811*, 3 vols, 1954–8, cited by Anis, 'al-Mu'arrikh al-rahil Muhammad Fu'ad Shukri', *al-Ahram* 20 December 1963.

114 Anis, 'al-Mu'arrikh al-rahil Muhammad Fu'ad Shukri', 13.

115 Majid Khadduri, *Modern Libya, A Study in Political Development*, Baltimore: John Hopkins Press, 1963, 101–4.

116 Shukri's memoirs, which may have shed light on this matter, were never published despite the suggestion of Anis at the time of Shukri's premature death, Anis, 'al-Mu'arrikh al-rahil Muhammad Fu'ad Shukri', *al-Ahram* 20 December 1963.

117 Adrian Pelt, *Libyan Independence and the United Nations, A Case of Planned Decolonization*, Yale UP, 1970, 437–8.

118 *Tatawwur al-sihafa al-misriyya, 1898–1981*, 4th edn, Cairo: Sijl al-'arab, 1982 (1st edn 1944).

119 J.J.G. Jansen, 'Ibrahim 'Abduh (b. 1913), His Autobiographies and His Political Polemical Writings', *Bibliotheca Orientalis* 37 (1980) 128–32.

120 Ghurbal, *Beginnings of the Egyptian Question*, ix–x.

121 Quoted Choueiri, *Arab History and the Nation-State*, 69.

122 Ghurbal, *Beginnings of the Egyptian Question*, xiii.

123 Crabbs, 'Politics, History, and Culture in Nasser's Egypt', 390.

124 Muhammad Anis, 'Shafiq Ghurbal wa madrasat al-tarikh al-misri al-hadith', 13, 17.

125 See, for example, Anwar al-Jundi, 'Hal yuktiba al-tarikh min jadid', *al-Risala* no. 1000 (1 September 1952) 985–6.

126 Fauzi M. Najjar, 'State and University in Egypt during the Period of Socialist Transformation, 1961–1967', *Review of Politics* 38 (1976) 58.

127 Interview with 'Abd al-'Aziz Nawwar; see also Crabbs, 'Politics, History, and Culture in Nasser's Egypt', 414.

128 *MTM* 11 (1963) lists tributes by 'Abd al-Karim and Muhammad Rif'at, among others.

129 *Tarikh al-hadara al-misriyya*, vol. 1, Cairo: Maktabat al-khusda al-misriyya, n.d.

130 al-Jumay'i, *Ittijahat al-kitaba al-tarikhiyya*, 172; Lam'i al-Muti'i, *Mawsu'at hadha al-rajul min misr*, Cairo, 1997, 206.

131 Interview with Ahmad 'Abd al-Rahim Mustafa.

132 Ahmad Husayn Tamawi, *Muhammad Sabri*, Cairo: al-Hay'a al-misriyya al-'ama li'l-kitab, 1994, 8; Tariq al-Bishri, *al-Haraka al-siyasiyya*, 439; Ramadan, *Misr fi 'asr al-Sadat*, vol. 2, 87.

133 al-Jumay'i, *Ittijahat al-kitaba al-tarikhiyya*, 176.

134 Crabbs, 'Politics, History, and Culture in Nasser's Egypt', 415 no. 6.

135 Interview with Ahmad 'Abd al-Rahim Mustafa; see also 'Hadith ma'a al-duktur Muhammad Sabri', *al-Katib* 9 (1961) 80–8 and Crabbs, 'Politics, History, and Culture in Nasser's Egypt', 403, 415.

136 For 'Abd al-Karim's résumé, see *Taqdir wa 'urfan li'l-ustadh al-duktur Ahmad 'Izzat 'Abd al-Karim*, Cairo, Jami'at 'Ain Shams, 1976, v–viii.

137 Promoted to Professor of Modern History in 1951, he served as Dean of Faculty of Arts (1961–4), Vice Rector (1964–8) and Rector (1968–9), before retiring as Professor Emeritus.

138 He features in neither of the discussions of Fauzi Najjar or Ahmed Abdalla on university politics of the 1960s.

139 Interview with 'Abd al-'Aziz Nawwar.

140 See Giuseppe Contu, 'Ahmad Izzat 'Abd al-Karim 1909–1980, storico arabo con-temporaneo', in Clelia Sarnelli Cerqua (ed.) *Studi arabo-islamici in onore di Roberto Rubinacci nel suo settantesimo cumpleano*, vol. 1, Napoli: Istituto Universitario Orientale, 1975, 236. For high school text, *Tarikh al-'alam al-'arabi fi al-'asr al-hadith*, Cairo, 1960, see Mark Krug, 'History Teaching in Nasser's Egypt', *Teachers College Record* 66 (November 1964) 130.

141 Interview with Ra'uf 'Abbas. He also influenced his younger colleagues: Salah al-'Aqqad credited 'Abd al-Karim with directing his own interest to the Gulf (Interview).

142 Typical of this new scholarship were the studies on landownership by Ra'uf 'Abbas and 'Asim al-Disuqi at 'Ain Shams which were supplemented by the work of 'Ali Barakat, a student of Muhammad Anis, at Cairo University.

143 A'da' al-Siminar, *Siminar al-dirasat al-'ulya li'l-tarikh al-hadith, 1955–75*, Cairo: Jami'at 'Ain Shams, 1976.

144 See further, Giuseppe Contu, 'La conscenza del mondo arabo moderno e contemporaneo attraverso gli studi storici di 'Ayn Shams: 1976–77', *Annali* (Istituto Universitario Orientale di Napoli) 39 (1979) 333–44.

145 Interview with Ahmad 'Abd al-Rahim Mustafa.

146 Interview with 'Abd al-Khaliq Lashin.

147 This issue led to a bitter and public clash between Lashin and 'Abd al-'Azim Ramadan. 'Asim al-Disuqi also suggests 'Abd al-Karim disliked criticism of the landowning class – part of the thrust of Lashin's thesis – since 'Abd al-Karim himself had married into it, Interview with 'Asim al-Disuqi.

148 'Asim al-Disuqi reported that 'Abd al-Karim proved an unsympathetic examiner for his own thesis which employed a Marxist framework and had insisted on the modification of some Marxist terminology in another student's thesis, Interview with 'Asim al-Disuqi.

149 For the following, see 'Asim al-Disuqi, 'Muhammad Anis wa duruhu fi ta'qil dirasat al-tarikh bi'l-jami'a al-misriyya', *MTM* 34 (1987) 3–13; Barakat, *QF*, 83–8.

150 Barakat, QF, 83. Some accounts mistakenly ascribe a University of London doctorate to Anis. The title of his thesis was 'Some aspects of British interest in Egypt in the late eighteenth century, 1775–1798', Roger R. Bilboul (ed.), *Retrospective Index to Theses of Great Britain and Ireland 1716–1950*, vol. 1, American Bibliographical Center, 1975, 70.

151 Barakat, *QF*, 83, citing the evidence of Anis' brother, 'Abd al-'Azim, himself a communist.

152 Ahmad 'Abd al-Rahim Mustafa, 'Muhammad Anis, Mu'arrikhan wa munadilan', *al-Hilal* 94 (November 1986) 60.

153 See, for example, Muhammad Anis, 'al-Nazra al-ishtirakiyya li-tarikh mujtama'na', *al-Ahram* 10 July 1963. Anis even attracted criticism from the *Sunday Times* of London, 'al-Madrasa al-thalitha kitabat al-tarikh', *al-Jumhuriyya*, 19 September 1963.

154 Muhammad Anis, 'Tarikhna al-qawmi fi al-mithaq', *al-Katib* 63 (June 1966) 69–74.

155 Kamal al-Din Rif'at was a second echelon Free Officer, then a member of the RCC, identified with the Left in government. As a member of the Tripartite Commission, he was closely involved in setting up the program and ideology of the ASU. This Commission was subsequently reorganized in December 1964 into the Secretariat for Ideology and Propaganda with Rif'at in 'exclusive control', John Waterbury, *The Egypt of Nasser and Sadat, The Political Economy of Two Regimes*, Princeton, UP, 1983, 319, 323 no. 5.

156 Kirk J. Beattie, *Egypt during the Nasser Years, Ideology, Politics and Civil Society*, Boulder, Co: Westview Press, 1994, 167; on Anis' membership of the Vanguard, Interview with 'Abd al-'Azim Ramadan.

157 Raymond Baker, *Egypt's Uncertain Revolution Under Nasser and Sadat*, Cambridge, Mass.: Harvard UP, 1978, 108.

158 See Fauzi M. Najjar, 'State and University in Egypt during the Period of Socialist Transformation, 1961–1967', *Review of Politics* 38 (1976) 77.

159 Baker, *Egypt's Uncertain Revolution*, 83–4 (danger of technocrats); Robert Springborg, *Family, Power and Politics in Egypt*, Philadelphia: University of Pennsylvania Press, 1982, 194 (ASU discussions); Rejwan, *Nasserist Ideology*, 186 (attacking Haykal). On Anis' visits to the Suez Canal in the late 1960s, see Crabbs, 'Politics, History, and Culture in Nasser's Egypt', 398.

160 Interview with Ra'uf 'Abbas. There are some notable exceptions to this generalization. 'Abd al-'Azim Ramadan, whose media output is even more prolific than that of Anis, became professor of history at Manufiyya; 'Ali Barakat held a position at the University of Mansura, then moved to the University of Hilwan; and Latifa Salim holds a position at Zagazig University. 'Abd al-'Aziz Nawwar suggested that Anis' students have been more prominent in the press (Interview).

161 A number of historians, among them 'Asim al-Disuqi, 'Abd al-Khaliq Lashin and Ra'uf 'Abbas, while not formally students of Anis, cited his influence on their work (Interviews).

162 'Ali Barakat, 'Fi al-tariq ila al-madrasa al-ijtima'iyya fi kitab tarikh misr hadith', *Fikr* 5 (March 1985) 59.

163 'Abd al-'Azim Ramadan, 'Madaris kitabat tarikh misr al-mu'asir', in 'Abd Allah (ed.), *Tarikh misr*, 62.

164 'Abbud Fawdah, 'Hadith al-madina: ma'a al-duktur Muhammad Anis', *al-Jumhuriyya* 17 May 1961; see also Crabbs, 'Politics, History, and Culture in Nasser's Egypt', 393.

165 Interview with 'Abd al-Rahim Mustafa.

166 'Abbud Fawdah, 'Hadith al-madina: ma'a Muhammad Shafiq Ghurbal', *al-Jumhuriyya* 8 May 1961.

167 Crabbs, 'Politics, History, and Culture in Nasser's Egypt', 393.

168 Ra'uf 'Abbas, for example, wrote his Masters thesis on the labour movement in Egypt from 1899 to 1952 under 'Abd al-Karim's supervision.

169 Quoted in Wagih Abdel-Ati, 'History in the Making', *al-Ahram Weekly* 28 May–3 June 1992.

170 Ahmed Abdalla, *The Student Movement and National Politics in Egypt, 1923–1973*, London: al-Saqi, 1985, 108.

171 Strictly speaking AUC did not have a History Department until the late 1990s.

172 The University of Asyut had been founded in 1957 but it was not until 1971 that the Faculty of Arts was established, Interview with 'Asim al-Disuqi.

173 Interview with 'Abd al-Hamid al-Batriq.

174 Interview with Salah al-'Aqqad.

175 Interview with Ahmad 'Abd al-Rahim Mustafa; Barakat, *QF*, 83.

176 Interviews with 'Abd al-'Azim Ramadan, Ra'uf 'Abbas and 'Ali Barakat.

177 Interview with 'Abd al-Khaliq Lashin.

178 Interview with Ra'uf 'Abbas Hamid.

179 Notable examples in the years immediately prior to 1952 were PhD graduates of the Universities of Birmingham (Muhammad Anis, 1950), Liverpool (Zaynab Rashid, 1949), London ('Abd al-Hamid al-Batriq, 1947) and Cambridge (Ahmad Shalabi, 1950–51); and with a *doctora d'état* at the Sorbonne (Salah al-'Aqqad, 1956; Jalal Yahya, 1958). For the situation before 1914, see Rif'at, *Awakening of Modern Egypt*, 228.

180 Interview with Salah al-'Aqqad; Halim suggests that the abrogation of the 1936 treaty in 1951 also restricted opportunities for postgraduate studies in England, Hala Halim, 'Alexandreus', *al-Ahram Weekly* 6–12 July 1995.

181 There were some exceptions. Mustafa al-'Abadi, an ancient historian, went to Cambridge University and obtained his doctorate in 1960 (Halim, 'Alexandreus', 16); 'Umar 'Abd al-'Aziz 'Umar graduated with a PhD from the University of London in 1966 for his thesis, 'Anglo-Egyptian relations and the construction of the Alexandria–Cairo–Suez Railway, 1833–58'. (P.M. Jacobs, *History Theses, 1901–1970*, University of London: Institute of Historical Research, 1976). Both later took positions at Alexandria University.

182 Badran, *Feminists, Islam, and Nation*, 9, 57.

183 Reid, *CU*, 113; Mervat Hatem, 'The Enduring Alliance of National and Patriarchy in Muslim Personal Status Laws: The Case of Modern Egypt', *Feminist Issues* 4 (spring 1986) 29, gives even lower figures, citing 12.4 per cent of women as literate in 1960.

184 For the following see Reid, *CU*, 52–6.

185 Ibid., 105–6.

186 By comparison, the private American University in Cairo had 15 women students enrolled in 1934, Badran, *Feminists, Islam and Nation*, 293n.

187 Badran, *Feminists, Islam and Nation*, 151.

188 Kathleen Howard-Merriam, 'Women, Education, and the Professions in Egypt', *Comparative Education Review* 23 (1979) 261.

189 For the following see Badran, *Feminists, Islam and Nation*, 177–8.

190 Reid, *CU*, 108–9.

191 Cynthia Nelson, *Doria Shafik, Egyptian Feminist: a Woman Apart*, American University in Cairo Press, 1996, 98–100.

192 Interview with Ra'uf 'Abbas.

193 al-Jumay'i, *Ittijahat al-kitaba al-tarikhiyya*, 143–4.

194 Zubayda Muhammad 'Ata and Khayriyya Muhammad Qasmiyya at Cairo University, and Nabila Muhammad Muhammad 'Abd al-Halim and Layla 'Ata Allah Hanna at Alexandria University (all in 1972); Fadila 'Abd al-Amīr al-Shami ('Ain Shams), Fatima Mustafa 'Amr (Women's College), Ismat Mahmud Ghanim (Alexandria) in 1973. Of these only Palestinian Qasmiyya worked on the modern period. For graduate lists see *MTM* 19 (1972) 345–59; *MTM* 20 (1973) 351–6; *MTM* 21 (1974) 333–40.

195 Interview with 'Abd al-Mu'nim al-Jumay'i; Sabagh had obtained her MA in 1961, 'Abd al-Mu'nim al-Jumay'i, *al-Ittijahat al-kitaba al-tarikhiyya*, 182.

196 It is worth noting that Latifa Salim was awarded a State Merit Award (social sciences) in 2001, 'That Time of Year', *al-Ahram Weekly* 28 June–4 July 2001.

197 Interview with Afaf Marsot; see also, 'Afaf Lutfi El-Sayyid: Student of Egypt's Past', *Newsletter of American Research Center in Egypt* 160 (winter 1993) 13–14.

198 Hanna graduated with a PhD from the University of Provence, 1988, and Sonbol from Georgetown University.

199 In April 1976 there were 2 women out of 17 participants (Sahila al-Rimawi, a Syrian, and Layla 'Abd al-Latif); in May 1977, 3 women out of 33 (Salwa 'Ali Milad; Layla Sabagh, Damascus; Khalifa al-Shatir, Tunis) Contu, 'La conscenza del mondo arabo moderno e contemporaneo attraverso gli studi storici di 'Ayn Shams: 1976–77', *Annali* (Istituto Universitario Orientale di Napoli) 39 (1979) 333–44.

200 A'da' al-Siminar, *Siminar al-dirasat al-'ulya li'l-tarikh al-hadith, 1955–75*, Cairo: Jami'at 'Ain Shams, 1976. Additional listings show 3 women (including one Syrian) out of 29 Master of Arts graduates; 1 Syrian woman out of 23 PhD students and four women from a total of 41 MA students.

201 Khalil was from the National Centre for Social Research and Wahba a political researcher of the Majlis al-Sha'b. A number of other Arab and Western female scholars participated in the conference discussions, Ahmad 'Abd Allah (ed.), *Tarikh Misr*, 426–33.

202 The three were Nelly Hanna (AUC), Amira Sonbol (Georgetown, USA) and Ghislaine Alleaume (CEDEJ), Muhammad 'Afifi (ed.), *al-Madrasa al-tarikhiyya al-misriyya, 1970–1995*, Cairo: Dar al-shuruq, 1997.

203 Interview with 'Abd al-Rahim Mustafa; on the student uprising Abdalla, *Student Movement*, 176–211.

204 Interview with 'Asim al-Disuqi.

205 Majdi al-Daqaq, 'Ba'd taqdim istiqalatahu al-hay'a al-'ulya li'l-wafd al-duktur Muhammad Anis yarwa qissataha ma'a hizb al-wafd al-jadid' *al-Musawwar* 25 May 1984; this prompted another historian to criticize the move as being against the Wafd's historical principles, Yunan Labib Rizq, 'Tahalluf didda tarikh', *al-Musawwar* 11 May 1984, 16–17.

206 Interview with Salah al-'Aqqad.

207 Despite Krämer's assertion ('History and Legitimacy: The Use of History in Contemporary Egyptian Party Politics', 20) Rizq has never belonged to a political party, Interview with Yunan Labib Rizq.

208 Ramadan, *Misr fi 'asr al-Sadat*, vol. 2, 332–43.

209 For a biting critique of Ramadan's shifting positions, see Muhammad Abu al-Asa'd, *al-Sihafa al-misriyya wa tazyif al-wa'y*, Cairo: Dar al-thaqafa al-jadida, 1988, 49–68.

210 Ramadan's ongoing series *al-Sira' al-ijtima'i wa'l-siyasi fi 'asr Mubarak* which first appeared in 1993 had reached its twelfth volume by April 2000.

211 G. Alleaume, 'L'Égypte et son histoire: actualité et controverses', *CEDEJ Bulletin* 20 (1986) 9–78.

212 See below Chapter 5.

213 Anis, 'Shafiq Ghurbal wa madrasat al-tarikh al-misri al-hadith', 16. For a full discussion of the history and activities of the Association see 'Abd al-Mun'im Ibrahim al-Disuqi al-Jumay'i, *al-Jam'iyya al-misriyya li'l-dirasat al-tarikhiyya, 1945–1985*.

214 *al-Sijl al-thaqafi* 2 (1949) 234.

215 *al-Sijl al-thaqafi* 2 (1949) 235 and 4 (1951) 319.

216 Reid, 'The Egyptian Geographical Society: from Foreign Laymen's Society to Indigenous Professional Association', *Poetics Today* 14 no. 3 (Fall 1993) 565–7.

217 The first work published by the Society was *Ibrahim Pasha (1789–1848)* which commemorated the centenary of Ibrahim's death, *Cahiers d'histoire égyptienne* 1 no. 3 (1948) 274. Among others that followed was 'Abd al-Rahman Zaki, *al-Tarikh al-harbi li-'asr Muhammad 'Ali al-kabir*, al-Jam'iyya al-misriyya li'l-dirasat al-tarikhiyya, 1950.

218 Sahar El-Bahr, 'The end of history?' *al-Ahram Weekly* 6–12 May 1999.

219 Amina Elbendary, 'History matters', *al-Ahram Weekly* 12–18 July 2001.

220 Interview with Mahmud Mitwalli.

221 'Ittihad al-mu'arrikhin al-'arab', *al-Katib* 58 (May 1974) 51–2.

222 Ibid., 52.

223 Interview with 'Abd al-'Aziz Nawwar; on al-Najjar, see Peter Gran, *Beyond Eurocentrism*, 84.

224 Interview with 'Abd al-'Aziz Nawwar.

225 Interview with Ahmad 'Abd al-Rahim Mustafa.

226 'L'Unione degli storici arabi', *Oriente Moderno* 58 no. 12 (December 1978) 861–2.

227 'al-Lajna al-da'ima li'l-a'lam al-'arabi...', *al-Ahram* 6 July 1993.

228 Interview with Ahmad 'Abd al-Rahim Mustafa.

2 HISTORY, INSTITUTIONS AND THE STATE

1 Temu and Swai, *Historians and Africanist History*, 127.

2 Jean Ellul, *Index des communications et mémoires publiés par l'Institut d'Égypte (1859–1952)*, Cairo: L'Institut Français d'Archéologie Orientale, 1952, xi.

3 L'Institut Égyptien, *Livre d'or de l'Institut Égyptien, 1859–1899*, Cairo, 1899, 8. The name L'Institut Égyptien had been adopted in deference to the original Institut.

4 Ellul, *Index*, xiii.

5 Ibid. xi–xiv.

6 An index of all articles published up until 1952 can be found in Ellul, *Index des communications et mémoires publies par l'Institut d'Égypte (1859–1952)*.

7 Donald Reid, 'The Egyptian Geographical Society: from Foreign Laymen's Society to Indigenous Professional Association', *Poetics Today* 14 no. 3 (Fall 1993) 553.

8 *Bulletin de l'Institut d'Égypte* 32 (1949–50) 400–1; Huzzayin later became president of the Institut in 1954 and served as Minister of Culture in 1965–66.

9 Ellul, *Index*, xiii no. 2.

10 Ibid., Plate VII.

11 *Bulletin de l'Institut d'Égypte* 32 (1949–50) 373. The Ministry's contribution was LE 4110 out of a total income of LE 4567.

12 For a fuller discussion, see Donald Reid, 'The Egyptian Geographical Society', *Poetics Today* 14 no. 3 (Fall 1993) 539–72.

13 Dehérain, 'Un Mécène Royal, S.M. Fouad 1er, Roi d'Égypte', in Hanotaux (ed.), *Histoire de la nation égyptienne*, vol. VII, xix–xxi.

14 Reid, 'The Egyptian Geographical Society: from Foreign Laymen's Society to Indigenous Professional Association', 540–3.

15 Ibid., 550.

16 Ibid., 562.

17 Dehérain, 'Un Mécène Royal, S.M. Fouad 1er, Roi d'Égypte', xxi.

18 Reid, 'The Egyptian Geographical Society', 555.

19 Yusuf Qattawi [Joseph Cattaui Pacha] (ed.), *L'Égypte, Aperçu historique et géographique gouvernement et institutions vie économique et sociale*. Cairo: L'Institut Français, 1926, 386.

20 For example, Angelo Sammarco, *La Marina egiziana sotto Mohammed Ali, il contributo italiano*, 1931; René Qattawi, *Le Règne de Mohamed Aly d'après les archives russes en Égypte*, 1931; for a bibliography of Douin's works see, René Qattawi Bey, 'Georges Douin (1884–1944)', 94–5.

21 Reid, 'The Rise of Professions and Professional Organization in Modern Egypt', 39. Their tone was also overwelmingly if not entirely male. There were no women members of the Institut d'Égypte nor probably of the Royal Geographical Society although Alexandra de Avierino was a member of the Société Archéologique d'Alexandrie in 1902.

22 Reid, 'The Egyptian Geographical Society', 566.

23 Crabbs, *WH*, 71.

24 Heyworth-Dunne, *History of Education*, 353.

25 Crabbs, *WH*, 101. The expulsion of Muhammad 'Abduh, for a time a member of its history faculty, seems consistent with this restrictive atmosphere.

26 By the 1920s the college had changed its name to the Higher Teachers' College (*Madrasat al-mu'allimin al-'ulya*) and subsequently became part of Cairo University, Crabbs, *WH*, 102. See also Reid, *CU*, 144 who suggests it was phased out in the 1930s.

27 For the following, see Reid, *CU*, 22–5.

28 Ibid., 26; J.E. Marshall, *The Egyptian Enigma, 1890–1928*, London: John Murray, 1928, 92.

29 The first modern university of Egypt has been known by three names. First called the Egyptian University (*al-jami'a al-misriyya*) when established as a private institution in 1908, it retained this name as a state institution until 1940 when it became Fu'ad I University. After 1952, it was changed to Cairo University. In general discussion I have preferred the current name but have also employed the appropriate name when demanded by historical context.

30 Reid, *CU*, 31.
31 Ibid., 35.
32 For some cases, ibid., 91–4.
33 Ibid., 26–8, 62; Crabbs, *WH*, 102.
34 For the following see Reid, *CU*, 75–9.
35 Ibid., 75.
36 Quoted from a speech published in *al-Siyasa* in 1925 by Abu Al-Futouh Ahmad Radwan, *Old and New Forces in Egyptian Education*, New York: Columbia University, 1951, 114.
37 The remark of Robert Graves, who taught at the University in 1926, overstates the case but conveys an interesting contemporary impression, 'The University was an invention of King Fu'ad's, who had always been anxious to be known as a patron of the arts and sciences. There had been a Cairo University before this one, but it had been nationalistic in its policy…', Robert Graves, *Good-bye to All That, An Autobiography*, London: Jonathan Cape, 1929, 411.
38 For a detailed discussion of these manoeuvres, see Reid, *CU*, 87–102.
39 Abdalla, *Student Movement*, 39–61.
40 Reid, *CU*, 130–1.
41 Fauzi M. Najjar, 'State and University in Egypt during the Period of Socialist Transformation, 1961–1967', 57 citing Louis 'Awad, *al-Jami'a wa'l-mujtama' al-jadida*, Cairo, 1963, 7.
42 Afaf Lutfi al-Sayyid Marsot, 'Survey of Egyptian Works of History', *American Historical Review* December 1991, 1427.
43 Dekmejian, *Egypt under Nasir*, 70.
44 Mustafa, 'Mu'arrikhan wa munadilan', 63.
45 'The Actor who ridiculed Isma'il', see Irene L. Gendzier, *The Practical Visions of Ya'qub Sanu'*, Cambridge, Mass.: Harvard UP, 1966, 3; Beattie, *Egypt during the Nasser Years*, 134.
46 Gamal Abdel Nasser, *The Philosophy of the Revolution*, Buffalo NY: Smith, Keynes & Marshall, 1959, 25.
47 Note Nasser's remark, 'most of the members of the Revolutionary Council were professors in the Staff College', *Philosophy of the Revolution*, 36.
48 Najjar, 'State and University in Egypt', 58.
49 Nasser and Kamal al-Din Husayn had for a time been law students, Reid, *CU*, 169.
50 Alexandria University enjoyed a different reputation, see Mursi Saad el-Din, 'Alexandria University: a beacon for half a century', *al-Ahram Weekly* 30 July 1992.
51 For a full discussion of the issue of state and university relations during the Nasser period, see Fauzi Najjar, 'State and University in Egypt', 57–87.
52 Najjar, 'State and University in Egypt', 58. There is some uncertainty about whether it was established before or after the coup in July, see Reid, *CU*, 262 no. 10.
53 Beattie, *Egypt during the Nasser Years*, 139–40.
54 Reid, *CU*, 170–1.
55 Najjar, 'State and University in Egypt', 66.
56 Abdalla, *Student Movement*, 118, 124.
57 Abdel-Malek, *Egypt*, 216–21.
58 Ibid., 189–221.
59 Of the 256 people on the Committee, 34 were professors, Waterbury, *The Egypt of Nasser and Sadat*, 317. I have been unable to establish if any of these were historians but Muhammad Anis is a likely candidate.
60 Rejwan, *Nasserist Ideology*, 266.

61 'History to be Rewritten', *The Times* 11 March 1957.

62 Ghurbal (ed.), *Tarikh al-hadara al-misriyya, al-'asr al-fir'auni*, vol. 1. Though the work is undated, 'Ukasha's reference in the preface to the death of Shafiq Ghurbal suggests a date of late 1961.

63 For an English translation, see Rejwan, *Nasserist Ideology*, 195–265.

64 For the following, Rejwan, *Nasserist Ideology*, 208–13.

65 Quoted in Rejwan, *Nasserist Ideology*, 222.

66 'Egyptian History to be "Purified" ', *The Times* 7 June 1963; Rejwan, *Nasserist Ideology*, 11 states that Anis was put in charge of the project but Muhammad Anis, 'al-Tarikh fi khidmat al-tatawwur al-ishtiraki, al-ishtirakiyya taqyim li-madina bi-qadrima ma hiya tanzim li-hadirna', *al-Ahram* 7 July 1963 suggests he was merely a member of the committee.

67 Jalal al-Sayyid, 'Tarikhna al-qawmi fi daw' al-ishtirakiyya', *al-Katib* 29 (August 1963) 90.

68 'al-Ishtirakiyya taqyim li-madina hiya tanzim li-hadirna', *al-Ahram* 7 July 1963; 'al-Nazra al-ishtirakiyya li-tarikh mujtama'na', *al-Ahram* 10 July 1963.

69 Anis, 'al-Ishtirakiyya taqyim li-madina hiya tanzim li-hadirna', 11.

70 Jalal al-Sayyid, 'Tarikhna al-qawmi fi daw' al-ishtirakiyya', 88.

71 Ahmad 'Abd al-Rahim Mustafa, 'Hawla i'adat taqyim tarikhna al-qawmi', *Ruz al-Yusuf* no. 1830 (8 July 1963) 12.

72 Muhammad al-Sharqawi, 'Fi dirasat tarikhna al-hadith', *al-Risala* 1036 (21 November 1963) 22–3 quoted and translated by Crabbs, 'Politics, History, and Culture in Nasser's Egypt', 395.

73 For a published record of these meetings, see Ahmad 'Abd al-Rahim Mustafa, 'Nadwat i'adat kitabat al-tarikh al-qawmi', *MTM* 13 (1967) 345–69, for al-Sa'ati's comment, 348.

74 Quoted in Reid, *CU*, 202–03.

75 Anis, 'Tarikhna al-qawmi fi al-mithaq', *al-Katib* 63 (June 1966) 69–74.

76 This is my overall impression after speaking with a number of academic historians.

77 The phrase is Dekmejian's, *Egypt under Nasir*, 70–81.

78 Dekmejian, *Egypt under Nasir*, 70; see also Crabbs, 'Politics, History, and Culture in Nasser's Egypt', 420, who describes the 'half-hearted conformity' imposed by the Revolution.

79 Interviews with 'Abd al-'Aziz Nawwar, Ra'uf 'Abbas.

80 Interview with Ahmad 'Abd al-Rahman Mustafa.

81 Sa'id 'Abd al-Fatah 'Ashur, *Thawrat sha'b*, Cairo: Dar al-nahda al-'arabiyya, 1965, Interview with Ahmad 'Abd al-Rahim Mustafa.

82 Louis 'Awad, *al-Ahram* 26 January 1971, quoted in Abdalla, *Student Movement*, 115–16.

83 Quoted in Abdalla, *Student Movement*, 117.

84 *al-Dimuqratiyya bayna shuyukh al-hara wa magalis al-taratir* ('Democracy between the Alley Patrons and the Councils of Clowns'), 1979, 153, quoted in Abdalla, *Student Movement*, 255 no. 58.

85 Najjar, 'State and University in Egypt', 65.

86 Gershoni and Jankowski, *Egypt, Islam and the Arabs*, 164–90.

87 The remark was made in response to a question put by 'Abd al-Rahman 'Azzam, later the first secretary-general of the Arab League, Rejwan, *Nasserist Ideology*, 58.

88 Ghada Hashem Talhami, *Palestine and Egyptian National Identity*, New York: Praeger, 1992. 9–10; P.J. Vatikiotis, *The Modern History of Egypt*, London: Weidenfeld and Nicolson, 1969, 476–7.

89 It is also known as the Institute of Arabic Studies and Research (*Ma'had al-dirasat wa-buhuth al-'arabiyya*).

90 William L. Cleveland, *The Making of an Arab Nationalist, Ottomanism and Arabism in the Life and Thought of Sati' al-Husri*, Princeton UP, 1971, 79–80.
91 These lectures were published as *Minhaj mufassal li-durus fi al-'awamil al-tarikhiyya fi bina' al-umma al-'arabiyya*, 1961; Ghurbal remained in the post until his death in 1961.
92 See interview with Ghurbal in Fawdah, 'Hadith al-madina, ma'a Shafiq Ghorbal'; al-Jumay'i, *al-Jami'a al-misriyya wa'l-mujtam'a 1908–1940*, 112.
93 Interview with 'Asim al-Disuqi.
94 Among the early theses were *al-'Arab wa'l-turk 1908–1916; Tarikh al-wahda al-'arabiyya hatta 1945; al-Mas'ala al-marakshiyya 1902–12; Yimin 'ala 'ahd al-imam Yahya 1911–1948*, all supervised by Shafiq Ghurbal (Anis, 'Shafiq Ghorbal wa madrasa al-tarikh al-misri al-hadith', 16).
95 Interview with Ra'uf 'Abbas.
96 Also known as the Arabic UNESCO; Georgie Hyde, *Education in Modern Egypt: Ideals and Realities*, London: Routledge & Kegan Paul, 1978, 210–11.
97 Najjar, 'State and University in Egypt', 61; Ra'uf 'Abbas believes this decision was not implemented (Interview).
98 Mahmud A. Faksh, 'The Consequences of the Introduction and Spread of Modern Education: Education and National Integration in Egypt', *Middle Eastern Studies* 16 no. 2 (1980) 52.
99 Abdel-Malek, *Egypt*, 219.
100 *Tarikh al-'alam al-'arabi fi al-'asr al-hadith*, Cairo, 1960.
101 *Dirasat fi al-mujtama' al-'arabi*, Cairo, 1961, see Reid, *CU*, 204.
102 Muhammad Sa'id al-'Aryan and Jamal al-Din al-Shayyal, *Qissat al-kifa bayna al-'arab wa'l-'isti'mar*, Cairo, 1960 cited in Dekmejian, *Egypt under Nasir*, 322 no. 50; 'Ali Husni al-Kharbutli, *al-Tarikh al-muwahhad li'l-umma al-'arabiyya*, Cairo, 1970; Jalal Yahya, *al-'Alam al-'arabi al-hadith mundhu al-harb al-'alamiyya al-thaniyya*, 1980, see Rejwan, *Nasserist Ideology*, 60.
103 Dekmejian, *Egypt under Nasir*, 69.
104 See Ihsan 'Abd al-Quddus' remarks and criticism on this point, Rejwan, *Nasserist Ideology*, 78–9.
105 Rejwan, *Nasserist Ideology*, 60–7.
106 Reid, *CU*, 206.
107 Arthur Goldschmidt Jr, *Modern Egypt, The Formation of a Nation-State*, Boulder, Co: Westview Press, 1988, 77.
108 Muhammad al-Sayyid Ghallab, 'al-Dirasat al-ifriqiyya – African Studies', *Majallat al-dirasat al-ifriqiyya* 1 (1972) 1.
109 Reid, *CU*, 198.
110 Quoted from *Philosophy of the Revolution*, 110–11 in Reid, *CU*, 198.
111 Abdel-Malek, *Egypt*, 218.
112 Ibid., 230–1, 421 no. 17–18; for many years Cairo University maintained a campus in Khartoum.
113 Ghallab, 'al-Dirasat al-ifriqiyya – African Studies', 1–8.
114 Reid, 'The Egyptian Geographical Society', 564.
115 Rejwan, *Nasserist Ideology*, 84 quoting Raja al-Naqqash gives 1963 as the date of the decision by the ASU to set up the Institute; Beattie states its doors opened in May 1965, *Egypt during the Nasser Years*, 180–2; Dekmejian, *Egypt under Nasir*, 147 agrees with Beattie.
116 Waterbury, *Egypt of Nasser and Sadat*, 323.
117 Beattie, *Egypt during the Nasser Years*, 180.
118 'Dur al-fikr fi al-mujtama' al-ishtiraki', *al-Katib* January 1965, 7–9 quoted by Rejwan, *Nasserist Ideology*, 5.

119 Beattie, *Egypt during the Nasser Years*, 205 no. 128.
120 Mustafa, 'Muhammad Anis, mu'arrikhan wa munadilan', 64.
121 These were first published in *al-Katib*, then later in book form with Rajab Haraz, 'Asim al-Disuqi, 'Muhammad Anis wa duruhu fi ta'qil dirasat al-tarikh bi'l-jami'a al-misriyya 1950–1986', *MTM* 34 (1987) 11; see also 'Ali Barakat, 'Fi al-tariq ila madrasa ijtima'iyya fi kitabat tarikh misr al-hadith, 1898–1952', 59.
122 Beattie, *Egypt during the Nasser Years*, 182.
123 Ibid., 212, 220.
124 For the following see Raymond Baker, *Sadat and After, Struggles for Egypt's Political* Soul, Cambridge, Mass.: Harvard UP, 1990, 179–204.
125 Interview with Ra'uf 'Abbas.
126 It is generally assumed Hasan was rewarded with this appointment for assistance rendered to the Free Officers prior to the 1952 coup (Interview with Ra'uf 'Abbas). Since 1980 'Abbas has been head of the History Unit.
127 'Abd al-Karim (ed.) *50 'aman 'ala thawrat 1919*, Cairo, c. 1970.
128 al-Sayyid Yassin (ed.), *Thawrat yuliu wa'l-taghyir al-ijtima'i, rabi' qarn ba'd 23 yuliu 1952*, Cairo: Markaz al-dirasat al-siyasiyya wa'l-istratijiyya bi'l-ahram, 1977.
129 Ra'uf 'Abbas Hamid (ed.), *Arba'un 'aman 'ala thawrat yuliu*, Cairo: Markaz al-dirasat al-siyasiyya wa'l-istratijiyya bi'l-ahram, 1992.
130 Baker, *Sadat and After*, 191.
131 Mayer, *The Changing Past*, 74; see also Ra'uf 'Abbas, 'Maktaba al-thawra al-'urabiyya', *al-Siyasa al-dawliyya* 64 (April 1981) 498.
132 Anwar al-Sadat, *Revolt on the Nile*, New York: John Day, 1957; *In Search of Identity*, New York: Harper and Row, 1978.
133 Interview with Ra'uf 'Abbas.
134 'Lajna tarikh thawra 23 yuliu', *al-Ahram* 11 October 1975. The presidential decree no. 475 (1976) was not published until May 1976.
135 Deputy Speaker of Majlis al-sha'b; he had been chairman of the commission that investigated and subsequently condemned the student movement of 1972–3, Abdalla, *Student Movement*, 202.
136 Former rector of al-Azhar.
137 Professor emeritus of modern history and former rector of 'Ain Shams University.
138 Director of Propaganda and Ideology, ASU. During the sixties he was a member of the Law Faculty at Cairo University and author of a work on the July Revolution which rejected Marxism 'as a purely materialistic philosophy', Rejwan, *Nasserist Ideology*, 102.
139 Professor in the Faculty of Economics and Political Science at Cairo University; president of Centre for Political and Strategic Studies at al-Ahram, and chief editor of its journal, *al-Siyasa al-dawliyya*; also editor of *al-Ahram al-iqtisadi*. He became Acting Minister of Foreign Affairs in 1977 and more recently served as secretary-general of the United Nations (Gabriel M. Bustros (ed.), *Who's Who of the Arab World*, 7th edn, Beirut: Publitec, 1984–5).
140 Professor of history at 'Ain Shams University.
141 Geographer and author of the monumental *Shakhsiyyat misr*, Cairo: Dar al-hilal, 1993.
142 Historian of Islamic history at Women's College, 'Ain Shams University.
143 Professor of law, Alexandria University.
144 Professor of ancient history, Alexandria University.
145 An ageing warhorse of the Watani Party, Abaza (b. 1898) served as chief editor of *al-Musawwar* for almost 40 years, a position from which he exercised considerable influence. '[A] sworn enemy of the Wafd under the old system,

one of the spokesmen of the minority parties of the right, a specialist in political double-talk... closely linked to the Misr complex' (Abdel-Malek, *Egypt*, 147), he was appointed as head of Dar al-Hilal in 1960 and later attacked Nasser's legacy (Baker, *Egypt's Uncertain Revolution Under Nasser and Sadat*, 1978, 152); see also Reid, *Lawyers and Politics in the Arab World, 1880–1960*, 116 no. 20.

146 Member of the Majlis al-sha'b. Originally a member of the Watani Party, Takla was a member of the Central Committee of ASU (1971) (*Who's Who Arab World*, 1984); politically a centrist, she was later a minister in Sadat's cabinet and a prominent member of Misr Party's foreign affairs committee; she broke with Sadat over Camp David and joined the Labour Party, Raymond A. Hinnebusch Jr, *Egyptian Politics Under Sadat, The Post-Populist Development of an Authoritarian-Modernizing State*, Cambridge UP, 1985, 168–9.

147 Member of the Majlis al-sha'b and later deputy speaker in 1979–80.

148 Former professor of Faculty of Religion.

149 The official decree published in May 1976 listed additional members, Husayn Khilaf, a specialist from the Arab League, Ahmad Khalifa of the National Centre for Social and Criminal Studies and Lieutenant General Jamal 'Askar, and omitted Jamal Hamdan. Mahmud Mitwalli, a historian, was later appointed as technical secretary.

150 Yunan Labib Rizq, 'Kitabat tarikh 23 yuliu bayna al-tahrim wa'l-ibaha', *al-Ahram* 27 September 1975.

151 Ramadan, *Misr fi 'asr al-Sadat*, vol. 2, 88–91.

152 'Amana 'ama wa 8 lijan li-tajmi' watha'iq al-thawra', *al-Ahram* 27 October 1975.

153 'Husni Mubarak yaftatihu a'mal lajna tasjil tarikh al-thawra', *al-Ahram* 13 October 1975.

154 Ibid.

155 Yunan Labib Rizq, 'Kitabat tarikh 23 yuliu bayna al-tahrim wa'l-ibaha'.

156 Ahmad 'Izzat 'Abd al-Karim, 'al-Hukuma wa-kitabat al-tarikh', *al-Ahram* 14 November 1975.

157 Sayyid Ahmad al-Nasiri, 'Ma huwa al-hadaf, kitabat tarikh al-sha'b am tarikh al-thawra?', *al-Ahram* 6 December 1975.

158 Sabri Suwaylim, 'Mata yantaha tasjil asrar al-thawra kamila?', *al-Ahram* 3 January 1977. The Committee divided the three volumes thus: vol. 1, 1919–52; vol. 2, 1952–67; vol. 3, 1967–72.

159 17 February 1976; one student to another: 'How do the historians know the reasons for the collapse of the Roman state... without asking anyone'?

160 'Kalimat Husni Mubarak fi awwal ijtima' li'l-lajnat tasjil al-thawra', *al-Ahram* 10 January 1976.

161 'al-Lajna al-'askariyya yastami'u ila aqwal al-fariq awwal Fawzi wa'l-fariq Murtaji', *al-Ahram* 6 January 1976.

162 Interview with Ahmad 'Abd al-Rahim Mustafa.

163 Interviews with Ra'uf 'Abbas and 'Abd al-'Aziz Nawwar.

164 Presidential decrees no. 392 (1978) (appointment of Subhi al-Hakim) and no. 439 (1985) (dissolution of committee).

165 According to 'Abd al-'Aziz Nawwar a small amount of material appeared in the newspaper *Mayu* (Interview); Richard B. Parker, *The Politics of Miscalculation in the Middle East*, Bloomington and Indianapolis: Indiana UP, 1993, 37 reports an anonymous source as saying that the committee 'have had difficulty finding key documents'. This seems unconvincing.

166 'Abbas has asked al-Hakim about the whereabouts of the collected documents but finds his professed ignorance less than convincing (Interview).

167 His death of a heart attack some years later was believed to have related to his treatment in prison, Interview with 'Abd al-Rahim Mustafa.

168 al-Jumay'i, *Ittijahat al-kitaba al-tarikhiyya*, 204.

169 Interview with 'Abd al-Khaliq Lashin.

170 As far as I am aware there is no general work on censorship in Egypt but for a specific study, see Samira Helmy Ammar, 'Censorship of English Language Books in Egypt 1952–1990', MA thesis, AUC, May 1990.

171 Reid, *CU*, 78 ('Abd al-Raziq), 121–2 (Husayn); Mehrez, *Egyptian Writers*, 20–4 (Mahfuz).

172 Crabbs, 'Politics, History, and Culture in Nasser's Egypt', 390.

173 'Abd al-Rahman al-Rafi'i, *Mudhakkirati 1889–1951*, Cairo: Kitab al-yawm, 1989, 102–4.

174 Barbara Carter, *The Copts in Egyptian Politics 1918–1952*, Cairo: AUC Press, 1986, 126 no. 180.

175 Abdel-Malek (*Egypt*, 392) stated that the materialist works of al-Shafi'i, Jirjis and 'Amr were 'thoroughly mutilated by the censor'.

176 Zakariyya Sulayman Bayumi, 'al-Ittijahat al-diniyya bayna 'ahdi 'Abd al-Nasir wa'l-Sadat wa athar harakatihum al-mu'asira 'ala tanawulu durahum qabla 1952', 414 in 'Abd Allah (ed.) *Tarikh Misr*. Bayumi adds that mere possession of these studies was regarded as proving hostility towards the government.

177 This is Crabbs' view, 'Politics, History, and Culture in Nasser's Egypt', 386–420.

178 *Tatawwur al-haraka al-wataniyya fi misr 1918–36*, Cairo, 1968; Interview with 'Abd al-'Azim Ramadan.

179 *Qadiyat Filastin, al-marhala al-harja 1945–56*, Cairo, 1968; Interview with Salah al-'Aqqad.

180 Interview with 'Asim al-Disuqi.

181 This is my impression from talking with a number of historians. Censorship of some works of fiction may suggest a different scenario, see Sonallah Ibrahim, 'The Experience of a Generation', *Index on Censorship* 9 (1987) 19–22.

182 Interview with Salah al-'Aqqad.

183 Bayumi, 'al-Ittijahat al-diniyya...', 414; Interview with Salah al-'Aqqad.

184 Interview with Rif'at al-Sa'id.

185 This figure is based on the estimates given to me by Salah al-'Aqqad and Ahmad 'Abd al-Rahim Mustafa (Interviews).

186 Yvonne Haddad, *Contemporary Islam and the Challenge of History*, 33.

187 Interview with Rif'at al-Sa'id.

188 Interview with Ra'uf 'Abbas.

189 The works in this instance were by Najib Mahfuz, Ihsan 'Abd al-Quddus and Yusuf Idris, Dina Ezzat, 'Guarding Literature', *al-Ahram Weekly* 10–16 August 1995.

190 Interview with Samir Murqus.

191 Interview with Ra'uf 'Abbas.

192 Amira Ibrahim, 'It's all there at Archives House', *al-Ahram Weekly* 28 May– 3 June 1992.

193 Crabbs, 'Politics, History, and Culture in Nasser's Egypt', 390.

194 Muhammad Sabri, *La Genèse de l'ésprit national égyptien*, 1924, 2–3.

195 Muhammad Sabri, *L'Empire égyptien sous Ismail*, 9.

196 Muhammad Anis, 'Turathna al-qawmi...ya wazir al-thaqafa! hal yusbaqna al-ajanib li-dirasat watha'iqna al-tarikhiyya?', *al-Ahram* 10 April 1963.

197 Mustafa, 'Muhammad Anis, mu'arrikhan wa munadilan', 62–3.

198 'Adil al-Husayni, 'al-Tarikh kidhab', 30–1.

199 'Su'al wa jawab ma'a al-duktur Muhammad Anis', *al-Jumhuriyya* 11 August 1962.

200 Muhammad Anis, 'Turathna al-qawmi...ya wazir al-thaqafa! hal yusbaqna al-ajanib li-dirasat watha'iqna al-tarikhiyya?' *al-Ahram* 10 April 1963.

201 'Abd al-'Azim Ramadan, 'Muhammad Anis', *al-Wafd* 18 September 1986; Salah al-'Aqqad, 'Muhammad Anis, mu'arrikhan wa mufkaran', *al-Ahram* 4 September 1986.

202 al-'Aqqad, 'Muhammad Anis, mu'arrikhan wa mufkaran'; al-Disuqi, 'Muhammad Anis wa duruhu fi ta'qil dirasa al-tarikh bi'l-jami'a al-misriyya, 1950–1986', 7.

203 Interview with Ra'uf 'Abbas.

204 Preface to 'Abd al-Karim (ed.), *50 'aman 'ala thawrat 1919*.

205 For example, Haykal's account of the events of 1967, *al-Infijar 1967*, Cairo: al-Ahram, 1990, included 149 pages of documents from a total of over 1000 pages.

206 Ra'uf 'Abbas Hamid (ed.), *Arba'un 'aman 'ala thawrat yuliu*, 6–7.

207 For recent discussions on the poor state and lack of accessibility of Egyptian state archives see Ra'uf 'Abbas, 'Himaya watha'iqina al-qawmiyya', *al-Hilal* May 2001, 9–15; Mona el-Gobashy, 'Shredding the Past', *Cairo Times* 19–25 April 2001.

208 Published in 1975, see Jansen, 'Ibrahim Abduh (b. 1913)', 131.

209 al-Husayni, 'al-Tarikh kidhab', 31.

210 This is often recognized explicitly in the title, see Ra'uf 'Abbas Hamid, 'al-Watha'iq al-baritaniyya wa tarikh misr', *al-Ahram al-iqtisadi* 888 (January 1986) 36–7.

211 Crabbs, 'Politics, History, and Culture in Nasser's Egypt', 391 no. 1 states that in 1904 there were 176 newspapers being published in Cairo alone.

212 For some further discussion, see Afaf Lutfi al-Sayyid Marsot, 'Survey of Egyptian Works of History', 1425–6; 'Abd al-'Azim Ramadan, *Mudhakkirat al-siyasiyyin wa'l zu'ama fi misr 1891–1981*, Cairo: al-Watan al-'arabi, 1984.

3 HISTORY IN THE STREET: THE NON-ACADEMIC HISTORIAN

1 Mustafa Tiba, 'Hawla awraq Hinri Kuriyil matlub taqyim mawdu'i li'l-tarikh al-hadith', *al-Hilal* 96 (November 1988) 48.

2 al-Jumay'i, *Ittijahat al-kitaba al-tarikhiyya*, has most openly acknowledged the part played by 'amateur historians' (*mu'arrikhun hawa*). While praising their contribution to Egyptian historiography he cautions at the same time that '[this] does not mean that everyone who tries writing history becomes a historian' (p. 69). Elsewhere al-Jumay'i defines a historian as one who writes history and can '...add to a new theory or examination to the science (*'ilm*) of history and the historical school' (p. 232).

3 Literally, 'the national school' in Egyptian usage. I have preferred to use the term 'the liberal school' to avoid confusion with other national discourses.

4 Donald M. Reid, *Lawyers and Politics in the Arab World*, Minneapolis: Bibliotheca Islamica, 1981, 101–3.

5 Reid, *Lawyers and Politics*, 42; among Khanki's works is *al-Kitab al-dhahabi li'l-mahakim al-ahliyya*, Cairo, 1938.

6 Published in Alexandria by Matba'at al-mahrusa, 6 vols, 1884.

7 *al-Mas'ala al-sharqiyya*, 2 vols, Cairo: Matba'at al-liwa', 1909 (orig. published 1898).

8 Muhammad Farid, *Kitab al-bahjah al-tawfiqiyya fi tarikh mu'assis al-'a'ila al-khidiwiyya*, Bulaq: al-Matba'a al-amiriyya, 1891, is a history of Muhammad 'Ali's reign; *Tarikh al-dawla al-'aliyya al-'uthmaniyya*, Cairo: Matba'at al-taqaddum bi-misr, 1912 (orig. published 1894) deals with the Ottoman Empire

from the time of Osman to the Treaty of Berlin in 1878 and, in the third edition, the narrative continues up until 1909, Crabbs, *WH*, 174–6.

9 Crabbs, *WH*, 163 no. 21.

10 Crabbs, *WH*, 173, describes *Kitab al-bahjah al-tawfiqiyya* as 'an apology for his [Muhammad 'Ali's] rule'.

11 Crabbs, *WH*, 151; 'Abd al-Rahman al-Rafi'i, *Mustafa Kamil, ba'th al-haraka al-wataniyya*, Cairo: 1939, 192–5.

12 al-Rafi'i, *Mudhakkirati*, 17. The Club was subsequently closed by the British in 1914.

13 Ibid., 24.

14 Crabbs, *WH*, 189–90.

15 Note Crabbs' remark on Sharubim, *WH*, 196 no. 5.

16 For the following, see Crabbs, *WH*, 191–5.

17 Jurji Zaydan, *Tarikh al-tamaddun al-islami*, vol. 1, Cairo, 1968, 12 quoted in Reid, *CU*, 35–6.

18 Jurji Zaydan, *Tarikh misr al-jadid min al-fath al-islami ila alan*, 2 vols, 1911; a later edition published in 1925 was titled, *Kitab tarikh misr al-hadith*, 2 vols, Cairo: Dar al-hilal, 1925.

19 Reid, *CU*, 35–6.

20 Choueiri, *Arab History and the Nation-State*, 66.

21 Ahmad 'Abd al-Rahim Mustafa, ' 'Abd al-Rahman al-Rafi'i, 1889–1966', *al-Hilal* 75 no. 1 (January 1967) 41.

22 Mohamed Fahmy, *La Verité sur la question d'Égypte*, Saint-Imier, 1913, cited in Choueiri, *Arab History and the Nation-State*, 108 no. 4. Among Lutfi al-Sayyid's historical writings are *Safhat matwiyya, min tarikh li'l-istiqlal fi misr min maris 1908 ila maris 1909*, Cairo: Maktabat al-nahda al-misriyya, 1946.

23 For sources on al-Rafi'i's life, see Ahmad 'Abd al-Rahim Mustafa, ''Abd al-Rahman al-Rafi'i wa tarikh al-haraka al-qawmiyya', *al-Majalla* 60 (1962) 22–7; Ahmad 'Abd al-Rahim Mustafa, ''Abd al-Rahman al-Rafi'i, 1889–1966', *al-Hilal* 75 no. 1 (January 1967) 40–7; Tariq al-Bishri, ''Abd al-Rahman al-Rafi'i, mu'arrikhan wa siyasiyyan', *al-Tali'a* (December 1971) 89–108 and al-Rafi'i's own memoirs, *Mudhakkirati 1889–1951*, 1989.

24 Ahmad 'Abd al-Rahim Mustafa, ' 'Abd al-Rahman al-Rafi'i', *al-Majalla*, 23.

25 Reid, 'The Rise of Professions and Professional Organization in Modern Egypt', *Comparative Studies in Society and History* 16 (1974) 41–5.

26 Reid, *Lawyers and Politics*, 51.

27 Nasser read the first three of al-Rafi'i's books on the national movement while at the Military Academy in 1937–8 and later taught history there himself, Abdel-Malek, *Egypt*, 208–9.

28 Crabbs, 'Politics, History, and Culture in Nasser's Egypt', 415.

29 Reid, *Lawyers and Politics*, 166–7.

30 Al-Rafi'i later felt defensive about having accepted the position, see Farhat J. Ziadeh, *Lawyers, the Rule of Law and Liberalism in Modern Egypt*, Stanford University, 1968, 158n.

31 Reid, *Lawyers and Politics*, 167; Mayer, *The Changing Past*, 37, 80 no. 7.

32 Mustafa, ' 'Abd al-Rahman al-Rafi'i', *al-Majalla*, 26.

33 Ibid., 22; he was also nominated for the Nobel Prize in 1964.

34 *Huquq al-sha'b*, 1912; *Niqabat ta'awun al-zira'iyya*, 1914, cited al-Rafi'i, *Mudhakkirati*, 32–8.

35 *Muqaddamat thawrat 23 yuliu 1952*, Cairo, 1957 and *Thawrat 23 yuliu 1952 – tarikhna al-qawmi fi sabi' sanawat 1952–1959*, Cairo, 1959.

36 *Misr al-mujahida fi 'asr al-hadith*, cited by Mayer, *The Changing Past*, 32.

37 al-Rafi'i, *Mudhakkirati*, 84.
38 al-Rafi'i certainly knew French; he had acted as a translator when working for *al-Liwa'*, *Mudhakkirati*, 23.
39 'Abd al-'Azim Ramadan, 'Madaris kitabat tarikh misr al-mu'asir', in 'Abd Allah, *Tarikh Misr*, 61.
40 Mustafa, "Abd al-Rahman al-Rafi'i', *al-Majalla*, 26; al-Rafi'i, *Mudhakkirati*, 102–4.
41 For example, Jalal al-Sayyid, 'Tarikhna al-qawmi fi daw' al-ishtirakiyya', 89 and Yunan Labib Rizq, 'Bayna al-mawdu'iyya wa'l-tahazzub fi kitabat al-tarikh al-azhab al-siyasiyya fi misr', 365–7 in 'Abd Allah (ed.) *Tarikh Misr*; see also the criticism of Rif'at and Ghurbal on his interpretation of the 'Urabi Revolution, Mayer, *The Changing Past*, 30–1.
42 al-Rafi'i, *Mudhakkirati*, 97.
43 al-Bishri, ' 'Abd al-Rahman al-Rafi'i ', 98–101.
44 'Hadith ma'a al-duktur Muhammad Sabri', *al-Katib* 9 (1961) 84.
45 'Hadith al-madina, ma'a Shafiq Ghurbal', *al-Jumhuriyya* 8 May 1961.
46 Smith, for example, prefers al-Rafi'i's account to the more recent interpretation of 'Abd al-'Azim Ramadan, see Charles Smith, *Islam and the Search for Social Order in Modern Egypt*, Albany: State University of New York Press, 1983, 207 no. 2.
47 Ismael and El-Sa'id, *Communist Movement in Egypt*, 12–13.
48 Salama Musa, *Ishtirakiyya*, 1913 quoted in ibid., 3–4.
49 al-Mansuri, *Tarikh al-madhahib al-ishtirakiyya*, cited in Ismael and El-Sa'id, *Communist Movement in Egypt*, 5–11; another writer at this time, Nicola Haddad, who wrote on a more theoretical level, was also significant.
50 Vernon Egger, *A Fabian in Egypt, Salamah Musa and the Rise of the Professional Classes in Egypt, 1909–39*, Lanham, MD: University Press of America, c. 1986, 75.
51 Among the many leftist intellectuals who studied abroad were Shuhdi 'Atiyya al-Shafi'i and 'Abd al-Razzaq Hasan, who obtained postgraduate degrees in Britain, and Yusuf Darwish, Fu'ad Mursi, Isma'il Sabri 'Abdallah, who studied in France. For connections between Egyptian communists and contacts in the British Army, see Richard Kisch, *The Days of the Good Soldiers, Communists in the Armed Forces WWII*, London & New York: Journeyman, 1985.
52 I have used the name Iskra here since it appears most frequently in the literature. However, the group was also known by its Arabic name, *al-Sharara* ('The Spark'), Interview with Hillel Schwartz.
53 Selma Botman, *The Rise of Egyptian Communism, 1939–70*, Syracuse UP, 1988, 47–54.
54 Abdel-Malek, *Egypt*, 23.
55 Ahmad Sadiq Sa'd, *Mushkilat al-fallah*, Cairo: Lajnat nashr al-thaqafa al-haditha, 1945, quoted in Barakat, *QF*, 80.
56 Elinor Burns, *British Imperialism in Egypt*, London: Labour Research Department, 1928. It was one in a series dedicated to a critical examination of British imperialism. On the Labour Research Department, see W. Kendall, *The Revolutionary Movement in Britain, 1900–21*, London: Wiedenfeld and Nicolson, 1969, 278–83.
57 Abdel-Malek, *Egypt*, 22.
58 A collection of articles written by Sadiq Sa'd at this time was republished as *Safhat min al-yasar al-misri fi a'qab al-harb al-'alamiyya al-thaniyya 1945–46*, Cairo: Madbouli, 1976.
59 Iskra had merged with the Egyptian Movement for National Liberation (HAMITU) to form HADITU in 1947. For a useful listing of leftist periodicals of this period see Botman, *Rise of Egyptian Communism*, 157–63.

60 Abdel-Malek, *Egypt*, 120.
61 Ibid., 121; both Duwayk, in the New Dawn group, and Sulayman, in Art et Liberté, a Trotskyite group of the late thirties, were active communists, Botman, *Rise of Egyptian Communism*, 14.
62 Abdel-Malek, *Egypt*, 395 no. 2.
63 For details on Shuhdi 'Atiyya al-Shafi'i, see Abdel-Malek, *Egypt*, 134 and Joel Beinin, 'The Communist Movement and Nationalist Political Discourse in Nasirist Egypt', *Middle East Journal* 41 no. 4 (Autumn 1987) 572–4.
64 Shuhdi 'Atiyya al-Shafi'i and 'Abd al-Ma'bud al-Jibayli, *Ahdafuna al-wataniyya*, Cairo, 1945, cited in Ismael and El-Sa'id, *Communist Movement in Egypt*, 47–51.
65 *Tatawwur al-haraka al-wataniyya al-misriyya 1882–1956*, Cairo, 1957. It was republished in 1983, Meijer, 'Contemporary Egyptian Historiography of the Period 1936–1942', xxi.
66 Beinin and Lockman, *Workers on the Nile*, 20.
67 Ibrahim 'Amr, *Ta'mim al-qanal*, Cairo, 1956.
68 Ibrahim 'Amr, *Thawrat misr al-qawmiyya*, Dar al-nadim, Cairo, 1957 and *al-Ard wa'l-fallah, al-mas'ala al-zira'iyya fi misr*, Dar al-misriyya, Cairo, 1958; for quote, Abdel-Malek, *Egypt*, 50.
69 First a member of the Egyptian Movement for National Liberation (HAMITU), Jirjis became the leader of a splinter group which formed al-'Usba al-marksiyya, and later Nawat al-hizb al-shuyu'i al-misri; see Ismael and El-Sa'id, *Communist Movement in Egypt*, 54 for background on these organizations.
70 *Dirasat fi tarikh misr al-siyasi mundhu al-'asr al-mamluki*, Dar al-misriyya, Cairo, 1958.
71 Abdel-Malek had been one of the leaders, with al-Shafi'i, of the Revolutionary Bloc that split from HADITU at the end of 1947. He fled to France in 1959, Abdel-Malek, *Egypt*, 459; Beinin 'The Communist Movement and Nationalist Political Discourse in Nasirist Egypt', 573.
72 Abdel-Malek, *Egypt*, 298.
73 Interview with Ra'uf 'Abbas; Rejwan, *Nasserist Ideology*, 8.
74 Rejwan, *Nasserist Ideology*, 8–9.
75 Beattie, *Egypt during the Nasser Years*, 185.
76 For example, Muhammad Rif'at wrote for *al-Katib* and 'Abd al-'Azim Ramadan for *al-Tali'a*.
77 Other journals, such as *al-Fikr al-mu'asir*, *Sawt al-'arab*, also served as forums for progressive thought.
78 'Awad, *al-Jami'a al-misriyya fi al-am al-thalith min al-thawra*, 3, quoted in Reid, *CU*, 171.
79 *Egypt: Portrait of a President, 1971–1981, The Counter-Revolution in Egypt, Sadat's Road to Jerusalem*, first published in Arabic in 1978, in French in 1979 and finally by Zed Books in English in 1981.
80 Interview with Ra'uf 'Abbas.
81 Salah 'Isa is the author of a number of histories such *as al-Burjwaziyya al-misriyya wa uslub al-muwafada*, 1900–1940, Cairo: al-Thaqafa al-wataniyya, 1980.
82 Shaden Shehab, 'First, a Dream', *al-Ahram Weekly* 24–30 August 1995.
83 Interview with Rif'at al-Sa'id; many of these articles were republished in *Safhat min tarikh misr, ru'ya al-'alaqa bayna tarikh wa'l-siyasa*, Cairo: Dar al-thaqafa al-jadida, 1984.
84 Rif'at al-Sa'id, *Mustafa al-Nahhas, al-siyasi wa'l-za'im wa'l-munadil*, Beirut: Dar al-qadaya, 1976; *Sa'd Zaghlul bayna al-yimin wa'l-yasar*, Beirut: Dar al-qadaya, 1976; *Hasan al-Banna, mu'assis jama'at al-ikhwan al-muslimin, mata ... kayfa wa-limadha?*, Cairo: Dar al-thaqafa al-jadida, 1984.

85 Among these works is the five volume *Tarikh al-haraka al-shuyu'iyya al-misriyya, 1900—1940*, Cairo: Shirkat al-amal, 1987–9.

86 In fact, al-Sa'id occupies an ambiguous position between academia and politics since, though primarily active in political work, he has some links with 'Ain Shams University and the American University in Cairo.

87 Beinin, 'The Communist Movement and Nationalist Political Discourse in Nasirist Egypt', 568 no. 1 describes al-Sa'id's work as 'highly partisan toward the current to which he belonged' [i.e. HADITU].

88 Abu Sayf Yusuf, *Watha'iq wa mawaqif min tarikh al-yasar al-misri, 1941–1957*, Cairo: al-Amal, 2000.

89 Taha Sa'd 'Uthman, *al-Tabaqa al-'amila wa'l-'amal al-siyasi*, vol. 3, Mu'assasa al-'uruba, 1988; Mahmud al-'Askari, *Safhat min tarikh al-tabaqa al-'amila*, Hilwan: Dar al-khidamat al-niqabiyya, 1995.

90 Joel Beinin 'Will the Real Egyptian Working Class Please Stand Up?', in Zachary Lockman (ed.) in *Workers and Working Classes in the Middle East, Struggles, Histories, Historiographies*, State University of New York Press, 1994, 265.

91 Center for Trade Union and Workers Services, 'Working with Reality', 2–3 (undated).

92 Jean Vallet, *Awda' 'ummal al-sina'a al-kabira fi al-qahira*, trans. Yusuf Darwish, Dar al-khidamat al-niqabiyya wa'l-ummaliyya, 1996 from the French 1911 original, *Contribution a l'étude de la condition des ouvriers de la grande industrie au Caire*, Valence, 1911.

93 It has published an Arabic translation of Beinin and Lockman's work, *Workers on the Nile*, a book which attempts to establish an autonomous political role for the workers' movement, see Joel Beinin, 'The Egyptian Regime and the Left: Between Islamism and Secularism', 25–6.

94 Lajna tathiq tarikh al-haraka al-shuyu'iyya al-misriyya hatta 1965, *Shahadat wa ru'a, min tarikh al-haraka al-shuyu'iyya fi misr*, Cairo, 5 vols, 1998–2001.

95 Mahmud Amin al-'Alim (ed.), *Qadaya fikriyya: Azmat al-nizam al-ra'smaliyya fi misr...limadha...wa-ila ayna* 3–4 (1986), *al-Tabaqa al-'amila al-misriyya... al-turath...al-waqi'...afaq al-mustaqbal* 5 (1987), *al-Islam al-siyasi – al-asas al-fikriyya wa'l-ahdaf al-'amaliyya* 8 (1989).

96 *Sab'un 'aman 'ala al-haraka al-shuyu'iyya al-misriyya, ru'ya tahliliyya-naqdiyya* 11–12 (1992). Another leftist journal, *al-Yasar*, which first appeared in February 1990, has featured regular historical articles.

97 The relationship between Islam and history, raising issues of authenticity and the character of modernity, is far too complex to address here. Even within contemporary Islam there have been different attitudes towards history. According to Haddad, one school of thought that holds that Islam achieved its full articulation in the past, has focused on the early Islamic period and has little interest in subsequent historical developments. Another trend seeks 'to provide a contemporary Western ethos to Islam' and relegates Islam to the private sphere beyond the public domain of Western secularism and therefore holds no particular Islamic view of history. Yet another trend seeks a rearticulation of 'Islam for modern man' and calls for its resumption in the modern world. It is this last view which seeks to reintroduce an Islamic interpretation into contemporary history with which I am principally concerned here. For a more extensive discussion of the above, see Haddad, *Contemporary Islam and the Challenge of History*, esp 8–11, and the typology of Islamic thought offered in Nazih Ayubi, *Political Islam, Religion and Politics in the Arab World*, London & New York: Routledge, 1991, 237.

98 'Abduh had been appointed to the history faculty of Dar al-'Ulum for a short time in 1878, Crabbs, *WH*, 101.

99 Among a number of discussions, see Israel Gershoni, 'Imagining and Reimagining the Past: The Use of History by Egyptian Nationalist Writers, 1919–1952', 12–19.

100 Charles D. Smith, 'The "Crisis of Orientation": The Shift of Egyptian Intellectuals to Islamic Subjects in the 1930s', *IJMES* 4 (1973) 382–410.

101 Quoted from *Fi manzil al-wahy*, 1937, in Gershoni, 'Imagining and Reimagining the Past: The Use of History by Egyptian Nationalist Writers, 1919–1952', 28.

102 Safran, *In Search of Political Community*, 137.

103 *'Abqarriyat Muhammad*, 1942; *'Abqarriyat 'Umar*, 1942; *'Amr ibn al-'As*, 1944 cited by Gershoni, 'Imagining and Reimagining the Past', 21.

104 The phrase is Smith's, *IJMES* 4 (1973) 382–410.

105 Gershoni, 'Imagining and Reimagining the Past', 21.

106 Ibid., 24.

107 They were joined to a lesser extent by Misr al-Fatat which was formed in 1933 on a more complex platform of nationalist and Islamic elements.

108 Richard P. Mitchell, *The Society of the Muslim Brothers*, London: Oxford UP, 1969, 189.

109 Mitchell, *Muslim Brothers*, 185–7. The last two publications were owned and edited by Salih 'Ashmawi, a leader of the Society in the early fifties.

110 For some general discussion, see Yunan Labib Rizq, 'Bayna al-mawduwiyya wa'l-tahazzub fi kitabat tarikh al-azhab al-siyasiyya fi misr', 369–70.

111 *al-Ikhwan al-muslimin* and *al-Wafd wa'l-islam*, both published in 1947, cited ibid., 370.

112 Abdel-Malek, *Egypt*, 438 no. 6; among al-Ghazzali's works are *al-Islam wa'l-istibdad al-siyasi*, c. 1950–1, *al-Islam wa'l-awda' al-iqtisadiyya*, 3rd edn, 1952, *Ta'ammulat fi al-din wa'l-haya*, 1951, cited Mitchell, *Muslim Brothers*, xviii.

113 For the works of Anwar al-Jundi, which include *al-Islam wa-harakat al-tarikh*, 1968, *Ma'alim al-tarikh al-islami al-mu'asir min khilali 300 wathiqa siyasiyya*, 1981 and many others, see Haddad, *Contemporary Islam and the Challenge of History*, 225 no. 6.

114 For example Ahmad Anwar al-Jundi, *Hasan al-Banna – hayat raju wa-tarikh madrasa*, 1946; Ahmad Anis al-Hajjaji, *al-Imam*, 1950–2, 2 vols; 'Abd al-Basit al-Banna, *Mata...ila...shahid al-Islam*, 1951, cited in Mitchell, *Muslim Brothers*, xvii–xviii.

115 Goldschmidt, *Biographical Dictionary of Modern Egypt*, s.v. ''Umar al-Tilmisani'.

116 In 1953, al-Ghazzali was dismissed from the Ikhwan following his clash with the new leader Hudaybi. He later taught at al-Azhar, and various universities and colleges in Saudi Arabia, Qatar, Algeria, see Arthur Goldschmidt, *Biographical Dictionary of Modern Egypt*, s.v. 'Muhammad al-Ghazzali'.

117 Mitchell, *Muslim Brothers*, 188 no. 9

118 *al-Ikhwan al-muslimin*, 26 September 1946, quoted by Mitchell, *Muslim Brothers*, 220.

119 Mitchell, *Muslim Brothers*, 220.

120 For these events, see Mitchell, *Muslim Brothers*, 105–62.

121 Abdel-Malek, *Egypt*, 262.

122 The committee, which comprised Shaykh Sadiq 'Arjun, Dr Muhammad Yusuf Musa, Dr 'Abd al-Hamid Yunis, Dr Muhammad Najjar and Qutb, was to deal with the following topics: 'Introduction to Islamic History', 'Islam at the Time of the Prophet', 'Islamic Expansion', 'Arrest of Islamic Expansion' and 'The Islamic World Today', Haddad, *Contemporary Islam and the Challenge of History*, 227 no. 21.

123 On this general policy of Sadat, see Waterbury, *Egypt of Nasser and Sadat*, 359–64.

124 Bayumi, 'al-Ittijahat al-diniyya bayna 'ahdi 'Abd al-Nasir wa'l-Sadat wa athar harakatihum al-mu'asira 'ala tanawulu durahum qabla 1952', 413.

125 There were other publications: a monthly, *al-I'tisam* and *al-Mukhtar al-islami*.

126 Baker, *Sadat and After*, 344 no. 1.

127 See Baker, *Sadat and After*, 262 quoting 'Abd al-Halim Eweiss and Abu Zayid, 'Islamic History in Schools: A War on Islam', *al-Da'wa* November 1978; 'Isam al-Din al-'Aryan addressed the matter of an Islamic interpretation of the meaning of history, Gilles Kepel, *The Prophet and Pharaoh, Muslim Extremism in Egypt*, Paris: al Saqi Books, 1985, 152.

128 'Umar Tilmisani, *Qala al-nas . . . wa lam aqal fi hukm 'Abd al-Nasir*, Cairo: Dar al-ansar, 1980, 83–4.

129 Kepel, *Prophet and Pharaoh*, 124; Says Baker, 'Virtually every issue of the journal carried reports of their part in Egypt's national struggles', *Sadat and After*, 347 no. 33.

130 Muhammad 'Abd al-Quddus, '10 Sanawat ba'd wafah taghiyyat misr', *al-Da'wa* September 1980; for the assessment of 'Abd al-Quddus, Baker, *Sadat and After*, 257.

131 *Ruz al-Yusuf* 7 July 1980, quoted in Baker, *Sadat and After*, 345 no. 11.

132 'Umar al-Tilmisani, *Dhikrayyat . . . la mudhakkirat*, Cairo: Dar al-islamiyya, 1985; for the others, see Baker, *Sadat and After*, 347 no. 38, 349 no. 89.

133 *Madhabih al-ikhwan fi sujun Nasir*, Cairo: Dar al-i'tisam 1977. Rizq also published an account of the death of 21 Brothers in a south Cairo gaol in 1957, see Kepel, *The Prophet and Pharaoh*, 28.

134 Despite a number of court rulings against the action of the government, *al-Sha'b* was still closed in mid-2001.

135 'Misr al-fatat: sittun 'aman min al-jihad', *al-Sha'b* December 1993.

136 Interview with Tariq al-Bishri.

137 Ibid.

138 Many of these articles were republished in a collected edition, Tariq al-Bishri, *Dirasat fi al-dimuqratiyya al-misriyya*, Dar al-shuruq, 1987.

139 Roel Meijer, 'Changing Political Perspectives in the Contemporary Historiography of the Period 1919–1952'. Paper presented at the conference 'Commitment and Objectivity in Contemporary Historiography of Egypt 1919–1952', Netherlands Institute of Archaeology and Arabic Studies in Cairo, 1987, 7.

140 Interview with Tariq al-Bishri.

141 For further discussion, see Chapter 5.

142 An article by al-Bishri was featured in the 60th anniversary of Misr al-Fatat issue of *al-Sha'b*, 'Ahmad Husayn min wajha nazr al-tarikh', 26–7.

143 'Articulating Discontent', *al-Ahram Weekly*, 6–12 February 1997.

144 On the work of Muhammad 'Imara, see Boullata *Trends and Issues in Contemporary Arab Thought*, 74–9; Leonard Binder, *Islamic Liberalism: A Critique of Development Ideologies*, Chicago & London: University of Chicago Press, 1988, 146–50.

145 For a discussion on Abdel-Malek's revised thought, see Boullata, *Trends and Issues in Contemporary Arab Thought*, 97–9.

146 Wadie Kirolos, 'Debate Drowns in Shouts', *al-Ahram Weekly* 2–8 March 1995.

147 *Ma'rid al-hasna' fi tarajim mashahir al-nisa'*, Alexandria, 1879, quoted in Badran, *Feminists, Islam and Nation*, 256 no. 53.

148 Mervat Hatem, 'Through Each Other's Eyes: Egyptian, Levantine-Egyptian, and European Women's Images of Themselves and of Each Other (1862–1920)', *Women's Studies International Forum* 12 (1989) 190.

149 These were recently republished by Dar al-hilal in 1999.

150 Quoted in Margot Badran, *Opening the Gates*, 218.

151 For a full discussion on this phenomenon, Beth Baron, *The Women's Awakening in Egypt*, Yale UP, 1994.

152 Nabawiyya Musa wrote for *al-Ahram* and *al-Muqattam* and Bahithat al-Badiyah for *al-Jarida* (Badran, *Feminists, Islam, and Nation*, 39, 54); Fatima Nim'at Rashid contributed to *La Semaine égyptienne*.

153 These were not only written by women. In fact, many of the historical articles carried by *L'Égyptienne* were by men such as Ahmad Shafiq, Ahmad Zaki and Muhammad Sabri, Badran, *Feminists, Islam, and Nation*, 104.

154 In the following year its Arabic language version, *al-Amal*, appeared.

155 Doria Ragaï (Shafik), *La Femme et de le droit religieux de l'Égypte contemporaine*, Paris: Paul Geuthner, 1940.

156 *Tatawwur al-nahda al-nisa'iyya fi misr min 'ahd Muhammad 'Ali ila 'ahd al-Faruq*, Cairo: Maktabat al-tawakul, 1945. 'Abduh's collaboration was required in part because of Shafiq's inability to write literary Arabic, Cynthia Nelson, *Doria Shafik, Egyptian Feminist, A Woman Apart*, Cairo: AUC Press, 1996, 129.

157 *al-Mar'a al-misriyya min al-fara'ina ila al-yawm*, Cairo: Maktabat misr, 1955.

158 Afaf Lutfi al-Sayyid Marsot, 'The Revolutionary Gentlewomen in Egypt', 261–76 in Lois Beck and Nikki Keddie (eds), *Women in the Muslim World*, Cambridge, Mass.: Harvard UP, 1978.

159 Margot Badran and Miriam Cooke (eds), *Opening the Gates, A Century of Arab Feminist Writing*, Bloomington and Indianapolis: Indiana UP, 1990; Nikki R. Keddie and Beth Baron (eds), *Women in Middle Eastern History*, New Haven and London: Yale UP, 1991; Beth Baron, *The Women's Awakening in Egypt*, 1994; Margot Badran, *Feminists, Islam, and Nation*, Cairo, AUC Press, 1996; Cynthia Nelson, *Doria Shafik, Egyptian Feminist, A Woman Apart*, AUC Press, 1996; Thomas Philipp is one of the few to cross the gender barrier, see his 'Feminism and Nationalist Politics in Egypt', 277–94 in Beck and Keddie (eds), *Women in the Muslim World*, 1978.

160 These include the New Woman Research Centre, Association of the Development and Enhancement of Women, Forum for Women in Development and the Centre for Egyptian Women's Legal Assistance.

161 Amina Elbandary, 'A voice of her own', *al-Ahram Weekly* 11–17 October 2001.

162 Malak Hifni Nasif, *al-Nisa'iyyat*, Cairo: Women and Memory Forum, 1998.

163 Huda al-Shadda, Sumaya Ramadan and Umayma Abu Bakr, *Zaman al-nisa' wa al-dhakira al-badila*, Cairo: Dar al-kutub, 1998.

164 Rashid al-Barawi, *al-Tafsir al-ishtiraki li'l-tarikh*, Dar al-khusda al-'arabiyya, 1968, 1. The situation may have been a little different at Alexandria University, as Mursi Saad El-Din (cultural attaché in London at the time) noted,

> During the immediate post-war period the number of post-graduates in medicine, sciences, literature, history, geography, indeed all disciplines, far exceeded those sent [to England and the rest of Europe] by Cairo University. When those post-graduates returned, it was natural that they carried with them socialist ideas, which prompted their immediate support of the revolution and its socialist measures. Alexandria University became a centre of radical ideas.
>
> ('Alexandria University: a beacon for half a century', *al-Ahram Weekly* 30 July 1992)

165 Barakat, *QF*, 83, 84 no. 73.

166 Interview with 'Abd al-'Azim Ramadan.
167 Muhammad Anis and al-Sayyid Rajab Haraz, *Thawrat 23 yuliu 1952*, Cairo: Dar al-nahda al-'arabiyya, 1965. The apparent failure of the authors to acknowledge the work of 'Amr, al-Shafi'i and Jirjis is puzzling and may be explained by the political difficulty of explicitly acknowledging the work of Marxist historians at this time.
168 Among these are Ra'uf 'Abbas, 'Asim al-Disuqi, Mahmud Mitwalli, and 'Ali Barakat at Cairo University (Interviews).
169 'Ali Barakat, 'Fi al-tariq ila madrasa ijtima'iyya fi kitabat tarikh misr al-hadith, 1898–1952', 59.
170 Choueiri notes the stronger 'Islamic tone' than in Ghurbal's earlier (English language) study, *Arab History and the Nation-State*, 102–3.
171 Reid, *CU*, 147.
172 Reid, *CU*, 147, 172, 198.
173 For the following see al-Jumay'i, *Ittijahat al-kitaba al-tarikhiyya*, 140–1.
174 'Dur al-Azhar fi hifaz 'ala al-tābi' al-'arabi li-misr iban al-hukm al-'uthmani'; 'Suwar min dur al-Azhar fi muqawama al-hamla al-faransiyya 'ala misr', ibid.
175 'Dur al-Azhar fi al-haya al-misriyya iban al-hamla al-faransiyya wa matla' al-qarn al-tasi' 'ashar, PhD, Faculty of Arabic Language, Azhar, 1973, al-Jumay'i, *Ittijahat al-kitaba al-tarikhiyya*, 141.
176 His doctoral thesis was first published in 1978 under the title, *al-Ikhwan al-muslimun wa'l jama'at al-islamiyya fi al-haya al-siyasiyya al-misriyya, 1928–48*. Other important works are *al-Ittijah al-islami fi al-thawra al-misriyya 1919*, 1983 and *al-Ikhwan al-muslimun bayna 'Abd al-Nasir wa'l-Sadat min al-manshiyya ila al-minassa, 1952–1981*, Cairo: Maktaba wahba, 1987.
177 Salah al-'Aqqad, Bayumi's supervisor, later regretted having accepted the thesis. However, he regarded Bayumi's study as being selective rather than misrepresentive of the historical record (Interview); see also the hostile remarks of 'Abd al-Rahim 'Abd al-Rahman 'Abd al-Rahim, 'al-Kitaba al-misriyya 'an thawrat 1919 bayna al-mawdu'iyya wa'l-iltizam', in 'Abd Allah (ed.), *Tarikh Misr*, 213 and the subsequent discussion, 215–21.
178 Shimon Shamir, 'Radicalism in Egyptian Historiography', 215–27.
179 For example, on one occasion, on being asked to write an Islamic version of the history of the labour movement in Egypt, Ra'uf 'Abbas' reply was '*mafish*!' ('There isn't one!'), Interview with Ra'uf 'Abbas.
180 Latifa Salim, *al-Mar'a al-misriyya wa al-taghyir al-ijtima'i 1919–1945*, 1984; Amal Kamil Bayumi al-Subki, *al-Haraka al-nisa'iyya fi misr ma bayna al-thawratayn 1919 wa 1952*, Cairo, 1987. Among work that had appeared in the interim were Ijlal Khalifa, *al-Haraka al-nisa'iyya al-haditha fi misr*, 1973; Muhammad Kamal Yahya, *al-Judhur al-tarikhiyya li-tahrir al-mar'a al-misriyya fi al-'asr al-hadith*, 1983; Bahiga Arafa, *The Social Activities of the Egyptian Feminist Union*, Cairo: Elias, 1973 (based on a BA thesis (AUC) submitted in 1954).

4 EGYPT FOR WHICH EGYPTIANS

1 Nancy E. Gallagher, 'The Life and Times of a Moroccan Historian: An Interview with Abdallah Laroui', *Journal of Maghrebi Studies* 2 no. 1 (1994) 25–6.
2 In this specific sense Crabbs is right to state, 'Egypt had arrived at a clearly articulated sense of national consciousness, and every Egyptian historian after 1922 was a nationalist', *WH*, 208.
3 'Abd al-Karim, 'Kalima 'an Shafiq Ghurbal', 12; Muhammad Anis, 'Shafiq Ghurbal wa madrasat al-tarikh al-misri al-hadith', 13.

4 Though delivered in English, they were apparently first published in Arabic as *Takwin al-misr* in 1957, and later in English as *The Making of Egypt, A Series of Ten Talks*, 2nd edn, Cairo: League of Arab States, nd.

5 Ghurbal, *The Beginnings of the Egyptian Question and the Rise of Mehemet Ali*, London: George Routledge, 1928.

6 Ghurbal, *The Egyptian Question*, 284.

7 Ibid.

8 *Tarikh al-mufawadat al-misriyya al-baritaniyya, bahth fi 'alaqat al-baritaniyya min al-ihtilal ila 'aqd mu'ahadat al-tahalluf 1882–1936*, vol. 1, Cairo, 1952.

9 Ibid., 49.

10 Muhammad Anis, 'Shafiq Ghurbal wa madrasat al-tarikh al-misri al-hadith', 17.

11 Barakat, *QF*, 77.

12 Ghurbal, *The Making of Egypt*, 55.

13 Mustafa, 'Muhammad Anis, mu'arrikhan wa munadilan', 60.

14 Jalal al-Sayyid, 'Tarikhna al-qawmi fi daw' al-ishtirakiyya', 88.

15 Choueiri, *Arab History and the Nation-State*, Part 2, 'The professional historians: managers of legitimation'; see also Barakat, *QF*, 77.

16 For Rif'at see Crabbs, 'Politics, History, and Culture in Nasser's Egypt', 401 no. 2; al-Sayyid, 'Tarikhna al-qawmi fi daw' al-ishtirakiyya', 89 criticizes Shukri's discussion of the 'Urabi Revolution for being only concerned with the actions of the French and British government and not the internal situation of 'the people's struggle' (*kifah al-sha'b*).

17 Barakat, *QF*, 76.

18 M. Sabri, *La Révolution égyptienne*, vol. 2, 208.

19 Ibid., 208–9.

20 Quoted in Barakat, *QF*, 77.

21 Sabri, *La Révolution égyptienne*, vol. 2, 15.

22 Note the subtitles, *Mustafa Kamil, ba'th al-haraka al-wataniyya, tarikh misr al-qawmi min sanat 1892 ila sanat 1908; Muhammad Farid, ramz al-ikhlas wa'l-tadhiyya, tarikh misr al-qawmi min sanat 1908 ila sanat 1919*, Cairo: Maktaba mustafa al-halabi, 1941.

23 al-Rafi'i, *Thawrat 1919, tarikh misr al-qawmi 1914–1921*, 4th edn, Cairo: Dar al-ma'arif, 1987, 16.

24 Barakat, *QF*, 78.

25 al-Rafi'i, *Muhammad Farid*, 377–9.

26 Yunan Labib Rizq, 'Bayna al-mawdu'iyya wa'l-tahazzub fi kitabat al-tarikh al-azhab al-siyasiyya fi misr', 367.

27 The two clashed heatedly in parliament on the issue of Sudan, al-Bishri, 'Abd al-Rahman al-Rafi'i', 88–108.

28 Hamada Mahmud Ahmad Isma'il, *Sina'at tarikh misr al-hadith, dirasa fi fikr 'Abd al-Rahman al-Rafi'i*, Cairo: al-Hay'a al-misriyya al-'ama li'l-kitab 1987, 240. The treaty received general support across the Egyptian political spectrum with the exception of the Watani Party. For al-Rafi'i's view of the treaty see his *Qawai'd al-mu'ahada, istiqlal am himayya*, Cairo, 1936.

29 Isma'il, *Sina'at tarikh misr al-hadith*, 242.

30 Barakat, *QF*, 78; Rizq, 'Bayna al-mawdu'iyya wa'l-tahazzub fi kitabat al-tarikh al-azhab al-siyasiyya fi misr', 366 calls al-Rafi'i a '*al-ta'zhim wa'l-ta'thim*' ('great deeds and crimes') historian.

31 Mustafa, "Abd al-Rahman Rafi'i', *al-Majalla*, 36.

32 Jalal al-Sayyid, 'Tarikhna al-qawmi fi daw' al-ishtirakiyya', 89–90.

33 My thanks to Dr 'Abd al-'Azim Ramadan for raising this point.

34 Mustafa, 'Nadwat i'adat kitabat al-tarikh al-qawmi', 353.

35 The sequel was *Tatawwur al-haraka al-wataniyya fi misr mundhu ibram mu'ahada 1936 ila nihaya al-harb al-'alamiyya al-thaniyya*, Beirut, 1970 (also published under the title *Tatawwur al-haraka al-wataniyya fi misr 1937–1948*), Interview with 'Abd al-'Azim Ramadan; for much of the following I rely on Meijer, 'Contemporary Egyptian Historiography'.

36 In addition to his Wafdist-nationalist interpretation of history Ramadan also claims to be a historical materialist and has produced historical studies written within the framework of class struggle. Nevertheless, he has generally stressed the centrality of the Wafd in the national movement and, particularly in regular columns of the revived party's newspaper, *al-Wafd*, has consistently given priority to political factors over economic and social forces. See Meijer, 'Contemporary Egyptian Historiography', 35–40; Ramadan, ''Ilm al-tarikh bayna al-mawdu'iyya al-dhatiyya', *al-Majalla al-tarikhiyya al-maghribiyya* 13–14 (January 1979).

37 Meijer, 'Contemporary Egyptian Historiography', 47.

38 Ibid., 40.

39 Ibid., 45.

40 Quoted in Afaf Lutfi al-Sayyid Marsot, *Egypt's Liberal Experiment, 1922–36*, Berkeley: University of California Press, 1977, 57.

41 The cardinal importance accorded to the leader in a Wafdist interpretation was demonstrated in a public historiographical controversy. The row was precipitated by the doctoral thesis of 'Abd al-Khaliq Lashin, a student at 'Ain Shams University, on the political life of Sa'd Zaghlul. Lashin drew extensively on the memoirs of Zaghlul and took a very critical view of the Wafd leader's political motives, portraying him as a man obsessed with the maintenance of power and his own reputation. 'Abd al-'Azim Ramadan rose to Zaghlul's defence and in a public and often bitter debate, he and Lashin slugged it out; see 'Abd al-Khaliq Lashin, 'al-Haqa'iq al-gha'iba nashr mudhakkirat Sa'd Zaghlul', *al-Hilal*, March 1987, 15–20, and 'Abd al-'Azim Ramadan and Ahmad 'Abd Allah, 'Hawla al-ma'raka ilati darat baynahama 'ala safhat al-suhuf bi-khusus taqwim dur al-za'im Sa'd Zaghlul', in Abdulla (ed.), *Tarikh misr*, 277–80.

42 Meijer, 'Contemporary Egyptian Historiography', 42.

43 Ibid., 49–54.

44 Ibid., 54.

45 Ibid., 40.

46 Ibid., 112.

47 Shuhdi 'Atiyya al-Shafi'i, *Tatawwur al-haraka al-wataniyya al-misriyya 1882–1956*, Cairo, 1957, 3, quoted in 'Asim al-Disuqi, 'Naqd al-madkhal al-akhlaqi fi taqwim waqa'i' al-tarikh: dirasa tatbiqiyya 'ala al-tarikh li-thawrat 1919', 205.

48 For the following I rely on 'Asim al-Disuqi, *Nahwa fahm tarikh misr al-iqtisadi wa'l-ijtima'i*, Cairo: Dar al-kitab al-jama'i, 1981, 5–17.

49 Ibrahim 'Amr, *Thawrat misr al-qawmiyya*, 40–52.

50 al-Disuqi, *Nahwa fahm tarikh misr*, 16.

51 Meijer, 'Contemporary Egyptian Historiography', 13.

52 Ahmad Nazmi 'Abd al-Hamid and Rashid al-Barawi, *al-Nizam al-ishtiraki – 'arad watahlil wa naqd*, Cairo: Maktabat al-nahda al-misriyya, 1946, 117–18, quoted in al-Disuqi, 'Naqd al-madkhal al-akhlaqi fi taqwim waqa'i' al-tarikh: dirasa tatbiqiyya 'ala al-tarikh li-thawrat 1919', 201.

53 Ibid.

54 See 'al-Disuqi, 'Naqd al-madkhal al-akhlaqi fi taqwim waqa'i' al-tarikh: dirasa tatbiqiyya 'ala al-tarikh li-thawrat 1919', 205.

55 Anis and Haraz, *Thawrat 23 yuliu 1952*, 143–6.

56 Meijer, 'Contemporary Egyptian Historiography', 16.

57 Anis and Haraz, *Thawrat 23 yuliu 1952*, 147–66.
58 For example, see Abdel-Malek, *Egypt*, 353–62.
59 For a discussion of these, see Peter Gran, 'Modern Trends in Egyptian Historiography: A Review Article', *IJMES* 9 (1978) 367–71.
60 al-Disuqi, 'Asim, *Nahwa fahm tarikh misr al-iqtisadi wa'l-ijtima'i*, 1981.
61 Ibid., 55–6.
62 Ibid.
63 'Asim al-Disuqi, *Misr al-mu'asira fi dirasat al-mu'arrikhin al-misriyyin*, Cairo: Dar al-hurriyya [c. 1976] 26, notes Anis' view that the Liberal Constitutionalists represented the large landowners and the Sa'dists, the capitalists, in the period after 1937.
64 Meijer, 'Contemporary Egyptian Historiography', 57.
65 Ibid., 83–97.
66 'Amr, *Thawrat misr al-qawmiyya*, 95–7.
67 For the following, see al-Disuqi, *Nahwa fahm tarikh misr*, 13–14.
68 Quoted in al-Disuqi, *Nahwa fahm tarikh misr*, 13.
69 al-Disuqi, *Nahwa fahm tarikh misr*, 13.
70 Ibid., 13–14.
71 Beinin, 'The Communist Movement and Nationalist Political Discourse in Nasirist Egypt', 578; see also al-Disuqi, *Nahwa fahm tarikh misr*, 14.
72 I am here only concerned with Anis' views as expressed during the first half of the 1960s. He later came to develop a more sympathetic view of the Wafd in his analyses of the February 1942 incident and the fire of Cairo of which Salah al-'Aqqad later wrote, 'Without doubt his writing on the fire of Cairo in January 1952 which aimed a blow at the nationalist forces had created a kind of mutual affection between Dr Anis and the Wafd', 'Muhammad Anis, mu'arrikhan wa mufakkiran', *al-Ahram* 4 September 1986. Anis would later be involved with the revived Wafd in the late 1970s.
73 Anis and Haraz, *Thawrat 23 yuliu 1952*, 205–10.
74 Ibid., 147–60. He did, however, mention the establishment of the Egyptian Communist Party in 1921 (138–41).
75 Beinin, 'The Communist Movement and Nationalist Political Discourse in Nasirist Egypt', 578. See also al-Disuqi, 'Naqd al-madkhal al-akhlaqi fi taqwim waqa'i' al-tarikh', 204 who makes the point less forcefully. Fawzi Jirjis' account similarly appears to make no mention of the communist role.
76 This was true of Fawzi Jirjis and Muhammad Anis but al-Shafi'i and Ibrahim 'Amr professed little open enthusiasm for the Arab world, Abdel-Malek, *Egypt*, 265.
77 For a discussion of the reaction of the communist movement to Nasser see Beinin, 'The Communist Movement and Nationalist Political Discourse in Nasirist Egypt', 574–83; Beattie, *Egypt during the Nasser Years*, 130–2.
78 Abdel-Malek, *Egypt*, 298 (published originally in French in 1962).
79 Abdel-Malek, *Egypt*, xxxi (from the preface of the English translation dated February 1968).
80 Among Rif'at al-Sa'id's many works note especially, *Tarikh al-haraka al-shuyu'iyya al-misriyya*, vols 1–5; Tariq al-Bishri, *al-Haraka al-siyasiyya fi misr, 1945–52*, 2nd edn, Cairo: Dar al-shuruq, 1983 (first published 1972).
81 Meijer, 'Contemporary Egyptian Historiography', 59.
82 Ibid., 66.
83 Quoted from al-Sa'id, *Tarikh al-munazzamat al-yasariyya al-misriyya, 1940–1950*, Cairo: Dar al-thaqafa al-jadida, 1976, 277 in Meijer, 'Contemporary Egyptian Historiography', 69. For a discussion of the views of other leftist writers on this committee, Abdalla, *Student Movement*, 71–4.

84 Meijer, 'Contemporary Egyptian Historiography', 60.

85 Ibid., 60–2.

86 This popular front concept was reflected in the links between some communists, particularly the New Dawn group, with the Wafdist Vanguard (the left wing of the Wafd) and the unsuccessful call for a combined front between HADITU and the Wafd, Ismael and El-Sa'id, *Communist Movement in Egypt*, 60.

87 For example, see the view of Muhammad Sid Ahmad in Meijer, 'Contemporary Egyptian Historiography', 119. It should be noted that al-Sa'id, an Egyptian of Muslim background, was a member of HADITU, a group whose moving spirit during the 1940s was an Egyptian Jew, Henri Curiel, and whose membership included many Jews of foreign nationality.

88 Mahmoud Hussein ['Adil Rif'at and Bahjat al-Nadi], *Class Conflict in Egypt 1945–1970*, New York and London: Monthly Review Press, 1973. It had been earlier published in French.

89 Hussein, *Class Conflict in Egypt*, 11–12.

90 Beinin, 'Will the Real Egyptian Working Class Please Stand Up?', 247–70 in Zachary Lockman (ed.), *Workers and Working Classes in the Middle East, Struggles, Histories, Historiographies*, State University of New York Press, 1994.

91 Beinin and Lockman, *Workers on the Nile*, 19–20.

92 On the former point, see the discussion held at the Egyptian Historical Society in December 1965, Mustafa, 'Nadwat i'adat kitabat al-tarikh al-qawmi', 351–6.

93 For *al-isti'mar al-dakhili* see Mitchell, *Muslim Brothers*, 218.

94 For an excellent discussion on this, see Haddad, *Contemporary Islam and the Challenge of History*, esp. 77–81, and on the writings of Sayyid Qutb, 162–8.

95 For the following, see Mitchell, *Muslim Brothers*, 264–7.

96 For this discussion I rely on the following works of Bayumi *al-Ittijah al-islami fi thawra al-misriyyat 1919*, 1983; *al-Ikhwan al-muslimun wa'l-jama'at al-islamiyya fi al-haya al-siyasiyya al-misriyya 1928–1948*, Cairo: Maktaba wahba, 1991 (first published 1978); and *al-Ikhwan al-muslimun bayna 'Abd al-Nasir wa'l-Sadat min al-manshiyya ila al-minassa, 1952–1981*, Cairo: Maktaba wahba, 1987.

97 Bayumi, *al-Ikhwan al-muslimun 1928–1948*, 21–4.

98 Meijer, 'Changing Political Perspectives . . .', 4.

99 For a discussion see, Crabbs, *WH*, 152–6.

100 Meijer, 'Changing Political Perspectives in the Contemporary Historiography of the Period 1919–1952', 6–9.

101 For the following I rely on 'Abd al-Rahim 'Abd al-Rahman 'Abd al-Rahim, 'al-Kitabat al-misriyya 'an thawrat 1919 bayna al-mawdu'iyya wa'l-iltizam', 212–14.

102 Bayumi, *al-Ittijah al-islami fi al-thawra al-misriyyat 1919*, 23, quoted by 'Abd al-Rahim, 'al-Kitabat al-misriyya 'an thawrat 1919 bayna al-mawdu'iyya wa'l-iltizam', 213.

103 'Abd al-Rahim, 'al-Kitabat al-misriyya 'an thawrat 1919 bayna al-mawdu'iyya wa'l-iltizam', 213.

104 For the following, see Meijer, 'Changing Political Perspectives in the Contemporary Historiography of the Period 1919–1952', 10.

105 *al-Haraka al-siyasiyya fi misr, 1945–52*, 2nd edn, Cairo: Dar al-shuruq, 1983.

106 Meijer, 'Contemporary Egyptian Historiography', 60–2.

107 al-Bishri, *al-Haraka al-siyasiyya fi misr, 1945–52*, introd., 2nd edn, 42, quoted by Roel Meijer, *History, Authenticity, and Politics: Tariq al-Bishri's Interpretation of Modern Egyptian History*, Occasional Paper no. 4, Amsterdam, Middle East Research Associates, 1989, 19.

108 Quoted in Meijer, *History, Authenticity, and Politics*, 19–20.
109 al-Bishri, *al-Haraka al-siyasiyya fi misr, 1945–52*, introd., 2nd edn, 35.
110 For the following, see Binder, *Islamic Liberalism*, 252–5.
111 Meijer, 'Contemporary Egyptian Historiography', 146.
112 Ibid., 134.
113 Meijer, *History, Authenticity, and Politics*, 28–31, cf. Binder, *Islamic Liberalism*, 255–8 which presents al-Bishri's earlier view of the Ikhwan.
114 Meijer, 'Contemporary Egyptian Historiography', 137–8.
115 Meijer, *History, Authenticity, and Politics*, 29–31.
116 Ibid., 31–2.
117 Ibid., 117.
118 Tariq al-Bishri, 'Awraq Hinri Kuriyil', *al-Hilal* 95 (April 1988) 18–25; Ra'uf 'Abbas (ed.), *Awraq Hinri Kuriyil wa'l-haraka al-shuyu'iyya al-misriyya*, Cairo, 1988; Ra'uf 'Abbas Hamid, 'Hinri Kuriyil', *al-Hilal* 96 (November 1988) 42–7; Muhammad Sid Ahmad, 'al-Yahud fi al-haraka al-shuyu'iyya al-misriyya wa'l-sira' al-'arabi al-isra'ili', *al-Hilal* 96 (June 1988) 21–7; Mustafa Tiba, 'Hawla awraq Hinri Kuriyil matlub taqyim mawdu'i li'l-tarikh al-hadith', *al-Hilal* 96 (November 1988) 48–53.
119 For the following, Meijer, 'Contemporary Egyptian Historiography', 127–31.
120 Binder, *Islamic Liberalism*, 261–2.
121 For this discussion see Meijer, *History, Authenticity, and Politics*, 14–18.
122 Binder, *Islamic Liberalism*, 276. This point is made in al-Bishri's work on Muslim–Copt relations, *al-Muslimun wa'l-aqbat fi atar al-jama'a al-wataniyya*, Cairo: Dar al-shuruq, 1982.
123 Meijer, *History, Authenticity, and Politics*, 33.
124 Bayumi, *al-Ikhwan al-Muslimun bayna 'Abd al-Nasir wa'l-Sadat min al-man-shiyya ila al-minassa, 1952–1981*, 1987.
125 Ibid., 146.
126 Ibid., 148.
127 Muhammad 'Abd al-Quddus, '10 Sanawat ba'd wafah taghiyyat misr', *al-Da'wa* September 1980, 46–8.
128 'Umar Tilmisani, *Qala al-nas . . . wa lam aqal fi hukm 'Abd al-Nasir*, 324–31.
129 Ibid., 83.
130 Bayumi, *al-Ikhwan al-muslimun bayna 'Abd al-Nasir wa'l-Sadat, 1952–1981*, 144.
131 Meijer, *History, Authenticity, and Politics*, 38.
132 The early work of Duria Shafiq, *La Femme et le droit religieux*, is an example of this approach.
133 See statements regarding the participation of women in Ghurbal, *Tarikh al-mufawadat*, 49, and Sabri, *La Révolution égyptienne*, vol. 2, 208. Al-Rafi'i, *Thawrat 1919*, 209, 234 quotes examples of specific demonstrations in which women took part, referring to the great majority of women as 'the wife of x'.
134 By contrast, the role played by the EFU in the peace movement of the 1930s seems relatively neglected in the liberal narrative.
135 Botman, *Rise of Egyptian Communism*, 22–6.
136 Beinin and Lockman, *Workers on the Nile*, 345.
137 Ismael and al-Sa'id, *Communist Movement in Egypt*, 18, 86; Botman, *Rise of Egyptian Communism*, 71. As one measure of female participation in the communist movement, al-Sa'id (*Tarikh al-haraka al-shuyu'iyya al-misriyya*, vol. 5) lists only one woman from the almost 40 individual testimonies collected. Similarly, in the series *Shahadat wa ru'a*, of the first five volumes only four accounts out of 53 are by women.

138 For example, Ahmad Taha Ahmad, *al-Mar'a kifahha wa 'amalha*, 1964 and Kamilya 'Abd al-Fattah, *fi sikulujiyyah al-mar'a al-'amila*, Cairo 1972 cited by Tucker, 'Problems in the Historiography of Women', 326.
139 Nikki Keddie, 'Problems in the Study of Middle Eastern Women, *IJMES* 10 (1979) 238.
140 For the following Bayumi, *al-Ikhwan al-muslimun*, 292–9.
141 To these we could add earlier women's organizations that used Islam to defend a traditional model for women. Among them were the Jam'iyyat tarqiyyat al-mar'a and the magazine of Fatima Rashid launched in 1908, Jam'iyyat ummahat al-mustaqbal and Nahdat al-sayyidat al-misriyyat (both established 1921) (Badran, *Feminists, Islam, and Nation*, 52).
142 Badran, *Feminists, Islam, and Nation*, 248.
143 See Tahia Abdel-Nasser, 'Recovered Memories', *al-Ahram Weekly* July 1999 (Book Supplement).
144 Mariz Tadros, 'Dad in the kitchen?', *Al-Ahram Weekly*, 13–19 September 2001.
145 Consider, for example, Mervat Hatem,'Through Each Other's Eyes', *Women's Studies International Forum* 12 (1989) 183–98.
146 Two studies, 'Imad Hilal, *al-Bagaya fi misr, dirasa tarikhiyya ijtima'iyya (min 1834–1949)*, Cairo: al-'Arabi, 2001 and 'Abd al-Wahab Bakr, *Mujtama' al-qahira al-sirri (1900–1951)*, Cairo: al-'Arabi, 2001, dealing with prostitution have very recently been published.

5 THE COPTS

1 Muhammad Neguib [Najib], *Egypt's Destiny*, London: Victor Gollancz, 1955, 194–5.
2 Dekmejian, *Egypt under Nasir*, 82.
3 Muhammad H. Haykal, *Autumn of Fury, The Assassination of Sadat*, London: Corgi, 1983, 174.
4 Sulayman Nasim, a Coptic historian of education, suggested 10 million Copts out of a total 56 million Egyptians as an approximate figure (Interview).
5 Interview with Rafiq Habib.
6 *Modern Egypt*, II, 205–6. Despite this statement Cromer elsewhere resorts to crass generalization in his description of the Egyptian population. After discarding a number of classifications, he writes, '...they may be classified as Moslems and Christians, a distinction which, being converted from terms of religious belief into those of political and social life, would differentiate the ignorant, conservative mass from the more subtle, more superficially intellectual, but, if the true Europeans be excluded, by no means more virile minority.' *Modern Egypt*, Vol. II, 168–9.
7 The first noteworthy case was the Egyptian Party set up in 1908 by Akhnukh Fanus. Later examples include the National Democratic Party (later the Christian Democratic Party) formed by Ramsis Jibrawi in June 1949; the Society of the Coptic Nation formed in 1952 (see below) and still later, Zaki Shinuda's Coptic Unity Party.
8 Amira Sonbol, 'Society, Politics and Sectarian Strife', 271 in Ibrahim M. Oweiss (ed.), *The Political Economy of Contemporary Egypt*, Washington: Center for Contemporary Arab Studies, 1990. Samir Murqus reported an advertisement which appeared in *al-Ahram* some years ago calling for a Coptic party but which came to nothing (Interview).
9 I use the term 'national' here to distinguish these newspapers from the majority of Coptic newspapers which have been religious or community publications. Most

notable were *al-Watan* (1877–1930) a proclerical, conservative daily hostile to the Wafd, and *Misr* (est. 1895) originally pro-British but later a supporter of the Wafd. It was a particularly strong advocate of Coptic interests under the editorship of Salma Musa in the late 1940s. For a detailed listing, *Coptic Encyclopedia*, s.v. 'Press, Coptic' (B.L. Carter).

10 *Watani* maintains strong relations with the Orthodox Church (members of the clergy contribute regularly to the paper's columns) and according to one informant receives financial support from Coptic communities abroad, Interview with Rafiq Habib.

11 Carter, *Copts in Egyptian Politics*, 212–20.

12 Dekmejian, *Egypt under Nasir*, 21. Two anecdotes have been invoked to capture attitudes towards Coptic participation in government service. The first is the story told of Sa'd Zaghlul, who, when asked why there were two Copts in his cabinet (as opposed to the more common practice of one), replied that since English bullets made no distinction between Muslim and Copt neither should he. The other, probably apocryphal, concerns the low number of Copts in the Ministry of Defence. After the 1956 war Nasser is reported to have asked for the proportion of Coptic casualties. On being told it was 3 per cent, he determined that Copts should be represented in the ministry in the same ratio (Interview with Rafiq Habib). The *Coptic Encyclopedia* notes succinctly, 'At present it is taken for granted that there are certain leadership and government positions to which Copts are not entitled.' s.v. 'Modern Egypt, Copts in' (Samira Bahr).

13 Nadia Ramsis Farah, *Religious Strife in Egypt, Crisis and Ideological Conflict in the Seventies*, Montreux: Gordon and Breach, 1986, 117.

14 Made during Sadat's address to Parliament on 14 May 1980, Haykal, *Autumn of Fury*, 228.

15 Haykal, *Autumn of Fury*, 248.

16 The trend has continued with the latest serious incident at al-Kosheh at the end of the nineties.

17 'Abd Allah (ed.), *Tarikh Misr*. The issue came closest to being addressed in Sadiq Sa'd's paper on the work of Tariq al-Bishri.

18 Even early in the twentieth century when Copts held some 45 per cent of all bureaucratic positions in government departments they were represented with only 6 per cent of positions in the Ministry of Education, Reid, *CU*, 149–51.

19 Salama Musa, 'Intellectual Currents in Egypt', *Middle Eastern Affairs* (August–September 1951) 270.

20 Sharubim served as President of Jami'yyat al-tawfiq al-qibtiyya, a leading Coptic organization, Crabbs, *WH*, 133. His daughter married the son of Butrus Ghali, prime minister of Egypt. Arthur Goldschmidt Jr, 'The Butrus Ghali Family', *Journal of the American Research Center in Egypt* 30 (1993) 183.

21 *al-Kafi fi al-tarikh misr al-qadim wa'l-hadith*, 4 vols, Bulaq: Matba'at al-kubra al-amiriyya, 1898–1900, see Crabbs, *WH*, 133–6.

22 Among the first Copts who became academic historians of the modern period were Yunan Labib Rizq and Sulayman Nasim.

23 By contrast, the private American University in Cairo engaged no Muslim in a full-time academic position until 1958, Reid, *CU*, 164.

24 The *thanawiyya 'amma* is the final high school exam.

25 Ra'uf 'Abbas, 'Hadhari inahum yatala'bun bi-mustaqbal al-watan wa yashkun fi amana al-aqbat bi'l-jami'a', *al-Ahali* 10 November 1993; 'Atabi' ma taqumun bihi min jahd mutamayyiz wa siyasatikum tahza bi-taqdir al-quwan al-sharifa', *al-Ahali* 24 November 1993.

26 Interview with Rif'at al-Sa'id; see also Salama Musa, 'Intellectual Currents in Egypt', 272.

27 The case of Jurji Zaydan at Cairo University in 1910, namely of a Greek Orthodox lecturing on Islamic history, resulted in protests and suggested there was significant Muslim opposition to the idea of a Christian teaching history, see Reid, CU, 35–6.

28 Interview with Yunan Labib Rizq. See for example, '"Abu Qarqas" ... wa sina'at al-munakh al-fitna al-ta'ifiyya', al-Yasar 5 (July 1990) 34–6 and '"Abu Qarqas" wa sina'at al-munakh (2), al-'Auda ila al-za'amat al-diniyya', al-Yasar 6 (August 1990) 31–3.

29 Interview with Yawaqim Rizq Murqus.

30 Lutfi al-Sayyid, Safhat matwiyya, min tarikh li'l-istiqlal fi misr min maris 1908 ila maris 1909, 33–4, quoted in Charles Wendell, The Evolution of the Egyptian National Image, From its Origins to Ahmad Lutfi al-Sayyid, Berkeley and Los Angeles: University of California Press, 1972, 239–40.

31 Marsot, Egypt's Liberal Experiment: 1922–1936, viii.

32 Muhammad 'Afifi, al-Aqbat fi al-'asr al-'uthmani, 1517–1798, Cairo, 1992. 'Afifi explained that he approached the subject 'as though he was not Egyptian' (Interview).

33 Ghali Shukri, al-Aqbat fi watan mutaghayyir, 7, quoted in David Sagiv, Fundamentalism and Intellectuals in Egypt, 1973–1993, London: Frank Cass, 1995, 135. 'Abdel-Malek, Egypt, 261 had made a similar complaint of the school curriculum of the early sixties as 'completely ignoring six centuries of Coptic history'.

34 'New History for the Millenium', al-Ahram Weekly 29 April–5 May 1999; the comment was made by Yunan Labib Rizq.

35 Later in the 1930s the Giza Movement, an advanced level of the Sunday School was set up, Edward Wakin, A Lonely Minority, The Modern Story of Egypt's Copts, William Morrow: New York, 1963.

36 Barbara Carter, The Copts in Egyptian Politics 1918–1952, Cairo: AUC Press, 1986, 119 no. 42.

37 Donald M. Reid, 'Archaeology, Social Reform and Modern Identity among the Copts' (1854–1952) 311–35 in Alain Roussillon (ed.), Entre réforme sociale et mouvement national, Cairo: CEDEJ, 1995.

38 Coptic Encyclopedia, s.v. 'Higher Institute of Coptic Studies' (Aziz S. Atiya).

39 This appeared in Misr, Carter, Copts in Egyptian Politics, 115.

40 Interview with Samir Murqus.

41 Ibid. Guest speakers have included Tariq al-Bishri and Muhammad 'Imara, figures both associated with the Islamic current.

42 Mona el-Nahhas, 'Controversy over Coptic University Plan', al-Ahram Weekly 13–19 February 1997.

43 Among Egyptian scholars featured are Mirrit Butrus Ghali, Samira Bahr, Yunan Labib Rizq.

44 Carter, Copts in Egyptian Politics, 114–15.

45 For example, see Mustafa El-Feki [al-Fiqi], Copts in Egyptian Politics 1919–1952, Cairo: General Egyptian Book Organization, 1991, 55.

46 Muhammad Sabri, La Révolution égyptienne, vol. 2, 207.

47 The proposal for separate representation was put forward by a Coptic notable, Tawfiq Dus; it was defeated by a convincing but not unanimous 15 votes to 7, Carter, Copts in Egyptian Politics, 133–42.

48 Jamal Badawi, 'al-Wafd bayt al-aqbat al-siyasi', al-Wafd 18 May 1995.

49 Mustafa El-Feki [al-Fiqi], Copts in Egyptian Politics 1919–1952, Cairo: General Egyptian Book Organization, 1991. This study was based on the PhD al-Fiqi

obtained from the University of London in 1977 titled, 'Makram Ebeid, A Coptic Leader in the Egyptian National Movement, A Case Study in the Role of the Copts in Egyptian Politics, 1919–1952'.

50 al-Fiqi, *Copts in Egyptian Politics*, 12–13.
51 Ibid., 183.
52 Ibid., 74.
53 Vatikiotis, *Arab and Regional Politics in the Middle East*, 254.
54 Barbara Carter, *The Copts in Egyptian Politics 1918–1952*, Cairo: AUC Press, 1986, 172, 177.
55 al-Fiqi, 178; Carter, *Copts in Egyptian Politics*, 193–4.
56 Carter, *Copts in Egyptian Politics*, 221.
57 On numbers see Carter, *Copts in Egyptian Politics*, 177.
58 Donald M. Reid, 'The National Bar Association and Egyptian Politics, 1912–1954', *International Journal of African Historical Studies* 7 (1974) 637.
59 Jamal Badawi, *al-Fitna al-ta'ifiyya fi misr, judhuruha wa asbabaha*, 2nd edn, Cairo: al-Zahra' li'l-a'lam al-'arabi, 1992.
60 Butrus Butrus Ghali (ed.), *al-Sha'b al-wahid wa'l-watan al-wahid, dirasa fi asul al-wahda al-wataniyya*, Cairo: Markaz al-dirasat al-siyasiyya wa'l-istratijiyya bi'l-ahram, 1982.
61 Al-Fiqi has since served in the Ministry of Foreign Affairs and as an adviser to President Mubarak.
62 al-Lajna al-misriyya li'l-wahda al-wataniyya, *al-Bayan*, nd; see also Aisha Rafea, 'Right to be Egyptian', *al-Ahram Weekly* 24–30 November 1994.
63 Khalid Muhyi al-Din (ed.), *al-Mas'ala al-ta'ifiyya fi misr*, Beirut: Dar al-tali'a, 1980.
64 Lajna al-difa' 'an al-thaqafa al-qawmiyya, *al-Mushkila al-ta'ifiyya fi misr*, Cairo: Markaz al-buhuth al-'arabiyya, 1988.
65 Together with articles which appeared in *al-Yasar* these were published in book form and dedicated to the ECNU, *Misr, muslimin wa aqbatan*, [Cairo]: np, 1993. Articles by 'Asim al-Disuqi and 'Abd al-'Azim Anis on *ta'ifiyya* also appeared in *al-Yasar* in 1990.
66 Ra'uf 'Abbas Hamed, 'The Copts under British Rule in Egypt, 1882–1914', *MTM* 26 (1989) 49–59.
67 Ibid., 59.
68 'Asim al-Disuqi, 'Judhur al-mas'ala al-ta'ifiyya fi misr al-hadith', 30–42 in Lajna al-difa' 'an al-thaqafa al-qawmiyya, *al-Muskila al-ta'ifiyya fi misr*, 1988.
69 Ibid., 35–6.
70 Ibid., 37.
71 Quoting Zaghib Mikha'il, ibid., 41.
72 Ibid., 41.
73 Muhammad Ghazzali, *Min huna na'alam*, Cairo, 1370 AH, 159 quoted by Bayumi, *al-Ikhwan al-muslimun wa'l-jama'a al-islamiyya fi al-haya al-siyasiyya al-misriyya, 1928–48*, 311.
74 Ra'uf 'Abbas Hamid, 'The Copts under British Rule in Egypt, 1882–1914', 57.
75 Mitchell, *The Society of the Muslim Brothers*, 222.
76 Quoted in Kepel, *The Prophet and Pharaoh*, 119.
77 Baker, *Sadat and After*, 257. The July and August 1981 issues of *al-Da'wa* contain detailed discussions of the Coptic issue. Baker, *Sadat and After*, 348 no. 51. Waguih Ghali, a Coptic novelist, mocks this attitude in *Beer in the Snooker Club*, New York: New Amsterdam, 1964, reprint, 1987, 77.
78 J.D. Pennington, 'The Copts in Egypt', *Middle Eastern Studies* 18 (1982) 173.
79 'Abd al-Rahim 'Abd al-Rahman 'Abd al-Rahim, 'al-Kitaba al-misriyya 'an thawrat 1919 bayna al-mawdu'iyya wa'l-iltizam', 212.

80 Binder describes it as 'both rare and courageous', Leonard Binder, *Islamic Liberalism: A Critique of Development Ideologies*, University of Chicago Press, 269.

81 Ibid., 273, 287; Meijer, *History, Authenticity, and Politics*, 39.

82 Binder, *Islamic Liberalism*, 248.

83 Ibid., 271.

84 Ibid., 260–3; Meijer, *History, Authenticity, and Politics*, 31.

85 Ahmad Zakariyya al-Shiliq, review of *al-Muslimun wa'l-aqbat fi atar al-jama'a al-wataniyya*, by Tariq al-Bishri, *al-Siyasa al-dawliyya* 68 (April 1982) 214.

86 Binder, *Islamic Liberalism* 276.

87 Meijer, *History, Authenticity, and Politics*, 40–1.

88 This is my impression from talking with a number of Coptic and Muslim interviewees.

89 Kyriakos Mikhail, *Copts and Moslems under British Control, A Collection of Facts and a Resume of Authoritative Opinions on the Coptic Question*, New York & London: Kennikat Press, 1911, reprint, 1971.

90 *Farraq tasud, al-wahda al-wataniyya wa'l-akhlaq al-qawmiyya*, 1950 quoted in 'Asim al-Disuqi, 'al-Fitna al-ta'ifiyya', *al-Yasar* 4 (June 1990) 32.

91 Jak Tajir [Jacques Tagher], *al-Aqbat wa'l-muslimin mundhu al-fath al-'arabi ila 'am 1922*, Cairo: np, 1951.

92 Carter, *Copts in Egyptian Politics*, 126 no. 180.

93 Mu'arrikh misri, 'Khitab maftuh ila rafi'a ra'is al-hukuma li-katib kabir ma'ruf', *Misr* 14 February 1952, 1,4. Given his association with the paper, this is possibly a pseudonym of Salama Musa or perhaps Ramsis Jibrawi.

94 Omayma Abdel-Latif, 'Keep State and Religion Separate', *al-Ahram Weekly*, 26 May–1 June 1994; cf. Klausner's statement, 'I meet vibrant, talkative Christians in church, but their public voice is muted.' Klausner, 'A Professor's-Eye View of the Egyptian Academy', *Journal of Higher Education*, 57 no. 4 (July/August 1986) 351.

95 Ahmed Khalifa, 'Copts are not a Minority', *al-Ahram Weekly* 24 May–1 June 1994; Sulayman Nasim, ' "Khirafa" al-aqlayya fi misr', *Watani* 17 May 1992.

96 Bulus Basili, *al-Aqbat: wataniyya wa tarikh*, Cairo, 1987.

97 Samira Bahr, *al-Aqbat fi al-haya al-siyasiyya al-misriyya*, 2nd edn, Cairo: al-Inglu al-misriyya, 1984; Zaki Shenuda, *Qibti shahid 'ala al-'asr*, Cairo, Nabil 'Adli Matias, 1992.

98 Milad Hanna, *Na'am aqbat wa lakinna misriyyun*, Cairo, 1980, and *Misr lakull al-misriyyun*, Cairo: Dar sa'd al-sabah, 1993; Ghali Shukri, *al-Aqbat fi watan mutaghayyir*, Cairo: Dar al-shuruq, 1991; Wilyum Sulayman Qilada, *al-Masihiyya wa'l-islam fi misr*, Cairo: Sina, 1993; Abu Sayf Yusuf, *al-Aqbat wa'l-qawmiyya al-'arabiyya*, Beirut: Markaz dirasat al-wahda al-tarikhiyya, 1987.

99 An important exception to this pattern is Anouar Abdel-Malek, a Copt whose more recent writings have been influenced by political Islam.

100 Usama Salama, 'Akadhib sawt amrika wa hujum 'ala al-hukuma madfu' al-ajr', *Ruz al-Yusuf* no. 3491 (8 May 1995) 24–5; see also Abu Sayf Yusuf, *al-Aqbat wa'l-qawmiyya al-'arabiyya*, 184–5.

101 Interview with Samir Murqus; see also his article, 'al-Tiyar al-masahi al-mustanir wa'l-amrikan al-mutaqibtin', *al-Ahali* 10 November 1982.

102 Salama Musa, 'Tarikh al-wataniyya al-misriyya, nashu'ha wa tatawwurha', *al-Hilal* 36 no. 3 (January 1928) 270.

103 *Coptic Encyclopedia* s.v. 'Political Parties, Egyptian Party' (Yunan Labib Rizq).

104 Samira Bahr, *al-Aqbat fi al-hayat al-siyasiyya al-misriyya*, 2nd edn, Cairo, 1984.

105 Ibid., 127.

106 Ibid., 128–9.
107 Ibid., 131.
108 Abu Sayf Yusuf, *al-Aqbat wa'l-qawmiyya al-'arabiyya*, 1987.
109 Ibid., 143–4; There were also calls for a revival of the Coptic language.
110 This view has also been expressed to me by a number of Coptic interviewees.
111 Bahr, *al-Aqbat fi al-hayat al-siyasiyya al-misriyya*, 148–9.
112 Ibid., 150–1.
113 Ibid., 152.
114 Ibid., 153.
115 Abu Sayf Yusuf, *al-Aqbat wa'l-qawmiyya al-'arabiyya*, 162.
116 Habib is the son of the late Dr Samuel Habib, former head of the Coptic Evangelical Church. During the 1990s he has also attracted considerable attention through his association with the unsuccessful attempt to gain legal recognition for al-Wasat, a centrist political party made up in part of some disaffected Ikhwan members, see Amira Howeidy, 'Third Time Lucky?', *al-Ahram Weekly* 10–16 June 1999.
117 Rafiq Habib, *al-Ihtijaj al-dini wa'l-sira' al-tabaqi fi misr* ('Religious Protest and the Class Struggle in Egypt'), Cairo: Sina, 1989. The next year his *al-Masihiyya al-siyasiyya fi misr* ('Political Christianity in Egypt') appeared.
118 Interview with Rafiq Habib.
119 A number of these reactions to Habib's work are collected in Rafiq Habib, *Ightiyal jil, al-kanisa wa-'awda muhakam al-taftish*, Cairo: Yafa, 1992, for Ghali Shukri's articles, see Habib, *Ightiyal jil*, 139–59; 'Hisan tarawada al-masihi fi misr (2)', *al-Watan al-'arabi* 166 (18 May 1990) 26–8; 'al-Sira' al-masihi – al-masihi fi misr (3)', *al-Watan al-'arabi* 167 (25 May 1990) 24–6.
120 Interview with Yawaqim Rizq Murqus.
121 Interview with Sulayman Nasim.
122 This sentiment was expressed in a number of interviews with Coptic intellectuals.
123 Carter, *Copts in Egyptian Politics*, 289 no. 163; Sonbol, 'Society, Politics and Sectarian Strife', 274; Interview with Wilyum Sulayman Qilada.
124 *Al-Ahram* 26 July 1954 provided front page coverage of the episode. It was also covered internationally coverage: 'Coptic Revolt Broken', *New York Times* 27 July 1954.
125 Ghali Shukri, *Egypt: Portrait of a President*, London: Zed Books, 1981, 271–3. First published in Arabic, it was later translated into French in 1979, and subsequently English. Wakin, *The Lonely Minority*, 95, had discussed the incident some 15 years before.
126 Haykal, *Autumn of Fury*, 164.
127 Carter, *Copts in Egyptian Politics*, 280; Sonbol, 'Society, Politics and Sectarian Strife', 275; Badawi, *al-Fitna al-ta'ifiyya fi misr*, 81–8.
128 Shukri, *Egypt: Portrait of a President*, 273; Interview with Ghali Shukri.
129 Bahr, *al-Aqbat fi al-hayat al-siyasiyya al-misriyya*, 143–5.
130 Abu Sayf Yusuf, *al-Aqbat wa'l-qawmiyya al-'arabiyya*, 141–7.
131 Rafiq Habib, *al-Ihtijaj al-dini*, 108–11.
132 Yunan Labib Rizq, *al-Azhab al-siyasiyya min misr 1907–1984*, Cairo: Kitab al-hilal, 1984, 65. Rizq is professor of modern history at the University of 'Ain Shams and one of the few Coptic academic historians in this discipline.
133 Views expressed to me in interviews with Sulayman Nasim and Wilyum Qilada.
134 al-Fiqi, *Copts in Egyptian Politics*, 183.
135 Girgis Guda Girgis, *al-Sadat...wa'l-aqbat*, Beverly Hills, CA: American Coptic Association, 1982, 17 quoted by Sonbol, 'Society, Politics and Sectarian Strife', 281 no. 15.

136 Cited by al-Fiqi, *Copts in Egyptian Politics*, 182.
137 Pennington, 'The Copts in Egypt', 165.
138 Carter, *Copts in Egyptian Politics*, 115. Some historians regard the period immediately *following* the arrival of the British in 1882 as representing a golden age for Copts, see Carter, *Copts in Egyptian Politics* 114 quoting Ramzi Tadrus.
139 al-Fiqi, *Copts in Egyptian Politics*, 193.

6 THE *MUTAMASSIRUN*

1 'Levantines, though not a separate nation, possess characteristics of their own which may almost be termed national...[they] are more or less Orientalised Europeans...[and] necessarily present every gradation of character, from the European with no trace of the Oriental about him, to the European who is so thoroughly orientalised as scarcely to have preserved any distinctive European characteristics.' Cromer, *Modern Egypt*, vol. II, 246–7.
2 Quoted in Wendell, *The Evolution of the Egyptian National Image*, 248.
3 Respectively Robert L. Tignor, 'The Economic Activities of Foreigners in Egypt, 1920–1950: From Millet to Haute Bourgeoisie', *Comparative Studies in Society and History* 23 (1980) 416–49; Marius Deeb, 'The Socioeconomic Role of the Local Foreign Minorities in Modern Egypt, 1805–1961', *IJMES* 9 (1978) 11–22; Yorgos A. Kourvetaris, 'The Greeks of Asia Minor and Egypt as Middleman Economic Minorities during the late 19th and 20th Centuries', *Ethnic Groups* 7 (1988) 85–111.
4 These different terms are clearly not exact equivalents. I have centred my discussion on the term *mutamassirun* because of its derivation from *misriyyun* ('Egyptian') and its recognition of an affiliation with greater Egyptian society; 'foreign minorities' implies no such sense.
5 I do not here propose to specifically discuss the substantial body of work on the Jews of Egypt except where it is germane to my argument although it clearly represents a significant part of *mutamassirun* historiography and shares many of its characteristics. The circumstances surrounding the establishment of Israel have further obscured a clear appreciation of the Jewish life in Egypt. For valuable discussions that evaluate Jews in Egypt according to their own terms, see Joel Beinin, *The Dispersion of Egyptian Jewry*, Berkeley: University of California Press, 1998; Gudrun Krämer, '"Radical" Nationalists, Fundamentalists, and the Jews in Egypt or, Who is a Real Egyptian?', 354–71 in G.R. Warburg and Uri Kupferschmidt (eds), *Islam, Nationalism, and Radicalism in Egypt and the Sudan*, New York: Praeger, 1983; Gudrun Krämer, *The Jews in Modern Egypt, 1914–1952*, London: I.B. Tauris, 1989.
6 A rough figure of 230,000 can be arrived at by adding the numbers in the 1917 census for Greeks, Italians, Jews and Armenians and the number of Syrians (35,000) given by Philipp (*Syrians in Egypt*, XI). This figure undoubtedly increased over the following decade. By comparison the combined British and French communities numbered just over 45,000 people (1917 census).
7 A preliminary calculation based on official census figures suggests at least a third and perhaps even a half of *mutamassirun* held Egyptian or Ottoman nationality and were therefore not beneficiaries of the Capitulations but this important issue requires further research.
8 'Abbas I was less encouraging in this respect, expelling many during his reign; Sa'id and Isma'il were more welcoming, Deeb, 'The Socioeconomic Role of the Local Foreign Minorities in Modern Egypt, 1805–1961', 14–15; see also Rouben Adalian,

'The Armenian Colony of Egypt during the Reign of Muhammad Ali (1805–1848)', *Armenian Review* 33 (1980) 115–44.

9 On Salvagos, see Kitroeff, *Greeks in Egypt*, 80–3; for Cicurel and Sidnawi, see Samir Raafat, 'Sednaoui', *Cairo Times* 29 May 1997.

10 Charles Issawi, *Egypt in Revolution*, Oxford UP, 1963, 30; Cromer, *Modern Egypt*, vol. II, 248.

11 Beinin and Lockman, *Workers on the Nile*, 49–57.

12 Afaf Lutfi al-Sayyid Marsot, *A Short History of Modern Egypt*, Cambridge UP, 1985, 115.

13 Hourani, *Arabic Thought in the Liberal Age*, 81.

14 Angelo Sammarco, *Il contributo degl'Italiani ai progressi scientifici e practici della medicina in Egitto sotto il regno di Mohammed Ali*, Cairo, 1928, *Gli Italiani in Egitto: Il contributo italiano nella formazione dell'Egitto moderno*, Alexandria, 1937; R. Radopoulos, *O Vasilefs Fouat o protos ke anagennomeni Egiptos*, Alexandria, 1930.

15 Henein Bey Henein in Yusuf Qattawi (ed.), *L'Égypte, Aperçu historique et géographique gouvernement et institutions, vie économique et sociale*, Cairo: L'Institut Français, 1926, 382.

16 Ibid., 380.

17 Rif'at, *Awakening of Egypt*, 226.

18 Egyptians were certainly aware of the privileges conferred by foreign citizenship and it was not unknown for them to be used for their own benefit. Early in the century Ahmad Lutfi al-Sayyid, at the suggestion of the khedive, had gone to Switzerland to obtain Swiss citizenship in order to establish a newspaper back in Egypt under the protection of the Capitulations, Wendell, *The Evolution of the Egyptian National Image*, 213. Some Egyptian landlords, including a speaker of the Majlis shura qawanin, held foreign nationality in the nineteenth century, Interview with Ra'uf 'Abbas. This recalls the *beratli*, the practice in the Ottoman Empire of selling foreign nationality for its financial and legal advantages.

19 'Abd al-Rahman al-Rafi'i, *Fi 'aqab al-thawra al-misriyya*, vol. 3, 285.

20 On the second point, note the comment of Pierre Cachia, 'Of all the foreign nationals we were acquainted with, I do not know any who had occasion to invoke legal immunity.' Pierre Cachia, *Landlocked Islands, Two Alien Lives in Egypt*, American University in Cairo Press, 1999, 175.

21 *Modern Egypt*, vol. II, 257.

22 Earl of Cromer, *Modern Egypt*, vol. II, 246–7. Twenty years later, reporting on the attitudes of British officers in the 1920s, Robert Graves conveyed an impression at odds with the Egyptian–foreigner dichotomy of the liberal school and the moral censure of Cromer. Recounting the views of British officials he noted that, 'None of them [i.e. British officials] took Egyptian nationalism seriously; there was no Egyptian nation they said. The Greeks, Turks, Syrians, and Armenians *who called themselves Egyptians* had no more right in the country than the British.' [my emphasis], Graves, *Good-bye to All That*, 418.

23 Albert Hourani, *Minorities in the Arab World*, London: Oxford UP, 1947, 25.

24 Interview with Ra'uf 'Abbas.

25 al-Disuqi, *Nahwa fahm tarikh misr*, 10.

26 Ibid., 16.

27 Nabil 'Abd al-Hamid Sayyid Ahmad, *al-Nashat al-iqtisadi li-'l-ajanib wa 'atharahu fi al-mujtama' al-misri min 1922 ila 1952*, Cairo: al-Hay'a al-misriyya al-'ama li'l-kitab, 1982.

28 Ibid., 8.

29 Ibid., 8–24.

30 Ibid., 470.
31 See, for example, Sulayman Muhammad al-Nukhayli, *al-Haraka al-'ummaliyya fi misr wa mawqif al-sihafa wa'l-sulta misriyya minha sanat 1882 ila sanat 1952*, Cairo, 1967, 93; Ra'uf 'Abbas, *al-Harakat al-'ummaliyya fi misr, 1899–1952*, Cairo, 1967, 45–65; Amin 'Izz al-Din, Tarikh *al-tabaqa al-'amila al-misriyya mundhu nash'atiha hatta thawrat 1919*, Cairo, 1967, vol. 1, 71–2. There is no detailed study on foreign workers.
32 I. Yannakakis, 'Aux origines du communisme égyptien 1920–1940', 94–9 in *Le Mouvement Communiste au Moyen-Orient*, Paris, 1984.
33 Ismael and El-Sa'id, *The Communist Movement in Egypt*, 33–4. Among the Greek Left, there was a division between those who were active in the 'Egyptian' communist movement and those who worked in a wholly Greek organization.
34 In fact international unions, i.e. those with both Egyptian and foreign members, continued at least until the 1930s and there was an active foreign working class in Egypt until the early 1960s. Note Ellis Goldberg's basis for differentiating Egyptian and foreign workers, *Tinker, Tailor and Textile Worker, Class and Politics in Egypt, 1930–1952*, University of California Press, 1986, 190 no. 1.
35 Mitchell, *Muslim Brothers*, 221–2.
36 Ibid., 272, 330.
37 Ibid., 222.
38 Jeffrey T. Kenney, 'Enemies Near and Far: The Image of the Jews in Islamist Discourse in Egypt', *Religion* 24 (1994) 253–70.
39 al-Bishri, *al-Haraka al-siyasiyya fi misr*, Introd., 2nd edn, 34–6.
40 al-Bishri, *al-Muslimun wa'l-aqbat*, 530.
41 al-Bishri has more recently been very critical in his attitude towards Jews in the communist movement, Tariq al-Bishri, 'Awraq Hinri Kuriyil', *al-Hilal* 95 (April 1988) 18–25.
42 Dekmejian, *Egypt under Nasir*, 84.
43 A number of scholars of *mutamassir* background have become Middle East scholars in the West but exhibit an émigré rather than a *mutamassir* perspective. They include economic historian Charles Issawi, Nadav Safran, and in a marginal sense, P.J. Vatikiotis, who studied in Cairo as a student. Issawi's description of himself reveals the complexity of identity and the inadequacy of national categories: 'So if you want a blood test, I am much more Damascene than anything else. Culturally I am Lebanese and Egyptian.' Gallagher, *Approaches to the History of the Middle East*, 48.
44 Krämer, *The Jews of Egypt*, 169–70.
45 For a catalogue, see Evgenios Michailidis, *Panorama*, Alexandria, 1972.
46 For a catalogue, see Evgenios Michailidis, *Vivliografia ton Ellinon Egiptioton*, Alexandria, 1966.
47 See Efthimios Souloyiannis, *I Thesi ton Ellinon stin Egipto*, Athens: Dimos Athineon, 265.
48 Among Greeks, those living in Egypt were distinguished from other Greeks by the term *Egiptiotes*. In this discussion I have employed the term 'Egyptian Greeks', though this should not be understood in terms of nationality.
49 *Panegiptia* 8 January 1931, 2.
50 A. Kasigonis (ed.), *al-Yunani al-Mutamassir–Egiptiotis-Ellin*, Alexandria, 1932–40.
51 G. Arvanitakis, *Sinoptiki istoria tis Egiptou*, Alexandria: Grammata, 1926; I. Petridis, *Misr-Yunan*, Alexandria: A. Kasigonis, 1934.
52 D. Sevastopoulou, *I Alexandreia pou fevgi*, Alexandria, 1953, 30–2.

53 On Nomikos, see Sotiri Mikha'ilidhis, 'Khristuf Numiku, 'Alim yunani fi tarikh al-'arab wa'l-islam wa'l-athar', *Deltion Ellino-Aravikon Sindesmos* 2 (no. 8), 14–12.

54 Kh. Nomikos, *Aravika istorimata*, Alexandria, 1920.

55 Athanasios Politis, *O Ellinismos ke I Neotera Egiptos*, vol. I. *Istoria tou Egiptiotou Ellinismou apo tou 1798 mekhri 1927*, vol. II. *Simvoli tou Ellinismou eis tin anaptixin tis Neoteras Egiptou*, Alexandria, 1927, 1930 (French edn, *L'Hellenisme et l'Égypte moderne*, 2 vols, Paris: Félix Alcan, 1929–30).

56 Among many was Tasos Palaiologos, *O Egiptiotis Ellinismos, istoria ke drasis (753 π.X.–1953)*, vol. 1, Alexandria, 1953.

57 Manolis Yalourakis, *I Egiptos ton Ellinon*, Athens, 1967.

58 Souloyiannis, *I Thesi ton Ellinon stin Egipto*, 265. One of the founders of ELIA in 1980, and its subsequent director, was Dimitris Kharitatos, himself an Alexandrian Greek.

59 For a full bibliography of Souloyiannis' work see his *I Thesi ton Ellinon stin Egipto*, 1999; Christos Hadziiosif, 'La Colonie grecque en Égypte, 1833–1856', unpublished thesis, Université de Paris-Sorbonne, 1980; Pandelis M. Glavanis, 'Aspects of the Economic and Social History of the Greek Community in Alexandria during the Nineteenth Century', PhD Thesis, University of Hull, 1989.

60 Alexander Kitroeff, *The Greeks in Egypt, 1919–1937: Ethnicity and Class*, 1989, vi. Unstated was the almost total silence by Egyptian historians on the subject.

61 Ibid., 42–7.

62 Ibid., 136–40.

63 Ibid., 140.

64 R. Ilbert and I. Yannakakis (eds), *Alexandrie 1860–1960, un modèle éphémère de convivialité: communautés et identité cosmopolite*, Editions Autrement, Paris, 1992 (later published in English as *Alexandria 1860–1960, The Brief Life of a Cosmopolitan Community*, Alexandria: Harpocrates, 1997). Amongst the contributors are Ilios Yannakakis, Katerina Trimi (the former is Egyptian-born, the latter of Egyptian Greek family) on the Greeks, Jacques Hassoun (an Egyptian Jew) on Jews, Édouard al-Kharrat, a Coptic writer and an interview with Yusuf Shahin. On Jews see also Jacques Hassoun (ed.), *Juifs du Nil*, Paris: Le Sycamore, 1981.

65 The Armenian community also has an active cultural life and record of publication in Egypt. Among a number of historians who have written on the Armenian experience in Egypt is Awetis Yapuchean, the longtime editor of *Arev*, an Armenian newspaper still published in Cairo. Among his works is *Egiptahay mshakoyti patmutiwn* ('The History of Egyptian–Armenian Culture'), 1981 (Interview with Awetis Yapuchean).

66 For a discussion of the concept of the fiction writer as an underground historian, see Mehrez, *Egyptian Writers Between History and Fiction*, 6–8.

67 Originally published in three volumes in Athens as *I Leskhi* (1960), *I Ariagni* (1962), *I Nikhterida* (1965). For the English translation, *Drifting Cities*, trans. K. Cicellis, New York: Alfred Knopf, 1974.

68 Tsirkas wrote a number of other novels and collections of poetry that draw on his life in Egypt, as well as a scholarly history, *O Kavafis ke I Epokhi tou*, Athens: Kedros, 1958.

69 Peter Levi, 'The World from Underground', *Times Literary Supplement* 14 November 1975, 1356.

70 For example, Evgenia Palaiologou-Petronda, *Sto Kero tou papous mou*, 1983; *I Loti tou pathous*, 1991; Eleni Voïskou, *Anixe tin porta* [c. 1963], Ioanna

Kotsaki, *I Agapimeni poli*, 1993; George P. Pierides, *Memories and Stories from Egypt*, Nicosia: Diaspora, 1992.

71 Robert Solé, *Le Tarbouche*, Paris: Le Seuil, 1992 (recently published in English translation under the title *Birds of Passage*, 2000), see review of Amin Malouf, 'Nostalgies du Nil', *Le Monde* 6 March 1992, 23. The best academic treatment of the Syrians in Egypt is by German historian, Thomas Philipp, *The Syrians in Egypt 1725–1975*, Stuttgart: Steiner Verlag Wiesbaden GmbH, 1985; see also Elisabeth Panfalone, 'Les Emigres libanais et syriens en Égypte (1724–1960): Une strategie de maintien d'une distinction minoritaire', DEA, 1992/93.

72 André Aciman, *Out of Egypt, A Memoir*, New York: Farrar Strauss Giroux, 1994. In 1995, *Out of Egypt* won the Whitting Writers Award for a *non-fiction* work but it has been subject to some criticism on this score, see Samir Raafat, 'André Aciman's "Out of Egypt"', *Egyptian Gazette* 21 December 1996, and 'Aciman Encore, Out of Egypt's Great Uncle Vili Resolved at Last', *Egyptian Mail* 1 February 1997.

73 See, for example, Tawfik al-Hakim, *Maze of Justice*, University of Austin Press, Austin, 1989, 53.

74 For example, Magdi Wahba, 'Cairo Memories', *Encounter* 62 no. 5 (May 1984) 74–9 and articles on the Greeks (Pascale Ghazaleh, 'Adrift in the City', *al-Ahram Weekly* 6–12 August 1998), and the Armenians (Supplement *al-Ahram Weekly* 20–26 May 1999).

75 Samir Raafat is the son of the late Dr Wahdi Raafat, an eminent constitutional jurist, and a relative of 'Ali Shamsi Pasha, a Wafdist Minister of Education of the 1920s. Personal communication with Samir Raafat, 26 May 1997.

76 For these articles see http://www.egy.com/history/source.html *The Egyptian Gazette – The Saturday Articles*.

77 Samir Raafat, 'The National Bank of Egypt (NBE) 1898–1998, The Men who Chartered the Bank', *Egyptian Mail* 11 May and 25 May 1996.

78 *Maadi 1904–62: History and Society in a Cairo Suburb*, Cairo: Palm Press, 1994.

79 For 'Ali Sabri see Ghali Shukri, *al-Muthaqqafun wa'l-sulta fi misr*, vol. 1, Cairo: 1990, 145–6.

80 Personal communication with Samir Raafat, 26 May 1997.

81 Ibid.

82 Ibid. Raafat has had more polemic articles rejected as 'too controversial' even in English, see Samir Raafat, 'Reforms We Have Done. Now We Must Perform' [http://www.egy.com/history/97-05-14.shtml]. It may also be significant that articles on foreign communities in the English language *al-Ahram Weekly* have not appeared in Arabic. See, for example, Pascale Ghazaleh, 'Adrift in the City', *al-Ahram Weekly* 6–12 August 1998, and the supplement on Armenians in Egypt in *al-Ahram Weekly* 20–26 May 1999.

83 Botman's comment typifies this view, 'Marxists from the Armenian, Italian, and Greek communities were tied to the communist parties in their own countries and were not directly active in the Egyptian political field', *The Rise of Egyptian Communism*, 5. There is as yet no integrated study of the Greek left in Egypt but see Anthony Gorman, 'Egypt's Forgotten Communists: The Post-War Greek Left', *Journal of Modern Greek Studies* 20 (2002) 1–27; I. Yannakakis, 'Aux origines du communisme égyptien 1920–1940', 91–103, and Yiannis Anastasiadis, *Mnimes apo ti drasi tou aristerou kinimatos tou Egiptiotou Ellinismou*, Athens, 1993.

84 On the criminal element, see 'Abd al-Wahab Bakr, *al-Bulis al-misri 1922–1952*, Cairo: Dar al-zahr, 1993, 196–7; on newspapers see Ibrahim 'Abduh, *Tatawwur al-sihafa al-misriyya, 1898–1981*, Cairo: Sijl al-'arab, 4th edn, 1982, 356–62.

85 There has been greater willingness on the part of some Western economic historians to offer a radical reassessment of the economic role of foreign resident capitalists and reconceptualize their relationship with Egyptian capitalists. Robert Tignor, *State, Private Enterprise and Economic Change in Egypt*, 243: 'Although many of the native-born Egyptian businessmen have been recognized and some of them lionized (notably Talaʿat Harb), many foreigners resident in Egypt also played important roles, which, though very meaningful to the whole process, have generally been ignored by later commentators. The names of Henri Naus, Michel Salvago, Yusuf Cicurel, and Yusuf Aslan Qattawi rarely appear in studies of modern Egypt, although their influence on events was enormous.' See also Robert Vitalis, *When Capitalists Collide, Business Conflict and the End of Empire in Egypt*, 1995; Marius Deeb, 'The Socioeconomic Role of the Local Foreign Minorities in Modern Egypt, 1805–1961', 11–22.

86 The recent works of Mahmud Muhammad Sulayman, *al-Ajanib fi misr, dirasa fi tarikh misr al-ijtimaʿi*, Cairo, Ein, 1996, Sayyid ʿAshmawi, *al-Yunaniyyun fi misr, dirasat tarikhiyya fi al-dur al-iqtisadi-al-siyasi, 1805–1956*, 1997, and Muhammad Rifʿat al-Imam, *Tarikh al-jaliyya al-armaniyya fi misr*, Cairo: al-Hayʾa al-misriyya al-ʿama liʾl-kitab, 1999 (whose analysis does not go beyond the beginning of the twentieth century) suggest there is at least an increased interest in the subject.

87 P.J. Vatikiotis, 'The New Western Historiography of Modern Egypt', 323 speaking of Greek radicals in Egypt.

88 Vitalis, *When Capitalists Collide*, 165.

BIBLIOGRAPHY

INTERVIEWS

'Abd al-'Azim Ramadan
'Abd al-'Aziz (Sulayman) Nawwar
'Abd al-Hamid Muhammad al-Batriq
'Abd al-Khaliq Lashin
'Abd al-Mun'im I. al-Disuqi al-Jumay'i
Abu Sayf Yusuf
'Afaf Lutfi al-Sayyid Marsot
Ahmad 'Abd al-Rahim Mustafa
Ahmad Zakariyya al-Shiliq
'Ali Barakat
'Asim al-Disuqi
Ghali Shukri
Hillel Schwartz (telephone)

Mahmud Mitwalli
Muhammad 'Afifi
Ra'uf 'Abbas Hamid
Rafiq Habib
Rif'at al-Sa'id
Salah al-'Aqqad
Samir Murqus
Sulayman Nasim
Tariq al-Bishri
Wilyum Sulayman Qilada
Yawaqim Rizq Murqus
Yunan Labib Rizq

NB: With the exception of Hillel Schwartz, all interviews were conducted in Cairo, the great majority of them between April 1993 and March 1994.

NEWSPAPERS

Egypt (all Cairo except where noted)

al-Ahali
al-Ahram
al-Ahram Weekly
Cairo Times
Egyptian Gazette
al-Jumhurriya
Misr
al-Sha'b
al-Yunani al-Mutamassir – Egiptiotis Ellin (Alexandria, 1932–40)

Other

Le Monde, Paris
New York Times
The Times, London

SOURCES IN ARABIC

'Abbas Hamid, Ra'uf. *al-Harakat al-'ummaliyya fi misr 1899–1952*. Cairo: Dar al-katib al-'arabi, 1967.

'Abbas Hamid, Ra'uf. 'Himaya watha'iqina al-qawmiyya', *al-Hilal* May 2001, 9–15.

'Abbas Hamid, Ra'uf. 'Hinri Kuriyil', *al-Hilal* 96 (November 1988) 42–7.

'Abbas Hamid, Ra'uf. 'Maktabat al-thawra al-'urabiyya', *al-Siyasa al-dawliyya* 64 (April 1981) 210.

'Abbas Hamid, Ra'uf. 'al-Watha'iq al-baritaniyya wa tarikh misr', *al-Ahram al-iqtisadi* 888 (20 January 1986) 36–7.

'Abbas Hamid, Ra'uf (ed.) *Arba'un 'aman 'ala thawrat yuliu*. Cairo: Markaz al-dirasat al-siyasiyya wa'l-istratijiyya bi'l-ahram, 1992.

'Abbas Hamid, Ra'uf (ed.) *Awraq Hinri Kuriyil wa'l-haraka al-shuyu'iyya al-misriyya*. Cairo: Sina, 1988.

'Abd al-Hamid, Ahmad Nazmi and al-Barawi, Rashid. *al-Nizam al-ishtiraki -'arad wa-tahlil wa naqd*. Cairo: Maktaba al-nahda al-misriyya, 1946.

'Abd al-Hamid Sayyid Ahmad, Nabil. *al-Nashat al-iqtisadi li'l-ajanib wa-atharuhu fi al-mujtama' al-misri min 1922 ila 1952*. Cairo: al-Hay'a al-misriyya al-'ama li'l-kitab, 1982.

'Abd al-Karim, Ahmad 'Izzat. 'kalima 'an Shafiq Ghurbal', *al-Majalla al-tarikhiyya al-misriyya* 11 (1963) 10–20.

'Abd al-Karim, Ahmad 'Izzat. 'Muhammad Shafiq Ghurbal, ustadh zil wa sahib madrasa', *al-Majalla al-tarikhiyya al-misriyya* 19 (1972) 25–31.

'Abd al-Karim, Ahmad 'Izzat (ed.) *50 'aman 'ala thawrat 1919*. Cairo: al-Ahram [*c.* 1970].

'Abd al-Karim, Ahmad 'Izzat; Abu al-Hamid al-Batriq and Abu al-Futuh Radwan. *Tarikh al-'alam al-'arabi fi al-'asr al-hadith*. Cairo, 1960.

'Abd Allah, Ahmad (ed.) *Tarikh misr: bayna al-manahij al-'alimi wa'l-sira' al-hizbi*. Cairo: Dar al-shuhdi li'l-nashr, 1988.

'Abd al-Rahim, 'Abd al-Rahim 'Abd al-Rahman. 'al-Kitaba al-misriyya 'an thawrat 1919 bayna al-mawdu'iyya wa'l-iltizam', 207–14 in Ahmad 'Abd Allah (ed.) *Tarikh misr: bayna al-manahij al-'alimi wa'l-sira' al-hizbi*. Cairo: Dar al-shuhdi li'l-nashr, 1988.

'Abduh, Ibrahim. *Tatawwur al-sihafa al-misriyya, 1898–1981*. 4th edn, Cairo: Sijl al-'arab, 1982.

Abu al-As'ad, Muhammad. *al-Sihafa al-misriyya wa tazyif al-wa'y*. Cairo: Dar al-thaqafa al-jadida, 1988.

A'da' al-Siminar. *Siminar al-dirasat al-'ulya li'l-tarikh al-hadith, 1955–75*. Cairo: Jami'at 'Ain Shams, 1976.

'Afifi, Muhammad. *al-Aqbat fi al-'asr al-'uthmani, 1517–1798*. Cairo, 1992.

'Afifi, Muhammad (ed.) *al-Madrasa al-tarikhiyya al-misriyya, 1970–1995*, Cairo: Dar al-shuruq, 1997.

Ahmad, Muhammad Sid. 'al-Yahud fi al-haraka al-shuyu'iyya al-misriyya wa'l-sira' al-'arabi al-isra'ili', *al-Hilal* 95 (June 1988) 21–7.

'Amr, Ibrahim. *al-Ard wa'l-fallah, al-mas'ala al-zira'iyya fi misr.* Cairo: Dar al-misriyya, 1958.

'Amr, Ibrahim. *Thawrat misr al-qawmiyya.* Cairo: Dar al-nadim, 1957.

Anis, 'Abd al-'Azim. 'al-Fitna al-ta'ifiyya...mas'uliyya man?!!', *al-Yasar* 3 (1990) 20–1.

Anis, Muhammad. *Dirasat fi watha'iq thawrat 1919, al-mursilat al-sirriyya bayna Sa'd Zaghlul wa 'Abd al-Rahman Fahmi.* Cairo: al-Hay'a al-misriyya al-'ama li'l-kitab, 1988.

Anis, Muhammad. 'Fu'ad Shukri', *al-Ahram* 30 December 1963.

Anis, Muhammad. 'al-Mu'arrikh al-rahil Muhammad Fu'ad Shukri', *al-Ahram* 20 December 1963.

Anis, Muhammad. 'Shafiq Ghurbal wa madrasat al-tarikh al-misri al-hadith', *al-Majalla* 58 (November 1961) 12–17.

Anis, Muhammad. 'al-Tarikh fi khidmat al-tatawwur al-ishtiraki, al-ishtirakiyya taqyim li-madina bi-qadrima ma hiya tanzim li-hadirna', *al-Ahram* 7 July 1963.

Anis, Muhammad. 'Tarikh: Tahia ila 'alim mu'arrikh fi mihnatihu, hal hat al-usatidha 'ala jami'atihum?', *al-Ahram* 10 April 1963.

Anis, Muhammad. 'Tarikh: Turathna al-qawmi...ya wazir al-thaqafa? hal yusbaqna al-ajanib li-dirasa watha'iqna al-tarikhiyya', *al-Ahram* 1 April 1963.

Anis, Muhammad. 'Tarikhna al-qawmi fi al-mithaq', *al-Katib* 63 (June 1966) 69–74.

Anis, Muhammad and Haraz, al-Sayyid Rajab. *Thawrat 23 yuliu 1952.* Cairo: Dar al-nahda al-'arabiyya, 1965.

al-'Aqqad, Salah. 'Muhammad Anis, mu'arrikhan wa mufakkiran', *al-Ahram* 4 September 1986.

al-'Aqqad, Salah. *Qadiyat filastin, al-marhala al-harja 1945–56.* Cairo, 1968.

'Ashur, Sa'id 'Abd al-Fatah. *Thawrat sha'b.* Cairo: Dar al-nahda al-'arabiyya, 1965.

'Aziz, Khayri. 'Mawqif 26 Yuliu 1956 min al-Tarikh', *al-Tali'a*, July 1965, 32–9.

Badawi, Jamal. *al-Fitna al-ta'ifiyya fi misr, judhuruha wa asbabahu.* Cairo: al-Zahra' li'l-a'lam al-'arabi, 1992 (first published 1977).

Bahr, Samira. *al-Aqbat fi al-haya al-siyasiyya al-misriyya.* 2nd edn, Cairo: al-Inglu al-misriyya, 1984.

Bakr, 'Abd al-Wahab. *Adwa' ala al-nashat al-shuyu'i fi misr 1921–1950.* Cairo: Dar al-ma'arif, 1984.

Bakr, 'Abd al-Wahab. *al-Bulis al-misri 1922–1952.* Cairo: Dar al-Zahr, 1993.

Barakat, 'Ali. 'Fi al-tariq ila madrasa ijtima'iyya fi kitabat tarikh misr al-hadith, 1798–1952', *Fikr* 5 (March 1985) 56–61.

Barakat, 'Ali. 'al-Tarikh wa'l-qadaya al-manhaj fi misr al-mu'asira', *Qadaya fikriyya* 11–12 (July 1992) 73–90.

Basili, Bulus (al-Qummus). *al-Aqbat: wataniyya wa tarikh.* Cairo, 1987.

Bayumi, Zakariyya Sulayman. *al-Ikhwan al-muslimun bayna 'Abd al-Nasir wa'l-Sadat min al-manshiyya ila al-minassa, 1952–1981.* Cairo: Maktaba wahba, 1987.

Bayumi, Zakariyya Sulayman. *al-Ikhwan al-muslimun wa'l-jama'a al-islamiyya fi al-haya al-siyasiyya al-misriyya, 1928–48.* Cairo: Maktaba wahba, 1991.

Bayumi, Zakariyya Sulayman. 'al-Ittijahat al-diniyya bayna 'ahdi 'Abd al-Nasir wa'l-Sadat wa athar harakatihum al-mu'asira 'ala tanawulu durahum qabla 1952', 413–14 in Ahmad 'Abd Allah (ed.) *Tarikh misr: bayna al-manahij al-'alimi wa'l-sira' al-hizbi.* Cairo: Dar al-shuhdi li'l-nashr, 1988.

Bayumi, Zakariyya Sulayman. *al-Ittijah al-islami fi thawra al-misriyyat 1919*. Cairo: Dar al-kitab al-jami'i, 1983.

al-Bishri, Tariq. '*Abd al-Rahman al-Rafi'i, mu'arrikhan wa siyasiyyan*', *al-Tali'a* December 1971, 88–108.

al-Bishri, Tariq. 'Awraq Hinri Kuriyil', *al-Hilal* 95 (April 1988) 18–25.

al-Bishri, Tariq. *Dirasat fi al-dimuqratiyya al-misriyya*. Cairo: Dar al-shuruq, 1987.

al-Bishri, Tariq. *al-Haraka al-siyasiyya fi misr, 1945–52*. 2nd edn, Cairo: Dar al-shuruq, 1983.

al-Bishri, Tariq. *al-Muslimun wa'l-aqbat fi atar al-jama'a al-wataniyya*. Cairo: Dar al-shuruq, 1982.

al-Daqaq, Majdi. 'Ba'd taqdim istiqalatahu al-hay'a al-'ulya lil-wafd al-duktur Muhammad Anis yarwa qissataha ma'a hizb al-wafd al-jadid' *al-Musawwar* 25 May 1984.

al-Disuqi, 'Asim. 'al-Fitna al-ta'ifiyya fi asul tawa'if al-mujtama' al-misri', *al-Yasar* 4 (June 1990) 32–4.

al-Disuqi, 'Asim. 'Judhur al-mas'ala al-ta'ifiyya fi misr haditha', 30–42 in Lajna al-difa' 'an al-thaqafa al-qawmiyya. *al-Mushkila al-ta'ifiyya fi misr*. Cairo: Markaz al-buhuth al-'arabiyya, 1988.

al-Disuqi, 'Asim. *Misr al-mu'asira fi dirasat al-mu'arrikhin al-misriyyin*. Cairo: Dar al-hurriyya, [c. 1976].

al-Disuqi, 'Asim. 'Muhammad Anis wa duruhu fi ta'qil dirasat al-tarikh bi'l-jami'a al-misriyya, 1950–1986', *al-Majalla al-tarikhiyya al-misriyya* 34 (1987) 3–13.

al-Disuqi, 'Asim. *Nahwa fahm tarikh misr al-iqtisadi wa'l-ijtima'i*. Cairo: Dar al-kitab al-jama'i, 1981.

al-Disuqi, 'Asim. 'Naqd al-madkhal al-akhlaqi fi taqwim waqa'i' al-tarikh: dirasa tatbiqiyya 'ala al-tarikh li-thawrat 1919', 193–206 in Ahmad 'Abd Allah (ed.) *Tarikh misr: bayna al-manahij al-'alimi wa'l-sira' al-hizbi*. Cairo: Dar al-shuhdi li'l-nashr, 1988.

'al-Duktur Muhammad Fu'ad Shukri, 1904–1963', *al-Majalla al-tarikhiyya al-misriyya* 11 (1963).

Farid, Muhammad. *Kitab al-bahjah al-tawfiqiyya fi tarikh mu'assis al-'a'ila al-khidiwiyya*. Bulaq: al-Matba'a al-amiriyya, 1891.

Farid, Muhammad. *Tarikh al-dawla al-'aliyya al-'uthmaniyya*. Cairo: Matba'at al-taqaddum bi-misr, 1912 (orig. published 1894).

Fawda, 'Abbud. 'Hadith al-madina: ma'a al-Duktur Muhammad Anis', *al-Jumhuriyya* 17 May 1961.

Fawda, 'Abbud. 'Hadith al-madina, ma'a Shafiq Ghorbal', *al-Jumhuriyya* 8 May 1961.

'Fu'ad Shukri', *al-Majalla al-tarikhiyya al-misriyya* 11 (1963).

Ghali, Butrus Butrus (ed.) *al-Sha'b al-wahid wa'l-watan al-wahid, dirasa fi asul al-wahda al-wataniyya*. Cairo: Markaz al-dirasat al-siyasiyya wa'l-istratijiyya bi'l-ahram, 1982.

Ghallab, Muhammad al-Sayyid. 'al-Dirasat al-ifriqiyya – African Studies', *Majallat al-dirasat al-ifriqiyya* 1 (1972) 1–8.

Ghurbal, Muhammad Shafiq. *Minhaj mufassal li-durus fi al-'awamil al-tarikhiyya fi bina' al-umma al-'arabiyya*. Cairo: Centre for Arabic Studies of the Arab League, 1961.

Ghurbal, Muhammad Shafiq. *Takwin misr 'abr al-'asur*. Cairo: al-Hay'a al-misriyya al-'ama li'l-kitab, 1990.

Ghurbal, Muhammad Shafiq. *Tarikh al-mufawadat al-misriyya al-baritaniyya, bahth fi 'alaqat al-baritaniyya min al-ihtilal ila 'aqd mu'ahadat al-tahalluf 1882–1936*. Vol. 1, Cairo: Maktabat al-nahda al-misriyya, 1952.

Ghurbal, Muhammad Shafiq (ed.) *Tarikh al-hadara al-misriyya, al-'asr al-fir'auni*. Vol. 1, Cairo: Maktaba al-nahda al-misriyya, 1961.

Habib, Rafiq. *Ightiyal jil, al-kanisa wa 'awda muhakam al-taftish*. Cairo: Yafa, 1992.

Habib, Rafiq. *al-Ihtijaj al-dini wa'l-sira' al-tabaqi fi misr*. Cairo: Sina, 1989.

Habib, Rafiq. *al-Masihiyya al-siyasiyya fi misr*. Cairo: Yafa, 1990.

'Hadith ma'a al-duktur Muhammad Sabri', *al-Katib* 9 (1961) 80–8.

Hamdan, Jamal. *Shakhsiyyat misr, dirasa fi 'abqariyyat al-makan*. Cairo: Dar al-hilal, 1993.

Hanna, Milad. *Misr lakull al-misriyyun*. Cairo: Dar sa'd al-sabah, 1993.

Hanna, Milad. *Na'am aqbat wa lakinna misriyyun*. Cairo, 1980.

Haykal, Muhammad Hasanayn. *al-Infijar – 1967*. Cairo: al-Ahram, 1990.

al-Hitta, Ahmad. *Tarikh al-zira'a al-misriyya fi 'ahd Muhammad 'Ali al-kabir*. Cairo, 1950.

Hunayyin, Jirjis. *al-Atyan wa'l-dara'ib fi al-qutr al-misri*. Bulaq: al-Matba'at al-kubra al-amiriyya, 1904.

al-Husayni, 'Adil. 'al-Tarikh kidhab', *Ruz al-Yusuf* 1777 (2 July 1962) 30–1.

Isma'il, Hamada Mahmud Ahmad. *Sina'at tarikh misr al-hadith, dirasa fi fikr 'Abd al-Rahman al-Rafi'i*. Cairo: al-Hay'a al-misriyya al-'ama li'l-kitab, 1987.

'Isa, Salah. *al-Burjuwaziyya al-misriyya wa uslub al-mufawada, 1900–1940*. Cairo: al-Thaqafa al-wataniyya, 1980.

'Ittihad al-mu'arrikhin al-'arab', *al-Katib* 158 (May 1974) 51–2.

'Izz al-Din, Amin. *al-Tabaqa al-'amila al-misriyya*. i. *mundhu nash'atiha hatta thawrat 1919* ii. *1919–29* iii. *1929–39*. Cairo: Dar al-sha'b, 1967–72.

al-Jabarti, 'Abd al-Rahman. *'Aja'ib al-athar fi al-tarajim wa'l-akhbar*. 3 vols, Beirut: Dar al-faris, nd.

Jirjis, Fawzi. *Dirasat fi tarikh misr al-siyasi, mundhu al-'asr al-mamluki*. Cairo: al-Dar al-misriyya, 1958.

al-Jumay'i, 'Abd al-Mun'im Ibrahim al-Disuqi. *Ittijahat al-kitaba al-tarikhiyya fi tarikh misr al-hadith al-mu'asir*, Cairo: Ein for Human and Social Studies, 1994.

al-Jumay'i, 'Abd al-Mun'im Ibrahim al-Disuqi. *al-Jami'a al-misriyya wa'l-mujtama', 1908–1940*. Cairo: Markaz al-dirasat al-siyasiyya wa'l-istratijiyya bi'l-ahram, 1983.

al-Jumay'i, 'Abd al-Mun'im Ibrahim al-Disuqi. *al-Jam'iyya al-misriyya lil-dirasat al-tarikhiyya*, Shubra: Matb'at al-jablawi, 1985.

al-Jundi, Anwar. 'Hal yuktiba al-tarikh min jadid', *al-Risala* 1000 (1 September 1952) 985.

al-Jundi, Anwar. 'Tathir al-tarikh', *al-Risala* 1002 (15 September 1952) 1043.

Kamil, Mustafa, *al-Mas'ala al-sharqiyya*. 2 vols, Cairo: Matba'at al-liwa', 1909 (orig. published 1898).

al-Kharbutli, 'Ali Husni. *al-Tarikh al-muwahhad li'l-umma al-'arabiyya*. Cairo, 1970.

Lajna al-difa' 'an al-thaqafa al-qawmiyya. *al-Mushkila al-ta'ifiyya fi misr*. Cairo: Markaz al-buhuth al-'arabiyya, 1988.

al-Lajna al-misriyya li'l-wahda al-wataniyya. *al-Bayan al-awwal*, nd.

Lajna tathiq tarikh al-haraka al-shuyu'iyya al-misriyya hatta 1965, *Shahadat wa ru'a, min tarikh al-haraka al-shuyu'iyya fi misr*, 5 vols, Cairo: Markaz al-buhuth al-'arabiyya, 1998–2001.

Lashin, 'Abd al-Khaliq. *Misriyyat fi al-fikr wa'l-siyasa*. Cairo: Sina, 1993.

Lashin, 'Abd al-Khaliq. 'al-Haqa'iq al-gha'iba nashr mudhakkirat Sa'd Zaghlul', *al-Hilal* 94 (March 1987) 15–20.

'al-Madrasa al-thalitha kitabat al-tarikh', *al-Jumhuriyya* 19 September 1963.

Mikha'il, Zaghib. *Farraq tasud, al-wahda al-wataniyya wa'l-akhlaq al-qawmiyya*. 1950.

Mikha'ilidhis, Sutiri. 'Khristuf Numiku, 'Alim yunani fi tarikh al-'arab wa'l-islam wa'l-athar', *Deltion Ellino-Aravikon Sindesmos* 2 no. 8, 14–12.

Mubarak, 'Ali. *al-Khitat al-tawfiqiyya al-jadida li-misr al-qahirah wa muduniha wa biladiha al-qadima wa'l-mashhura*. 20 vols, Bulaq, 1306 AH (1889–90).

Muhyi al-Din, Khalid. *Wa alan atkallim*. Cairo: Markaz al-dirasat al-siyasiyya wa'l-istratijiyya bi'l-ahram, 1992.

Muhyi al-Din, Khalid (ed.) *al-Mas'ala al-ta'ifiyya fi misr*. Beirut: Dar al-tali'a, 1980.

Murqus, Samir. '"al-Majlis al-milli", madiyya...hadara...mustaqbalahu', *Majalla madaris al-ahad* January/February 1984.

Murqus, Samir. 'Tarikh khidmat madaris al-ahad wa'l-atharaha al-ta'limi fi al-fatra min 1900–1950', *Majalla madaris al-ahad* November/December 1984.

Musa, Salama. 'Tarikh al-wataniyya al-misriyya, nashu'ha wa tatawwurha', *al-Hilal* 36 no. 3 (January 1928) 267–71.

Mustafa, Ahmad 'Abd al-Rahim. ''Abd al-Rahman al-Rafi'i 1889–1966', *al-Hilal* 75 (January 1967) 40–7.

Mustafa, Ahmad 'Abd al-Rahim. ''Abd al-Rahman al-Rafi'i' wa tarikh al-haraka al-qawmiyya', *al-Majalla* 60 (January 1962) 22–7.

Mustafa, Ahmad 'Abd al-Rahim. 'Hamla al-mubakhir wa san'u al-tigha fi al-siyasa wa fi al-tarikh', *al-Hilal* 94 (March 1987) 10–14.

Mustafa, Ahmad 'Abd al-Rahim. 'Hawla i'adat taqyim tarikhna al-qawmi', *Ruz al-Yusuf* 1830 (8 July 1963) 12.

Mustafa, Ahmad 'Abd al-Rahim. 'Muhammad Anis, mu'arrikhan wa munadilan', *al-Hilal* 94 (November 1986) 60–7.

Mustafa, Ahmad 'Abd al-Rahim. 'Nadwat i'adat kitabat al-tarikh al-qawmi', *al-Majalla al-tarikhiyya al-misriyya* 13 (1967) 345–69.

Mustafa, Ahmad 'Abd al-Rahim. 'Shafiq Ghorbal mu'arrikhan', *al-Majalla al-tarikhiyya al-misriyya* 11 (1963) 255–78.

al-Muti'i, Lam'i. *Mawsu'at hadha al-rajul min misr*. Cairo: Dar al-shuruq, 1997.

al-Naqqash, Salim. *Misr li'l-misriyyin*. 6 vols, Alexandria: Matba'at al-mahrusa, 1884.

Nasim, Sulayman. '"Khirafa" al-aqlayya fi misr', *Watani* 17 May 1992.

Nasim, Sulayman. *Siyagha al-ta'lim al-misri al-hadith 1922–52, dur al-qawa al-siyasiyya wa'l-ijtima'iyya wa'l-fikriyya*. Cairo: al-Hay'a al-misriyya al-'ama li'l-kitab, 1984.

al-Nukhayli, Sulayman Muhammad. *al-Haraka al-'ummaliyya fi misr wa mawqif al-sihafa wa'l-sulta misriyya minha sanat 1882 ila sanat 1952*. Cairo, 1967.

Qilada, Wilyum Sulayman. *al-Masihiyya wa'l-islam fi misr*. Cairo: Sina, 1993.

al-Rafi'i, 'Abd al-Rahman. *Fi 'aqab al-thawra al-misriyya*. 3 vols, Cairo: Maktaba al-nahda al-misriyya, 1947–51.

al-Rafi'i, 'Abd al-Rahman. *al-Jam'iyyat al-wataniyya, sahifa min al-tarikh al-nahdat al-qawmiyya*. Cairo: Matba'at al-nahda, 1922.

al-Rafi'i, 'Abd al-Rahman. *Misr, 3 – al-sha'b al-watani*. Cairo: Dirasat qawmiyya, 1979.

al-Rafi'i, 'Abd al-Rahman. *Mudhakkirati 1889–1951*. Cairo: Kitab al-yawm, 1989.

al-Rafi'i, 'Abd al-Rahman. *Muhammad Farid, ramz al-ikhlas wa'l-tadhiyya, tarikh misr al-qawmi min sanat 1908 ila sanat 1919*. Cairo: Maktaba Mustafa Al-Halabi, 1941.

al-Rafi'i, 'Abd al-Rahman. *Muqaddamat thawrat 23 yuliu 1952*. Cairo, 1957.

al-Rafi'i, 'Abd al-Rahman. *Mustafa Kamil, ba'th al-haraka al-wataniyya*. Cairo, 1939.

al-Rafi'i, 'Abd al-Rahman. *Qawa'id al-mu'ahada, istiqlal am himayya*. Cairo: Matba'a al-azhar, 1936.

al-Rafi'i, 'Abd al-Rahman. *Thawrat 1919, tarikh misr al-qawmi 1914–1921*. 4th edn, Cairo: Dar al-ma'arif, 1987.

al-Rafi'i, 'Abd al-Rahman. *Thawrat 23 yuliu 1952 – tarikhna al-qawmi fi sabi' sanawat 1952–1959*, 1959.

Ramadan, 'Abd al-'Azim. ''Ilm al-tarikh bayna al-mawdu'iyya al-dhatiyya', *al-Majalla al-tarikhiyya al-maghribiyya* 13–14 (January 1979) 43–53.

Ramadan, 'Abd al-'Azim. 'Madaris kitabat tarikh misr al-mu'asir', 59–68 in Ahmad 'Abd Allah (ed.) *Tarikh misr: bayna al-manahij al-'alimi wa'l-sira' al-hizbi*. Cairo: Dar al-shuhdi li'l-nashr, 1988.

Ramadan, 'Abd al-'Azim. *Misr fi 'asr al-Sadat*. 2 vols, Cairo: Madbouli, 1989.

Ramadan, 'Abd al-'Azim. *Mudhakkirat al-siyasiyyin wa'l zu'ama fi misr 1891–1981*. Cairo: al-Watan al-'arabi, 1984.

Ramadan, 'Abd al-'Azim. *Tatawwur al-haraka al-wataniyya fi misr 1918–36*. Cairo: Madbouli, 1983.

Ramadan, 'Abd al-'Azim. *Tatawwur al-haraka al-wataniyya fi misr mundhu ibram mu'ahada 1936 ila nihaya al-harb al-'alamiyya al-thaniyya*, Beirut, 1970.

Ramadan, 'Abd al-'Azim and Ahmad 'Abd Allah. 'Hawla al-ma'raka ilati darat baynahama 'ala safhat al-suhuf bi-khusus taqwim dur al-za'im Sa'd Zaghlul', 277–80 in Ahmad 'Abd Allah (ed.) *Tarikh misr, bayna al-manahij al-'alimi wa'l-sira' al-hizbi*. Cairo: Dar al-shuhdi li'l-nashr, 1988.

Rif'at, Muhammad. 'Kalima al-ustadh Muhammad Rif'at', *al-Majalla al-tarikhiyya al-misriyya* 11 (1963) 7–9.

Rizq, Jabir. *Madhabih al-ikhwan fi sijun Nasir*. Cairo: Dar al-i'tisam, 1977.

Rizq, Yunan Labib. '"Abu Qarqas"..wa sina'at al-munakh al-fitna al-ta'ifiyya', *al-Yasar* 5 (July 1990) 34–6.

Rizq, Yunan Labib. '"Abu Qarqas" wa sina'at al-munakh (2), al-'auda ila al-za'amat al-diniyya', *al-Yasar* 6 (August 1990) 31–3.

Rizq, Yunan Labib. *al-Azhab al-siyasiyya min misr 1907–1984*. Cairo: Kitab al-hilal, 1984.

Rizq, Yunan Labib. 'Bayna al-mawdu'iyya wa'l-tahazzub fi kitabat al-tarikh al-azhab al-siyasiyya fi misr', 363–74 in Ahmad 'Abd Allah (ed.) *Tarikh misr; bayna al-manhaj al-'ilmi wa'l-sira' al-hizbi*. Cairo: Dar shuhdi li'l-nashr, 1988.

Rizq, Yunan Labib. 'Tahalluf didda al-tarikh', *al-Musawwar* 11 May 1984 16–17, 65.

Sa'd, Ahmad Sadiq. *Mushkilat al-fallah*. Cairo: Dar al-qarn al-'ishrin, 1945.

Sa'd, Ahmad Sadiq. *Safhat min al-yasar al-misri fi a'qab al-harb al-'alamiyya al-thaniyya 1945–46*. Cairo: Madbouli, 1976.

al-Sa'id, Rif'at. *Hasan al-Banna, mu'assis jama'at al-ikhwan al-muslimin, mata.. kayfa wa-limadha?* Cairo: Dar al-thaqafa al-jadida, 1984.

al-Sa'id, Rif'at. *Misr muslimin wa'l-aqbatan.* [Cairo]: np, 1993.

al-Sa'id, Rif'at. *Mustafa al-Nahhas, al-siyasi wa'l-za'im wa'l-munadil.* Beirut: Dar al-qadaya, 1976.

al-Sa'id, Rif'at. *Sa'd Zaghlul bayna al-yimin wa'l-yasar.* Beirut: Dar al-qadaya, 1976.

al-Sa'id, Rif'at. *Safhat min tarikh misr, ru'ya al-'alaqa bayna tarikh wa'l-siyasa.* Cairo: Dar al-thaqafa al-jadida, 1984.

al-Sa'id, Rif'at. *Tarikh al-haraka al-shuyu'iyya al-misriyya, 1900–1940.* 5 vols, Cairo: Shirkat al-amal, 1987–9.

al-Sa'id, Rif'at. *Tarikh al-munazzamat al-yasariyya al-misriyya, 1940–1950.* Cairo: Dar al-thaqafa al-jadida, 1976.

Salama, Usama. 'Akadhib sawt amrika wa hujum 'ala al-hukuma madfu' al-ajr', *Ruz al-Yusuf* no. 3491 (8 May 1995) 24–5.

Salim, Latifa Muhammad. *al-Mar'a al-misriyya wa al-taghyir al-ijtima'i 1919–1945.* Cairo: al-Hay'a al-misriyya al-'ama li'l-kitab, 1984.

Sami, Amin. 'Lamma kuntu mu'alliman', *al-Hilal* 45 (1937) 610–12.

Sami, Amin. *Misr wa'l-nil min fajr al-tarikh ila alan.* Cairo: Dar al-kutub al-misriyya, 1938.

Sami, Amin. *Taqwim al-Nil.* 6 vols, Cairo: Dar al-kutub al-misriyya bi'l-qahira, 1916–36.

Sarhank, Isma'il. *Haqa'iq al-akhbar 'an duwal al-bihar.* 3 vols, Cairo: Matba'at al-amiriyya bi-bulaq, 1896, 1898, 1923.

al-Sayyid, Ahmad Lutfi. *Safhat matwiyya, min tarikh li'l-istiqlal fi misr min maris 1908 ila maris 1909.* Cairo: Maktabat al-nahda al-misriyya, 1946.

al-Sayyid, Jalal. 'Tarikhna al-qawmi fi daw' al-ishtirakiyya', *al-Katib* 29 (August 1963) 87–92.

al-Shafi'i, Shuhdi 'Atiya. *Tatawwur al-haraka al-wataniyya al-misriyya 1882–1956.* Cairo, 1957.

al-Shafi'i, Shuhdi 'Atiya and al-Jibayli, 'Abd al-Ma'bud. *Ahdafuna al-wataniyya.* Cairo: al-Risala, 1945.

Shafiq, Ahmad. *Hawliyyat misr al-siyasiyya.* 6 vols, Cairo, 1924–31.

Sharubim, Mikha'il. *al-Kafi fi al-tarikh misr al-qadim wa'l-hadith.* 4 vols, Bulaq: al-Matba'at al-kubra al-amiriyya, 1898–1900.

Shinuda, Zaki. *Qibti shahid 'ala al-'asr.* Cairo: Nabil 'Adli Matias, 1992.

al-Shiliq, Ahmad Zakariyya. Review of *al-Muslimun wa'l-aqbat fi atar al-jama'a al-wataniyya,* by Tariq al-Bishri, *al-Siyasa al-dawliyya* 68 (April 1982) 211–16.

Shukri, Ghali. *al-Aqbat fi watan mutaghayyir.* Cairo: Dar al-shuruq, 1991.

Shukri, Ghali. *al-Muthaqqafun wa'l-sulta fi misr.* Vol. 1, Cairo, 1990.

Shukri, Ghali. 'Hisan tarawada al-masihi fi misr (2)', *al-Watan al-'arabi* 166 (18 May 1990) 26–8.

Shukri, Ghali. 'al-Sira' al-masihi – al-masihi fi misr (3)', *al-Watan al-'arabi* 167 (25 May 1990) 24–6.

Shukri, Muhammad Fu'ad. *Bina' dawla misr Muhammad 'Ali.* Cairo, 1948.

Shukri, Muhammad Fu'ad. *Misr fi matla' al-qarn al-tasi' 'ashar.* 1801–11, 3 vols, 1954–8.

'Su'al wa jawab ma'a al-duktur Muhammad Anis', *al-Jumhuriyya* 11 August 1962, 10.

al-Subki, Amal Kamil Bayumi. *al-Haraka al-nisa'iyya fi misr ma bayna al-thawratayn 1919 wa 1952*. Cairo: al-Hay'a al-misriyya al-'ama li'l-kitab, 1986.

al-Tahtawi, Rifa'ah Rafi'. *Kitab manahij al-albab al-misriyya fi mabahij al-adab al-'asriyya*. Cairo: Matba'at shirkat al-ragha'ib, 1912.

Tamawi, Ahmad Husayn. *Muhammad Sabri*. Cairo: al-Hay'a al-misriyya al-'ama li'l-kitab, 1994.

Tajir, Jak. *al-Aqbat wa'l-muslimin mundhu al-fath al-'arabi ila 'am 1922*. Cairo, np, 1951.

Taqdir wa 'Urfan li'l-ustadh al-duktur Ahmad 'Izzat 'Abd al-Karim. Cairo, Jami'at 'Ain Shams, 1976. (*Studies in Modern History, Didicated [sic] to Prof Dr Ahmed Ezzat Abdul Karim*. Ain Shams University Press, 1976).

Tiba, Mustafa. 'Hawla awraq Hinri Kuriyil matlub taqyim mawdu'i li'l-tarikh al-hadith', *al-Hilal* 96 (November 1988) 48–53.

Tilmisani, 'Umar. *Dhikrayyat....la mudhakkirat*. Cairo: Dar al-islamiyya, 1985.

Tilmisani, 'Umar. *Qala al-nas...wa lam aqal fi hukm 'Abd al-Nasir*. Cairo: Dar al-ansar, 1980.

Yahya, Jalal. *et al. al-'Alam al-'arabi al-hadith mundhu al-harb al-'alamiyya al-thaniyya*. Cairo, 1980.

Yassin, al-Sayyid (ed.) *al-Thawra wa'l-taghir al-ijtima'i, ruba' qarn ba'd 23 yuliu 1952*. Cairo: Markaz al-dirasat al-siyasiyya wa'l-istratijiyya bi'l-ahram, 1977.

Yusuf, Abu Sayf. *al-Aqbat wa'l-qawmiyya al-'arabiyya*. Beirut: Markaz dirasat al-wahda al-tarikhiyya, 1987.

Yusuf, Abu Sayf. *Watha'iq wa mawaqif min tarikh al-yasar al-misri, 1941–1957*. Cairo: al-Amal, 2000.

Zaydan, Jurji. *Kitab tarikh misr al-hadith*. (orig. title *Tarikh misr al-jadid min al-fath al-islami ila alan*) 2 vols, Cairo: Dar al-hilal, 1925.

SOURCES IN ENGLISH, FRENCH, GREEK AND ITALIAN

Abbas Hamed, Raouf [Ra'uf]. 'The Copts under British Rule in Egypt, 1882–1914', *al-Majalla al-tarikhiyya al-misriyya* 26 (1989) 49–59.

Abdalla, Ahmed. *The Student Movement and National Politics in Egypt, 1923–1973*. London: al-Saqi, 1985.

Abdel-Malek, Anouar. *Egypt: Military Society*. New York: Random House, 1968.

Aciman, André. *Out of Egypt, A Memoir*. New York: Farrar Strauss Giroux, 1994.

Adalian, Rouben. 'The Armenian Colony of Egypt During the Reign of Muhammad Ali (1805–1848)', *Armenian Review* 33 (1980) 115–45.

'Afaf Lutfi El-Sayyid: Student of Egypt's Past', *Newsletter of American Research Center in Egypt* 160 (Winter 1993) 13–14.

Ahmed, Jamal Mohammed. *The Intellectual Origins of Egyptian Nationalism*. London: Oxford UP, 1960.

Akbarzadeh, Shahram, 'Nation-building in Uzbekistan', *Central Asian Survey* 15 no. 1 (1996) 23–32.

Alleaume, Ghislaine. 'L'Égypte et son histoire: actualité et controversies', *CEDEJ Bulletin* 20 (1986) 9–78.

Ammar, Samira Helmy. 'Censorship of English Language Books in Egypt 1952–1990'. MA thesis. AUC, May 1990.

Anastasiadis, Yiannis. *Mnimes apo ti drasi tou aristerou kinimatos tou Egiptioti Ellinismou* ('Memories from the Activity of the Egyptian–Greek Left Movement') Athens, np, 1993.

Anderson, Lisa. 'Legitimacy, Identity, and the Writing of History in Libya', 71–91 in Eric Davis and Nicolas Gavrielides (eds) *Statecraft in the Middle East, Oil, Historical Memory, and Popular Culture*. Miami: Florida International University Press, 1991.

Aroian, Lois Armine. *The Nationalization of Arabic and Islamic Education in Egypt: Dar al-'Ulum and al-Azhar*. American University in Cairo, 1983.

Artin, Ya'qub. *L'Instruction publique en Égypte*. Paris, 1890.

Artin, Ya'qub. *La Propriété foncière en Égypte*. Cairo, 1908.

Atiya, Aziz S. (ed.) *The Coptic Encyclopedia*. 8 vols, New York: Macmillan, 1991.

Ayalon, David. 'The Historian al-Jabarti', 391–402 in B. Lewis and P.M. Holt (eds). *Historians of the Middle East*. London: Oxford UP, 1962.

Ayalon, David. 'The Historian al-Jabarti and His Background', *Bulletin of the School of Oriental and African Studies* 23 (1960) 217–49.

Ayubi, Nazih. *Political Islam, Religion and Politics in the Arab World*. London & New York: Routledge, 1991.

Badran, Margot. *Feminists, Islam, and Nation*. Cairo: AUC Press, 1996.

Badran, Margot and Cooke, Miriam (eds) *Opening the Gates, A Century of Arab Feminist Writing*. Bloomington and Indianapolis: Indiana UP, 1990.

Baker, Raymond. *Egypt's Uncertain Revolution under Nasser and Sadat*. Cambridge, Mass.: Harvard UP 1978.

Baker, Raymond. *Sadat and After, Struggles for Egypt's Political Soul*. Cambridge, Mass.: Harvard UP, 1990.

Baram, Amatzia. *Culture, History & Ideology in the Formation of Ba'thist Iraq 1968–89*. New York: St Martin's Press, 1991.

Baron, Beth. *The Women's Awakening in Egypt*. New Haven & London: Yale UP, 1994.

Barraclough, Geoffrey. *Main Trends in History*. New York and London: Holmes & Meier, 1979.

Beattie, Kirk J. *Egypt During the Nasser Years, Ideology, Politics and Civil Society*. Boulder, Co: Westview Press, 1994.

Beinin, Joel. 'The Communist Movement and Nationalist Political Discourse in Nasirist Egypt', *Middle East Journal* 41 no. 4 (Autumn 1987) 568–84.

Beinin, Joel. *The Dispersion of Egyptian Jewry*. Berkeley: University of California Press, 1998.

Beinin, Joel. 'The Egyptian Regime and the Left: Between Islamism and Secularism', *Middle East Report* 185 (November–December 1993) 25–6.

Beinin, Joel. 'Will the Real Egyptian Working Class Please Stand Up?', 247–70 in Zachary Lockman (ed.) *Workers and Working Classes in the Middle East, Struggles, Histories, Historiographies*. State University of New York Press, 1994.

Beinin, Joel and Lockman, Zachary. *Workers on the Nile: Nationalism, Communism, Islam, and the Egyptian Working Class, 1882–1954*. London: I.B. Tauris, 1988.

Berque, Jacques. *Egypt, Imperialism & Revolution*. Trans. Jean Stewart, New York & Washington: Praeger, 1972.

255

Bilboul, Roger R. (ed.) *Retrospective Index to Theses of Great Britain and Ireland 1716–1950.* Vol. 1, American Bibliographical Center, 1975.

Binder, Leonard. *Islamic Liberalism: A Critique of Development Ideologies.* Chicago & London: University of Chicago Press, 1988.

al-Bishri, Tariq. 'Mouvement National et Mouvement Islamiste', *Peuples Méditerraéens* 21 (October–December 1982) 23–30.

Blattner, E.J. *Who's Who in Egypt and the Middle East.* Cairo: Minerbo, 1949.

Boia, Lucian (ed.) *Great Historians of the Modern Age.* New York: Greenwood Press, 1991.

Botman, Selma. *The Rise of Egyptian Communism, 1939–70.* Syracuse UP, 1988.

Botman, Selma. 'Women's Participation in Radical Egyptian Politics 1939–1952', 12–25 in Magda Salman *et al. Women in the Middle East.* London & New Jersey: Zed Books, *Khamsin* series, 1987.

Boullata, Issa. *Trends and Issues in Contemporary Arab Thought.* Albany: State University of New York Press, 1990.

Brown, Nathan J. *Peasant Politics in Modern Egypt, The Struggle Against the State.* New Haven and London: Yale UP, 1990.

Burns, Elinor. *British Imperialism in Egypt.* London: Labour Research Department, 1928.

Bustros, Gabriel M. (ed.) *Who's Who of the Arab World.* 7th edn, Beirut: Publitec, 1984–5.

Cannon, John (ed.) *The Blackwell Dictionary of Historians.* Oxford: Blackwell, 1988.

Carter, Barbara. *The Copts in Egyptian Politics 1918–1952.* Cairo: AUC Press, 1986.

Chejne, Anwar G. 'The Concept of History in the Modern Arab World', *Studies in Islam* 4 (1967) 1–31.

Chejne, Anwar G. 'The Use of History by Modern Arab Writers', *Middle East Journal* 14 (Autumn 1960) 382–96.

Choueiri, Youssef M. *Arab History and the Nation-State, A Study in Modern Arab Historiography 1820–1980.* London & New York: Routledge, 1989.

Christian, David. 'Marat Durdyiev and Turkmen Nationalism', 57–81 in Aleksandar Pavkovic *et al.* (eds) *Nationalism and Postcommunism, A Collection of Essays.* Aldershot: Dartmouth, 1995.

Cleveland, William L. *The Making of an Arab Nationalist, Ottomanism and Arabism in the Life and Thought of Sati' al-Husri.* Princeton NJ: Princeton UP, 1971.

Contu, Giuseppe. 'Ahmad Izzat 'Abd al-Karim 1909–1980, Storico arabo contemporaneo', 219–38 in Clelia Sarnelli Cerqua (ed.) *Studi arabo-islamici in onore di Roberto Rubinacci nel suo settantesimo cumpleano.* Vol. 1, Napoli: Istituto Universitario Orientale, 1975.

Contu, Giuseppe. 'La conoscenza del mundo arabo moderno e contemporaneo attraverso gli studi storici di' Ayn Shams 1976–77', *Annali* (Istituto Universitario Orientale di Napoli) 39 (1979) 333–44.

Crabbs, Jack A. Jr. 'Politics, History, and Culture in Nasser's Egypt', *IJMES* 6 (1975) 386–420.

Crabbs, Jack A. Jr. *The Writing of History in Nineteenth-Century Egypt, A Study in National Transformation.* Detroit: Wayne State University & Cairo: AUC Press, 1984.

Crabitès, Pierre. *Americans in the Egyptian Army.* London: George Routledge, 1938.

Crabitès, Pierre. *Ibrahim of Egypt*. London: George Routledge, 1935.

Crabitès, Pierre. *Ismail, The Maligned Khedive*. London: George Routledge, 1933.

Deeb, Marius. 'The Socioeconomic Role of the Local Foreign Minorities in Modern Egypt, 1805–1961', *IJMES* 9 (1978) 11–22.

Dehérain Henri, 'Un Mécène Royal: Le Roi Fouad Ier', iii–xxxii, in Gabriel Hanotaux (ed.) *Histoire de la nation égyptienne*. Vol. VII, Paris: Libraire Plon, 1931–40.

Dekmejian, R. Hrair. *Egypt under Nasir, A Study in Political Dynamics*. University of London Press, 1971.

Delanoue, Gilbert. *Moralistes et politiques musulmans dans l'Égypte du XIXe siècle*, vol. 1, Cairo: IFAO, 1982.

'Divers Historiens et Archèologues'. *Précis de l'histoire d'Égypte*. 3 vols, L'Institut Français D'Archéologie Orientale du Caire, 1932–3; vol. 4, Rome, 1935.

Dodwell, Henry Herbert. *The Founder of Modern Egypt, A Study of Muhammad 'Ali*. Cambridge UP, 1931.

Cromer, Earl of. *Modern Egypt*. 2 vols, London: Macmillan, 1908.

Enteen, George M. *The Soviet Scholar-Bureaucrat, M.N. Pokrovskii and the Society of Marxist Historians*. Pennsylvania UP, 1978.

Egger, Vernon. *A Fabian in Egypt, Salamah Musa and the Rise of the Professional Classes in Egypt, 1909–39*. Lanham, MD: University Press of America, *c.* 1986.

Ellul, Jean. *Index des communications et mémoires publiés par l'Institut d'Égypte (1859–1952)*. Cairo: L'Institut Français d'Archéologie Orientale, 1952.

Fahmy [Fahmi], Muhammad. *La Verité sur la question d'Égypte*. Saint-Imier, 1913.

Faksh, Mahmud A. 'The Consequences of the Introduction and Spread of Modern Education: Education and National Integration in Egypt', *Middle Eastern Studies* 16 no. 2 (1980) 42–55.

Farah, Nadia Ramsis. *Religious Strife in Egypt, Crisis and Ideological Conflict in the Seventies*. Montreux: Gordon and Breach, 1986.

Faris, Nabih Amin. 'The Arabs and Their History', *Middle East Journal* 8 (1954) 155–62.

El-Feki [al-Fiqi], Mustafa. *Copts in Egyptian Politics 1919–1952*. Cairo: General Egyptian Book Organization, 1991.

El-Feki, Mustafa. 'Makram Ebeid, A Coptic Leader in the Egyptian National Movement, A Case Study in the Role of the Copts in Egyptian Politics, 1919–1952'. PhD thesis. University of London, 1977.

Gallagher, Nancy E. (ed.). *Approaches to the History of the Middle East: Interviews with Leading Middle East Historians*. Reading: Ithaca, 1994.

Gallagher, Nancy E. 'The Life and Times of a Moroccan Historian: An Interview with Abdallah Laroui', *Journal of Maghrebi Studies* 2 no. 1 (1994) 25–6.

Gendzier, Irene L. *The Practical Visions of Ya'qub Sanu'*. Cambridge, Mass.: Harvard UP, 1966.

Gershoni, Israel. 'Imagining and Reimagining the Past: The Use of History by Egyptian Nationalist Writers, 1919–1952', *History and Memory* 4 no. 2 (1992) 5–37.

Gershoni, Israel. 'New Pasts for New National Images: The Perception of History in Modern Egyptian Thought', 51–8 in Shimon Shamir (ed.) *Self-Views in Historical Perspective in Egypt and Israel*. Tel Aviv University, 1981.

Gershoni, Israel and Jankowski, James P. *Egypt, Islam and the Arabs, The Search for Egyptian Nationhood, 1900–1930*. New York & Oxford: Oxford University Press, 1986.

Ghali, Waguih. *Beer in the Snooker Club*. New York: New Amsterdam, 1964, reprint, 1987.

Ghorbal [Ghurbal], Shafik. *The Beginnings of the Egyptian Question and the Rise of Mehemet Ali*. London: George Routledge, 1928.

Ghorbal [Ghurbal], Shafik. Mohammed. *The Making of Egypt, A Series of Ten Talks*. 2nd edn, Cairo: League of Arab States, nd.

Goldberg, Ellis. *Tinker, Tailor and Textile Worker, Class and Politics in Egypt, 1930–1952*. University of California Press, 1986.

Goldschmidt Jr, Arthur. *Biographical Dictionary of Egypt*. Cairo: AUC Press, 2000.

Goldschmidt Jr, Arthur. 'The Butrus Ghali Family', *Journal of American Research Center in Egypt* 30 (1993) 183–8.

Goldschmidt Jr, Arthur. *Modern Egypt, The Formation of a Nation-State*. Boulder, Co: Westview Press, 1988.

Gorman, Anthony. 'Egiptiotis Ellin', *Ta nea tou ELIA* 58 (summer 2001) 13–18.

Gorman, Anthony. 'Egypt's Forgotten Communists: The Post-War Greek Left', *Journal of Modern Greek Studies* 20(2002) 1–27.

Gran, Peter. *Beyond Eurocentrism, A New View of Modern World History*. Syracuse UP, 1996.

Gran, Peter. 'Commitment and Objectivity in Italian Road Historiography: The Case of Egyptian Writing after World War II', Unpublished paper, 1987. (Arabic translation in Ahmad ʿAbd Allah (ed.) *Tarikh misr*. Cairo: Dar al-shuhdi lil-nashr, 1988, 87–94.)

Gran, Peter. 'Modern Trends in Egyptian Historiography: A Review Article', *IJMES* 9 (1978) 367–71.

Graves, Robert. *Good-bye to All That, An Autobiography*. London: Jonathan Cape, 1929.

Guha, R. and Spivak, G.C. (eds). *Selected Subaltern Studies*. Oxford UP, 1988.

Haddad, Yvonne Y. *Contemporary Islam and the Challenge of History*. Albany: State University of New York, 1982.

Hagg, Tomas (ed.) *Nubian Culture Past and Present*. Stockholm: Almqvist and Wiksell International, 1987.

Hanotaux, Gabriel (ed.) *Histoire de la nation égyptienne*. 7 vols, Paris: Libraire Plon, 1931–40.

Hassoun, Jacques (ed.) *Juifs du Nil*. Paris: Le Sycamore, 1981.

Hatem, Mervat. 'The Enduring Alliance of Nationalism and Patriarchy in Muslim Personal Status Laws: The Case of Modern Egypt', *Feminist Issues* 6 (1986) 19–43.

Hatem, Mervat. 'Through Each Other's Eyes: Egyptian, Levantine-Egyptian, and European Women's Images of Themselves and of Each Other (1862–1920)', *Women's Studies International Forum* 12 (1989) 183–98.

Haykal, Muhammad H. [Heikal, Mohamed] *Autumn of Fury, The Assassination of Sadat*. London: Corgi, 1983.

Heyworth-Dunne, J. *An Introduction to the History of Education in Modern Egypt*. London: Frank Cass, 1968.

Hinnebusch, Raymond A. Jr. *Egyptian Politics Under Sadat, The Post-Populist Development of an Authoritarian-Modernizing State*. Cambridge: Cambridge UP, 1985.

Hourani, Albert. *Arabic Thought in the Liberal Age 1798–1939*. Oxford UP, 1970.

Hourani, Albert. *Minorities in the Arab World*. London: Oxford UP, 1947.

Hussein, Mahmoud. *Class Conflict in Egypt 1945–1970*. New York and London: Monthly Review Press, 1973.

Hussein [Husayn], Taha. *The Future of Culture in Egypt*. New York: Octagon, 1975.

Hyde, Georgie. *Education in Modern Egypt: Ideals and Realities*. London: Routledge & Kegan Paul, 1978.

Ibrahim, Sonallah. 'The Experience of a Generation', *Index on Censorship* 9 (1987) 19–22.

Ilbert, Robert and Ilios Yannakakis (eds), *Alexandrie 1860–1960, un modèle éphémère de convivialité: communautés et identité cosmopolite*. Editions Autrement, Paris, 1992 (later published in English as *Alexandria 1860–1960, The Brief Life of a Cosmopolitan Community*. Alexandria: Harpocrates 1997).

Inalcik, Halil. 'Some Remarks on the Study of History in Islamic Countries', *Middle East Journal* 7 (1953) 451–5.

L'Institut Égyptien, *Livre d'or de l'Institut Égyptien, 1859–1899*. Cairo, 1899.

Ismael, Tareq Y. and Rifa'at El-Sa'id. *The Communist Movement in Egypt, 1920–1988*. Syracuse UP, 1990.

Issawi, Charles. *Egypt in Revolution*. Oxford UP, 1963.

Jacobs, P.M. *History Theses, 1901–1970*. University of London: Institute of Historical Research, 1976.

JanMohamed, Abdul R. and Lloyd, David. 'Introduction: Toward a Theory of Minority Discourse: What is to be Done?', 1–16 in Abdul R. JanMohamed and David Lloyd (eds) *The Nature and Context of Minority Discourse*. New York and Oxford: Oxford UP, 1990.

Jansen, J.J.G. 'Ibrahim Abduh (b. 1913), His Autobiographies and His Political Polemical Writings', *Bibliotheca Orientalis* 37 (1980) 128–32.

Jewsiewicki, Bogumil and Newbury, David (eds). *African Historiographies, What History for Which Africa*. Beverly Hills, CA: Sage, 1986.

Keddie, Nikki R. 'Problems in the Study of Middle Eastern Women', *IJMES* 10 (1979) 225–40.

Keddie, Nikki R. and Baron, Beth (eds). *Women in Middle Eastern History*. New Haven and London: Yale UP, 1991.

Kendall, W. *The Revolutionary Movement in Britain, 1900–21*. London: Wiedenfeld and Nicolson, 1969.

Kenney, Jeffrey T. 'Enemies Near and Far: The Image of the Jews in Islamist Discourse in Egypt', *Religion* 24 (1994) 253–70.

Kepel, Gilles. *The Prophet and Pharaoh, Muslim Extremism in Egypt*. Paris: al Saqi Books, 1985.

Khalaf, Samir. 'The Growing Pains of Arab Intellectuals', *Diogenes* 54 (1966) 59–80.

Kisch, Richard. *The Days of the Good Soldiers, Communists in the Armed Forces WWII*. London & New York: Journeyman, 1985.

Kitroeff, Alexander. *The Greeks in Egypt, 1919–1937, Ethnicity and Class*. London: Ithaca, 1989.

Klausner, Samuel Z. 'A Professor's-Eye View of the Egyptian Academy', *Journal of Higher Education* 57 no. 4 (July/August 1986) 345–69.

Kourvetaris, Yorgos A. 'The Greeks of Asia Minor and Egypt as Middleman Economic Minorities during the late 19th and 20th Centuries', *Ethnic Groups* 7 (1988) 85–111.

Krämer, Gudrun. 'History and Legitimacy: The Use of History in Contemporary Egyptian Party Politics'. Paper presented at the conference 'Commitment and Objectivity in Contemporary Historiography of Egypt 1919–1952', Netherlands Institute of Archaeology and Arabic Studies in Cairo, 1987. (Published in Arabic translation in Ahmad ʿAbd Allah (ed.) *Tarikh misr: bayna al-manahij al-ʿalimi wa ʾl-sira ʿal-hizbi.* Cairo: Dar al-shuhdi lil-nashr, 1988, 275–84.)

Krämer, Gudrun. *The Jews in Modern Egypt, 1914–1952.* London: I.B. Tauris, 1989.

Krämer, Gudrun. '"Radical" Nationalists, Fundamentalists, and the Jews in Egypt or, Who is a Real Egyptian?', 354–71 in G.R. Warburg and Uri Kupferschmidt (eds) *Islam, Nationalism, and Radicalism in Egypt and the Sudan.* New York: Praeger, 1983.

Krug, Mark M. 'History Teaching in Nasser's Egypt', *Teachers College Record* 66 (1964) 128–37.

Lane, E.W. *Manners and Customs of the Modern Egyptians.* London: East-West, 1978.

Laroui, Abdallah. *The Crisis of the Arab Intellectual, Traditionalism or Historicism?* University of California Press, 1976.

Levi, Isaac G. 'Angelo Sammarco (1883–1948)', *Bulletin de l'Institut d'Egypte* 31 (1949) 205–7.

Levi, Peter. 'The World from Underground', *Times Literary Supplement* 14 November 1975, 1356.

Lewis, Bernard. 'History-Writing and National Revival in Turkey', *Middle Eastern Affairs* 4 nos. 6–7 (1953) 218–27.

Lewis, Bernard and Holt, P.M. (eds) *Historians of the Middle East.* London: Oxford UP, 1962.

Lockman, Zachary (ed.) *Workers and Working Classes in the Middle East, Struggles, Histories, Historiographies.* State University of New York Press, 1994.

Marshall, J.E. *The Egyptian Enigma, 1890–1928.* London: John Murray, 1928.

Marsot, Afaf Lutfi al-Sayyid. 'Egyptian Historical Research and Writing on Egypt in the 20th Century', *MESA Bulletin* 7 no. 2 (1973) 1–15.

Marsot, Afaf Lutfi al-Sayyid. *Egypt's Liberal Experiment, 1922–36.* Berkeley: University of California Press, 1977.

Marsot, Afaf Lutfi al-Sayyid. 'The Revolutionary Gentlewomen in Egypt', 261–76 in Lois Beck and Nikki Keddie (eds), *Women in the Muslim World.* Cambridge, Mass.: Harvard UP, 1978.

Marsot, Afaf Lutfi al-Sayyid. 'Survey of Egyptian Works of History', *American Historical Review* (1991) 1422–34.

Marsot, Afaf Lutfi al-Sayyid. *A Short History of Modern Egypt.* Cambridge UP, 1985.

Masselos, Jim. 'The Dis/appearance of Subalterns: A Reading of a Decade of Subaltern Studies', *South Asia* 25 no. 1 (1992) 105–25.

Mayer, Thomas. *The Changing Past, Egyptian Historiography of the Urabi Revolt, 1882–1983.* Gainsville: University of Florida Press, 1988.

Mehrez, Samia. *Egyptian Writers between Fiction and History.* Cairo: AUC Press, 1994.

Meijer, Roel. 'Changing Political Perspectives in the Contemporary Historiography of the Period 1919–1952'. Paper presented at the conference 'Commitment and Objectivity in Contemporary Historiography of Egypt 1919–1952', Netherlands

Institute of Archaeology and Arabic Studies in Cairo, 1987. (Published in Arabic translation in Ahmad ʿAbd Allah (ed.) *Tarikh misr: bayna al-manahij al-ʿalimi waʾl-siraʿ al-hizbi*. Cairo: Dar al-shuhdi lil-nashr, 1988, 28–35.)

Meijer, Roel. 'Contemporary Egyptian Historiography of the Period 1936–1942: A Study of Its Scientific and Political Character'. Amsterdam, 1985.

Meijer, Roel. *History, Authenticity, and Politics: Tariq al-Bishri's Interpretation of Modern Egyptian History*. Occasional Paper no. 4, Amsterdam, Middle East Research Associates, 1989.

Mikhail, Kyriakos. *Copts and Moslems under British Control, A Collection of Facts and a Resume of Authoritative Opinions on the Coptic Question*. New York & London: Kennikat Press, 1911, reprint, 1971.

Mitchell, Richard P. *The Society of the Muslim Brothers*. London: Oxford UP, 1969.

Mitchell, Timothy. *Colonising Egypt*. Cairo: AUC Press, 1989.

Mitchell, Timothy. 'The Invention and Reinvention of the Egyptian Peasant', *IJMES* 22 (1990) 129–50.

Moussa [Musa], Salama. 'Intellectual Currents in Egypt', *Middle Eastern Affairs* 2 (1951) 267–72.

Nasser, Gamal Abdel. *The Philosophy of the Revolution*. Buffalo NY: Smith, Keynes & Marshall, 1959.

Najjar, Fauzi M. 'State and University in Egypt During the Period of Socialist Transformation, 1961–1967', *The Review of Politics* 38 (1976) 57–87.

Neguib [Najib], Mohammed. *Egypt's Destiny*. London: Victor Gollancz, 1955.

Nelson, Cynthia. *Doria Shafik, Egyptian Feminist, A Woman Apart*. American University in Cairo Press, 1996.

Nomikos, Khristophoros. *Aravika istorimata* ('Arab Narratives'). Grammata: Alexandria, 1920.

Palaiologos, Tasos P. *O Egiptiotis Ellinismos, istoria ke drasis (753 π.χ.–1953)* ('Egyptian Hellenism, History and Activity 753 B.C–1953'). Vol. 1, Alexandria, 1953.

Panfalone, Elisabeth. 'Les Emigres libanais et syriens en Egypte (1724–1960): Une strategie de maintien d'une distinction minoritaire'. DEA, 1992/93.

Parker, Richard B. *The Politics of Miscalculation in the Middle East*. Bloomington and Indianapolis: Indiana UP, 1993.

Pelt, Adrian. *Libyan Independence and the United Nations, A Case of Planned Decolonization*. Yale UP, 1970.

Pennington, J.D. 'The Copts in Egypt', *Middle Eastern Studies* 18 (1982) 158–79.

Philipp, Thomas. 'Feminism and Nationalist Politics in Egypt', 277–94 in Lois Beck and Nikki Keddie (eds.) *Women in the Muslim World*. Cambridge, Mass.: Harvard UP, 1978.

Philipp, Thomas. *The Syrians in Egypt 1725–1975*. Stuttgart: Steiner Verlag Wiesbaden GmbH, 1985.

Pierides, George P. *Memories and Stories from Egypt*. Nicosia: Diaspora, 1992.

Politis, Athanase G. *O Ellinismos ke i Neotera Egiptos* ('Hellenism and Modern Egypt'). vol. I. *Istoria tou Egiptiotou Ellinismou apo tou 1798 mekhri 1927*, vol. II. *Simvoli tou Ellinismou eis tin anaptixin tis Neoteras Egiptou*, Alexandria, 1927, 1930 (French trans. *L'Hellenisme et l'Égypte moderne*. 2 vols, Paris: Félix Alcan, 1929–30).

Politis, Athanase G. *Les Rapports de la Grèce et de l'Égypte pendant le règne de Mohamed-Aly, 1833–1849*. Cairo, 1930.

Qattawi [Cattaui], René. 'Georges Douin (1884–1944)', *Bulletin de l'Institut d'Egypte* 27 (1946) 89–95.

Qattawi [Cattaui], René. *Le Règne de Mohamed-Aly d'après les archives russes en Égypte*. Cairo, 1931.

Qattawi, Yusuf [Cattaui Pacha, Joseph] (ed.) *L'Égypte, Aperçu historique et géographique gouvernement et institutions vie économique et sociale*. Cairo: L'Institut Français, 1926.

Radopoulos, Radamanthos G. *O Vasilefs Fouat o protos ke anagennomeni Egiptos* ('King Fu'ad I and Reborn Egypt') Alexandria, 1930.

Radwan, Abu al-Futouh Ahmad. *Old and New Forces in Egyptian Education*. New York: Columbia University, 1951.

Raafat, Samir. *Maadi 1904–62: History and Society in a Cairo Suburb*. Cairo: Palm Press, 1994.

Raafat, Samir. *The Egyptian Gazette – The Saturday Articles* [http://www.egy.com/history/source.html].

Reid, Anthony and Marr, David (eds) *Perceptions of the Past in Southeast Asia*. Singapore: Heinemann Educational Books, 1979.

Reid, Donald M. 'Archaeology, Social Reform and Modern Identity among the Copts (1854–1952)', 311–35 in Alain Rousillon (ed.), *Entre réforme sociale et mouvement national*, Cairo: CEDEJ, 1995.

Reid, Donald M. *Cairo University and the Making of Modern Egypt*. Cairo: AUC Press, 1991.

Reid, Donald M. 'Cairo University and the Orientalists', *IJMES* 19 (1987) 51–75.

Reid, Donald M. 'The Egyptian Geographical Society: from Foreign Laymen's Society to Indigenous Professional Association', *Poetics Today* 14 no. 3 (Fall 1993) 539–72.

Reid, Donald M. *Lawyers and Politics in the Arab World, 1880–1960*. Minneapolis: Bibliotheca Islamica, 1981.

Reid, Donald M. 'The National Bar Association and Egyptian Politics, 1912–1954', *International Journal of African Historical Studies* 7 (1974) 608–46.

Reid, Donald M. 'The Rise of Professions and Professional Organizations in Modern Egypt', *Comparative Studies in Society and History* 16 (1974) 24–57.

Rejwan, Nissim. *Nasserist Ideology, Its Exponents and Critics*. Jerusalem: Israel Universities Press, 1974.

Rifaat [Rif'at] Bey, Muhammad. *The Awakening of Modern Egypt*. London: Longmans, Green, 1947.

Rossi, Ettore. 'In Memoriam, Angelo Sammarco (1883–1948)', *Oriente Moderno* 28 (October–December 1948) 198–200.

Sabry, M. (Muhammad Sabri). *La Revolution égyptienne*. 2 vols, Paris: Librairie J. Vrin, 1919–21.

al-Sadat, Anwar. *Revolt on the Nile*, New York: John Day, 1957.

al-Sadat, Anwar. *In Search of Identity*, New York: Harper and Row, 1978.

Safran, Nadav. *In Search of Political Community, An Analysis of the Intellectual and Political Revolution of Egypt, 1804–1952*. Cambridge, Mass.: Harvard UP, 1961.

Sagiv, David. *Fundamentalism and Intellectuals in Egypt, 1973–1993*. London: Frank Cass, 1995.

Salibi, Kamal. *A House of Many Mansions: The History of Lebanon Reconsidered*. Berkeley: University of California Press, 1988.

Salman, Magda *et al. Women in the Middle East.* London & New Jersey: Zed Books, *Khamsin* series, 1987.

Sammarco, Angelo. *Il contributo degl'Italiani ai progressi scientifici e practici della medicina in Egitto sotto il regno di Mohammed Ali.* Cairo, 1928.

Sammarco, Angelo. *Gli Italiani in Egitto: Il contributo italiano nella formazione dell'Egitto moderno.* Alexandria, 1937.

Sammarco, Angelo. *La Marina egiziana sotto Mohammed Ali, Il contributo italiano.* Cairo, 1931.

Sammarco, Angelo. *Le Règne du Khédive Ismaïl de 1863 à 1875.* Cairo, 1937.

Sevastopoulou, Despina. *I Alexandreia pou fevgi* ('The Alexandria which is gone'), Alexandria, 1953.

Shafik, Doria Ragaï. *La Femme et de le droit religieux de l'Égypte contemporaine.* Paris: Paul Geuthner, 1940.

Shamir, Shimon. 'Radicalism in Egyptian Historiography', 215–27 in Gabriel R. Warburg and Uri M. Kupferschmidt (eds) *Islam, Nationalism, and Radicalism in Egypt and the Sudan.* New York: Praeger, 1983.

Shamir, Shimon. 'Self-Views in Modern Egyptian Historiography', 37–49 in Shimon Shamir (ed.) *Self-Views in Historical Perspective in Egypt and Israel.* Tel Aviv University, 1981.

Sharabi, Hisham. 'The Crisis of the Intelligentsia in the Middle East', *The Muslim World* 47 (July 1957) 187–93.

el-Shayyal, Gamal el-Din. 'Historiography in Egypt in the Nineteenth Century', 403–21 in B. Lewis and P.M. Holt (eds) *Historians of the Middle East.* London: Oxford UP, 1962.

el-Shayyal, Gamal el-Din. *A History of Egyptian Historiography in the Nineteenth Century.* Faculty of Arts, no.15, Alexandria: Alexandria UP, 1962.

al-Shiliq, Ahmad Zakariyya. Review of *al-Muslimun wa'l-aqbat fi atar al-jama'a al-wataniyya*, 1982 by Tariq al-Bishri, *al-Siyasa al-dawliyya* 68 (April 1982) 211–16.

Shoukri, [Shukri], Ghali. *Egypt: Portrait of a President.* London: Zed Books, 1981.

Smith, Charles D. 'The "Crisis of Orientation": The Shift of Egyptian Intellectuals to Islamic Subjects in the 1930s', *IJMES* 4 (1973) 382—410.

Smith, Charles D. *Islam and the Search for Social Order in Modern Egypt: a Biography of Muhammad Husayn Haykal.* Albany: State University of New York Press, 1983.

Solé, Robert. *Le Tarbouche.* Paris: Le Seuil, 1992.

Sonbol, Amira. 'Society, Politics and Sectarian Strife', 265–81 in Ibrahim M. Oweiss (ed.) *The Political Economy of Contemporary Egypt.* Washington: Center for Contemporary Arab Studies, 1990.

Souloyiannis, Efthimios. *I Thesi ton Ellinon stin Egipto* ('The Position of Greeks in Egypt'), Athens, Dimos Athineon, 1999.

Springborg, Robert. *Family, Power and Politics in Egypt: Sayed Bey Marei – his Clan, Clients, and Cohorts.* Philadelphia: University of Pennsylvania Press, 1982.

Talhami, Ghada Hashem. *Palestine and Egyptian National Identity.* New York: Praeger, 1992.

Taylor, A.J.P. *A Personal History.* London: Hamish Hamilton, 1983.

Temu, Arnold and Bonaventure Swai. *Historians and Africanist History: A Critique, Post-Colonial Historiography Examined.* London: Zed Press, 1981.

Tignor, Robert L. 'The Economic Activities of Foreigners in Egypt, 1920–1950: From Millet to Haute Bourgeoisie', *Comparative Studies in Society and History* 23 (1980) 416–49.

Tignor, Robert L. *State, Private Enterprise and Economic Change in Egypt*. Princeton NJ: Princeton UP, 1984.

Tsirkas, Stratis. *Drifting Cities*. trans. K. Cicellis New York, Alfred Knopf, 1974 (orig. published in Greek as *Akivernites polities*, Athens: Kedros, 1960, 1962, 1965).

Tsirkas, Stratis. *O Kavafis ke i epokhi tou* ('Kavafy and His Age'). Athens: Kedros, 1958.

Tucker, Judith E. 'Problems in the Historiography of Women in the Middle East: The Case of Nineteenth-Century Egypt', *IJMES* 15 (1983) 321–36.

'L'Unione degli storici arabi', *Oriente Moderno* 58 (December 1978) 861–2.

Vatikiotis, P.J. *Arab and Regional Politics in the Middle East*. London: Croom Helm, 1984.

Vatikiotis, P.J. *The Modern History of Egypt*. London: Weidenfeld and Nicolson, 1969.

Vatikiotis, P.J. 'The New Western Historiography of Modern Egypt', *Middle Eastern Studies* 27 no. 2 (April 1991) 322–8.

Vatikiotis, P.J. 'State and Class in Egypt: A Review Essay', 875–89 in C.E. Bosworth *et al.* (eds) *The Islamic World, From Classical to Modern Times, Essays in Honor of Bernard Lewis*. Princeton, N.J.: Darwin Press, 1989.

Vitalis, Robert. *When Capitalists Collide, Business Conflict and the End of Empire in Egypt*. Berkeley: University of California Press, 1995.

Vryonis, Speros, Jr. *The Turkish State and History, Clio Meets the Grey Wolf*. Thessaloniki: Institute for Balkan Studies, 1991.

Wahba, Magdi. 'Cairo Memories', *Encounter* 62 no. 5 (May 1984) 74–9.

Wakin, Edward. *A Lonely Minority, The Modern Story of Egypt's Copts*. New York: William Morrow 1963.

Waterbury, John. *The Egypt of Nasser and Sadat, The Political Economy of Two Regimes*. Princeton NJ: Princeton UP, 1983.

Wendell, Charles. *The Evolution of the Egyptian National Image, From its Origins to Ahmad Lutfi al-Sayyid*. Berkeley and Los Angeles: University of California Press, 1972.

Wiet, Gaston. 'Jacques Tagher', *Cahiers d'histoire égyptienne* 4 (October 1952) 163–5.

Wilson, P.W. 'A Challenging Biography of Egypt's Ismail', *New York Times Book Review* 24 June 1934, 4.

Yalourakis, Manolis. *I Egiptos ton Ellinon* ('Egypt of the Greeks'). Athens, 1967.

Yannakakis I. 'Aux origines du communisme égyptien 1920–1940', 91–103 in *Le Mouvement communiste au Moyen-Orient*. Paris, 1984.

Ziada [Ziyada], Muhammad Mostafa. 'Modern Egyptian Historiography', *Middle Eastern Affairs* 4 (1953) 266–71.

Ziadeh, Farhat J. *Lawyers, the Rule of Law and Liberalism in Modern Egypt*. Stanford, CA: Stanford University, 1968.

INDEX

265